Gun Culture
in Early Modern
England

LOIS G. SCHWOERER

GUN
CULTURE
IN EARLY MODERN
ENGLAND

UNIVERSITY OF VIRGINIA PRESS

Charlottesville and London

In Memory of Paul

University of Virginia Press

© 2016 by the Rector and Visitors of the
University of Virginia

Printed in the United States of America
on acid-free paper

First published 2016

1 3 5 7 9 8 6 4 2

LIBRARY OF CONGRESS CATALOGING-IN-PUBLICATION DATA
NAMES: Schwoerer, Lois G.
TITLE: Gun culture in early modern England / Lois G. Schwoerer.
DESCRIPTION: Charlottesville : University of Virginia Press, 2016. | Includes
bibliographical references and index.
IDENTIFIERS: LCCN 2015046035| ISBN 9780813938592 (cloth : acid-free
paper) | ISBN 9780813938608 (ebook)
SUBJECTS: LCSH: Firearms—Social aspects—England—History. |
Firearms—Political aspects—England—History. | Firearms industry and
trade—England—History. | Great Britain—Social conditions. | Great
Britain—Politics and government—1485–1603 | Great Britain—Politics
and government—1603–1714.
CLASSIFICATION: LCC TS533.4.G7 S39 2016 | DDC 683.400942—dc23\
LC record available at http://lccn.loc.gov/2015046035

Cover art: A detail from a portrait of Endymion Porter
by William Dobson, c. 1642–45. (© Tate, London 2016)

CONTENTS

ACKNOWLEDGMENTS

Writing this book was an adventure that took me into fields, sources, and scholarship that I had not visited before. Finishing it gives me the opportunity to thank the many people who listened patiently, asked insightful questions, and made the journey a pleasure.

I worked in libraries and visited museums in the United States, England, and Europe. I am grateful to the expert help I received at these places. The Folger Shakespeare Library was my research headquarters. I applaud Elizabeth Walsh and the Reading Room staff for maintaining the Library's traditional ambience and high level of service. My special thanks go to Georgianna Ziegler, Louis B. Thalheimer Head of Reference, for her limitless support and expertise. I also express my appreciation to the Library of Congress, the First Federal Congress Project at the George Washington University, the Huntington Library where Mary Robertson, Curator of Manuscripts, gave me valuable assistance, and the Metropolitan Museum of Art in New York.

I met with the same courtesies in England. In London I worked at the British Library, the College of Arms where Archivist Lynsey Darby provided exceptional assistance, the Guildhall Library, the Public Record Office, the National Gallery of Art, the National Portrait Gallery, the Tate Gallery Britain, the Victoria and Albert Museum, and The Worshipful Company of Gunmakers whose Archivist Derek Stimpson shared his wide knowledge of guns and proofing. I used resources at the Bodleian Library and Christ Church College Library in Oxford and the Royal Armouries Museum in Leeds where conversation with Graeme Rimes marked a turning point in my preparation. On the Continent, in Vienna, at the Heeresgeschichtliches Museum, the exhibit of early guns was comprehensive and informative. At the Armeria Reale in Turin, Italy, Director Giuseppina Romagnoli arranged my visit, and Curator Marconi dismantled an early gun to demonstrate its operation. I am grateful to each of these persons.

Conversations with many colleagues have sharpened this study. Fellow researchers who comprise the ever-changing Folger community expressed interest and provided help, especially Jackson Boswell, Ian Gadd, Elizabeth

Hageman, Paul Hammer, Tim Harris, Bruce Janacek, Gerard Kilroy, Carole Levin, Pamela Long, John McDiarmid, Barbara Mowat, Lena Cowen Orlin, Linda Levy Peck, John Pocock, Aisha Pollnitz, Nigel Ramsey, and David Trim. Elizabeth Hageman and David Trim read most of an early draft, and Hageman read later versions of two chapters. Bruce Janacek, Jean Moss, Linda B. Salamon, and Melinda Zook commented on one or two early chapters. Members of the scholarly community at the Huntington Library—Susan Amussen, Barbara Donagan, Cynthia Herrup, Alan Houston, and David Underdown—also offered interest and comment. I am grateful to Ian Archer, Geoff Egan, John Schofield, and Justine Taylor for doing the same in London. Special acknowledgment goes to Tim Wales, a remarkably skilled and indefatigable research assistant.

David Cressy allowed me to read before its publication his article, "Saltpeter, State Security and Vexation in Early Modern England," *Past and Present*, no. 212 (2011): 73–111. Both article and subsequent book, *Saltpeter: The Mother of Gunpowder* (Oxford University Press, 2013), were important additions to the topic. Patrick Charles extended the same courtesy regarding his essay, "The Faces of the Second Amendment," *Cleveland State Law Review*, vol. 60 (2012), 1–55. I am grateful to Cressy and Charles.

The award of a Folger Library Short-Term Fellowship and a Huntington Library Short-Term Mellon Fellowship advanced my work. I thank these two libraries. I am honored that the Folger named me a Scholar-in-Residence.

Two women, then PhD History candidates at the George Washington University, ably assisted me: Lindsey Moore as a research assistant at the beginning of the project, and Natalie Diebel, who constructed spreadsheets of data drawn from Harold Blackmore's *Gunmakers of London 1350–1850* (York, PA: George Shumway, 1986). Adrienne Shevchenko, then a staff member of the Folger Institute, expanded the spreadsheets, and they became a valuable research tool.

I presented conference papers at the Chicago-Kent College of Law, the Folger Library, the Huntington Library, the Mid-West Conference on British Studies, the National Press Club, the North American Conference on British Studies, the Pacific Coast Conference on British Studies, the Renaissance Society of America, Smith College, Hilda Smith's retirement conference, and Stanford University. I thank the participants at these events for engaging in lively discussions.

The paper presented at the Chicago-Kent College of Law, "To Hold and Bear Arms: The English Perspective," was published in the *Chicago-Kent Law Review* in 2000. I thank the *Review* for permission to use it in a slightly modified version as chapter 10. The paper presented at Smith's retirement conference, "Women and Guns in Early Modern London," appeared in *Challenging Orthodoxies,* eds. Sigrun Haude and Melinda S. Zook (Farnham, Surrey: Ashgate, 2014), 33–52. I thank Ashgate for permission to excerpt a portion of it in chapters 2, 8, and 9.

I joined historians of the late-eighteenth-century history of the United States in submitting amici curiae to the Supreme Court in three cases: *Salim Ahmed Hamden v. Donald H. Rumsfeld* (2006), *the District of Columbia v. Dick Anthony Heller* (2008), and *Otis McDonald v. City of Chicago, Illinois* (2010). It was gratifying to bring early modern English history to bear on these contemporary matters.

Finally, I express my appreciation to the anonymous readers of my manuscript for the University of Virginia Press. Their comments and suggestions were most helpful. I also thank my editors and the staff at the Press for transforming the manuscript into a book with expert ease.

Introduction

Interrogating Early Modern English Gun Culture

TWO HORRIFIC GUN MASSACRES IN Great Britain twenty or more years ago first ignited my interest in the subject of this book. One occurred on 19 August 1987 in Hungerford, England; the other on 13 March 1996 in Dunblane, Scotland. Both were widely reported in British and American newspapers. In Hungerford, Michael Ryan went on a rampage, randomly killing sixteen people (including his mother, which he said was a mistake) and wounding fifteen others before shooting himself. In Dunblane, Thomas Watt Hamilton, armed with 4 handguns and 743 rounds of ammunition, walked into the village's Elementary School. In four minutes, he fired 105 bullets, killed sixteen children, all five or six years old, and one teacher; wounded ten other children and three teachers; and then killed himself. The media continued to report the aftermath of these events —the outcry, expressed in the Snowdrop Petition against privately owned firearms (initiated by residents of Dunblane and named for the only flower in bloom at the time), and the outrage of others against restrictions on the ownership and use of guns. All this led me, as a historian of early modern England, to wonder what the English government and people in that earlier era thought about guns and gun possession. These questions lay unexplored in my mind for almost ten years as other projects preempted them, but they never completely faded. They lingered on and became the initial reason for this book.

The origins of England's early modern gun culture rest on two initiatives. First in importance were the efforts of King Henry VIII (1509–1547). More famous for his six wives than his interest in firearms, the King revitalized and expanded a small gun industry that had existed in the country since the fourteenth century. He did so because he wanted a native business that would lessen dependence on Continental supplies and provide weapons in greater quantity and of higher quality than available in England to enable him to pursue an aggressive foreign policy against France. He also needed firearms to quell domestic violence in a nation destabilized by increasingly deep religious divisions, socioeconomic inequalities and resentments, and challenges to monarchical authority, especially from northern England, Scotland, and Ireland. Building on the work of his royal predecessors, King Edward III (1327–1377) for one, Henry ordered an increase in the number of artillery (cannon) and military handguns and placed both in the military organizations of the nation—the ancient county militias, the moribund feudal array, and the ad hoc armies mobilized for foreign engagement and then disbanded. To jumpstart the gun industry and better train Englishmen, he also lured gunfounders and gunmakers from the Continent and settled them mostly in London.[1]

The presence of military weapons had an unintended consequence. Men in Germany, as early as 1480, recognized that handguns could be used for personal pleasures, such as hunting and shooting.[2] Men in England, perhaps independently, came to same conclusion, for in 1514, a statute forbade them to use "hand gonnes" to hunt unless they possessed a yearly income of 300 marks.[3] This was the second initiative that advanced the gun industry. It came not from Henry VIII, but from people in the gun business. Although the king personally liked handguns, took instruction in their use, and collected them, he disallowed his subjects to possess and use them if their income did not meet a certain level. He had no part in their manufacture. The King's moves, however, provided the context for creating a business of making handguns for domestic use. Without Henry VIII's initiatives, handguns for personal pleasures would not have appeared when they did.

These two initiatives, then, one from Henry VIII, the other from gunmakers, laid the groundwork for two gun cultures: a military gun culture and a domestic gun culture. Although military gun culture plays a part, the focus of *Gun Culture in Early Modern England* is on domestic gun culture. My aim is to discover, describe, and analyze the nature of that culture, and the book does so by asking three major questions. First, how did English men, women and children of all socioeconomic standings learn about and respond to firearms? How did the presence of guns affect their lives? Drawing in people from across a wide socioeconomic range allows this study to train multiple perspectives on firearms. Second, what was the relationship between the government and the gun industry? What was the government's policy respecting its subjects and handguns? And third, what did Article VII of the Bill of Rights that embodied the constitutional settlement of the Revolution of 1688–89, also known as the Glorious Revolution, intend and mean? Article VII reads "That the Subjects which are Protestants may have Armes for their defence Suitable to their Condition and as allowed by Law." Did this Article grant to all English

Protestant subjects an individual right to arms? Was it the progenitor of the Second Amendment to the Constitution of the United States?

This book rests on several premises. One is that military and civilian gun cultures existed easily together in early modern England. No impenetrable barrier separated them, and men across society participated in both. Aristocrats, for whom war, military service abroad, and leadership of the local militia were a way of life for much of the era, were also the ones whose favorite sports were hunting and shooting. They had the money to buy beautifully decorated guns for collecting, gift giving, and decorating. During the years when peace prevailed, they lived as civilians and used firearms as civilians did. Periods of peace in the sixteenth and early seventeenth centuries, changes in their education and concepts of duty, and the advent of England's professional standing army at the Restoration in 1660 widened the distinction between the military and civilian spheres.[4] Still, aristocrats remained important to both gun cultures.

Middling, plebeian, and poor men also bridged the gap between the two cultures. Barred by their income to possess and operate a handgun legally, many men learned about firearms through military service. All soldiers saw and heard artillery and military handguns when they were fired on the battlefield. If a soldier were chosen to be a gunner,[5] he received instruction in the care and operation of either artillery or a military handgun. Some of the handguns that soldiers fought with were equally effective in hunting and shooting. When the men returned home at the end of their service, they brought knowledge of guns with them. In this way, men down the social scale learned about guns and participated in both cultures.

Another bridge between the two cultures was that the process of making handguns for military use and for personal pleasures was the same: a gunmaker put together the various parts which he or she got from other gun workers. Furthermore, whether working on a military or a domestic gun, gunmakers belonged to the same Worshipful Company of Gunmakers. Making artillery and military handguns provided the most employment for members of the gun industry, but guns for domestic uses also brought employment. In short, military and domestic gun culture did not occupy separate universes.

A second premise is that although men dominated military and domestic gun cultures, as they did many other aspects of life in the era, women had a role to play in both. Dismissing the prescriptive terms of the ideal woman of the period, who was expected to lead a sheltered life focused on her husband, children, and household, women of all social standings accepted firearms. Aristocratic English women did not hunt or shoot with guns and were less enthusiastic about them in general than their European counterparts. Still, some highborn women fought with firearms in the Civil Wars; others in London during a tense political crisis carried small guns in their muffs. Female authors wove guns into their prose and poetry, and still other women found domestic uses for gunpowder, the essential ingredient in guns. Women down the social scale, mostly artisanal widows, worked in the gun industry, making and repairing guns. Women servants in London households learned to operate a firearm.

Third, guns affected the lives of children from all social strata in multiple ways, depending on their social standing. Fathers, mothers, and friends gave young boys miniature guns and encouraged their use. Some toy guns were so carefully crafted that they contained gunpowder and a tiny pellet as the bullet. Children unwittingly transmitted attitudes about guns. They were important in creating and sustaining the domestic gun culture.

Fourth, a theme that threads through this study is that domestic gun culture softened the terror of firearms. The use of guns in sports, collecting, gift giving, decorating, and so on, and the pleasure people took in using guns, veiled their lethal purposes and possibilities. The same effect resulted from the role of artisanal women in gunmaking and the part guns and gunpowder played in the lives of well-to-do women. Street names and shop signs that advertised guns shops strengthened that sense. The fact that toy guns became a favorite plaything among little boys of all social standings further reinforced this theme.

The study of "cultures" of various kinds is not new in early modern English studies. Historians have long written about "political culture," "religious culture," and "print culture." I propose to add "gun culture"—words that are commonplace in the twenty-first century. What do the words mean? The etymology of the term is problematic. Neither the *Oxford English Dictionary* nor any dictionary of slang includes it. I conjecture that it first surfaced in the United States in the 1970s, years of keen and partisan interest in the Second Amendment to the United States Constitution. In the course of researching and writing this book, I talked with friends in the United States and England about the words. The survey, of course, was not scientific, but it yielded remarkably similar responses. People agreed that the words described a positive view of guns and an environment in which people own and use them in hunting, target shooting, the protection of person and property, and the exchange of gifts; believe in the right of the individual to own, possess, and use them; and oppose laws that restrict them.[6] My informants were agreed that the United States has a gun culture, whereas Great Britain does not.

To this, I always rejoined that all nations that have guns have a gun culture specific to them.

This definition of "gun culture," although important for the little it reveals about contemporary views, does not figure in this book. The word *culture* carries many connotations, as Peter Burke has helpfully shown,[7] but the definition I use refers to the assumptions and habits that people across society create in response to living with and thinking and talking about some issue. These attitudes develop coherency, viability, and definition. They are transmitted over time from one generation to the next. In early modern England, a civilian gun culture with its own unique characteristics developed in tandem with a military gun culture. Historians have shown very little interest in civilian gun culture. Among academic historians, only one scholar, J. R. Hale, the distinguished military historian, has addressed some of the issues that are part of this study. In an article published in 1965, "Gunpowder and the Renaissance: An Essay in the History of Ideas," Hale undertook to "watch the conscience of Christendom adjusting itself to the use" of firearms.[8] He presented examples, some drawn from England but most from Italy during the Renaissance era, to show the gradual acceptance of guns. Lisa Jardine, a professor of Renaissance Studies, is the only writer (so far as I know) who has used the term *gun culture* in print respecting the early modern era, and she limited that use to portraits of Elizabethan men with a gun.[9] No scholar has asked, at least in published work, the questions that are necessary to understand how a domestic gun culture emerged in England and what its characteristics were.

To my surprise and disappointment, literate English people did not write at length about their view and use of guns for domestic pleasures. My research uncovered no manuscript or printed tract of thoughtful reflection on or full-throated discussion of this topic. Only a few remarks surfaced. Two different kinds of literate persons, however, did discuss their attitude toward military guns. First, Continental humanists, Francesco Petrarch (1304–1374), Ludovico Ariosto (1474–1533), and Desiderius Erasmus (1466–1534), and English literati Sir Thomas More (1478–1535) and John Milton (1608–1674) held negative views of guns. They decried artillery and military handguns for killing people and animals and devastating countryside and cities, charged them with destroying chivalric principles, called them the Devil, and urged their destruction. Their work was much admired by literate English people but had no influence on government policy. It stands apart from the written views of literate subjects that I sought.[10]

A second group were active military men or men deeply interested and well read in military affairs. In the last decades of Queen Elizabeth I's reign, they printed almost two hundred tracts about war, strategy, and weaponry.[11] They included Barnabe Rich (1540–1617), Sir John Smythe (1534[?]–1607), and Sir Roger Williams (1539/40–1595). Their purpose was to debate the relative merits of the long bow and the gun, but all of them wrote in hopes of influencing national policy to strengthen the country's defenses. Although these individuals were not literate laypersons, their work holds interest for military gun culture.

A range of primary evidence compensated for the absence of essays and correspondence. The archival records of The Worshipful Company of Gunmakers provided data about the men and women who made, repaired, and decorated guns and struggled for almost a century to win incorporation of their own company. In like manner, the archives of the Company of Armourers and the Company of Blacksmiths revealed how their members fought the gunmakers persistently and furiously to defeat that effort. Wills contained data on the economic success or failure of gunmakers. Laws and proclamations showed what the monarch, the Privy Council, and members of Parliament thought about disallowing firearms to English subjects according to income. One may tease out the response of subjects from these records and from law cases. The gun licenses that Tudor monarchs issued revealed the government's determination to control firearms and to use them for their own financial and political advantage. The response of persons who bought or received a gun license furthered understanding of their attitude toward guns. The gun licenses uncovered an intrepid lady, Anne, Dowager Countess of Oxford, who, so far as is known at present, was the only woman to receive a gun license that enabled her to arm servants who were otherwise unqualified to use a gun.

In addition to these conventional sources, visual material was of great value. The Agas Map of London (printed 1562/63) is a striking example of the data a map can provide. A print of a gunmaking shop vivified the activities of gunmakers. Portraits of men, one woman, Teresia, Lady Sherley (1590–1668),[12] and of children holding a gun gave powerful proof of how much people of wealth admired guns and wanted to advertise that fact. They are rich testimony to the dissemination of guns and the development of a gun culture. Coats-of-arms offered further examples. They showed that some men identified so closely with a firearm that they used it to illustrate their name and family lineage.

In like manner, material culture provided evidence of how people regarded guns. Early modern guns are on view at many museums, among them the Royal Armoury Museum in Leeds, the Tower, and the Wallace Collection in London, the Metropolitan Museum of Art in New York City, and the Armeria Reale in Turin, Italy. Some guns are works of art—encrusted with precious and semi-precious jewels, incised with pictures often showing ancient myths, and damascened, that is, incised with designs whose lines are filled with gold or silver. These gorgeous guns speak to their owners' appreciation and admiration of firearms, their desire to identify with them and use them as a status symbol. Guns used in hunting, target shooting, and for protection were usually simple and unadorned. In addition to guns, a gentleman's toiletry case fashioned as a pendant in the shape of a tiny wheel-lock pistol and intricately decorated offers concrete evidence of its owner's appreciation and admiration of the gun. Known as the Pasfield Jewel, the toiletry case is on display at the Victoria and Albert Museum. Toy handguns and cannon, unearthed over the past thirty years or so in archaeological digs in the River Thames in London and other places in England, are still another form of material culture. They provide a unique perspective on how adults valued guns and on the toys that children played with.

Among secondary works, Howard L. Blackmore's *Gunmakers of London 1350–1850* (1986) and his *Gunmakers of London 1350–1850, A Supplement* (1999) deserve special acknowledgment. These two volumes contain biographical vignettes of over two thousand men and women who were connected with the gun industry in London from 1350 to 1850.[13] Other studies about gunfounders and gunmakers employed by the Ordnance Office, Huguenot gunmakers, and alien gunmakers in London provided additional data.[14] To work with all these data, two computer experts created spreadsheets to meet my specific needs.[15] The spreadsheets include the men's names, date of birth and death (when known) or date when "flourished," the location of their workshop or home (when known), membership in the Armourers' Guild and the Blacksmiths' Guild, relationship with the Ordnance Office, and other details. The material is arranged alphabetically, chronologically, and by location. Separate spreadsheets for women were organized in the same way. The spreadsheets are searchable and can yield statistical information. This is a bonus, because very little statistical data are available for the era. Given the nature of the evidence, most of the people who figure in this account are faceless. But not all. A few individuals otherwise unknown or little known to history can be introduced. Among them are Anne, Dowager Countess of Oxford, already mentioned; Hester Shaw, a London midwife and "whistle-blower" regarding the storage of gunpowder in the city; and Lady Teresia Sherley, also previously mentioned, the only English woman whose portrait shows her holding a gun. Other individuals include Christopher Morris, the first person to serve as Lieutenant of the Office of Ordnance; John Redhall, a lad about fifteen years old who was involved in a gun accident; and John Silk, the wealthy, energetic, "street-smart" gunmaker who helped lead and finance the effort to win recognition of the Worshipful Company of Gunmakers.

The reader will recognize that the point of view of this study is "English" rather than "British," even though a few examples are British. Other historians may want to place the questions raised here in a British context and uncover the gun cultures of Scotland, Ireland, and Wales. The decision to limit this study to England is justified by the meaning I give to gun culture. The European continent has a small part to play. The dates of early Modern England are conventionally 1485–1715, but I have strayed beyond them. There was a medieval and fifteenth-century background to the story of guns, and I draw some examples from later years in the eighteenth century. Attention to the meaning of Article VII of the Bill of Rights 1689 and the present-day scholarly disputes over it brings this study into the modern world.

Another obvious point is that only the military organizations that operated on land figure in this book. The maritime experiences of English men and some women are not included. This decision finds justification in the fact that the early modern navy, naval warfare, and maritime gunnery are topics as large and complicated as the one that occupies this study.

Although gunpowder is the essential ingredient in the operation of a firearm, and saltpeter is the most important of the three substances that make up gunpowder, neither receives careful attention in this book. Gunpowder and saltpeter followed a different line of development from that of guns. They stand apart from my major interests. Numerous scholars have written about them, but two recent studies are especially valuable: David Cressy's *Saltpeter: The Mother of Gunpowder* and Jack Kelly's *Gunpowder, Alchemy, Bombards, and Pyrotechnics: The History of the Explosive that Changed the World*.[16] For my purposes, gunpowder appears when it is pertinent to the topic, as, for example, in its remarkable domestic uses and as the vital element in salutes and fireworks.

Ten chapters address the development of early modern English gun culture. Chapter 1 recounts how a viable native gun-making business was set up. King Henry VIII encouraged Continental gunfounders and gunmakers to emigrate to jump-start the business and train English gunfounders and gunmakers in return for lodging and contracts. The second initiative, taken in tandem with the King's effort by the gunmakers themselves, was making guns for domestic uses. The chapter includes a narrative of the gunmakers' long struggle to win a royal charter for their own company and persuade the City of London to accept it. Chapter 2 deals with the business of gunmaking, focusing on the entrepreneurial and employment opportunities that guns opened up for men of all economic standing and for women, mostly widows of artisanal background. Individuals found work as independent gunmakers and as members of the Company of Gunmakers. The Company extended marks of approval to some women. Chapter 3 canvasses the many laws and proclamations that regulated guns for private use by limiting subjects' legal access to them on grounds of their annual income. Multiple reasons explain the restrictions, but a hierarchical social structure and its accompanying attitudes, and the fear that subjects of modest or poor means would use firearms in riots and revolts were the most important. The chapter describes the response of subjects on whom the restraints fell. Chapter 4 focuses on the gun licenses, which were devised by Henry VIII, used by the Tudors, and abandoned by the Stuarts. They granted certain privileges regarding the use of domestic guns. The chapter discusses the advantages they brought to crown and subject, and shows that they served as another gun control measure. Chapter 5 investigates how service in the nation's military institutions provided a pathway to guns. Nobles and aristocrats served as officers and in the cavalry, while men down the social scale were foot soldiers, a service that introduced them to artillery and military handguns. Military service helped spread knowledge of firearms throughout society. Chapter 6 shows that both military guns and guns for personal use affected London, which initially felt their presence more than any other city in England. Gunfounding, gunmaking, and commercial activities associated with firearms had a multiple effect on the city, which also suffered from gun crime, gun accidents, and devastating gunpowder explosions. It was the "Gun Capital of England" until the turn of the eighteenth century.

Chapter 7 addresses the effect of firearms on the social and personal lives of men. The cultural assumptions of aristocrats drew them toward military service and war, and their local political responsibilities required leadership of the county militias. They were also leaders in civilian gun culture, incorporating firearms into hunting and shooting, their favorite sports, making them part of their art collections, and giving them as gifts. Guns affected them more deeply and in more ways than any other social group. Men down the social scale also wanted firearms and expressed opposition to the restrictions placed on their possessing and using them. Chapter 8 deals with the relationship of wealthy and middling-status women with guns and gunpowder. English ladies were not interested in hunting with a gun or practicing target shooting, as were their European counterparts. But both European and English aristocratic women used guns in war—the Civil Wars in England and the wars of religion in Europe—and also employed them in acts of violence. Some women writers, poets, and playwrights wove the gun into their work. Women also felt the impact of gun crime and of gun and gunpowder accidents. Chapter 9 shows that guns had a role to play in the lives of early modern children. Well-to-do parents gave toy guns to their sons and included guns in the boys' portraits. Changes occurred in the curriculum of a few schools to accommodate learning about guns. Children of lesser means also had toy guns, as archaeological digs in the River Thames and other places prove. "Child's play" with guns, however, had a dark side that included accidents and crime. Chapter 10 examines the intention and meaning of Article VII of the Declaration of Rights. It offers a close reading of Article VII, its wording, context and drafting. The chapter concludes that Article VII did not grant an individual right to all English Protestant subjects to possess a gun, and that it was not the progenitor of the Second Amendment to the Constitution of the United States.

Two appendices present information that readers may find useful. The first describes the appearance and operation of early guns and defines unfamiliar terms that readers will encounter in this book. The second explains how the new device got its name, *gun*, and the effect of that word on the English language.

I hope this book will attract people who are interested in early modern England, whether lay readers, students, academic scholars, or military historians. My experience researching early modern gun culture has taught me that academic history and military history have stood apart from each other far too long and to the detriment of both. I also aspire to reach people who want to know something of the remote historical background of some current gun issues.

ONE · Re-creating and Developing a Gun Industry

A ROBUST, NATIVE GUN INDUSTRY was essential to the formation and growth of early modern England's gun culture. Both kinds of weapons—artillery and handguns for military use and handguns for personal pleasures—depended on such an industry to survive and thrive. Its history was intricate and contingent and occupies this first chapter. The first part focuses on the two initiatives that created and developed the gun business. First were the efforts of King Henry VIII who built on the work of his predecessors to upgrade the production of artillery and military handguns. Although they hold great importance for the industry, the nation, and England's role internationally, the king's contributions have received only glancing treatment in studies of Henry VIII.[1] Manufacturing handguns for domestic uses followed in the context of the king's efforts and was driven by ambitious and forward-looking members of the industry. The market for domestic guns was never as large or important as that for military guns, but producing guns for personal use took up the slack when the government's military orders declined in time of peace.

The second part of the chapter shifts attention to the campaign by gunmakers to achieve an independent gunmakers' company or guild that would represent their interests. When gunmakers first settled in London in the early sixteenth century, there was, of course, no gunmakers' guild. Since they needed guild membership to practice their craft, they joined guilds whose work was compatible with their own: the Armourers' Guild, the Blacksmiths' Guild, and, in the case of a few men, the Joiners' Guild. The Armourers and the Blacksmiths, occasionally joined by the Joiners, bitterly opposed the gunmakers' efforts to create a guild of their own, for the departure of the gunmakers meant a reduction in their income and status. After years of bruising battles, on 14 March 1638, King Charles I (reigned 1625–49) finally granted gunmakers a charter for their own company, which they named "The Worshipfull Company of Gunmakers."[2] It took another twenty-five years or so to persuade the Court of Aldermen of the City of London to recognize their guild. The gunmakers' efforts to establish their own company reveals the intense competiveness of these early entrepreneurs and craftsmen, the tactics on both sides to win help from the central government and the city of London, the strategy of leaders, and the use of bribes.

When King Henry VIII succeeded to the throne in 1509, he inherited a supply of ordnance, an established practice of making and storing firearms in the Tower, and the control of guns by royal authority. This was the legacy of the his royal predecessors who started in the fourteenth century to promote the slender gun industry that was emerging. Three are noteworthy. King Edward III (reigned 1327–77) responded to the advent of the Hundred Years' War in 1345–46 by calling on gunfounders and gunmakers in London and Sussex to make new guns, repair old ones, fabricate one hundred ribalds, and prepare them all for transport to the Continent.[3] The ribald was a small cannon that became a deadly weapon when mounted on the four sides of a cart and fired in sequence as the cart was turned. This murderous engine was called a Ribaudequin.[4] Edward III's use of the ribald indicates that he and people at court or in his military were abreast of the new gun technology. The king also engaged a bellfounder, William Wodeward, "the most important" gunfounder at the time, to make sixty cannon for the Crécy-Calais campaign in 1346.[5] Both England and France brought cannon to this battle, but may have used them only for their acoustical value to frighten the enemy.[6] Whatever the role of guns, Edward III won Calais in 1347 as a part of the settlement at the end of a bruising and lengthy siege.

Edward III continued to promote guns by establishing three new gun offices, thereby creating a kind of rudimentary administration. In 1362 he set up a new post, "The King's Smith," appointed Stephen atte Marsh to it, and supplied him with a suitable robe to indicate his importance.[7] In 1369 he appointed William Byker, a gunfounder, to another new position oddly named "Engineer of the War Slings" and charged him with making artillery. The government was attentive to safety, for Byker's equipment included gloves of plate and armor for his forearms and legs to protect him in his job.[8] The next year, in 1370, the king organized a new sub-department in the Tower for distributing guns. He appointed John Derby to it and gave him an impressive title: clericus pro officio gunnormum regis (clerk of the office of the king's guns), presumably to signify the importance of his work.[9]

The second early king who advanced England's gun industry was Edward IV (reigned 1461–83), who, David Grummitt's study maintains in contrast to traditional scholarship, "not only expanded but systematically modernized" the English gun industry, now located in Calais.[10] Deeply interested in military technology, Edward called upon William Rosse (who held an office in Calais) to assist him in increasing gunpowder weaponry and consolidating his control of guns.[11] When Edward died in 1483, the gunpowder weaponry of Calais, and by extension of "England as a whole," was comparable to that of contemporary states, Grummitt argues.[12]

The third major monarch who strengthened the nation's gun industry before Henry VIII was his father, King Henry VII (reigned 1485–1509). In 1490, five years after winning his crown at Bosworth Field, Henry VII hired artisans from the Continent to make guns in the Tower under the supervision of the royal household.[13] At about the same time, he actively encouraged the production of ordnance in Ashdown Forest in East Sussex, entering into multiple contracts with gunfounders there.[14] Further evidence of Henry VII's efforts followed in 1492, when he empowered James Hede to make saltpeter in England and followed that with the award of another patent for making saltpeter in 1501.[15] One assessment concluded that the "seeds of an English domestic gunfounding industry . . . can be found in the reign of Henry VII."[16] Another holds that above all Henry VII re-established the Tower as the nation's supply depot and reasserted royal control over making and storing ordnance.[17]

This strong platform, which King Henry VIII inherited, puts his initiatives in perspective, but does not diminish their importance. Almost immediately, the king, over the objections of his counselors, began preparing for war against France.[18] He did so not because England was threatened, but mostly because he wanted to win a prominent position on the international stage for himself. Larger than life in physique, strength, and ego, the king aspired to fulfill in his own person the ideal of a Renaissance prince, who, among other things, was expected to excel in martial skills and chivalric courage. According to one biographer, Henry modeled himself on his royal ancestors: Edward I, Edward III, and Henry V, all of whom had won fame fighting on the Continent.[19] He also sought to become the equal of his contemporaries, King Charles VIII of France (reigned 1483–98) and the Emperor Maximilian I (reigned 1493–1519). War was the way to achieve these goals. Other considerations reinforced Henry's determination to start a war. He looked to expand England's position in international affairs.[20] He took seriously his claim to the French throne, regarding it as a point of honor.[21] The encroachment of the French on the Netherlands alarmed Henry, for it endangered England's cloth trade and threatened the Netherlands' assistance in transporting English armies across the Channel and supplying their food.[22] Multiple reasons besides the desire for glory and honor reinforced Henry's international ambitions.

To achieve his objectives required military strength. The king apparently judged immediately that the quantity of artillery he inherited was not large enough nor its quality high enough to meet his needs. Moving in 1509, Henry ordered an upgrade in the numbers and excellence of England's artillery train.[23] Also in 1509, influenced, it is said, by King James IV of Scotland (1473–1513), Henry turned to Europe to purchase artillery.[24] Thomas Spinelly, Cardinal Thomas Wolsey's agent in Flanders, negotiated a contract with Hans Poppenruyter, the chief gunfounder at Malines (one of the best foundries in Europe at this time).[25] The relationship continued, and Poppenruyter repaired guns, made guns, and constructed the twelve huge bombards—each so heavy that it took fourteen horses to move it—that Henry VIII dubbed "The Twelve Apostles."[26] Florentine merchants in London also supplied Henry's military needs. In 1511–12, Peter Corsi sold Henry handguns with a "mould to each at 9 s. the piece" and "hagbusshes of iron with chambers."[27] John Cavalcanti provided Henry with harquebuses and "touche powder" for handguns in 1513–14.[28] To understand further how the best guns operated, Henry journeyed in 1518 to Southampton, where the Venetian fleet lay at anchor. Fascinated, the king ordered its guns fired again and again and marked their ranges.[29]

To strengthen England's native gun industry, a major goal, Henry tried to persuade Europeans who were thought to excel in gunfounding or gunmaking to immigrate to England. It is said (without proof) that Henry's "envious emulation" of the Emperor Maximilian was the reason for his importing "'Almain' or foreign armourers and gun-founders from France and the Low Countries to form schools for the production of war material in England in about the year 1515."[30] Equally plausible is that Henry (or his delegate) discussed possible candidates with the Florentine merchants in London. The king also sent agents to Europe to identify candidates and negotiate arrangements. In May 1543, Thomas Seymour, Henry's brother-in-law, wrote that he was in touch with a gunfounder in Makelen (a city near Muiden in the Netherlands) about making "small pieces." This unidentified gunfounder said that he was under contract, but starting in midsummer he could produce about five hundred pieces by Michaelmas. He asked that a piece made by Peter Baude (a French gunfounder favored by Henry) be sent to Antwerp to serve as a model.[31] What happened to Seymour's contact is unknown, but it opens a window on negotiations between a Dutch gunfounder and the English court. On 5 August 1544, Sir John Russell, who had managed the king's business on numerous occasions, reported to Sir William Paget (the principal secretary of state)[32] that Jeronymo, a gunfounder and "one of the foremost ... here," was willing to serve Henry. Russell thought him reliable. Discussions ensued: Jeronymo insisted that he receive £50, and Henry gave him a "letter of retainer" for one hundred harquebuses.[33] Fifteen days later, Russell wrote Paget again, this time expressing doubts about Jeronymo's trustworthiness, saying that Jeronymo had gone to Flanders, but will return by Boulogne "where he may be examined."[34] Apparently, the vetting was satisfactory, for Jeronymo migrated to England, where his name was changed to Hieronymus and then Anglicized to Jeremy the Stranger.[35] Another man involved in recruitment, William Damesell (Henry's agent in the Netherlands),[36] informed Paget on 29 August 1544 that he had been in touch with Domnical Irisco, a gunmaker, who said he had sent the king the two hundred arquebuses as promised. But Henry had ordered two thousand guns.[37] We do not know what happened after this exchange. These examples provide an idea of the kind of recruitment strategy that Henry and his agents undertook.

In another effort to advance the gun industry, Henry helped the alien gunfounders who arrived in London. He provided housing in the Tower and also furthered their careers. In the 1520s, Henry gave Peter Baude, who was working as a gunner[38] in the Tower, a building known as the "Bell House" to serve him as a gunfoundry. Located in Houndsditch, this structure had been used for making artillery since 1511.[39] With some help, Baude enlarged the "Bell House" to accommodate his expanded operation. The Ordnance Office highly regarded his work, for it paid him £20 in 1528 for making brass ordnance at Houndsditch.[40] Henry's gift advanced Baude's career and helped integrate him into English society.

Henry's government also forwarded the careers of English gunfounders. Two brothers, John and Robert Owen, whom Baude had trained in gunfounding, located in the Houndsditch area sometime before 1531. John Stow reported that the brothers "gate ground there to build upon, and to inclose for the casting of Brasse." He maintained that John Owen was the first Englishman to make brass ordnance.[41] The Owens' work won Henry's approval, and in 1537 he gave the brothers a pension of 8 pence a day[42] and in 1540, on the eve of war with France, the "Bellfounders house." Thanks to the government, they prospered. One brother became prominent enough for his death on 6 July 1553 to be noticed by the diarist Henry Machyn.[43] The Owens' children, continuing in their fathers' footsteps, also succeeded. In 1589, their foundry business was identified by the "Signe of the Guuilden Gonn in Houndsditch," and their house was known by a similar sign.[44] They became "unto the Dayes of King James most ready and exquisite Gunmakers."[45] The critical factor in the success of these men was the assistance of the government.

The king also sought to promote the health of the gun industry in the counties, especially in Sussex. Gunfounders and gunmakers had worked there since the fourteenth century, and King Henry VII had encouraged émigré gunfounders to settle in the Ashdown Forest. Joan Thirsk found that the industry did not prosper then.[46] But in 1543 with war on the horizon and the Dutch threatening to ban the export of iron to England, Henry sent Baude to Sussex to train Ralph Hogge (d. 1585), a gunfounder, in the "very difficult and complicated procedures necessary for casting a gun."[47] Hogge had only a local reputation at that time, but probably persons known in government circles recommended him. Brian Hogge, a relative, perhaps his brother, had worked at the Ordnance Office for many years. William Levett (d. 1554), a gunfounder in Sussex, had employed him. Levett's word would have carried weight. The son of a wealthy landowner, Levett, known as "Parson Levett," had earned a degree in canon law at Oxford University and became a Church of England cleric. His position as deputy receiver of the king's revenue in Sussex in 1533 gave him entrée to persons in London. In May 1535, Levett inherited the lease of the ironworks and furnaces belonging to his deceased brother John, a life-changing event for him. He worked the mills and enjoyed success. In 1539–40 he supplied the Office of Ordnance with iron shot; in 1541 he obtained the post of the king's "goonstone maker"; and that same year received £200 in advance for casting shot. By 1543, Levett was a leading Sussex gunfounder. So prominent was he that when Baude arrived in Sussex to teach Hogge the techniques of making cast iron guns in a blast furnace, he and Hogge worked under the direction of Levett.[48] They enjoyed great success, being the first in England to make a cast-iron cannon in one piece, that is, with the breach and barrel together as an integral whole.[49] Henry VIII's sending Baude to Sussex had significant economic and military consequences. The gunfounding industry prospered, thereby enhancing the region's economy and contributing to the king's military needs.

This narrative of Henry VIII's efforts to develop a robust gun industry shows the active involvement of the monarchy and the court in the process. The king's aggressive foreign policy required artillery and military handguns, and Henry took steps to assure their supply. He induced Continental gunmakers to immigrate to England to jumpstart the industry and train Englishmen, and he took care of their interests once they came. War and unsettled domestic conditions made the production of military guns essential throughout his reign. Henry's efforts were decisive because he himself was actively involved. Succeeding monarchs followed his lead in similar and different ways, as the need for military guns was ongoing. The industry was deeply dependent on the government and on war for orders.

The second initiative that promoted the gun industry was making handguns for domestic use. It followed within the context of and in tandem with manufacturing artillery and military handguns. Gunmakers themselves promoted this departure. The practice of using a firearm for hunting was introduced on the Continent before Henry VIII ascended the throne. As early as 1480, an illustration in a German book showed hunters shooting waterfowl with a harquebus, an early military gun.[50] In 1504 another book illustration depicted the Emperor Maximilian I, a man whom Henry VIII much admired, using a matchlock handgun to hunt a chamois (a goat-like antelope). The handgun the Emperor used in hunting was the same kind of gun his soldiers used in war.[51] In England, a 1514 game law provided the first evidence that guns were used in hunting; it banned anyone without an annual income of 300 marks from using them.[52] The 1514 law, however, had little effect. In a 1528 proclamation, Henry decried the "newfangle[d] and wanton[53] pleasure that men now have in using . . . handguns."[54] Twelve years later in another proclamation, Henry scolded people for shooting handguns in cities and towns and charged that they endangered residents "in the open street or in their own houses, chambers or gardens."[55] Upbraiding, however, did not stop the spread of handguns for personal pleasures. Steven Gunn argued (and I agree) that the use of handguns moved from town to countryside and on to remote areas.[56] Gunn also noticed that the relatively cheap cost of handguns—averaging 8s. 3d.—enabled people down the social scale to buy them.[57] Gunmakers were correct in judging that there was a market for handguns for domestic purposes. The use of handguns for hunting and shooting and then over time for many other uses spread through society, as discussed in subsequent chapters. These two initiatives, by the king himself and by workers in the industry, laid the foundation of an English gun industry.

Gunmakers took the lead in another area of importance to the business of gunmaking. They provided the energy, strategy, and financing for a campaign to achieve an independent gunmakers' company. In the absence of a gunmakers' guild and to satisfy the requirement of guild membership to work in London, gunfounders and gunmakers joined existing guilds whose work was compatible with their own: the Armourers' Guild, the Blacksmiths' Guild, and in a few instances the Joiners' Guild.[58] The three guilds were ancient: the Armourers had been in existence since 1322 and was chartered in 1453; the Blacksmiths was mentioned in 1299 and chartered in 1571; Joiners traced their origins back to the fourteenth century and won a charter also in 1571. Between 1500 and 1750, approximately 172 gunmakers joined the Armourers' Guild, and about 236 enrolled in the Blacksmiths' Guild.[59] There are no figures for how many became affiliated with the Joiners. Why gunmakers would enlist in the Joiners' Guild may puzzle readers. Actually, the work of joiners had much to offer gunmakers. Their craft required skill in making a tight joint between pieces of wood, and that dexterity is the key to the gunmakers' interest. In fact, when Richard Campbell wrote about the London companies in 1757, he described a gunmaker as a "Compound of the Joiner and the Smith; he works both in Wood and Iron." Campbell also observed that gunmaking "is a very ingenious Business, requiring . . . a nice Hand at forming a Joint to make his Work close."[60] Gunmakers entered the London economy through these guilds, and their presence brought income to them.

Recognizing the financial advantages from gunfounding and gunmaking, the Armourers and Blacksmiths vied with each other, from about 1570, over which one had the sole right to make and sell guns, search for and impound illegal ones, and examine, proof, and guarantee their quality. The right to proof guns was the major point of contention—because it was lucrative. No gun made in London or within a ten-mile radius and no imported gun was to be sold until it had been proofed and stamped, that is, until it had passed a "quality assurance test."[61] This test involved an examination of the metal to judge its quality, of the barrel and the bore to assure the absence of cracks and tiny holes, and of the bore to measure its size and proper "windage" with respect to the missile. The firearm was then fitted with a cartridge holding a charge more powerful than one that would normally be used and test-fired three times. If the gun passed, a proofmark was stamped on it. The cost of proofing was borne by the owner, an arrangement confirmed by the Gunmakers' charter granted in 1638 and discussed below. The cost varied over time and depended on the kind of gun. In 1698, the Gunmakers' Company established the charge at 10 pence for an arquebus, 8 pence for a birding or fowling piece "and Other Guns of that quallity," and 6 pence for a dag and pistol.[62] These figures reflected an increase in the cost imposed in 1675 because maintaining the proof house cost the Company so much.[63] The proofing provided income, which explains the competition between the Armourers and the Blacksmiths and the determination of the Gunmakers to have their own company.

In January 1581, gunfounders and gunmakers petitioned the Privy Council to grant them "A Corporacon, and to be one Company Incorporate."[64] Except for Thomas Parker, a member of the Armourers' Company, the men who organized the petition are unknown.[65] But the petition reveals their political astuteness. The petitioners complained that defective guns were "daylie brought into and soulde" in England and Ireland and painted a dismal picture of the harm they did. Many "subiectes are deceased and sustayne much losse," soldiers are "dayly murdered, lamed and spoyled," and enemies of the queen are emboldened. Such a situation was unnecessary, they declared, for "within Her Majesties saide Realms" were men [meaning themselves] who "doe and can verie artificially, strongely and well, make, worke, and bore" guns. Appealing to sympathy, they described themselves as "a greate number of poore men," undone for "lacke of worke." This point stretched the truth. The Armourers found out (through their member Parker) that "to bring . . . [the petition] to passe," the gunmakers planned to give Francis Russell, the Earl of Bedford, 100 calivers (a long-barreled harquebus) and "a nother as manye who was not Named."[66] A caliver ranged in price from 12 to 30 shillings.[67] Assuming that the gunmakers presented 200 fine calivers (100 to Bedford and 100 to the unnamed person) and each was priced at 30 shillings, the value of the gifts came to £300, a significant sum. Giving a gun and money or both to help achieve a goal threads through this chapter and others. The effort to inspire sympathy, whether true or not, was a politically clever move.

Another shrewd feature of the petition was the suggestion that the Master of the Office of Ordnance, Ambrose Dudley, the Third Earl of Warwick (c. 1530–1590), and his successors, should be the "governors" of the new gun company.[68] Arguably designed to ingratiate themselves with Warwick, this idea also identified the new company with the Ordnance Office. In still another politically astute move, gunmakers sent a petition to Sir Francis Walsingham (c. 1532–1590), the queen's Principal Secretary, entreating his assistance and saying they had "opened theire greefes" to Warwick.[69] The gunmakers approached Walsingham because they knew that he was the "primary point of contact for . . . suitors to the crown."[70] Despite these efforts, their petition failed.

What explains the failure of this carefully drafted petition? The opposition of the Armourers and the Blacksmiths was the principal reason. Both companies began a campaign to defeat the effort. Both wanted to claim all the rights over the manufacture, repair, and proof of guns. Both were as politically astute as the gunmakers. In January 1581, the Armourers "caused a bill to be drawn and put into the Parliament House."[71] The purpose of the legislation was to give the Armourers and the Joiners who joined them, joint control of the manufacture and sale of guns in London.[72] The Armourers appealed for assistance in getting their bill passed to high-placed men: the Lord Chancellor, Sir Thomas Bromley (c.1530–1587), and the Speaker of the House of Commons, Sir John Popham (c.1531–1607). Their bill must have had merit, for Bromley, a member of the Privy Council, active in the House of Commons, and recognized for his legal acumen, liked it enough to "recommend it" to Popham. Like Bromley, Popham was a renowned lawyer, equally well-placed. Appointed solicitor-general in 1579 and attorney-general in 1581, and elected speaker of the House of Commons also in 1581, he, too, looked with favor on the bill, describing it as "both neadfull and nessessarye." He used his influence to push it forward.[73] The Armourers were assiduous in keeping their bill before Popham, "attend[ing him] day by day, sometimes twice a day."[74] This seemingly hopeful response from people in a position to achieve results must have led the Armourers to expect success. But the bill was lost.

The Armourers' bill failed at least partly because of the actions of their competitors, the Blacksmiths. For their part, the Blacksmiths were just as eager as the Armourers to win the principal place in the gun industry, and they embarked on a countercampaign. William Hopkins, a Warden of the Blacksmiths from 1562 to 1563, "laboured [with others] against the Bill."[75] The Blacksmiths also approached Sir Walter Mildmay (1520/21–1589), the Chancellor of the Exchequer, a privy councilor, and a man much admired at court for his fiscal expertise. In an effort to discredit the Armourers with Mildmay, the Blacksmiths disparaged their work, saying that "none cowld mak no Gonnes nor any that could mak any ege tolles but one. Nethr cowld make any Armor, wth divers other untrewthes."[76] The Armourers tried to counter these libelous words by securing their own audience with Mildmay to explain the nature of their business and insist on their ability.[77] There was no resolution to this unseemly struggle. Very likely the attempts of the Blacksmiths and Armourers to win over men high-placed in Parliament, law, and fiscal matters cancelled each other out. And, in the end, the gunmaker's petition was lost in the conflict.

A promising turn of affairs for the gunmakers occurred eight years later, in 1589, when a report and a petition were submitted to Queen Elizabeth's government.[78] The report assessed the 1588 general muster that had been ordered to repulse the widely feared landing of men launched from the Spanish Armada. Prepared by the officers responsible for the muster, the report complained that "divers Muskettes, Callyvers, horsemens peeces, and dagges" that were issued to soldiers were "defective and insufficient for service." The bore of the guns was either crooked or the wrong size for the "bullettes," and the result was "oftentimes maymyinge or killing the partie Usinge the same and the Imynent and inevitable danger of all theis neare thereunto of what place callinge decree or estate soever." Attached to this disturbing report was a petition from twenty-one gunmakers, headed by William Hopkins (also active in the 1580 petition) and a Mr. Smythe, who was described as a maker of "smale ordinauns" in the Tower. Hopkins had enjoyed a long, varied, and successful career, and undoubtedly, his name carried weight.[79] Over the years, he had worked as "Maker of the Guns for the Queen" on a retainer of 16 pence per day, served as a Warden of the Blacksmiths' Company from 1562 to 1563, become a

Master Smith in the Tower of London, supplying ordnance with several kinds of guns from 1587 to 1588, and identified himself with gunmakers in 1589. He would have been known to people associated with the gun industry as well as men in government. The petitioners' purpose was to persuade Elizabeth and her advisers that they were well-qualified to deal with the issues described in the report. They assured the queen of their skill in gunmaking and the "credit and good opinion" that they enjoyed in "theire Art and profession."

The government responded to this overture with a lengthy "Draft Proclamation for Gunmakers." The author or authors of this document, which was remarkable for its implicit endorsement of the gunmaking industry, were not identified, but almost certainly William Cecil, Lord Burghley (1520/21–1598) was one, if not the only, author. The "Draft Proclamation" used the arguments of the report and the petition to develop a model for a gunmakers' guild. It announced the appointment of Hopkins "to have the viewe searches and triall of all and everye" gun[80] (in other words to proof them) and enjoined justices of the peace and other officers to assist him in imposing the rules and in arresting and punishing offenders responsible for defective guns.[81] The "Draft Proclamation" imposed many rules, among them standardization of barrels and bores, regulation of apprentices, and guidelines for fines for disobedience. The rules covered all gunmakers in London and its suburbs for seven miles around. It was a comprehensive and workable statement, but, for unknown reasons, it was neither proclaimed nor passed into law. Perhaps representatives of the Armourers and the Blacksmiths used their influence to persuade high-placed people that it was ill-advised. Although it was in the interests of the nation to strengthen the organization of gunmakers, the government allowed this effort to languish. Elizabeth died in 1603, and James I, who was less interested in guns at the beginning of his reign than later on, succeeded. The "Draft Proclamation" was forgotten.

Deteriorating relations with Spain renewed the English government's concern to augment its supply of military armaments and revived the interest of the Armourers and the Blacksmiths in claiming authority over guns. Between 1627 and 1637 they waged another battle of petitions that was just as fierce and ugly as the previous ones. Each side continued to vie with the other to win a monopoly over viewing, proofing, and repairing guns in England and Wales.[82] Each claimed this as their "immemorial right." In May 1637, gunmakers reentered the contest. They appointed "certeine Antients" to use "all Convenient speed" to procure a charter.[83] Escalating the effort, on 4 June 1637, a few gunmakers led by Henry Rowland, appealed directly to King Charles I to grant them a charter.[84] They decried the Blacksmiths as "men ignorant altogether of the arte of Gunnmaking." The Company of Blacksmiths, with the temporary support of the Armourers, countered with its own petition, begging the government to deny the request, declaring that otherwise they would become destitute.[85] At this point, King Charles I stepped in, no doubt because hostile relations with Scotland added urgency to settling the matter. If war should come, fractious relations among artisans responsible for founding, making, and proofing guns would be highly detrimental to England's position. The king referred the case to the Attorney General John Bankes (1589–1644) and the Solicitor General Sir Edward Littleton (1589–1645). Joined by Thomas Gardiner, the Recorder of London, these men met with representatives from the gunmakers and the Blacksmiths' Company. Finally, on 29 January 1638, they announced their decision: to grant incorporation to the gunmakers, but permit the Company of Blacksmiths to continue to exercise its former rights respecting guns.[86] On these terms, on 14 March 1638, Charles I listed one hundred and twenty-six men as members of the new company and granted them a royal charter under the Great Seal as "The Worshipful Company of Gunmakers," making them "One Body Corporate and Politick in Deed and in Name." The Worshipfull Company of Gunmakers ranked as the seventy-third guild created in London.

The Company's charter was a long, highly detailed document.[87] Beginning with high praise for London gunmakers for having supplied the government with firearms for many years and for having achieved an "exquisite" ability in their craft, the charter went on to criticize in harsh terms the "inexpert" and "unskilfull" "Blacksmiths and others" whose defective guns had inflicted "much harm and danger" on many "Loyal Subjects" (79). To shape the new company, the charter appointed its first master, two wardens, and ten assistants and specified their duties. Thereafter the members of the company chose these officers. The charter limited the company's authority to London, the city's liberties, and a four-mile compass (80–87). To exercise the "Art of Gunmaking," it stated that a person must serve a seven-year apprenticeship, present a Proof Piece, and receive the approval of the Wardens and Assistants "as an expert and able Workman." On being admitted to the company, each individual was required to take an oath of loyalty to the king, of obedience to the master and wardens, and of submission to the ordinances of the company, and swear to attend Quarter-Days and other meetings (89).[88] The charter gave the new Gunmakers' Company extensive powers to supervise the trade, advance the art of gunmaking, train future gunmakers, assure reliable production of "good and serviceable Handguns for Military Service and otherwise" (in recognition of a domestic market), and guarantee proper proofing. The company gained "full power" to search, proof, and mark guns of all kinds—whether made domestically or imported. Included was a proofmark for the company, the letters

GP topped with a crown, to be stamped on every proofed gun. The cost of proofing was to be borne by the owner of the gun (87). The Lord Mayor and Aldermen of London were ordered to enroll the charter (91). On the face of it, gunmakers could not have asked for more; many points in the charter were the same ones the gunmakers had requested.

In its final paragraph, however, the charter undermined previous provisions: no gunmaker in the Company of Blacksmiths should be forced either to join the new Company of Gunmakers or be debarred from the "power of search and Tryal that they now have by their Charter" (91–92). This was the compromise worked out in the meetings that Bankes, Littleton, and Gardiner had had with delegates from the Gunmakers and the Blacksmiths. Clearly, the government was unable to come to a decisive decision. Predictably, conflict continued.

Members of the Armourers Guild and Blacksmiths' Guild relentlessly renewed their efforts to block the Company of Gunmakers. They tried to prevent London's Mayor and Court of Aldermen from enrolling the new charter. Enrollment of the charter was necessary to achieve recognition of the Gunmakers as a company. Despite a letter from the Master of the Ordnance (Mountjoy Blount, First Earl of Newport [c.1597–1666]) endorsing the enrollment, the influence of the well-established Armourers and Blacksmiths with London officials was overwhelming. The charter was not enrolled.[89]

Fifteen years later, after the Civil Wars, leaders of the Gunmakers' Company reopened the matter. This time, John Silk, a prominent gunmaker and a politically shrewd individual who was willing to use money to accomplish his ends, devised a scheme to test the legal standing of the Gunmakers' Company. On 28 August 1651, in an effort "the better to capacitate the Company," Silk applied to London authorities to grant him freedom of the city by redemption through the Gunmakers' Company.[90] The idea was that success in this ploy (described as "a deliberate move to cause trouble")[91] would prove that the Gunmakers were a free London company. Silk won over London Alderman Foot to this plan, agreeing to pay him £30 if it worked.[92] The Blacksmiths learned of the move and persuaded the Lord Mayor in 1654 to arrest Silk as a "foreigner." The Lord Mayor complied and arrested and jailed Silk, but other London officials objected. The City released him and did not pursue the charge.[93] In the meantime, the struggle between the united Armourers and the Blacksmiths and the Gunmakers continued. In 1652, the Armourers and Blacksmiths tried to undercut an unidentified petition that the Gunmakers had submitted to the City of London. On 19 January, 1653, the two companies shared the expenses they had incurred in this effort.[94] In response, the Gunmakers' Court of Assistants renewed their determination and undertook to identify "some person" to help them obtain the charter's enrollment. After searching for two years, in 1655 they persuaded William Smith of Lincoln's Inn to assist them. Described as a gentleman, Smith was well-qualified to take on this job: he had served as clerk to the Town Clerk of London and secretary to John Sadler, Master of Requests to the Lord Protector. In the agreement worked out between them, Smith received the post of Clerk of the Gunmakers' Company for life with a salary of £8 per year, plus fees.[95] He set to work on the problem, but his path was not smooth, for opposition did not abate. On 10 March 1656, the Armourers took steps to bolster the reputation of their gunmakers by preparing a petition to show their "Skill & Care in that Manufacture." The petition aimed to forestall the idea that all gunmakers should be members of the Gunmakers' Company. It held that gunmakers in the Armourers' Guild "dislike[d] to be of the Company of Gunmakers" and that they would not shift their membership.[96] The Blacksmiths' Company agreed with this position, but at least one of its members objected. Edward Burrows had been made free of the Blacksmiths' Company in 1629, but had also worked for the Gunmakers' Company. In 1656, he told the Blacksmiths that he "cared not a fart" for their orders, transferred out of the Company, and was made free of the Gunmakers' Company two years later.[97] The Armourers' petition did not achieve the desired result. In the meantime, Smith succeeded in getting Silk admitted by redemption and the Gunmakers' charter enrolled on 5 June 1656. The Company of Gunmakers paid the City Chamberlain 46s. 8d. for his assistance.[98]

In 1663, after another dustup with their old enemies, the Gunmakers presented a petition to the Court of Aldermen aimed at solidifying their position. They held that when their charter was enrolled, its provisions applied only to persons working in the industry at that time. But now, twenty-five years later, the company was well established, and to assure excellent training, all persons wishing to become a gunmaker should be bound as an apprentice only to the Gunmakers' Company. Members of the Court of Common Council were persuaded and issued an order to that end.[99] By 1663, the Gunmakers had a charter, recognition by London, and the legal authority solely to train apprentices.

It took about eighty years to win a royal charter for a Company of Gunmakers and persuade London authorities to enroll the company's charter. Henry VIII's initial steps had been swift and undisputed, coming as they did from the king. Making handguns for domestic use had not engendered fierce opposition. But the next phase in the history of the industry was complicated and ugly. For the Armourers and Blacksmiths, the loss of income motivated their unceasing opposition. For the Gunmakers, their need to establish their own identity as well as advance their economic interests were ongoing incentives to win their own company. The Armourers and the Blacksmiths contested, step by step, their every effort, sometimes winning, sometimes losing, always slowing down the process. It took patience, confidence, shrewd political moves, the influence of a man hired for the job, and gifts of money to win a charter in 1638, enrollment of the charter by the City of London in 1657, and recognition that Gunmakers alone had the right to prove all handguns in 1663. Their struggles and successes became part of the developing military and domestic gun cultures.

The narrative of the company's further history to the present may be followed elsewhere in publications already mentioned. The company continues today in a modern world that has an ever-pressing need of firearms. With approximately three hundred members, it is one of few guilds engaged in the same kind of work for which it was founded in the seventeenth century.

TWO · Economic Opportunities for Men and Women

THE ADVENT OF GUNS HAD A significant economic impact. It created new entrepreneurial and employment opportunities for men across the social spectrum and for women (mostly widows) of artisanal status. Jobs were one reason English civilians assimilated guns so readily. International wars, domestic uprisings, and civil wars fueled a demand for artillery and for military handguns. Through the Ordnance Office, the department responsible for military supplies among numerous other tasks related to the military, the government hired gunfounders and gunmakers to make artillery and military handguns, the major source of income for members of the industry. This relationship contributed significantly to creating England's military gun culture. The demand for military weaponry, however, was not constant; it waxed and waned, depending on England's foreign policy, response to domestic turmoil, and forward-looking leadership. Guns for hunting and marksmanship, protection of person and property, collecting and gift giving, and other civilian activities helped to maintain a market for firearms and employment in the gun industry in peacetime. Manufacturers of lighter, shorter guns for women and young people, and artisans who transformed guns into objects of art added other elements to the civilian gun economy. Making and marketing these guns assisted the integration of guns into their lives and was an essential component in creating the nation's domestic gun culture.

War or threat of war was the context within which the military gun business developed. Fortunately for the industry, war was endemic over the era, famously the bloodiest period in European history until the twentieth century. During the sixteenth century, peace prevailed on the Continent for less than ten years, and in the seventeenth century for only four.[1] England fared batter. Protected always by the English Channel, often by financial penury, and sometimes by shrewd foreign policies, the country was at war in Europe for just eighty-seven of two hundred and twenty-nine years of the era. For example, England fought France in 1513, from 1522 to 1523, during the 1540s, from 1557 to 1558, from 1689 to 1697, and from 1702 to 1714. She fought Spain in the late sixteenth century, and in the middle of the seventeenth century she and the Netherlands engaged in three short wars. Domestic violence in the sixteenth century involved a range of issues—religious, political, social and economic—and was both persistent and widespread.[2] The amateur county militia was mustered to deal with such problems and, of course, was armed. In the mid-seventeenth century, the Civil Wars, involving England, Ireland, and Scotland, rent the nation from 1641 to 1648. In short, hostilities of one kind or another, international and domestic, repeatedly required military hardware and kept the gun business thriving. There were, however, periods of peace when the industry suffered setbacks.

The Ordnance Office, the department of the government responsible for providing supervision and development of the nation's military weaponry, assuring a supply of equipment for the army and navy, and training gunners, was also the government's agent for hiring people from the gun community.[3] The office was both the principal employer and principal customer of gunfounders, gunmakers, and others in the gun business. It hired both men and women. Located in the Tower, Ordnance had a long history. It evolved over the fourteenth century out of the Privy Wardrobe, an offshoot of the Royal Household. In 1414, King Henry V appointed the first known Master of Ordnance, Nicholas Marbury, with instructions to requisition artisans and military stores.[4] King Henry VIII expanded this department physically, ordering rooms made for administrative offices in the White Tower and a residence for the Master of the Ordnance in the Brick Tower.[5] The government bought up storehouses in the adjacent street, the Minories, to hold firearms, gunpowder, and supplies. The London antiquarian John Stow recorded that the king dissolved the nunnery in the Minories in 1539 and in its place built "faire and large storehouses for armour, and habiliments of warre, with diuerse worke houses seruing to the same purpose."[6] In 1546, funds were allocated to construct a new building on the Tower grounds to store and guard the nation's "artillery Ordinaunce" and provide a room for the king's guns.[7]

By 1535, holding high office at Ordnance seemed desirable. When the then-Master, Sir William Skiffington, died, an observer noticed competition for the post, remarking that "divers suitors" sought the appointment.[8] In 1544, Henry upgraded the status of the Office of Master by appointing Sir Thomas Seymour, his brother-in-law, to the position. Seymour held the post, described as a "striking mark of royal favor," until 1547, when he resigned because of his ennoblement and promotion to Lord High Admiral.[9] By appointing a family member, Henry transformed the Mastership into a prestigious position. Speculation holds that Henry took this step to equalize the social rank between the Lord Admiral (the chief officer of the Navy) and the Office of Master at Ordnance.[10] The Office of Master, however, did not carry the handsome perquisites of the Lord Admiral's position, which included other high posts in the Army or Navy and an ex-officio place on the Privy Council.[11] The annual salary of the new Ordnance Master was only £151 11s., which was in keeping with the low salaries of officeholders during the era, but not large enough alone to be an inducement to sixteenth-century aristocrats.[12] The mark of royal favor and the opportunity for influence were apparently compensation enough.

Throughout the era, a noble or an aristocrat continued to hold the position. Among such men in the sixteenth century was Ambrose Dudley, Third Earl of Warwick, who shared the post with the poet Sir Philip Sidney from 1585 to 1586.[13] Robert Devereux, Second Earl of Essex, Elizabeth I's favorite, was Master from 1597 to 1600. The pattern persisted. At the end of the seventeenth century, Henry Sidney, First Earl of Romney, held the position from 1693 to 1702, and John Churchill, First Duke of Marlborough, held it from 1702 to 1712 and 1714 to 1717.[14] The presence alone of men of such notable achievement and outstanding reputation enlarged the reputation of the Ordnance Office. It also publicly underlined the government's wholehearted acceptance of firearms.

Henry VIII also created a new office, the "Lieutenant of the Ordnance." In effect, this post was an additional upgrade of the office of Master, for its purpose was to spare the Master the drudgery of supervising the daily activities of the department. As the chief executive officer, the Lieutenant of the Ordnance received a salary of £72 a year, just about half the Master's salary.[15] The background of Christopher Morris, the first to hold this office, suggests Henry's initial intentions in creating the post. Morris had had extensive practical experience with guns.[16] Starting out in the Ordnance Office in 1513 as a gunner responsible for testing firearms, Morris moved on to the post of gunner on one of the king's great galleys, and then was sent to Tournai for further instruction in artillery. In 1527, Henry promoted him to the position of Master Gunner in the ordnance office, and in that capacity he supervised training in gunnery and assessed the nation's guns. He won promotion again in 1536 when he was made Master of Ordnance. For his exemplary service in this role, the king knighted him in 1539. In 1544, however, he was moved into the new office of Lieutenant of the Ordnance. Morris was clearly well qualified to be Lieutenant, but not Master, as that post was newly designed. His career is a nice example of the upward mobility that the revitalized gun industry created and the Ordnance Office realized.

Men who followed Morris, however, were men of wealth and high rank. Sir William Pelham, for instance, was Lieutenant from 1576 to 1587, and Sir George Carew from 1592 to 1608, when he was promoted to Master of the Ordnance and elevated to the title of First Lord Carew of Clapton. Sir Roger Allison followed Carew as Lieutenant from 1608 to 1616. In the late seventeenth century, four men who held the post were Privy Councilors, and one, Lord George Granville, was a peer.[17]

Restyling the titles of the new Ordnance officers was another indication that the government aimed to inflate their status. In the early seventeenth century, the master and lieutenant became the "Master-General" and the "Lieutenant-General."[18] Titles are important in a bureaucratic organization, especially one associated with the military. These changes signaled to other departments in the bureaucracy and to the public the importance of the Office's work.

The appointment of noble and aristocratic men to the two most important positions at the Office of Ordnance was consequential. The social standing that an aristocratic Master and Lieutenant brought to their offices would have weakened the snobbish attitude toward the work of the Ordnance Office that some people held. At the Restoration court, Henry Hyde, the First Earl of Clarendon (1609–1674), expressed this attitude well. Comparing the Ordnance Office with the Treasury department, he observed disparagingly that Ordnance dealt "only with smiths and carpenters and other artificers and handicraftsmen," whereas Treasury had "much to do with the nobility and chief gentry of the kingdom."[19] Although this evidence is from the seventeenth century, the attitude surely existed earlier. With nobles or wealthy aristocrats leading the department, Ordnance and its offices looked more attractive. The appointments were desirable for their access to the king, to patronage, and, for some, to the money to be made from corrupt dealings. Such appointments helped to advance the reputation of the entire gun industry. They also showed the seriousness of the government in promoting gunpowder-fired weaponry.

Positions beneath the level of Master and Lieutenant multiplied as the use of guns in military institutions expanded. They, too, offered employment opportunities for well-to-do and educated men. The Surveyor of the Ordnance, third in the hierarchy of the Ordnance Office, was responsible for quality control, uncovering "corruption and graft," and keeping records (in duplicate).[20] During the reign of Elizabeth I, Sir John Davis, a member of the Earl of Essex's circle, regarded the position as so desirable that he campaigned for it. In 1598, Davis asked for the Earl's support on grounds that his "former studies in artillery" and his expectation of making further contributions to that field well qualified him for the position.[21] Successful in the effort, Davis served as Surveyor-General of the Ordnance from 1599 to 1602. In the early seventeenth century, Sir John Kay occupied the position from 1608 to 1623, the longest-serving Surveyor in the early seventeenth century.[22] In the last half of the century, Sir Jonas Moore Sr. and his son held the office, one after the other, from 1679 through 1685, while William Bridges was also long-serving, holding the office from 1702 to 1714. Wealthy men were pleased to occupy this position.

Men who ranked below the status of gentleman also found jobs in the Ordnance Office. Those knowledgeable about artillery qualified for the post of Master Gunner, a job under the Crown that was added between 1485 and 1506.[23] The Master Gunner's duties, which earned him £70 annually (only a little less than the Lieutenant's salary), were extensive. They included training and certifying all the gunners in England and keeping records of them. He also proofed heavy ordnance and military arms, maintained the Artillery Garden north of the Tower, and kept a record of the ordnance stored in the government's forts and ships and its condition.[24] Regarded as the "crown's chief technical expert on . . . artillery," the Master Gunner often also held the job of proof master at a salary of £24 a year.[25] This brought his total annual income to £94, a respectable sum surpassing the salary of the Lieutenant-General and indicating the importance and inherent danger of his work. In addition, in the late seventeenth century, the Master Gunner sometimes earned a fee of ten guineas when asked to fire sixty-two guns on royal occasions.[26] The post of Master Gunner would have attracted men who were knowledgeable about firearms and possessed the requisite education in mathematics and geometry. Elizabeth I's Master Gunner requested and won a coat of arms (chapter 7).

The gunners, like the Master Gunner, came from the middling ranks of seventeenth-century society; the post was considered unsuitable for men from the lower social orders.[27] The number of gunners posted throughout the country must have been very large, for in one year of Elizabeth I's reign ninety-five men won appointment by the queen's letters patent serving just in the Tower of London.[28] They were paid out of the Exchequer on a descending scale, perhaps according to seniority or in testimony to their skill. Of the ninety-five men, thirteen earned 12 pence per day; nine, 8 pence; and sixty-five, 6 pence. The post was coveted: six men, styling themselves as "humble suters," petitioned the queen to appoint them to the position.[29]

In 1537, Henry VIII chartered a Fraternity of Artillery or Gunners in the Tower of London partly to provide systematic training for aspiring gunners.

Elizabeth I continued the effort.[30] Organized as a guild with masters, journeymen, and apprentices, the fraternity operated out of the Ordnance Office. Men at the apprenticeship level, called Scholars, Scrollers, or Servitor Gunners, received standardized instruction. They were required to attend classes, take notes, and pass examinations. A small number of their notes has survived, among them those of John Lad and Christopher Lad (brothers, it is assumed) who together in 1586 wrote and illustrated them.[31] The notes reveal that the students studied a wide range of subjects, including how to "know the goodness of all manner of gunpowder,"[32] how to use a quadrant to calculate the trajectory of a bullet,[33] and how to measure the height and weight of the shot and figure the amount of required powder.[34] The topics were difficult and the instructions complicated. To be accepted into the program, the apprentice needed a sound basic education, some knowledge of mathematics and geometry, and some familiarity with firearms. If youthful aspirants to a career as a gunner successfully completed this program, the Master Gunner and others could be assured they were well trained.

Other jobs essential to running a bureaucratic department offered further new opportunities for employment. Among them were clerk, supplier, craftsman, basket maker, bowyer, and blacksmith. One of the employees, Andrea Bassano, a member of a large Italian family of musicians, stands out. In about 1540, Andrea's grandfather, Jeronimo Bassano, and his sons, moved from Venice to England, where they prospered as instrument makers and musicians at the courts of King Henry VIII and Queen Elizabeth I. Andrea's father and his brothers continued this tradition. Andrea, however, apparently did not have the interest or perhaps the talent to be a musician. He turned instead to the Office of Ordnance for employment. From 1593 to 1603, Bassano and Samuel Garrett supplied canvas to Ordnance, and Andrea alone did so from 1620 to 1625. He was also responsible with other men for supplying "Emptions (miscellaneous ships' supplies)" from 1620 to 1625.[35] In about 1614, he and three other men worked as ordnance clerks at an annual salary of £20. His appointment as clerk showed no terminal date, whereas that of the other two specified a date, perhaps indicating Ordnance regarded him with favor. After 1625, Bassano disappears from the records I have seen, until 6 May 1645, when, as a "Commissioner appointed by a Committee of Parliament for taking the Remains of the Stores in the Offices of the Ordnance and Armory," he petitioned the House of Lords to be appointed Lieutenant of Ordnance, a Place "shortly to be void." He offered his experience as qualification for the position, citing his "Twenty-four years and upwards" as a clerk at Ordnance and pointing out that he was also a "Deputy to Mr. Morrice, one of the Officers."[36] "Mr. Morrice" was undoubtedly Francis Morrice, Clerk of the Ordnance from

1608 to 1625, an important post, not to be confused with an Ordnance clerk. Morrice was also appointed to Sir Lionel Cranfield's Reform Commission in 1618. To be Morrice's deputy was to occupy a position of consequence. Their Lordships concurred with the petition and sent it on to the House of Commons, which received it on 9 May 1645, when members noted that the Lords had given their assent to the petition.[37] The record, however, is silent about the final disposition of Bassano's petition. Bassano's career at the Office of Ordnance illustrates how the son of a second-generation immigrant family might prosper and shows that working in the gun business was an attractive option.

In sum, the Office of Ordnance offered desirable employment to aristocrats to fill positions at the highest levels of its operation and to educated men skilled in artillery and mathematics to occupy important posts lower in the bureaucracy. It also opened jobs to men, such as Bassano, who were willing to take on jobs as clerks and suppliers. This employment pattern lifted the reputation both of the Office of Ordnance and firearms.

Gunfounders, gunmakers, gunsmiths, and other artisans associated with guns also found work with the Ordnance Office. All of them were artisanal or lower in social status.[38] Their jobs were to make and repair guns, make and refresh gunpowder, and perform other tasks associated with guns for the government's military needs. The number of qualified persons who were available for such jobs grew slowly but steadily. From 1500 to 1525, eight or ten gunmakers were active in London, but as Henry VIII's project of luring Continental gunmakers to England took hold, the number grew to about nineteen gunmakers from 1525 to 1550.[39] During the reign of Queen Elizabeth I, from 1575 to 1600, a time of internal unrest and international challenge, it surged to about 134. In the seventeenth century, from 1625 to 1650, when the Thirty Years' War raged in Europe and the Civil Wars in the British Isles, approximately 365 gunmakers were counted, and from 1675 to 1715 (years of domestic upheaval followed by war) the number increased to about 450. For the twenty-five years between 1740 and 1765, only about 109 gunmakers worked in London, a figure no doubt reflecting both a more peaceful period and the establishment of a robust gun industry in Birmingham and other places. Altogether, approximately 2,069 gunmakers were in London from about 1500 to about 1765.

Among these gunmakers were about 123 women who were associated with the business of guns. Only 25 women worked in gunmaking from about 1550 to 1638, the years before London gunmakers received a charter. From 1640 to about 1765, the total membership of the Company of Gunmakers was about 1,400 persons and included about 95 women. Thus, during these years a little over 6 percent of the Company's members were women. It is, of course, no surprise that women worked in a craft, were enrolled in a guild, or if a widow continued at least a portion of her husband's business. Approximately 28 percent of London gunmakers—625 men and 65 women—worked for Ordnance at some time in their lives during the era. Thus, a little more than 10 percent were women, almost all of whom were widows of men who had worked at Ordnance. Gunmaking posed no physical challenge to women, as the nature of gunmaking, described in Appendix A, shows. However, no woman was associated with gunfounding, also described in the Appendix. Gunfounding would have posed a serious physical challenge. While no woman was a gunfounder, women were blacksmiths. The work of a blacksmith approached that of a gunfounder, and for a woman to be a blacksmith is also noteworthy.[40] At Ordnance, women made or repaired guns for military use, just as their husbands had done. For women in the seventeenth century to associate themselves with gunmaking, an enterprise connected with a product identified with war, violence and men, thereby violating social norms, is noteworthy. It is a further illustration of the attractiveness of working in the gun industry. Furthermore, this intimate involvement with firearms arguably had an unintended consequence: it softened the idea of the lethal nature of firearms, making them seem a part of everyday life.

Detailed information about the number of men and women connected with guns at the Office of Ordnance during the decade 1593–1603 is available in a printed chart.[41] The office employed sixty-eight persons: twelve blacksmiths, including three women; eight gunfounders, all men; forty-one gunmakers, including four women; and seven persons identified only as "craftsmen" and including one woman. Thus, eight women—all widows—comprised about 12 percent of the hires. For example, Isabel Hopkins, the widow of William Hopkins, an accomplished man with a successful career, continued a portion of his business, working at Ordnance as blacksmith and a gunmaker, starting in 1592. In 1597, she won her own contract repairing muskets and continued at Ordnance until 1600.[42] Among the four women gunmakers was Jane Staunton, the widow of Geoffrey Staunton of Tower Wharf, a gunmaker who had supplied Ordnance with calivers from 1570 to 1577, who continued his business repairing and making muskets and calivers from 1593 to 1603.[43] In August 1599, she received £28 7s. 6d. for thirty muskets, the same rate that Ordnance paid men for the same task.[44] Another woman gunmaker, Jane Woodruffe, probably the widow of John Woodruffe, a Master of the Blacksmiths Company (1597–99) who worked for Ordnance in 1581 and again from 1596–1600, repaired arms for Ordnance in 1603.[45] Although listed under the category of "craftsmen," Mary Longworth, in fact, worked as a gunmaker, continuing a portion of her late husband's business by repairing guns for Ordnance in 1602.[46]

Some women found jobs at the Office of Ordnance that were only indirectly related to making or repairing guns. Two women worked as a cooper and a girdler.[47] Other women were apparently on contract: Elizabeth Bennet supplied shovels and spades, while Mary Jonson provided brass.[48] Katherine Byworth had an independent business: she "operat[ed] five loading trucks" that carried "gonners stores" from the Office of Ordnance to the Wharf, picked up a load of iron and other items, and brought them back to the Office.[49] Whether working directly at making or repairing guns or in auxiliary areas, women changed the employment picture at the Office of Ordnance. It must have been startling (at least initially) for men to see a woman working as a gunmaker or a blacksmith and, in at least one proved instance, earning a man's salary for the same work. As a group, women gained experience. Some undoubtedly earned a reputation for good work, for they won their own contract after a year or two of employment and they continued to be assigned to work for Ordnance after the Company of Gunmakers received a charter in 1638.

Another chart prepared and printed for the years 1627–63 shows the number of military firearms that Ordnance ordered from the Gunmakers' Company: 48,259 matchlock guns, 55,181 snaphance guns, 18,135 pairs of snaphance pistols, 14,606 unspecified firearms, and 11,677 miscellaneous guns, for a total of 147,858 guns. The total value of the orders came to £170,132, a large sum, but the orders were spread over thirty-six years.[50] The figures can be broken down. Ordnance ordered 27,257 muskets in 1640 because of unrest in Scotland and England.[51] The table illustrates the obvious: in time of war or fear of war, orders for military arms were robust, while in time of peace, they were not, and the income of members of the gun industry suffered accordingly. Unfortunately, the table does not identify the individual gunmakers or their individual shares of the income.

During the tabulated years, 1627 to 1663, the Office gave the Gunmakers' Company orders to repair 81,583 guns. That number included 12,077 unspecified guns, 30,854 matchlock guns, 21,063 snaphance guns, 59 dags, and other firearms of various kinds. The total value of the order was £21,440.[52] Thus the Company took in a total revenue of £191,572 from Ordnance contracts for making military guns and repairing them over thirty-six years. Despite the limitations of the table, it indicates that, overall, Gunmakers did well during these years.

In 1657, the Gunmakers' Company successfully concluded an agreement with the Ordnance Office, whereby the Office would no longer negotiate work contracts with individual gunmakers, but deal directly with the Company, which, in turn, would hand out the work according to seniority and ability.[53] This arrangement strengthened the Company's internal structure and functioning, but limited the power of individuals over their work and, therefore, incomes. Women did not seem to suffer from the change in hiring arrangements, for the Company assigned them to work for Ordnance, as women gunmakers had done before the agreement. For example, Mary Fisher, the widow of George Fisher, who was a Master of the Company of Gunmakers from 1677 to 1695 and a contractor to Ordnance for twenty-one years from 1662 to 1683, followed her husband to Ordnance, where she worked for twelve years, from 1695 to 1707.[54] Elizabeth Ridgway, the widow of William Ridgway, who had a twenty-one year history—from 1640 to 1661—of contracts with the Office of Ordnance, held a job at the office for six years, from 1663 to 1669.[55] Ellen Smith, the widow of Thomas Smith, who had been an Ordnance Contractor for nineteen years, from 1631 to 1650, continued his business there from 1651 to 1653.[56] Employment of women gunmakers at Ordnance continued apace through the first two decades of the eighteenth century. For example, Mary Watkinson, the widow of John Watkinson, a gunmaker to Ordnance from 1687 to 1694, immediately followed her husband as a gunmaker to Ordnance in 1694 and worked there until 1705.[57] Mary Fort, the widow of Thomas Fort, a Gunmaker to Ordnance from 1693 to 1711, carried on her late husband's business at Ordnance during 1714 and 1715.[58] Finally, Dorothy Smithet took on the work of her husband, George Smithet, holding a position as a gunmaker at the Office of Ordnance from 1719 to 1720.[59] This long record of women gunmakers' employment at the Ordnance Office reinforces the assumption that, during the era, the women performed the tasks they were assigned to the satisfaction of their supervisors, thereby recommending the ongoing employment of women by the Office.

Artisanal women were active and productive members within the new Worshipful Company of Gunmakers. Their number was small: out of a company membership of about 1,500 persons from 1640 to 1770, there were only 97 women. Of them 24 may be regarded with obvious qualifications, I argue, as master gunmakers.[60] Women who merit this recognition included Ursula Barnes, Winifred Blemir, Mary Brook(s?), Elizabeth Dark, Margaret Groome, Elizabeth Hodgson, Mary Stace, Mary Tough, and Mary Widnes. However, I found no evidence that a woman presented a proof piece (the usual final step in reaching the level of Master), no woman became a freeman or held a guild office, and no woman represented the guild in public affairs. But they participated in the central work of the guild: making and repairing guns and, above all, training apprentices.

Women trained both male and female apprentices. The apprentice was sometimes a family member, which was also the case with male gunmakers. Sarah Gibbs, the widow of Richard Gibbs, took on their son Joseph as an apprentice. After an apprenticeship of seven years, he became free of the company in 1730.[61] Richard Kipling, son of Charles Kipling, was apprenticed in 1735 to his widowed mother, Hester Kipling, who not only continued her husband's business but also worked at the Hudson's Bay Company as a gunmaker.[62] Other apprentices, however, were unrelated to the woman gunmaker or her family. For example, on 2 May 1667, Ursula Barnes took on Thomas Wells as an apprentice.[63] Elizabeth Hodgson, widow of Thomas Hodgson, accepted James Buttery, the son of Joseph Buttery, a mercer in Surrey, as an apprentice bound for seven years starting 1 December 1692.[64] Richard Loder/ Loader was apprenticed to Elizabeth Thomas, the widow of Ralph Thomas, on 11 January 1705.[65] Thomas Haynes, son of John Haynes of Croydon Surrey, a husbandman, was bound for seven years to Thomas Towle, but in 1692 was "translated to Margaret Groome," the widow of Collins Groome.[66] Mary Tough accepted William Penington as an apprentice on 4 October 1704.[67] No member of the Gunmakers' Company objected to these arrangements. Indeed, the Company recognized the skill and work of some women when, in December 1692, the Court of Assistants formally gave two women— Elizabeth Hodgson and Margaret Groome—"liberty" to bind apprentices.[68] It is possible, of course, that other women who were training apprentices were officially recognized, too. Whatever their status, women were responsible for the training. One must assume that the officers of the company were confident that these women were competent and able to perform well this important task, which affected the skill of future gunmakers and the reputation of the Company.

Winifred Blemir, Mary Brooks, and Mary Stace, all widows of prominent and successful gunmakers, carried on their husbands' businesses for a number of years. Blemir's husband, Henry Blemir, had Ordnance contracts that Winifred continued for fourteen years from 1688 to 1702. Brooks managed Robert Brooks's Ordnance contracts from 1690 to 1694, and Mary Stace continued Joseph Stace's business from 1690 to 1698.[69] Ordnance must have been pleased with their work to have retained them for so long.

The three women just mentioned won recognition by the Company when they were invited in August 1690 to the annual Stewards' feast, a social occasion. Invitations for the event were assembled on 7 August and arranged under the title of "Persons invitable (of their rank) to the Stewards feast."[70] The names of Blemir, Brooks, and Stace were included with a marginal note explaining that the three women were "late of the Assistants,"[71] which meant to say that their late husbands were members of the Board of Assistants.[72] Mrs. Blemir and Mrs. Brooks, along with Mrs. Brooks's daughter, received further honor by being seated at Table One with the Master, the Assistants, and the wives of the Assistants.[73] Blemir, Brooks, and Stace were the only women besides the wives of officers to attend the gala. The invitation was undoubtedly a salute to their late husbands, but perhaps also recognized their contributions as gunmakers.

Twelve women paid the Gunmakers' Company the quarterly tax known as Quarterage that members owed the guild.[74] Among the women and the dates of their payment were Ursula Barnes (1663–72),[75] Mary Banckes (1673), and Ann Maskall (1721 and 1734). Mary Tough made forty Quarterage payments by 1702.[76] Elizabeth Towle made twelve Quarterage payments by 1692, and she paid Quarterage again in 1709.[77] Paying Quarterage was an obligation of the membership, and the fact that the twelve women paid the tax (albeit irregularly) arguably suggests that the Company recognized them as full members and expected the payment, and that these women, regarding themselves as members, complied with this obligation.

Late in the seventeenth century, the Gunmakers' Company took the unusual step of admitting to apprenticeship through indenture two single young women, Mary Sleg and Dorothy Green. Neither one had a family connection to gunmaking.[78] Mary Sleg was the daughter of a deceased tailor, John Sleg, from St. Botolph Aldgate. Apprenticed on 19 January 1687/88 to Thomas Towle for seven years, she was "transferred" to Mary Widnes on 8 February 1687/8.[79] Sleg was among twenty-five apprentices admitted in 1688. Dorothy Green came from Newcastle-upon-Tyne, where her deceased father, Peter Green, had worked as a carpenter. Apprenticed first to Thomas Towle and his wife, Elizabeth, for seven years by indenture dated 26 September 1690, on 2 October 1690, Green was "translated" also to Mary Widness.[80] Green was among the thirty-nine apprentices admitted in 1690.[81]

The admission of these young women is a noteworthy fact. Steve Rappaport stressed the absence of opportunity for single women in sixteenth-century London guilds, citing the step taken by the ancient company of Weavers to secure an ordinance that denied apprenticeship to single and married women, and forbade any woman but the widow of a weaver to learn the craft.[82] Other guilds held virtually the same attitude, as indicated by the fact that of the 32,000 apprentices in seven companies that Rappaport studied only 2 percent were women, and they were "mostly widows."[83] According to Hilda Smith's findings, however, a change occurred in the seventeenth century: in 1661, the Weavers admitted sixty-seven women as apprentices and from 1709–21 admitted twenty-four women as apprentices.[84] The Gunmakers' Company was apparently in the forefront of this tactic, but there may have been other guilds that did the same thing. The topic invites more research.

The Gunmakers' Company treated its women members with respect in other ways. For example, women were apparently invited to attend company meetings that were, of course, dominated by men. Occasionally they contributed to the discussion. This can be inferred from the record of a meeting of the Court of Assistants in January 1657, when Susan Davison had the confidence and spirit to express her views. The widow of John Davison, Susan complained before the court that John Abruck, her late husband's apprentice but now described as her "servant," had not "fully served his time" (that is, completed his apprenticeship) and therefore should not be admitted to the Company. The court took Davison's charge seriously and three months later, on 30 April, having "fully heard & debated" the issue, ruled that Abruck should pay Davison 30 shillings and "discharge all fees & charges" for his making free. Abruck accepted the ruling and was admitted to the Company.[85] Davison had won the men's attention. They recognized her allegation as valid and acted on it.

In other instances showing the women's self-interest, Agnes Appleby, the widow of Robert Appleby, who had held the office in the Royal Household of making leather cases for guns, pistols, and longbows, petitioned the Gunmakers' Company in 1612 that she be given his office.[86] The response to Appleby's petition is unknown, but her confidence in presenting it remains significant. More than a century later, in 1739, when Sarah Blanckley received the administration of the estate of her late husband, Samuel Blanckley, who had served the Company as Beadle, she boldly asked that she take his place in that office. A beadle was responsible for organizing guild meetings and had ceremonial duties that required him to carry a mace. He was one of only three officers who reported directly to the Master of the Company. The request was too much for the assembly, which rejected it out of hand, saying it was "quite unprecedented."[87] Again, their rejection does not diminish the brave confidence of Sarah Blanckley. Frances Brazier, the widow of John Brazier, was also a forceful woman. Not only did she apply in 1769 for her late husband's contract with the Hudson's Bay Company and work for them until 1774, she also won his contract with the East India Company, for which she worked at the same time in 1773.[88] Women enjoyed certain advantages from their association with the Company of Gunmakers. For example, in 1663, Mrs. Ridgway received in full the monies due to her late husband, while the widow of John Eckret was allowed a half year of her husband's pension.[89] At least one widow found a new husband in the Company: gunsmith Josiah Bird's widow, Contented Bird, married gunsmith William Green in 1637.[90] Like other guilds, the company provided social welfare assistance. Elizabeth Coleman, the widow of John Coleman, was given 10 shillings, "Being in great want," in 1717.[91] The widow of Henry Crips received a pension of 10 shillings per week "in consideration of house & shedds built at his own charge near ye West End of ye Chappell in ye Tower."[92] Finally, in 1726 Mary Fisher, the widow of George Fisher, received half a guinea from the Poor Box.[93] It would seem that membership in the Gunmakers' Company had its benefits.

Another source of income for gunmakers came from guns that legally qualified English subjects (and undoubtedly unqualified ones, too) bought for domestic use. Statutes and proclamations restricting domestic guns to the wealthy failed to dampen the interest of the public in possessing handguns. In a 1528 proclamation, King Henry VIII excoriated his subjects for buying guns for personal use and expressed his angry alarm at the number of guns in private hands.[94] Steven Gunn found that handguns for domestic use multiplied in the 1540s and 1550s.[95] A proclamation and a petition indicates that a strong market for domestic guns also existed at the end of the century. On 21 December 1600, Queen Elizabeth and her Privy Council issued a proclamation charging that, despite the law, "common and ordinary persons" carry and shoot guns.[96] "Pistols, birding pieces, and other like short pieces and small shot "were especially dangerous and heinous," the proclamation declared, because they were used to commit mayhem on the highways and lay "waste . . . [to] game throughout all parts of the realm." The edict condemned the insolence of "mean and base person[s]" who take "pheasants, partridges, and such other sort of fowl and game as should serve" men of wealth and high position. It called for their punishment. The government's condemnation of subjects' using "pistols and birding pieces" suggests not only how difficult it was to enforce gun restrictions but how popular guns were.

Gunmakers opposed the proclamation, for they profited from the sale of domestic guns. They petitioned Sir Robert Cecil, Lord Burghley, to persuade Elizabeth to rescind it.[97] This petition, the third one sent to the queen on similar themes, claimed that orders for "martial pieces" had declined and that they had suffered a severe downturn in their business. Forced (the petition read) to make "fowling pieces, birding pieces, and other pieces of pleasure" to maintain themselves, the gunmakers insisted that by forbidding the use of such pieces the proclamation would destroy their trade. This claim, a ploy to inspire sympathy which they had used in an earlier petition, was not convincing. England had been fighting with Spain and Ireland since 1585.[98] The Ordnance accounts for 1599 show numerous purchases "from multiple gunmakers."[99] The queen did not withdraw the proclamation. English subjects bought and used guns for personal pleasures and in doing so supported that part of the gun business.

Production of domestic guns varied. It was apparently strong in the 1620s as evidenced by John Browne, who, outraged in 1625 over not being paid by the government, "departed into the country with determination to employ himself in such works for the subject as would yield him ready money."[100] His confidence indicates a strong domestic marker. During the Civil Wars, of course, the focus was on guns for military purposes, but at the end of the conflict, domestic production picked up again. William Burton, the Proof Master of the Gunmakers' Company, reported in 1655 that he proofed 2,128 birding guns and 1,771 pistols.[101] The report does not provide the price of the birding guns and pistols, but, depending on the decoration and the reputation of the designer, a birding gun cost between 3 shillings and £5,[102] a pistol between 1 shilling and £5.[103] If one assumes that the birding guns and pistols averaged £2, then the gunmakers who produced the items took in £7,798. Over the next eight years, the Company of Gunmakers turned out a large number of guns for domestic use—between 300 and 600 guns per month, or a total of between 28,800 and 57,600 guns.[104] The number spiked in 1660 and 1661 to over 1,000 guns per month, reaching 1,512 guns in March 1661. Then, production fell back to between 300 and 568 guns per month from January 1663 to June 1663. Neither the kind of gun nor its price is indicated, but these figures show that the market for domestic guns was robust between 1655 and 1663. Since these years spanned the last years of Cromwell's government and the early part of the Stuart Restoration, it seems likely that weapons were bought for political reasons and protection as well as sport.

Domestic guns continued to be attractive items in the early eighteenth century. As a summary example, William Brazier, who twice served as Master of the Gunmakers' Company, proofed approximately twenty-nine thousand handguns between 1721 and 1731.[105] The figures make clear that guns for private use were popular across the era and brought an income to the gun business. Unfortunately, the figures do not indicate how many guns an individual bought or how many individuals bought them. They do not help to answer the question of how many individuals owned or possessed guns. For the early modern period, we may never have a statistically acceptable answer.

Some members of the Company of Gunmakers undertook marketing strategies aimed at exciting interest in guns, stimulating sales, and enlarging profit. From 1663 to 1665, Stephen Andrews aggressively advertised his guns by "hawking his wares" around the streets of London.[106] The Gunmakers' Company disapproved of this tactic and imposed a penalty for "selling guns as a hawker." They included the prohibition in the Ordinances of the Company, drawn up in 1670, as one of thirty-seven new regulations.[107] Less flamboyant gunmakers sought other ways to reach prospective customers: they placed advertisements in the relatively new newspapers. In 1661 William Edwards, a bandoleer-maker employed by the Ordnance Office, took out an ad in *Mercurius Publicus*, No. 37, to apprise readers of the excellence of his bandoleers.[108] At about the same time in the 5–12 December 1661 issue of *Mercurius Publicus*, William Martindale informed readers that at his shop "At the sign of the Stirrop in Chiswell-Street," he made and sold a wide range of guns, from the "pocket Pistol to the whole Cannon." On offer were guns "charged with three or four several charges, also swords with pistols."[109] The last item—a sword with a pistol attached—was an old-fashioned design, probably aimed at antique gun collectors. Perhaps these efforts helped to bring Martindale to the attention of the court, for he became King Charles II's Gunsmith-in-Ordinary in 1662.[110]

Advertising grew, reinforcing the link between guns and the press. In 1692, men who held the patent for lacquering on iron (to protect guns and other metal items from rust) gave notice of the three places where they worked: the "Japan Warehouse in the west end of the Royal Exchange," a house on St. James's Street, and the "Japan House in Hoton beyond Moorfields."[111] The *Post Man and the Historical Account* advertised in its 6 March 1712 edition that "108 new Firelocks with Bayonets" made by Andrew Dolep were to be sold "at a reasonable rate" at "Mr Maynards, Gunsmith, in Grafton-street, Soho."[112] In 1721, Isaac Bleiberg, Gun-Maker, placed a notice in two editions of the *Daily Post* four days apart, informing readers that he had moved to a new address in Holland Street and was offering "a considerable Quantity of fine Arms . . . at very reasonable Rates."[113]

No doubt the most effective advertising of all were the gun shops in London where a customer might buy guns and gun accessories. Their number multiplied over the era, testifying to the steady growth of a market for guns. In 1656, a report prepared by the Company of Gunmakers counted twenty-eight gun shops.[114] Searches for defective or illegally imported guns that the Company carried out in 1692 and in 1693 added the names and addresses of shopkeepers who sold defective or unproved guns.[115] Another report by the company in 1704 listed eighty shopkeepers, including six women, with addresses for many.[116] These data showed that over the years gun shops pervaded the city: in St. Paul's Churchyard, in Westminster Hall, at St. James's Market, at "Charing Cross over ag[ain]st St. Martins Lane," "At a Stall on this side of St. Martins Lane," along the Minories, on Tower Hill, at Holborn, at St. John, Wapping. A resident or a visitor to London could readily purchase a gun, have a gun repaired at some shops, have a gun lacquered, and, as Samuel Pepys did, persuade a gunmaker to explain how a gun worked.[117] Advertising and the presence of gun shops increased public interest in firearms and surely stimulated sales.

The financial success of gunmakers and gunsmiths reflected individual initiative, personal skill, timing, and, surely, luck. Some men made a great deal of money; their personal stories are full of telling details about the gun economy. Robert Silk (John Silk's son) enjoyed a long career in the gun industry and financial success. He held offices in the Gunmakers' Company, serving as Master three times, worked for Ordnance for thirty-four years, Hudson's Bay Company for seventeen years, and the Royal African Company for eighteen. His appointment in 1689 as Chief Gunmaker in the Tower of London was further indication of his skill and reputation.[118] Silk signed his will on 7 February 1701 and died within the year, leaving handsome bequests. His second wife, Mary Silk, received items that were specified in their prenuptial contract: £1,000, £20 for mourning clothes, her watch, and all her rings and jewelry that did not belong to Silk's first wife. Each of Silk's three sons received leases on several pieces of property: the eldest, John, was given the lease on a house in which Silk had lived as well as leases on several tenements. Abraham, the second son, inherited leases on four houses located in Middlesex. The youngest boy, Tobias, got the lease on the house in which Silk was living when he died, leases on two adjoining houses, and £600 when he completed his apprenticeship. Silk's daughter Martha received the lease on one property, £200, and two diamond rings that had belonged to her mother. Silk also left gifts of money to relatives, friends, and servants. Any monies remaining after his debts and legacies were paid were to be divided equally among his children. He willed at least twelve properties and large sums of money. There is no doubt that the gun business allowed Silk to prosper handsomely.

Thomas Carlile also did well. Apprenticed to Roger Carlile in the Blacksmiths' Company in 1660, Thomas shifted to the Gunmakers' Company, became free of that company in 1667, and was elected Assistant in 1682. In 1684, he worked as a gunmaker at the Hudson's Bay Company.[119] His will, dated 10 March 1686, left a third of his personal estate to his wife Elizabeth and two-thirds to be divided among their daughter and two sons.[120] Although the value of the personal estate was not specified, it must have been substantial, for the legacies were designed to meet the needs of his wife and children and took into account a future marriage for his daughter. The appraisal of the estate a year later, on 27 April 1687, contained more detailed information.[121] Carlile was described as "of St. Lawrence Jewry" which located his residence in the eastern part of London near the famous ancient church of that name.[122]

The house was spacious, with two cellars, two garrets, a "lower room," a room "up one pair of stairs," a kitchen, and another room up two flights of stairs. The itemized furnishings suggest that the family lived comfortably. They included china, pictures, and woolens and linens, as well as fireplace accessories such as a fender, a fire shovel, and a pair of bellows. Canisters of tea and chocolate indicate that there was money to spend on luxuries. Other household items such as beds and chairs surely existed but were not listed. Birding guns, pistols, muskets, and "four old guns" were itemized, and the whole was appraised at approximately £170. Carlile owned another house located at Walham Green, Fulham, and its contents were valued at about £65. Furthermore, Carlile remembered three close men friends with gifts of messuages (that is, houses with outbuildings and land). Again, no value was indicated, but it was probably significant. Carlile left his father-in-law 15 shillings and his brother-in-law 5 shillings, and he forgave other friends a debt. Further indications of his wealth were that he left £60 in ready money and creditors owed him £225 in bills and bonds. His career as a gunmaker had enabled him to accumulate a comfortable estate, provide for his wife and children, express in tangible terms the high regard in which he held his closest friends, and testify to his generous spirit.

Robert Brook was another "Citizen and Gunmaker of London" who could look back on a satisfying career, one that brought him financial security. He became free of the Gunmakers' Company in 1660 and Master in 1679, and in 1670 won appointment as Gunmaker-in-Ordinary to King Charles II. A resident of the Minories, he held contracts with Ordnance from 1661 to 1689, worked for the East India Company in 1682, and in 1683 made a Barbary gun and lock for the King of Fez and Morocco.[123] At about the age of fifty, he drew up his will on 7 January 1688/9, an unsettled time when the Revolution of 1688–89 was unfolding.[124] Noting that he had already given his daughter Mary £400 on her marriage to Anthony Wilden, Esq., he willed her £20 more and "released" to her husband the money he had disbursed in support of her "clothes, diet, lodging and other necessaries." To his second daughter, Susan, described as a spinster, he also willed £400. Brook made his wife Mary his executrix, and left everything else to her, specifying goods, chattels, ready money, plate, debts, household stuff, leases and "Estate whatsoever both Reall and Personall." Mary continued his business.

On the other hand, many male gunmakers achieved only modest financial success. Peter Banks of Radcliffe (a parish of Stepney) furnishes an example. An active member of the Company of Gunmakers, Banks was elected an Assistant in 1656 and then Master in 1666. He worked for Ordnance from 1662 to 1669 and for the Hudson's Bay Company in 1668.[125] Banks left a house in

Ham, Surrey, whose contents were valued at about £44 and a house in Rad-cliffe in which the total goods, including his tools worth £16, were valued at only £36.[126] The financial success of another resident of Stepney, a gunsmith named George Woodruffe, was apparently derailed by his debts, which were described as "sperate and desperate." Although his house included two cham-bers, a long room, a back room, a kitchen, and a cellar, Woodruffe left only a "Boltinge Mill and cloathes" and tools used by a gunmaker valued at £2. His total estate, appraised on 3 June 1661, was worth only £43.[127] William Parsons, a gunmaker who worked for the Board of Ordnance from 1665 to 1678 and lived on Rood Lane in London, attained still less financial security. He left goods whose total value was appraised at just a little over £22.[128]

One man, William Sowerby of St. Paul Shadwell, Middlesex, a gunmaker, holds interest because he was able to turn bankruptcy to his own advantage. Apprenticed in 1696, Sowerby submitted his proof piece in 1706 and worked for Ordnance from 1709 to 1715 and for the Royal African Company in 1722. Despite this record of employment, he was recorded as bankrupt in July 1723 and ordered to appear at the London Guildhall in August 1723 when his cred-itors were to "come prepared to prove their debts."[129] Apparently, Sowerby took advantage of bankruptcy to create a new lease on life and work, for in 1727 he won election to the post of assistant in the Company of Gunmakers. Presumably, he continued to work as a gunmaker until he faded from the record in 1731.[130]

The wills and property appraisals give a snapshot of the financial attain-ment of persons associated with the gun industry and provide details sugges-tive of how they lived and something of their cultural values. Notably absent is any mention of books, pamphlets, or tracts on religion and politics.

Guns brought new entrepreneurial and job opportunities to men across the socioeconomic spectrum—to nobles, aristocrats, gentlemen, men of mid-dling status, artisans and low status men—and to artisanal women. Whether employed on the basis of an individual contract or through the Company of Gunmakers, workers in the gun industry found their best employer in the Ordnance Office, in other words, the government. As the premier, perma-nent military establishment, the Ordnance Office was the lynchpin in the supply system of military weapons, receiving orders from the Privy Council and dealing with guilds and craftsmen in filling them. Gunmakers did quite well financially when war occurred or threatened, but suffered in times of peace. Guns for domestic uses, hunting, target shooting, gift giving, and for protection and crime, however, helped to sustain the industry then. Women gunmakers, numbering under 10 percent of the total number of gunmakers, worked for the Ordnance Office before and after the creation of the Worshipful Company of Gunmakers. They were regular members of the company; they trained apprentices, made and repaired guns, and attended company meetings. A few received marks of acceptance and recognition. Toward the end of the seventeenth century, the company admitted as apprentices two single young women who apparently had no familial connection with the Gunmakers. The gun industry made a significant difference in entrepreneurial and employment opportunities in London throughout the era and in other parts of the nation, such as Bristol and Birmingham, when gunmaking became an active industry outside the capital city.

THREE · Regulating
Domestic Guns with
"Good and Politic
Statutes"

ALMOST AS SOON AS GUNS became available in the early sixteenth
century, the English government imposed on its subjects whose
income was beneath a prescribed level an array of regulations
that limited their possession and use of firearms.[1] Using statutes and proclamations, the authorities amplified the effort begun in the Middle Ages to
prevent persons at the lower rungs of society from having access to weapons.
Their reasons for doing so were multiple and diverse and require a complete
review. Sometimes proclamations applied restrictions, such as the permissible
targets for gun practice or the length of the allowed firearm, to all persons
of "whatever condition."[2] However, the government's determination to limit
guns to persons of wealth was a defining characteristic of the gun culture that
was evolving. The response of English subjects on whom the restrictions fell
was an equally important component of the nation's gun culture.

Statutes and proclamations were the major instruments the government
used to announce constraints on firearms. They provide unrivalled evidence of
the viewpoint of monarchs, nobles, aristocrats, and well-to-do urban leaders.
Statutes embodied the majority opinion of members of the House of Lords
and the House of Commons and, of course, of the monarch. Proclamations
were issued in the name of the monarch with the advice of the Privy Council. They generally reinforced statutes and, although they did not carry the
same legal weight as statutes, subjects were expected to obey them.[3] To ensure
people's notice and respect, proclamations carried marks of importance. They
bore the imprint of the Great Seal and the signatures of the monarch and
members of the Council. They were printed, proclaimed at an appropriate
place in a more or less elaborate ceremony, and posted in public places. The
rhetoric they employed in making an announcement was carefully crafted: it

commanded, instructed, harangued, scolded, recalled past laws, pleaded for obedience, and begged for help in imposing the orders. Proclamations often emphasized and sometimes extended the means of enforcement and enlarged the penalties to be imposed on the disobedient. Despite these efforts, the multiplicity of statutes and proclamations addressed to the same end testified to problems of enforcement and of compliance that the government faced.

Prominent among the government's reasons for limiting firearms to the well-to-do was dismay over the violation of royal and aristocratic hunting privileges and property, a concern that had a long lineage, going back to the late fourteenth century. In 1389 during the troubled reign of King Richard II (1377–99), the landed elite in Parliament was successful in passing the first comprehensive Game Law, which established that field sports were a function of wealth and social status, not royal prerogative. Early medieval kings had assumed that hunting was a royal sport and that ownership of the game of the realm was part of their prerogative. Hunting, regarded as a symbol of royal power, was saturated with ritual and myth designed to underscore monarchical authority.[4] Kings limited field sports to a small minority of subjects by using the ancient forest laws and granting franchises in the form of rights of park, chase, and free warren. The forest laws referred to large tracts of land set aside by the monarch as his private preserve. To hunt in the monarch's land required his permission. A person holding a franchise for a park (an enclosed area) or a chase (an unenclosed area) had the authority to grant permission to others to hunt therein.[5] The law of 1389 upended these royal assumptions and practices, but imposed new restrictions. It barred from hunting any person who did not have an annual income of 40 shillings and any priest who could not command an annual living of £10.[6] It singled out "Artificers, Laborers and Servants, and Grooms," scolded them for hunting on the Sabbath when they should "be at Church, hearing Divine Service," accused them of using hunting as a screen to meet and conspire "to rise and disobey their allegiance," and forbade them to keep dogs, nets, or "other" devices. The penalty was imprisonment for one year.

The act of 1389 blatantly targeted the poor, partly because of a major uprising eight years earlier, the Peasants' Revolt of 1381.[7] That event terrified the well-to-do and briefly destabilized King Richard II's government. The Game Law of 1389 aimed to protect the elite against domestic insurrection, while at the same time defending their sport and preserving game for royal, noble, and aristocratic enjoyment. It was compatible with still other early laws, such as the Assize of Arms (1181) and the Statute of Winchester (1285), which equated the possession of weapons with wealth and sought to regulate them. Inherent in these laws was the assumption that disloyalty was linked with poverty, a viewpoint characteristic of a hierarchical society. The Game Act of 1389 was a precursor to later laws and proclamations limiting hunting according to wealth; its essence was retained and firearms added to the weaponry when they became available.

The words "hand gonnes" appeared for the first time in a 1514 game law that banned the use of guns and crossbows in hunting to anyone without an annual income of 300 marks and imposed a penalty of forfeiture of the weapon and a fine of £10 for each violation.[8] To help strengthen its enforcement, the instrument empowered "every of the King's [qualified] subjects" to seize the offender's gun or crossbow and keep it "for their own use" and offered a share of the fine. In the absence of efficient and reliable local machinery for enforcing laws, calling on qualified subjects to assist in implementing the law and rewarding them by sharing the penalty were common tactics.

The violation of hunting restrictions remained a problem for the elite, and efforts to impose restraints continued. In 1523, the government passed a new law that replaced two central provisions of the 1514 act and softened its terms.[9] This statute reduced the annual income required of a person to keep and use crossbows and handguns from 300 marks (the equivalent of £200) to £100 and reduced the penalty for violating the law from £10 to 40 shillings (or £2). In the absence of evidence, one may speculate that the government, recognizing the growing popularity of firearms for personal use and the severe difficulty in implementing the previous requirements, decided greater success lay in the new terms. Whatever the reasoning, the £100 threshold remained throughout the early modern era. In December 1528, a proclamation decried the "newfangle[d] and wanton pleasure that men now have in using crossbows and handguns" and blamed these devices for the unlawful destruction of deer.[10] Exasperated that "good and politic statutes" were ignored, the king and members of the Privy Council ordered that "no manner of person have, shoot in, or keep any crossbow or gun in their houses or any other places." Violators were warned that they would suffer imprisonment without bail at the king's pleasure. Thirteen years later, in an effort to reach a category of people who were presumed guilty of violating hunting laws, an act entitled "Concerning Crossbows and Handguns" (1541) extended the restriction to servants on large estates forbidding them to shoot game or fowl and setting the penalty for doing so at confiscation of the gun and restoring the fine to £10.[11] Following on in 1545, proclamations banned subjects of all degrees from hunting and hawking when Henry VIII was in residence at Hampton Court or the palace at Westminster, explaining that the king wanted to keep the creatures "for his own disport and pastime."[12] In 1547, King Edward VI complained that his deer in Grafton had been hunted and "disquieted" day and night by dogs, crossbows, and handguns and ordered that "such engines" be confiscated and offenders punished.[13]

In a further effort at enforcement of hunting laws, King Edward VI's government in 1548 set up a new system of registering individuals who were qualified to use guns.[14] Such persons were instructed to appear before their local mayor and justices of the peace at the next Quarter Session and have their names written down properly by the Clerk of the Peace. This arrangement was justified on grounds that it would enable the king to discover how many "mete and hable men" there were in each county on whom he might call to defend the nation should "occasion" require. It set a penalty of 20 shillings per shot for an unregistered person caught hunting with a gun. To what extent qualified men honored this requirement is clouded. William Lambarde (1536–1601), an expert in law and local government, implied in his book on the office of the justice of the peace (1582) that initially the registration went forward, but that it had since lapsed. In a kind of note to himself, Lambarde wrote, "But learne of others whether this part is to have continuance still, or else did onely extend to such persons as had licenses at that time."[15] Michael Dalton, citing Lambarde, made virtually the same point in 1618, when he wrote: "but quaere if this be now in use."[16] It seems that after a brave start the registration project languished, and no one demanded that it continue. The idea of a register, however, highlights the government's desire to strengthen its control over who was qualified to shoot, while the failure of the project underscores the weakness of the local bureaucracy and the intransigence of shooters.

Anger over civilian subjects' violation of hunting rights receded in the reign of Queen Elizabeth as international wars and a host of domestic problems occupied the government. However, the queen and her Privy Council returned to the issue with a vengeance in a proclamation of 21 December 1600. Employing extreme language, the document railed against "common and ordinary persons" who disregard "divers good laws and statutes" prohibiting their "carrying and shooting in guns" such as pistols, birding pieces, and other short pieces used in hunting. The result was the "exceeding great waste and spoil" of game, which "belongeth to men of the best sort and condition" and should be reserved for the "delight . . . of her majesty, the nobility and other men of quality."[17] This official remark powerfully illustrated the attitude of the crown and wealthy men toward the question of whom in society should be allowed to hunt. It also bound men of "the best sort and condition" to the queen in their mutual love of hunting.

King James I, an ardent sportsman and passionate hunter, shared Elizabeth's views.[18] He was the first monarch to appoint gamekeepers to "preserve the king's game" and, drawing upon his royal prerogative, gave them the power to keep unauthorized "persons of meane qualitie" away from royal estates and prevent them from hunting game anywhere in the kingdom.[19] The king pushed the House of Commons in 1610 to pass laws that assured that "none but gentlemen" should hunt. James said candidly "it is not fit that clowns [i.e., plebeians] should have these sports."[20] The king's remark encapsulated the attitudes of a hierarchical society: people at the lower reaches of society should not be allowed to participate in this sport. As a twentieth-century historian wittily remarked, the laws "protected pheasants from peasants."[21]

Sixty years later, in 1671, King Charles II's Parliament passed the most severe of all the game laws.[22] "A Bill to preserve the Game" raised the landed property qualifications for a person to possess and use a gun to hunt. The effect was to exclude all but the wealthiest subjects. Further, for the first time the law excluded persons whose wealth came from nonlanded sources, such as trade or stocks or offices. Thus, individuals of great wealth, but not wealth derived from land, were legally barred from shooting and hunting. It allowed all qualified hunters to practice the sport any place they pleased, whereas those who were unqualified could not hunt, even on their own land. Finally, it empowered lords of manors above the rank of esquire to appoint gamekeepers with the authority to search for and seize all guns, and "other engines" illegally used in shooting.

This law concealed motivation that had little to do with firearms per se. Its very passage testified to the increasing political and social power of the landed gentry. By its terms, the qualified aristocracy shared with the monarch the right to hunt wherever it wished and to take whatever steps it deemed appropriate to preserve game. Further, Game Law scholars argue that the drafters were equally interested in using the law to discriminate against the urban "moneyed" interest to which many country gentlemen were in debt. The law testified to a cultural perspective that held land and persons whose wealth and standing were rooted in the countryside in higher esteem than merchants, lawyers, and bankers whose wealth was accumulated by urban activities. The law was another indication of the power of the leaders of the countryside.[23] Taken all together, the laws and proclamations that restricted hunting starkly reveal the willingness of persons at the topmost reaches of England's hierarchical society to use their political power to further their own interests.

Although efforts were made, the enforcement of statutes and proclamations restricting hunting faced difficulties. One was that gun licenses, which were first issued by King Henry VIII and continued through the sixteenth century, undermined those laws. They are discussed in the next chapter. Briefly, the purpose of gun licenses was to negate the effect of restrictive laws. Persons who held a license, either on their own account or by gift, escaped the limitations. It is reasonable to think that these circumstances weakened the willingness of people who were not favored with a license to observe the government's proscriptions against them.

The major challenge, however, was the reaction of subjects on whom the hunting restrictions fell. Persons whose income was modest or negligible felt that game was not the property of the wealthy landowner or of the king (as the old theory would have it), but rather of the person who brought it down. God, they maintained, "made the game of the land free and left it free."[24] They needed no gift of hunting rights or license to bag game for they regarded it as "the property of those who can take it." They used their gun to hunt more effectively and bring more protein and variety of food to their tables. In Bury St. Edmunds, the governor of the jail declared that "there was a general understanding amongst the lower orders of people that there is no crime in [poaching]" game.

The response of such men included grudging acceptance, willful disobedience, angrily expressed outrage, and written request for change. A defiant person could circumvent the restrictions by ignoring the law and taking a chance at not being caught. In 1550, the clerk of the peace in Norfolk noted that many unqualified men hunted in violation of the law. His records showed that of the men who were not legally qualified to shoot only three possessed a license. He also said that sixty men were out shooting every day in violation of the law and "none of them [was] worth more than £4 a year in land."[25] The implication of the clerk's report was that the laws were not being enforced by the local authorities.

The fact is that bold disobedience of the hunting laws was constant throughout the period. A nice example is William ap Thomas, a labourer from Ludlow. In 1554, he was charged with shooting a handgun in violation of the law, was tried, and fined 20 shillings. Three years later, in 1557, he was back in court, charged with the same misdeed, tried, and fined again.[26] On 26 July 1593, at the Chelmsford assizes Thomas Wood, yeoman, was before the court because he was unqualified to shoot at a doe with a fowling-piece.[27] In 1616, an indictment in Essex targeted an unqualified clothier, who was caught shooting doves with a handgun.[28] In 1632, a yeoman was summoned before the Warwickshire Quarter Sessions and indicted for using a gun to kill a pigeon on the Sabbath, which was against the law.[29] In 1639, a husbandman, William Cotterell of Bentlier Heath, faced the charge of shooting with a gun contrary to the statute.[30] The state papers of Charles I's reign record multiple attacks on the king's deer.[31] In 1627, two years after Charles ascended the throne, "rude people" were said to have "killed the greatest part of the deer in Leicester forest."[32] In 1640, persons targeted the "red and roe deer" in Windsor Forest and

Whittlewood Forest. Two years later Windsor Forest was again the scene of "great Destruction and Killing of His Majesty's Deer ... The People of the Country, in a continuous and tumultuous Manner, ... killed a Hundred" of the royal "fallow deer and red deer."[33] After the Restoration, in 1669 and 1670, a number of unqualified laborers in Kent were presented at the Assize Court for using a handgun to hunt pheasants and hares, while three men without the proper income were charged with using a gun.[34] Many cases were tried in Essex in the decade of the 1680s, probably because William Holcroft was not only a justice of the peace but also a verderer of Waltham Forest. He recorded in "His Booke" that he brought in men who carried or shot a gun in the forest, carried a concealed gun, or kept a gun and bullets and bullet molds in their houses, acts against the laws.[35] Similar situations occurred in Somerset. In 1696 at the Grand Inquest in Warwickshire, James Drinkewater of Moreton Baggott, was presented for keeping a gun "not being qualified" and destroying game.[36] In short, many court cases confirm that men at the lower levels of society who responded to the government's efforts to restrict their hunting by ignoring the law, were caught and punished. There must have been many more men who violated the laws but escaped detection.

Defiant anger was a second way to express objection to being denied the right to hunt with a gun. In July 1598, Joseph Stileman wrote to Sir Robert Cecil about a "crew of ill-disposed fellowes [in Devon] who carry guns & cross-bows who say they will not leave any deer in Theobald's park and Cheston park."[37] Such insolence was matched by Thomas Dell, who got himself in trouble for opposing Oliver Cromwell's commission of a local lord to confiscate all "dogs and engines for destroying the game of partridge." Dell said contemptuously that "he cared not for the commission nor he that set it out."[38] George Knitstall, a poacher, who was hunting partridges to serve at his "public house," told a Hertfordshire landowner in 1678 that if he were denied leave to hunt "he would take leave" and that he "did not care a straw for all the justices."[39] In 1720, Daniel Underdowne refused to allow the constable of Folkestone in Kent to search his house for nets and guns, which he admitted he possessed, declaring that "he thought he had as much Right to keep Guns and Netts as any Others."[40]

A third rejoinder to the restrictive laws was to make a case for their repeal in writing. In 1571, "Saul," the pseudonym of a pamphleteer, dismissed these laws out of hand, declaring that he ardently wished that "the saveguard of our deare Countrie might be of more price to us, then the savinge of a fewe wildfoule."[41] Another written request for repeal of the restrictions was made within the context of an organized resistance. Early in 1536, the leaders of the Pilgrimage of Grace used the Pontefract Articles, their petition to the authorities to deal with a series of important religious, political, and economic grievances, to call for a repeal of restrictive gun laws.[42] The Pilgrimage of Grace, one may recall, was an uprising in northern England involving five counties and parts of two more, aimed primarily at King Henry VIII's attack on the Catholic Church and the dissolution of the monasteries. Drawing in people from across the social spectrum, including "all the flower of the North" (as Thomas Howard, the Third Duke of Norfolk [1473–1554] put it), the insurrection attracted over thirty thousand partisans, most of them Catholic.[43] Deeply alarmed, the king sent an army led by the Duke of Norfolk to confront the rebels. With his army initially outnumbered and some soldiers sympathetic to the insurgents, Norfolk, as instructed by the king, agreed to negotiate. The duke offered a general pardon, a promise to restore the suppressed abbeys, and a pledge that a free parliament would be summoned and grievances discussed. In response, one of the rebels' most important leaders, Robert Aske, a lawyer, drew up a bargaining document, the Pontefract Articles, which listed twenty-four demands.[44] Among the demands for fundamental change in religion and government was Article 10, which asked that the statutes limiting possession of handguns and crossbows to the well-to-do be repealed, except insofar as they applied to the killing of the king's red and fallow deer in his forests or parks.

The uprising was a serious threat to the government, and all along Henry VIII intended to suppress it. The king seized on a fresh rebellion, led by Sir Francis Bigod, which occurred after the pardon offered for the first uprising, as an excuse to move against the rebels. With his army enlarged, his confidence restored, and directions from the king explicit, Norfolk moved against the rebels, and the Pilgrimage of Grace ended in a bloody rout. The main leaders, including Aske, who were implicated in the new rebellion, were sent to London where they were tried and executed.[45] But Article 10 of the Pontefract Articles remains important. It provides striking evidence that as early as 1536 the restrictive gun laws were unpopular with men across society in the northern part of England. That a request to repeal gun restrictions should appear in a document focused on broad religious, political, and economic complaints against the government is remarkable, indicating how deep was the dislike of the government's laws and proclamations to restrict hunting. Article 10 was lost, along with the other demands in the Pontefract Articles.

A third written objection came from the county leaders of Kent in their response to the government's request for comment on a proposal to increase the number of guns and gunners in the counties that was drafted and promoted in 1569 by William Cecil, Queen Elizabeth I's principal minister.[46] The Musters Commissioners wrote that nothing was "like to doo more good" to achieve that end than to allow "everie man" to shoot whenever he wanted to and at anything he pleased, so long as he did not violate someone else's rights.[47] Recognizing that the suggestion flew in the face of long-standing laws, Kent officials pointed out that the repeal of 33 Henry VIII. c. 6 (1541), along with other weighty matters, "offer" reason enough to "Calle . . . a Parliament." But, then, apparently realizing how long the legislative process would take, they proposed that the queen issue a proclamation, which they said would "partely" accomplish the same end. This extraordinarily radical proposal would have overturned the nation's centuries-long practice of restricting weapons to the wealthy. It won no traction at all and disappeared, but this does not diminish its importance for revealing the presence of an extremely negative view of the restrictive laws.

None of these instances of defiant disobedience, oral denunciation, and written requests for repeal of the restrictions resulted in change. The habit of deference, the condition of powerlessness and poverty, and the absence of effective leadership were powerful limitations on any demand for alteration in gun laws.

A second reason for the government's campaign of regulating its subjects' relationship to guns was to re-ignite fondness for the longbow. This effort was also complex and it, too, suffered from contradictions. A kind of historical mystique enveloped the longbow. English people generally believed, as a law put it, that the longbow was God's gift to England, the reason for the nation's many military victories, the source of national pride, and the promoter of manly health.[48] The effort to recover this attitude began in 1511, when Parliament passed a law that required householders to supply boys between seven and seventeen years of age with a bow and arrows and enforce regular practice.[49] Every town was responsible for setting up butts, seeing to it that young men and others practiced regularly, and appointing bowyers. To favor the interests of the bow-making industry, the price of bows and arrows was lowered in hopes of stimulating sales. In 1526 and often thereafter, the authorities blamed the decline of archery on the growing popularity of "unlawful" and "immoral" games, such as tennis, bowling, cards, and quoits, which they maintained undermined the health of young men, sabotaged the defenses of the nation, and served as shield for planning seditions, conspiracies, and robberies.[50] That same year, the king addressed a proclamation to local leaders in London and Middlesex directing them to enforce the laws against unlawful games. His instruction was that no person, whatever his status, shall be allowed to play these games. Local officers were assured that the disobedient would be punished "without favor or any manner of redemption."[51] The apparent hope was that young men, barred from tennis and bowling, would return to the more healthy sport of shooting the bow and arrow.

There was another subtext, however, to the government's effort to staunch the decline of archery. Henry VIII's 1528 proclamation hinted at it, when it blamed "the newfangle[d] and wanton pleasure that men now have in using of crossbows and handguns" as one reason archery had fallen out of favor.[52] C. G. Cruickshank, the historian of Elizabeth's army, argued that encouraging archery was "a campaign against the non-military use" of the gun, a way to siphon off that fascination with firearms.[53]

The laws and proclamations calling for renewed interest in archery met a mixed reception. On the one hand, local leaders in Buckinghamshire, Derbyshire, Essex, Oxfordshire, Warwickshire, and Wiltshire were cooperative and took steps to comply with the government's instructions.[54] In Essex, from 1573 to 1574, fifty-nine men were hauled before the authorities for failure to practice with the bow. In Peterborough, not only were residents fined for not practicing, but the town's constables were also fined for failing to enforce practice. Oxfordshire and Buckinghamshire made good on their intentions to obey the law, so that in 1588 these two counties had slightly more archers than gunners. Leaders in Derbyshire were known for conscientiously raising and training archers. Recently Steve Gunn has significantly enlarged this picture, showing that from about 1500 to the middle of the sixteenth century interest in archery was more robust than has been assumed. For example, towns such as Dover and Exeter kept their butts in good repair, in Bristol a painter was paid to decorate the posts close to the butts, and Warwick installed posts and rails to surround butts in two places, all in an effort to encourage their residents to practice archery.[55] Diverse reasons explain this obliging cooperativeness.[56] The cost of bows and arrows was considerably less than that for firearms. The fines collected from individuals for not shooting the longbow sweetened the local treasury. In addition, in some quarters the public agreed with the government that preserving archery had moral and social advantages: promoting the health of young men, keeping them occupied and uninterested in immoral games, and preserving the weapon traditionally associated with England's greatness.

Unfortunately for the government, however, its efforts to inspire young men to practice with the longbow were not popular. Why should young men "steadfastly ignore" the urgings of the government to take up the longbow, England's traditional weapon?[57] One reason, no doubt, was that they regarded the longbow as hopelessly old-fashioned and out-of-date. A bow and arrow were not nearly as exciting as a gun. They offered neither the noise, the fire, the danger, nor the destructive power of a firearm, and, they required skill, strength, and long practice that their critics claimed were now too difficult for the nation's youth. By contrast, the gun was a device men liked and enjoyed. A second explanation offered by local officials in Dorset held that young men disdained the longbow because "the harquebuz are of better accompt."[58] The Council made the same point in 1577, saying that people think archery is useless because they "see the caliver so much embraced at present."[59]

The reference point in these remarks was the government's policy of embedding guns in the arsenal of weapons used by the militia and its military and naval forces, at the same time it promoted and insisted upon the use of the bow. The strategy was blatantly duplicitous; one hand of the government deliberately concealed what the other hand was doing. There was a history to this duplicitous tactic. In the early sixteenth century, Henry VIII armed his pseudo-feudal army with guns at the same time that he deplored, indeed railed against, the lack of interest in the longbow. Queen Elizabeth I and her government urged young men to practice with the longbow, while at the same time she expanded the use of firearms in the newly established Trained Bands. Her government imposed a desperate measure in 1569 when it forbade trained archers "to learn the use of firearms."[60] In 1572, Elizabeth's Privy Council issued an order for the most physically able tradesmen in London to meet three times a week at Mile's End or St. George's Fields to learn how to use a gun.[61] By the end of the century, bows and bills were described forthrightly as "being unfytt weapons for this time."[62] The fact that the government took these steps would have been known to men in the militia and to the interested public and undoubtedly would have stimulated interest in firearms.

A third reason that archery seemed useless was arguably related to the debate in the last decade of Queen Elizabeth's reign over the relative merits of the longbow versus the gun as the weapon of choice in war. The context of the debate was war, remembered war, and threat of war. All of the discussants wrote in hopes of influencing national policy in the direction of strengthening the country's defenses and preparing the nation more effectively for war. The best-known advocate of the longbow was Sir John Smythe, who was distantly related to Queen Elizabeth I. Smythe addressed his tract *Certain Discourses Military* (1590) to "the Nobility of the Realm." Appealing to their high social status, he stressed that over the past twenty years men of the "common sort" had disparaged the longbow and aimed to "teach us the Arte Militarie." Smythe denounced the "hastie and furious Wordes" such men used and showed in his tract that the arguments of educated gentlemen rested on learned references to ancient, English, and contemporary history and to the

Bible and the Koran. From this elevated perspective, Smythe promoted the longbow and decried the gun.

Rejecting "as frivolous" the argument that English men are not as strong as they were in the heyday of the longbow, Smythe maintained that one may see "as many sons as tall or taller than their fathers, or bigger and stronger, as they . . . see lower, slenderer, and weaker [ones]."[63] The bow is more effective than a gun, he declared, for an archer can shoot four to five arrows to one bullet, whereas if the gunner tries to fire more rapidly, he misses the target. Besides, inclement weather disables guns more than it does bows and arrows. Guns do not work at all if the gunpowder is wet and the matches soggy. Additionally, when guns are fired, Smythe wrote surprisingly, they do less damage in "terrifying, wounding, and killing both horses and men" than the bow.[64] He explained that the cut caused by an arrow is much more dangerous and difficult to cure than a gunshot wound.[65] In Smythe's view, the bow had a "farre greater effect [in battles] than any other weapon that ever was or shall be invented."[66] These points conformed to the public posture of the government, but not to their policy, which was to arm the military forces of the nation with guns. Smythe's *Certain Discourses Military* was not the wave of the future.

In response, men championing the gun offered the first extended public defense of cannon and military guns. Battle-hardened soldiers who had fought against France and Spain and civilian armchair observers widely read in the military history of England, Greece, and Rome, submitted their case in seventy-eight[67] printed pamphlets. Their most persuasive argument was the technological superiority of the gun. In 1594, Humphrey Barwick maintained in his *Concerning The Force And Effect Of . . . Manuall Weapons Of Fire* that "the terrible force of the great and small shot" overwhelms the longbow.[68] Another reason to favor the gun, he argued, was that it saves lives. When arrows fail to decide a battle, he explained, soldiers turn to other weapons, but when guns are used, they give up because of the "terrible force of the great and small shot."[69] Thus the battle is shortened and lives saved by guns. Barwick offered an effective historical perspective on war and weaponry. Incredulously he wrote, "What! shall we refuse the Cannon and fall to the Ram againe?" His advice was to let the past rest. Weapons used at that time were the best available, but they are "trifles in respect to things now in use." Driving home the point, he declared that "Then was then and now is now." "The wars are much altered since the fiery weapons first came up."[70]

Robert Barret was of like mind and reinforced Barwick. Admitting in his *Theorike and Practike of Modern Warres*, published in 1598, that volleys of arrows may come thick, Barret maintained that they do little damage compared to the volleys of a musket or harquebus which "goeth with more terrour, fury and execution." Archers were simply no match for "Pistoletiers."[71] Directly contradicting Smythe, Barret declared that an arquebuser discharges more bullets more rapidly than a bowman can shoot arrows.[72]

The context of this debate had several components. One was the memory of the historic role that the longbow had played in English victories against the French, as at Crécy, Poitiers, and Agincourt, and the sense of national pride in the skill of those earlier bowmen. A second element was the government's anxiety over the presence of firearms among people at the lower end of the social spectrum and the feeling that practicing with the longbow kept young men occupied in a healthy sport and away from mischief, both political and social. Another factor was the ambivalent role of the Privy Council: on the one hand, it issued proclamations praising the longbow and requiring young men to practice it, but on the other, it quietly moved ahead with orders to Lords-Lieutenant to replace bows with guns.

The printed tracts in favor of the gun were more numerous, powerful, and persuasive than those arguing for the outdated longbow. They may well have persuaded readers and others who heard about them that the gun was superior and inclined them to discount the urgings of the government to practice with the longbow. Renewing interest in archery ceased to be an issue at the beginning of the seventeenth century, and the government discontinued its long-standing program of promoting the longbow. That once favored weapon was used in the Civil Wars, but only "to some extent" and "perhaps" because firearms were in short supply.[73] The gun had triumphed.

The English government had even less success in implementing its laws and proclamations that suppressed what it called "illegal" and "immoral" games, which it held responsible for the decline in interest in the longbow. The 1526 proclamation that Henry VIII addressed to London officials ordering them to enforce the laws against games on all persons, regardless of rank, met with wide resistance.[74] "The people murmured" and blamed the proclamation on Cardinal Thomas Wolsey (Henry VIII's principal adviser at this time), who, some thought, exercised too much power over the king and the government. They said that the Cardinal "grudged at every man's pleasure saving his own." The government was unmoved, however, and the proclamation remained.[75] Apparently, however, licenses were granted for gaming houses, for a statute passed in 1555 voided them on grounds that "idle and misruled persons use gaming houses as a cover for conventicles, seditions and conspiracies."[76] Then, in 1567, Queen Elizabeth's government offered a compromise. It licensed tennis courts not in London but Oxford, where at a "yeoman's house" "gentlemen and other honest persons might play," but barred "vagabonds, apprentices and servant players against their masters' will."[77] In 1573, Alice Toldervey received a license for twenty-one years to keep a tennis court "at her mansion house" or another convenient place for the use of gentlemen and other honest persons only.[78] Young Oxford scholars playing against their masters' will were also disallowed.[79] Thereby, the government indulged men of some wealth in their desire to play at "immoral games," while putting those games off limits to "apprentices" and "light persons." This step must have enraged those apprentices and so-called "light persons" who enjoyed playing games, too. The queen's remedy suggests how intrusive the government was in the personal lives of its subjects, always in the interests of the well-to-do. In any case, the effort to revive love of the bow by controlling games people could play did not meet with success.

A third reason for restricting gun ownership and possession was to protect the public. The proclamation of 27 July 1540, addressed to the Mayor and Sheriffs of London, scolded people who shoot handguns in "unmeet places" such as cities and towns without "regard or respect where their pellets do fall or light down after their shot" and charged that residents were endangered "in the open street or in their own houses, chambers or gardens." It limited the shooting of all persons, whatever their status and "notwithstanding" the king's "license," to marks and butts set up for that purpose.[80] The coincidence of this proclamation and the execution of Thomas Cromwell, King Henry VIII's chief minister and an ardent religious reformer, scheduled for the next day, 28 July 1540, on Tower Hill, strongly suggests, even in the absence of direct proof, that the proclamation aimed to limit demonstrations and protect the public from the "hazard" of gunfire. The next year, parliament passed "An Acte concerning crossbows and Handguns" to deal with "little shorte handguns and little hagbuttes," which were responsible, the law said, for "detestable and shameful murders, robberies, felonies, riot and route." The solution was to set the length of a handgun at no less than "one whole yarde" and of a demyhake at a minimum of three-quarters of a yard.[81] Imposing a legal length made it almost impossible to conceal the weapon. Further to address the safety of the public, other provisions in the 1541 act disallowed anyone to shoot in or within a quarter of a mile from any city or market town and to ride on a highway with a loaded gun or a bent crossbow, except in time of war (the same kind of restriction promulgated by the 1328 Statute of Northampton).

The contingent nature of some gun laws is well illustrated by this same 1541 law. The law actually exempted certain subjects from the restrictions on guns that it had just imposed. Thus, it allowed persons living outside urban areas to keep guns of the prescribed length to protect themselves, their family and their house. Residents living within five miles of the seacoasts, within twelve miles of the borders of Scotland, and on the Channel Islands were also spared the restrictive features of the law. The exemptions are explained by international circumstances: in 1541 England was on the verge of war with France, and the government needed to encourage strategically located people to become expert shooters.

In February 1544 when Henry VIII was fighting on two fronts, against Scotland and France, another proclamation dramatically illustrated how closely related to its military needs were the government's restrictions on guns. This proclamation gave "licence and lib[er]tie" to all native born subjects sixteen years old and older to "shoote in handgonnes & hagbusshes" notwithstanding "any Statute heretofore to the Contrary."[82] These suddenly empowered subjects, however, were not permitted to shoot animals or fowl near royal residences or shoot in any urban area except at butts or banks set up for that purpose. Allowing all native-born subjects sixteen years and older to possess and use a gun was an extraordinary and dramatic change in policy, and probably explains why the proclamation cited the Act for Proclamations of 1538 as its authority.[83] Predictably, as the international situation changed, the government's policy respecting its subjects' gun possession and use also changed. A proclamation of 1546 cancelled the 1544 proclamation and returned gun restriction to the status quo ante.[84] Peace prevailed, the proclamation explained, and the "licence and liberty" granted subjects were no longer necessary. The proclamation excepted subjects who possessed a gun license, but ordered local officials to ensure that hunters did indeed have such a license.

In 1548, shortly after Edward VI ascended the throne, Parliament stiffened the reimposition of gun regulations with a law that candidly assessed Henry VIII's 1544 proclamation, saying it had promoted idleness and "light conversation" and caused "daylye" damage to "houses, dovecots, and Churches."[85] Undoubtedly, the unstated but underlying reason for reinstating gun restrictions was the fear that firearms would promote lawlessness and worse—riots and uprisings against the authorities.

The contradictions in these laws partly reflected the nature of England's military defense in the sixteenth century. In the absence of a standing army and a police force and with a militia that was less effective than desirable, the government needed its ordinary subjects to be experienced in handling guns so that they were prepared to help protect the nation in the event of domestic turmoil or international challenge. The contradictions also exposed the long-standing and deep-seated fear of allowing people of little wealth to possess and use guns. Income was the guarantee of loyalty to the government, the protection against riot and uprising. The hierarchical structure of society and the attitude of the well-to-do toward persons at the lower end of society conflicted with the security needs of the nation. These consider-ations help explain the contradictions in some of the laws and proclamations regulating guns.

The safety of the monarch was an ongoing concern and a fourth major rea-son for regulating guns. The dag or "pocket dag," that small, easily concealed handgun often mentioned, was especially dangerous, and authorities focused on it. First to address this matter directly was King Edward VI, who issued a proclamation on 23 January 1549 that banned anyone, no matter his station, from carrying a dag within the court or three miles around it.[86] The penalty was imprisonment at the pleasure of the king. Edward's proclamation was a response to alarming events that had happened at court and in the country-side. It followed by a week the bizarre incident involving Thomas Seymour, Baron Seymour of Sudeley (1509–1549), the jealous and ambitious brother of Edward Seymour, the Protector Somerset. Allegedly, Sudeley was intent upon persuading the young King Edward to place him in the role held by his brother. To that end, he entered the king's private apartments on the night of 16 January 1549, using a key he had secured. The noise awakened Edward's little dog, which, of course, barked furiously. In great alarm, Sudeley, who was armed with a gun, shot the dog, and that finally aroused the royal guards.[87] Somerset ordered his brother arrested, and, although two out of three judges ruled that Sudeley had not committed treason, he was attainted and executed as a traitor in 1549.[88] The incident underlined the vulnerability of the mon-arch and the dangers inherent in a concealable weapon. Concurrent rebel-lions in the countryside further increased the sense of alarm and insecurity. In 1548 and 1549, serious uprisings erupted that opposed the enclosure of common land and the imposition of a new Prayer Book that moved the re-cently established Anglican church further toward Protestantism. Enclosure deprived the small farmer of land on which to grow crops or feed animals or both. The new Prayer Book offended people who opposed the Henrican reformation. Protests began in Somerset, moved to Wiltshire, Hampshire, Kent, Sussex, Essex, and East Anglia, and spread and intensified, extending to Cambridgeshire and north to Yorkshire. Known today as "Kett's Rebellion" in East Anglia, they created a severe crisis.[89]

Alarm over the potential dangers threatening the monarch intensified during Elizabeth's reign. Complex and dangerous international and domestic developments explain an almost paranoid anxiety over the safety of the queen. Observers feared that Elizabeth, now the leader of the Protestant world, would fall victim to a Catholic assassin. Murders of high-placed political lead-ers on the Continent by assassins driven by religious hatred gave urgency to these anxieties. For example, in February 1563, Francis Duke of Guise, a Catholic leader, was shot while hunting by a Huguenot, Jean de Poltrot de Mere, and died six days later.[90] In 1584, the Protestant William I of Orange (1533–1584), known as William the Silent, was killed by Balthazar Gerard, a double agent acting for King Phillip II, the leader of the Catholic cause.[91] Coming into the presence of the lightly guarded prince, Gerard pulled a wheel-lock multiple-firing pistol[92] from his clothing and shot William dead before anyone could intervene. This episode was a particularly frightening example of what might await another Protestant ruler. It was reinforced by the assassination of Henry III, King of France, in 1589, even though he was stabbed rather than shot. Domestic incidents were even more serious. In 1570, Pope Pius V excommunicated and deposed Elizabeth by a Papal Bull and thereby sanctioned Catholic assassination attempts on her. Among the foiled conspiracies, the Ridolfi Plot of 1571 was the most serious, involving Thomas Howard, the Fourth Duke of Norfolk (1538–1572), Mary Queen of Scots, Bernardino de Mendoza, the Spanish ambassador, a Florentine banker (Ridolfi), Philip II of Spain, and the Pope. The aim was to assassinate Elizabeth and replace her with Mary Queen of Scots, who would marry Norfolk, incite a rebellion of Catholics in northern England, and invade England. William Cecil, Lord Burghley, the queen's principal adviser, detected this elaborate scheme. It was derailed and Norfolk was executed.[93] Other plots were organized for the same purposes and involved some of the same parties. For example, a serious conspiracy was forestalled in November 1583 when Francis Throckmorton, who was suspected of involvement, was arrested. Under torture he implicated Mendoza, Mary, Henry Percy, the Earl of Northumberland, and Philip Howard, the Earl of Arundel, who were supporting a French plan to invade England. Sir Francis Walsingham (c. 1532–1590) and Burghley averted this plot.[94] There were other plots or suspected plots, but enough has been said to show that Elizabeth's government had reason enough to fear for her safety.

Alarm over the danger led to a succession of proclamations to ban the dag and forbid carrying a concealed weapon. A selection of them reveals the government's determination and the obdurate disobedience of English subjects. In 1559, a proclamation issued the year after Elizabeth's accession, when her control of the realm was still problematic, complained that in violation of King Henry VIII's law "many men do daily ride with handguns and dags" under the established legal length, and that such "lewd and evil persons" have committed "great and notable robberies and horrible murders." The queen called on all subjects to obey the law and on local justices of the peace "exquisitely" to enforce it.[95] The same point reappeared in a proclamation of 1575, which identified owners of inns, alehouses, and hotels and ordered them to seize any gun that a guest brought in and call in the constable to arrest the offender. The penalty for the hotelier's failure to do so was sharp: disbarment from keeping a hotel or alehouse for a year and imprisonment.[96] Still another proclamation followed in July 1579, which banned the dag absolutely, saying that in peacetime it was fit only for "thieves, robbers, and murderers."[97]

The proclamation empowered local officials to search for and seize pocket dags in private houses and the shops and houses of artificers, and to give the owner a receipt for them with the promise of compensation. For the first time, this proclamation sought to get to the bottom of the problem of dags by regulating the work of gunmakers: it forbade them to make, repair, or sell pocket dags, under threat of imprisonment.

Anxiety over the safety of the queen was still an issue in 1594. A proclamation that year ordered the immediate arrest and imprisonment of anyone caught violating the ban on shooting within two miles of wherever the queen was in residence.[98] This proclamation required that the queen and Privy Council be apprised of the event so "that some further extraordinary punishment" might be devised against "such [an] audacious person." In a further effort to make the system work, the government ordered officials in every county and city to certify in writing to the Star Chamber within eight days and thereafter on a yearly regularized schedule how the proclamation had been implemented.

Determination to restrict concealed weapons continued in the next century as the struggle between Catholic and Protestant interests intensified. In 1613, when rumors circulated about the threatening movements of the Spanish fleet and a shipment of pocket pistols from Spain, James I issued a proclamation that re-imposed regulations on the length of guns, banned the carrying of a dag, and demanded that persons who possessed such a weapon either break it "in pieces" or turn it in to a local office.[99] One contemporary, Sidney Montague, expressed his wholehearted approval of the proclamation against carrying short pistols, writing from London on 27 January 1612/13 that pocket pistols "are made for no good" and that he hoped "God will subvert them all."[100]

However, banning dags remained an intractable problem. In 1616, still another proclamation addressed the same issue, this one attempting to rid the nation of dags by again banning their manufacture and sale and by drying up demand by disallowing anyone from wearing or carrying them under pain of imprisonment and censure in the Court of Star Chamber. King James I described the weapons as "odious and noted Instruments of murther and mischiefe" and as "utterly unserviceable for defence, Militarie practise, or other lawful use."[101] This proclamation was the last one regarding civilians carrying dags. After this the question faded without explanation. Perhaps the authorities recognized that neither laws or proclamations, threats or invective had the desired effect of banning short pistols. Yet, despite alleged threats and foiled attempts, no English monarch was assassinated in the early modern period.

The laws and proclamations regulating guns provide one of the best and most authentic records of how upper status English people viewed firearms and how men of modest means and the poor responded to the limitations that were imposed on them. The presence of guns created many problems for early modern English governments. Monarchs and persons of authority in court and parliament worried about the destruction of the game and disruption of the hunting of wealthy members of society. They were concerned to assure the security of the monarch and the safety of the people. They blamed the decay of archery on guns. All these considerations underlay their persistent effort to keep firearms out of the hands of people of humble means. They had only modest success. A change in custom and lifestyle led people to indulge in—or want to indulge in—a "newfangle[d] and wanton pleasure in using handguns." This cultural change threaded through all levels of society and proved difficult to overcome.

For their part, plebeian men responded to the restrictions with a range of reactions, including resentment, outrage, oral protests, and written objections, including a petition. In opposing the restrictions, no one claimed that a "right" to a firearm was among the "rights and liberties" of English subjects. No serious revolt against the government because of gun restraints occurred. The sense of deference, absence of leadership, poverty, and the overwhelming authority and power of the government protected the status quo. These sharply different positions respecting guns by aristocrats on the one hand and subjects of modest or poor means on the other hand were clearly articulated. They were foundation stones of the gun culture that emerged in early modern England. The attitude of aristocrats, reflected in laws and proclamations, played out in the settlement of the Revolution of 1688–89 and in the poaching laws of the eighteenth and early nineteenth centuries.

FOUR · Domestic Gun
Licenses Issued
"As if under the
Great Seal"

AN UNPRECEDENTED PROVISO appeared at the end of the law that
Henry VIII's Parliament passed in 1514 restricting hunting with
a handgun for the first time. There, in a sentence or two, English
subjects were assured that the restrictive terms of the act shall "not extend or
be hurtful to any person(s) to whom it shall please the king or his heires to licence by his plagard to shote in cross bows and handgonnes." Licensees might
keep the weapons in their houses "for the defence of the same." Moreover, the
proviso held that "every suche licence by the King's placard or his heires to be
made shall be as good and effectual in the lawe . . . as though it were under the
great seale."[1] That this law gave the king and his heirs the power to license persons to shoot guns may surprise twenty-first-century readers for whom gun
licensing is such a fraught issue. But the word "license" is misleading, for the
meaning and purposes of a gun license were different in the sixteenth century
from what they are today. A sixteenth-century phenomenon, the gun license
disappeared in the early seventeenth century without recorded explanation.
So far as I know, the last one was dated 1604. This chapter explores what a
Tudor gun license was, how it worked, why it was introduced, what it reveals
about Tudor government and society, and what it contributes to the creation
of early modern gun culture.

The proviso in the act of 1514 in effect enlarged the prerogative of Henry
VIII and his heirs by giving them the authority to license whomsoever they
pleased to use crossbows and guns, notwithstanding restrictions in the law,
and further elevated the status of the royal license by making it "as good and
effectual in the lawe . . . as though it were under the great seale." This meant
that the monarch's license did not require the stamp of the Great Seal to be
implemented.[2] The proviso has not caught the attention of Henry VIII's

biographers, historians of Tudor history, or constitutional historians of that era, but endowing the monarch's license with authority as if it were passed under the Great Seal could theoretically have established a precedent for a considerable extension of royal power. That authority, however, was not used for anything but granting licenses to shoot with a crossbow and a gun. This proviso illustrates from another perspective the role guns played in the government's calculations.

Tudor monarchs made available two kinds of crossbow and gun licenses. One kind granted to a person who possessed an income of the required value[3] to possess a gun a license that gave him the authority to license a servant or a friend who was otherwise disqualified by reason of his income to shoot with a gun or crossbow. The second kind of license was granted directly to persons who were disqualified from shooting a crossbow or gun because of their income. Whatever the economic position of the person to whom a license was issued, whether qualified by income or not, the permission was restricted. All licenses set out in detail permissible and impermissible targets. Moreover, the licenses that empowered a person to license a servant or friend placed the responsibility for enforcement in the hands of that person, the licensee. Legislation of 1533 specifically held that lords who held a license were responsible for their tenants.[4] The licenses operated, therefore, as a kind of gun-control measure, specifically identifying permissible kinds of fowl and game that could be hunted, the level of income required, and the punishments for disobedience. At the same time, they created an implied supervisory responsibility for well-to-do licensees.

The specification of permitted targets and locations formed the bulk of all gun licenses. The "Forme for a placarde [or license] to be graunted to any person to shoote in Crosse bowes and handgunnes" from the reign of Queen Elizabeth I provides an example.[5] The person who was granted a license could shoot "at any tree, butt, bancke or mark and at any manner of wyld bestes whatsoever Except Dere redd or fallowe, and at all sortes of fowle" (naming a total of nineteen) and "all other wyldefowle whatsoever excepte heron" of a certain type that were restricted by a law of King Henry VIII.[6] The licensee was allowed to keep his "Crossebowes and handegunnes" in his house or wherever else he pleased, but he was not allowed to shoot "any manner of gonne" within five miles of any of the queen's houses, within any city borough or market town, or within two furlongs of areas used for hawking with river hawks. Failure to observe the restrictions on shooting beast or fowl or on the locations where shooting was forbidden risked voiding the license and incurring a fine of £10 for each incident. By specifying exactly at what a person might shoot, the government laid down markers on which enforcement could be based, thereby further widening the government's control of gun use.

The government's purposes in issuing gun licenses must be conjectured, for no explanation of this motive has survived.[7] First, officials undoubtedly recognized the growing popularity of the gun and wanted to exploit it for their own financial advantage. After all, early modern governments licensed many things and activities that brought money into the Treasury. Both King Henry VII and King Henry VIII had issued licenses to use crossbows.[8] So, why not guns? The government's practice of voiding current licenses by laws in 1523, 1533, and 1541, only to continue issuing them, supports the thought that raising money was a strong consideration.[9] Further to the point, other charges were added to the basic cost (of perhaps 10 shillings) of a license. Thus, the gun law of 1541 ordered that licensees must bind themselves in the Court of Chancery by posting a recognizance of £20 (a substantial sum) as an insurance that the licensee would obey the specified limitations in his or her license.[10] The money was to be set aside "to the King's use." The same law established a fine of "at least" £10 for a violation. The recognizance and the fine (should a violation occur, of course) considerably increased the cost of a gun license—to the financial advantage of the government. Moreover, the proclamation of 1546 (which restored previous restrictions on the use of firearms) provided an exception for subjects who had a royal license, but it commanded all local officials to rigorously ensure that hunters did indeed have a license.[11] A law of King Edward VI strengthened this by ordering in 1548 that the names of persons qualified to shoot guns be submitted to the Mayors and Justices of the Peace, and that the Clerk of the Peace in the counties keep a register of such persons.[12] The same law set a penalty of 20 shillings for each shot by an unregistered person.[13] Finally, in 1604, another license was offered to allow the licensee to use hail shot (which had been banned) to bring down fowl suitable as "hawke's meat" only.[14] This law established the cost of the license and the recognizance at 12 pence.[15] These bureaucratic arrangements respecting licenses for the newly popular gun suggest the government's seriousness about controlling licenses and collecting money from them.

How much income the government actually realized from gun licenses is unknown. No figure showing the cost of a license appears on surviving copies, and it is not otherwise recorded. However, it may have been 10 shillings, for "Saul" (the ardent gun proponent and tract writer already noticed) set 10 shillings as the amount to be charged for a gun license in the scheme that he recommended to the government.[16] "Saul" was so knowledgeable about the relationship between the government and guns that it is reasonable to think that he was using the government's figure. The number of licenses issued is also unknown, but the 1511 statute respecting crossbows commented on the "many men [who] have opteyned licences to shote in Crossbowes by placards" issued by Henry VII.[17] Surely the popularity of guns was equal to, if not greater than, that of crossbows. One may reasonably think that many licenses were purchased—far more than have survived—and that with a basic cost of perhaps 10 shillings per license a robust traffic would have been profitable.

A second probable reason for the government's interest in issuing gun licenses was that they operated as a control measure. The £20 recognizance fee and the £10 fine secured the observation of the specified targets. Moreover, men who were granted the right to license others were expected to enforce the restrictions on them, as already noted. Gun licenses were an indirect way of expanding the reach of the central government in the control of firearms.

Third, political leaders looked upon gun licenses as a way of rewarding worthy subjects. On 23 July 1552, King Edward VI, who had knighted Sir John Cheke the year before, "thought it fit . . . to add some farther royal testimonies of his favour to him." Among the marks of approval that the king chose was "grant[ing] him a patent" to allow one of his household servants the privilege of shooting with crossbows and guns, notwithstanding laws to the contrary. John Strype, whose biography of Cheke was first published in 1705, reported that the king wanted these gifts to "qualify [Cheke] the better to bear the post" of knighthood.[18]

Fourth, the government also regarded gun licenses as a device for winning or enlarging the good will of persons who received them. William Cecil recommended granting a gun license as a kind of reward and did so to win people over to his 1569 scheme. He wanted the men who took on responsibilities for his project to become members of a county corporation authorized to issue gun licenses. In addition, he proposed that the corporation be empowered to license "noble [men] and other pryncipall persons" to license their servants to shoot with guns. He was especially concerned that those who needed "the handgonne for killinge of hawkes meate" should have them.[19] These points suggest that he viewed a gun license as a way of winning and keeping their cooperation. It is a reasonable assumption that these several considerations—money, expanded control, reward, and the promotion of friendly interpersonal relations between the court and its high and mighty subjects—were at the bottom of the decision to grant Henry VIII and his heirs the power to issue gun licenses as if under the Great Seal.

What advantages did a gun license bring to wealthy men whose income already qualified them to own a gun? Again, one must speculate, for no evidence has survived regarding what these men really thought about licenses.

GUN CULTURE IN EARLY MODERN ENGLAND

Almost certainly well-to-do men in the country resented the restraints that prevented their servants from legally using a gun or crossbow to hunt. Such restrictions would have disrupted the smooth running of their estates. Moreover, if servants on an estate did hunt with crossbow or gun in violation of a law or proclamation, their masters were open to the charge of complicity in breaking the law. They would also have resented the restrictions that fell on their less-wealthy friends—presumably yeomen and husbandmen in the neighborhood—with whom they hunted from time to time. Those restrictions undermined such relationships. Given the authority to issue a gun license, well-to-do gentlemen could oil the wheels of county society and endear themselves to their friends by extending the privilege of using the crossbow and gun.

Licenses also offered a legal gun for the protection of persons and property: that is, licensed servants were legally able to help protect the manor against poachers and other intruders, human and animal. In the 1540s, Anne, Dowager Countess of Oxford (1499–1559), persistently asked Henry VIII for a gun license to enable to arm her servants to protect her and her property, citing assaults on her property and perceived danger to her person, on which more shortly. John, Abbot of Faversham, who lived in the country, wrote to Thomas Cromwell on 20 February 1532, complaining that he was "marvelously annoyed with rooks, crows, choughs, and buzzards, which not only destroy my doves, but the fruit of my orchard." He asked for a "license for my servants to have handguns and crossbows to destroy the said ravenous fowls."[20] Such purposes as these were likely the major reasons why the well-to-do favored licenses.

The approximately thirty surviving licenses went to politically and socially elite men who held office in state or church or were prominent in their counties, granting them the authority to license unqualified persons, to men down the socioeconomic ranks and to at least one woman of high social standing, Anne, Dowager Countess of Oxford, to license her servants.

The dowager countess received a gun license from King Henry VIII's government in June 1546.[21] The license was like other licenses, except that it contained a pardon for "all acts done by [her] upon the King's grant by word of Mouth on 31 May 1542" to license two of her servants to use guns. The oral grant and the pardon for its use suggest urgency about the matter. The oral grant implies that the dowager countess was on friendly terms with the king and moved easily about the court, which was true. Anne Howard de Vere came from the highest reaches of English society.[22] She was the daughter of Thomas Howard, the Second Duke of Norfolk (1443–1524), a military man who as the Earl of Surrey famously defeated the Scots at the battle of Flodden

Field, also serving both King Henry VII as lord treasurer and King Henry VIII as a diplomat. At his death, Norfolk was described as the "richest and most powerful peer in England."[23] Her mother, Agnes Tilney, was the duke's second wife. Thus, Anne was the half-sister of Thomas, the Third Duke of Norfolk, who succeeded their father in 1524. In 1519, when twenty years old, Anne married John de Vere (1499–1526), the Fourteenth Earl of Oxford, also twenty years of age. De Vere's father died in 1513, and John had been placed in the custody of the Duke of Norfolk in May 1514 at fifteen years old. John and Anne would have known each other as young people growing up in the same household. Their marriage, however, was a disaster. De Vere's unbridled behavior, "extravagance," and unkind treatment of his wife were so outrageous that both King Henry VIII and Thomas, Cardinal Wolsey, tried to rein him in. In 1523, the king ordered De Vere to leave his own household and return to the care of Norfolk, and Wolsey specifically instructed the young man to "lovingly, familiarly and kindly intreat and demean him towards [his] wife."[24] This counsel, which Anne later referred to as the Cardinal's "gracious goodness," won her abiding gratitude.[25] These interventions offer a glimpse of the court's attempts to protect a young, abused, noble lady.

Whether or not her husband changed his behavior is unknown and beside the point, as he died on 12 July 1526 without legitimate issue. His title went to his second cousin, also named John de Vere. This John de Vere, the Fifteenth Earl of Oxford (1482–1540), was said to have hovered around his cousin's deathbed waiting to come into his inheritance. He was determined to revenge himself on Anne for some previous attempts by her to thwart his efforts to obtain certain properties belonging to her husband. He immediately tried to intimidate her by destroying her property and game. However, although young and a very recent widow, Anne was not without resources. On 11 August 1526, a month after her husband's death, she wrote to Cardinal Wolsey telling him that the Fifteenth Earl of Oxford, accompanied by a force of five hundred men with "bows bent," had invaded her property, killed her deer, destroyed her house, beaten her servants and taken "all [her] goods."[26] A fortnight later, on 22 August, when Wolsey's considerable efforts proved unavailing, she wrote a similar account to her half-brother, the Third Duke of Norfolk, and enlisted the help of the powerfully placed Charles Brandon, Duke of Suffolk.[27] These two men, with others, urged Wolsey to further action.

Whatever further actions Wolsey took probably resolved the countess's immediate problems, for her appeals for protection stop. But within six or seven years, Anne suffered renewed difficulties and began writing about them regularly to Thomas Cromwell, who as Wolsey's counselor probably knew about her previous correspondence. On 22 January 1533, in a letter to Cromwell, the dowager countess referred to lewd persons living "near me, who, but for your help would never leave me in peace." She pointed to Sir Alexander Irlam, parson of Otton Belcham (a parish in Essex, close to Sudbury), charging that "in my husband's time, [he] conspired with others to poison me and to kill and steal my deer."[28] These were serious accusations and, although perhaps overstated, apparently moved Cromwell to respond. That he did so is implied in a letter of April 1533 that Rowland Lee, a former chaplain of Wolsey's, wrote to Cromwell.[29] Describing the dowager countess as a "woman of high wit," Lee told Cromwell that she expected to arrive at court within the week "intend[ing] to be merry with you . . . at supper" and to "thank you for your goodness."[30] Unfortunately the letter does not reveal what Cromwell did to assist Anne.

The troubles of the dowager countess surfaced again in 1542 when the king granted her the oral gun license mentioned above. Three years later in 1545, a fragmentary, largely illegible letter from Sir William Petre to Sir William Paget (the two principal secretaries) revealed that her difficulties had returned. Petre's letter reported, "A contention is fallen between my lord of Oxford and my ladie. He alleging that she hath . . . [The] "matter is committed to be hearde to my lorde Great Master and my lorde."[31] Presumably, the "contention" did not go to court, but maybe Petre's memorandum to Paget helped persuade the king to act. In June 1546, Henry granted Anne a written gun license, which contained a pardon for anything she had done under the oral license.[32] We do not know what steps she took under either the oral or the written license, nor is there information about whether the alleged attacks on her person and property were staunched. However, we do know that her person was not seriously harmed, for the dowager countess lived on to the age of sixty, dying in 1559.

This story about Anne Howard de Vere and her gun license merits attention because, among other reasons, it offers insight into why a person would want a license and what uses he or she might make of it. The contextual evidence shows that Anne intended to arm two of her servants to help protect herself and her property. The dowager countess and John, Abbot of Faversham, are the only licensees for whom the available evidence shows as much. But there may well have been other licensees who wanted a license for the same reasons.

A broad range of people acquired gun licenses. Some held office about the monarch and would have come into close contact with the king or queen. For example, Sir Thomas Henneage, described in the license as "the chief gentleman of the Privy Chamber," received a license in 1546 to appoint his servants and friends to shoot at certain game and fowl "at all tymes" and to keep crossbows and handguns in his house.[33] Sir John Gates, knight, a gentleman of the Privy Chamber during the reign of King Edward VI, was licensed to appoint "anyone of his servants" to shoot at specified targets and also to take his weapons to be repaired, provided he carried Gates's license with him, "ready to show."[34] Sir Richard Southwell (1502/3–1564), an active administrator under King Henry VIII and a member of the Privy Council and Master of the Ordnance during the reign of Queen Mary I, obtained a gun license from the queen on 7 January 1557.[35] Two churchmen, Nicholas, bishop of Worcester, and Andre Perne, dean of the cathedral of Ely, also secured gun licenses—the bishop in 1553, and the dean in 1563.[36] Prominent men in Bedford, Northampton, and Norfolk also obtained gun licenses.[37]

Other licensees were neither high placed politically nor especially wealthy. Among them were men who held menial jobs at court: the clerk of Queen Mary I's scullery, Alexander Horden, obtained a license on 31 January 1557.[38] Queen Elizabeth I's Master of the Hawkes, Henry Lord of Hunsdon, the queen's kinsman, was given permission in 1567 to license "any person for any length of time" to shoot, but only at birds suitable for hawks' meat.[39] That same year Henry Macwilliam, a Gentleman Pensioner, received a "Licence for life" to carry a crossbow, handgun, and other specified weapons and to use them to shoot at specified targets. His license also gave him authority to appoint one of his servants to do likewise.[40] Queen Elizabeth I granted Thomas Goad, whose surname links him to the Goads in Berkshire and Cambridgeshire, but who cannot be otherwise identified, a license for life in 1571.[41] Toward the end of her reign, Elizabeth issued a license on 6 July 1601 to Sir Robert Dormer, then the overseer of the queen's hawks (or a deputy authorized by him) to "take up at customary prices" hawks found at ports and rivers "thought fit for the queen," and to shoot such birds and fowl for hawk's meat with a crossbow or handgun or "any other kind of shot."[42] The license underscores the queen's lifelong interest in shooting with hawks and her use of licenses to assure their well-being.

At least one man from the middling rungs of the social scale, who had no connection to government, petitioned to be granted a license.[43] Probably in 1583, Richard Justice, a former soldier who cited his "long service in the wars" to recommend himself, petitioned the Privy Council for a license to keep "game" for the exercise of the caliver and pike, arguing that it was "an exercise very laudable for the training of able men for service." The response of the Council is not known. Other men received a license, among them, William Davye, a.k.a. William Bird, a "yoman," who obtained a license in 1555, empowering him for life to shoot a crossbow or handgun.[44] Twenty years later, in 1604, Anthony Land of Moulsham, Essex, a yeoman, obtained a license for a gun for shooting certain specified fowl used for "hawkes meat, onlie."[45]

Londoners as well aspired to be hunters and shooters: a license was issued in 1556 to William Mason, a merchant tailor of London, giving him the right for his lifetime to "shoot from time to time in a handgun or cross bow" at birds, fowls, and dead marks and to keep his gun in his house.[46]

Whatever the advantages of licenses to the government and to persons who received them, the Stuart monarchs discontinued the practice in the early years of the seventeenth century. There is no evidence of royal gun licenses being granted after Anthony Land's in Essex in 1604, and no explanation why the government terminated them.

Gun licenses offer a unique perspective on several aspects of Tudor society and government. First, the discovery of gun licenses fortuitously uncovered the story of Anne, Dowager Countess of Oxford, the only woman known at this time to hold a gun license and one of only two licensees to want a license specifically to help protect person and property. The story of Anne and her gun license rewards us with a glimpse of the problems a noble, property-owning, well-connected widow faced, her response to them, and the help she received. Thanks to the work of Barbara Harris, many early aristocratic women have been rescued from the dim recesses of the past. Now, this feisty, intrepid dowager countess may be added to them.

Second, although we know nothing of who sponsored the idea in 1514 of issuing gun licenses as "though it were under the great seale," Henry's chief advisers (later the Privy Council) and the Parliament endorsed the idea. The move suggests that the leading men of the court were practical. Aware of the sporting and hunting interests of their politically and socially important subjects and of the growing popularity of firearms throughout the nation, they undertook to exploit the situation. A gun license, with the authority it conveyed to the licensee, was a desirable thing to have; granting it could further reward a man whom the monarch regarded with favor, begin or deepen friendly relationships between the government and its prominent subjects, or reward men of modest income in and out of court circles.

Moreover, through fees, recognizances, and fines, a gun license brought money into the government's coffers. In addition, by specifying the targets permitted to the licensee, a license introduced another way to limit shooting. It also added another layer, albeit a thin one, to the slender bureaucracy tasked with enforcing laws that restricted gun use. The sixteenth-century relationship between the Crown and aristocratic leaders in the countryside, and between the latter and their servants and neighbors, looks a little different when viewed through the lens of gun licenses. This lens reveals from another perspective the control of guns that the government tried to impose on English subjects, and offers an additional insight into early modern gun culture.

FIVE · Military Service

A Pathway to Guns

S ERVICE IN ENGLAND's military institutions was a major pathway
that successive generations of men of all social standing traveled
during the early modern era. It brought aristocrats as well as middling, plebian and the poor into proximity to firearms and played a central
role in embedding guns in English society. Opportunities to participate in
military life abounded, for the Tudor-Stuart era was awash in violence on
both the international and domestic scenes. This chapter shows how English
subjects' participation in armies and the county militias helped spread knowledge of guns in and beyond the two percent of society legally allowed to have
them.

King Henry VIII inherited a feudal array in theory and set about to recon-
struct and use it to forward his policy of war. Multiple considerations, personal, diplomatic, dynastic, and economic (as already discussed) moved the
king to provoke war with France in 1512, 1522, and again in 1544.[1] Royal prerogative gave the king power over international affairs and authority to muster
armies and lead them into battle.[2] Using this prerogative and drawing upon
principles in medieval feudalism that men who held land from the monarch
or a great lord owed them certain military services, Henry revitalized and
reorganized the body. He demanded that leading nobles, aristocrats, gentry,
and others assist him by raising "contract armies." These armies rested on the
"affinities" in the counties, which the king created as his predecessors Richard
II and Edward IV had done. An "affinity" was a group of local men "of power
and worship" that the king and court cultivated and bound to themselves.
Their dependents and servants could be mustered in time of war to form the
basis of an army, and their service "lay at the heart" of Henry's reform.[3] A
"contract" army was raised for the 1512 campaign against France, with the Earl
of Shrewsbury sending 4,355 men, the Earl of Derby 511, and Lord Ferrers
420. The town of Boston provided 23 men, and the Bishop of Carlisle dis-

patched 51. At the king's command, 5,000 mercenaries were added, bringing the total to between 33,000 and 35,000 men.[4]

Thirty years later Henry again required the "gentlemen of England from the King's Council downwards" to contribute to "the Army against France."[5] A 1544 Muster Book shows that he charged the Lord Privy Seal with 100 horsemen and 1,200 footmen. The Duke of Suffolk "certify[ed]" that he would supply 100 horsemen with demilances and javelines" on good horses or good geldings, 100 archers, and 300 billmen. The Bishop of Winchester promised to deliver 100 horsemen and 200 footmen. Aristocrats were, of course, centrally important in this "quasi-feudal" army, but an "unprecedented number of their tenants and servants" (as many as 28,000) accompanied them.[6] In addition, Henry's army was augmented by 4,000 militia men (in violation of the law restricting the service of militiamen to their own county). Numbering 48,000 men at its peak, the 1544 army is said to be the "largest and most powerful" English army up to the reign of King William III (1689–1703).[7]

Guns were an important part of the weaponry of Henry's "bastard feudal" armies. In 1512, the king deployed "enough cannon to conquer Hell," wrote the Venetian Ambassador in excited terms.[8] In fact, Henry brought across the English Channel huge pieces of ordnance, including bombards (stone shooting guns), serpentines (a type of cannon), 120 "organs" (a multi-barreled device that fired murderous grape shot), as well as 100 "hagbusshes and a like number of "handgunys."[9] When invading France in 1544, the king's army arrived with 250 big guns and fired more than 100,000 rounds of "iron balls, and stones, and lead, all flying in the fastest and most deadly way."[10] Henry equipped 2,000 of the 28,000 infantrymen with handguns and arranged that laws against their possessing and using them as civilians because their income did not come up to the required level be set aside to allow the men to practice shooting before arriving on the battlefield.[11] Thus, these 2,000 men learned how to shoot a gun, which in private life they could not legally do. The other 26,000 infantrymen were introduced to guns and probably gained some knowledge of them. All these men would have brought back to their families and friends what they learned about firearms when they returned home from war. The composition of the foot of Henry VIII's "quasi-feudal" armies and the king's arrangements for their training to shoot provide answers to the question of how lower status men in the early sixteenth century learned about guns, which laws and proclamations barred them from legally possessing or using in civilian life.

Henry VIII's bastard-feudal force lasted through the sixteenth century. Queen Elizabeth I actually used it in 1569, 1588, and 1599. But recruitment was complex, difficult, and ineffective; the system was fundamentally flawed by erratic communication, imperfect records, denial by tenants of a military responsibility, and the disappearance of some great families and monasteries.[12]

Aristocrats in these armies played an important part in assuring that firearms would be used by officers and cavalry men. They regarded fighting wars as their way of life, and contemporaries reinforced the idea. As Keith Thomas put it, "for high-ranking men the supreme end of life was the performance of deeds of military prowess."[13] The traditional weapon for cavalrymen was the lance, and initially they viewed firearms, which were increasingly assigned them, with contempt. The chivalric code, a composite of virtue (meaning courage), honor, courtesy, selflessness, generosity in victory, and fortitude in defeat, with its deep Renaissance literary and cultural roots, had long defined the honorable way of fighting. A chivalric knight believed that one-on-one, eye-to-eye combat with an edged weapon was the only fair and noble way of fighting. They thought it contemptible for a lowly foot soldier, who might be crouching behind a tree or a bush, to aim his gun at a distant target and, if successful, wound or kill a man of wealth and social position without giving him a chance to fight and prove his honor and virtue.

Disdain for such a device used in such a way was not new; rather it continued a long tradition that went back to the Greeks and reappeared with each new version of a missile weapon.[14] The ban on the crossbow issued by Pope Urban II in 1096 and again by Pope Innocent III in 1139 because it upset the social order and was "unsporting" illustrates the point. The press, English authors, and the stage helped to keep the idea alive. For example, Ludovico Ariosto, a Renaissance literary figure and author of *Orlando Furioso: The Frenzy of Orlando*, a romantic epic, was vehemently against guns for reasons just described. His work was popular in England: Christopher Marlowe's *Tamburlaine* (1590) was filled with its themes. Sir John Harington published the first English translation in 1591, and Robert Greene adapted the story for the stage. It played in 1591 and 1599 before audiences that included Queen Elizabeth.[15]

The work of Shakespeare, Spenser, and Milton in the seventeenth century showed its influence.[16] Other writers were also appalled by the use of guns in war. The great English historian, William Camden (1551–1623), wrote in his *Remaines Concerning Britain* (1614) that "by murthering afar off" a firearm was the "enemy of true valour and manful couragiousness" and declared that "now" a man is "thought the most unfortunate, and cursed in his mother's womb, who dyeth by great shot." He memorialized Thomas Montacute, the Fourth Earl of Salisbury, as the first English gentleman to die by a bullet in 1428.[17] It is ironic that this English historian should castigate guns when he surely knew that the longbow was just as guilty of "murthering afar off" as a firearm.

But he was not alone. Arguing from the viewpoint of a military man defending the soldier and urging the proper use of firearms, Samuel Buggs regretted in a tract (a so-called sermon) printed in 1622 that when guns are employed "many a brave spirit dies by the hand of a Boy or as ignobilie as Abimelech by the hand of a Woman."[18] This view of guns continued: as late as 1635 David Persons lamented that "the bravest and most venturous fellows without much proofe of their undoubted courage [fall] prostrate on the ground" before a volley of shot.[19] By then such an observation was an anachronism.

Aristocratic scorn rested on another consideration: the technological limitations of a firearm fitted with a matchlock which initially was all that was available to them (see Appendix A). Pictures exist from the fifteenth century of men on horseback carrying a gun, but it was, in fact, very difficult for a rider to fire a matchlock gun. Humphrey Barwick, one of the military men writing at the end of Elizabeth's reign, pointed out that while there were many men who could ride well or shoot well, very few could "rightly use both together."[20] To ignite the priming powder, the rider had to direct a smoldering cord soaked in saltpeter to a little pan holding the priming powder which was affixed to the side of the firearm. It took two hands to do this. The maneuver was almost impossible while astride an active horse in battle; it required the rider either to dismount or stand in the stirrups to fire, both of which endangered him.

Technological developments, however, overtook and solved this problem. By the 1540s the new wheel-lock mechanism (see Appendix A) was in wide use in the cavalry.[21] When fitted with a wheel lock, the pistol could be primed in advance and made ready for shooting before the cavalryman mounted his horse. The rider could prepare two, three, even six guns ready to fire, hang them on his person or saddle, and use them, one by one, needing but one hand to do so, as his horse took him into battle, and then turned back so the rider could reload.

In England influential persons recommended that cavalrymen learn to shoot on horseback. Sir Humphrey Gilbert in his instrumental *Queene Elizabethes Achademy* (1570) advocated that in his proposed academy there should be "one good horseman to teache noble men and gentlemen to ride . . . a ready horse . . . and to skirmish on horsebacke with pistols."[22] Queen Elizabeth made the same point in her call in 1573 for what later became the Trained Bands. She specified that selected men be "taught and trained for to use, handle and exercise their horses, armour shot and other weapons both on horseback and on foot."[23] William Cecil also thought that men should be skilled in using a gun on horseback: in 1585 he drafted a note to the Lords-Lieutenant asking them to "Train shot on horseback."[24]

To implement these ideas a printed manual in English was needed that would instruct cavalrymen in simple terms and in detail how to shoot effectively on horseback. None was available until 1632, when John Cruso (fl. 1595–1655) published *Militarie Instructions for the Cavallrie. Or Rules and directions for the Service of the Horse*, the first of his four military books. Born in Norwich of Dutch parents, Cruso had had some military experience as a captain of the Dutch or Walloon Company in the Norwich trained bands.[25] He explained that his book filled a critical need because classical writers ignored the cavalry, later authors targeted only knowledgeable readers, no book on the subject was written in English, and no book offered the "first rudiments for the handling of arms" on horseback. Using works by Dutch military writers, drawing on Dutch martial experiences, and assuming little or no knowledge on the part of the reader, Cruso published a cogently written and lavishly illustrated book to fill this need.[26] Combining text with realistic pictures, the book took a cavalryman through all the basic steps he needed to learn to manage a gun on horseback: spanning his guns, mounting his horse, and giving fire. Cruso recommended that a cavalryman be "active and nimble," a man of "spirit and resolution," and above all a person who "loveth (and knoweth) what belongeth to a horse."[27] Thus, the cavalryman, armed with a wheel-lock pistol and skilled in using it, was eventually responsible for "driving the knight in armor from the battlefield."[28] Cruso's military works are considered important because they were the "first to make the new continental . . . military literature" accessible to English readers.[29]

The positive battlefield experiences of aristocrats and men closely associated with them may also have promoted the acceptance of firearms as a weapon of war. For example, the awesome power of firearms fascinated some individuals. An English gentleman, Sir Thomas Coningsby, recalled witnessing the battle at Rouen in 1591 when a cannonball went through one house and then landed on another. He confessed his admiration, writing that "were yt not for charytie it were a pleasure to behold."[30] It is reasonable to think that other English officers—and soldiers—felt the same way. Moreover, guns were the first acoustical weapon, and the fearsome noise they made aroused a positive emotional response in some men. A Scottish poet, George Lawder, captured this feeling when he wrote in 1629 how he longed to "heare the Cannons thundering voice / In terror threaten ruin: that sweet noyse / Rings in my eares more pleasing than the sound of any Musickes consort can be found."[31] His poem perhaps reflected not only what he felt, but also what he had observed in others' response. Men who found the sound of gunfire exhilarating no doubt would have endorsed the use of guns in warfare. On the other hand, in 1544 it was reported that Scotsmen fighting along the border with England did not like the sound of gunfire at all and would not "bide within the hearing of guns."[32] Later in the century, Sir Roger Williams dismissed the idea that the noise of gunfire was pleasurable, writing that it was the "rawe men or light-headed [fellows who] delight to heare the peece-cracke."[33]

In the last half of the sixteenth century, the dominance of aristocrats as officers was challenged by a minority view that military leaders should be chosen on grounds of their accomplishments and promise, not their ancestry or social status. An ancient Greek, Onosander (first century A.D.), had offered this proposition in *Of the Generall Captaine and of his Office*, which Peter Whitehorne translated and published in 1563. Thirty years later, William Garrard, a veteran of the Spanish wars, emphatically rejected "high titles . . . [and] favors of the Prince" as criteria for appointment to high military office (*Arte of Warre* [1591]). Following on, Matthew Sutcliffe, in *The Practice, Proceedings and Lawes of Armes* (1593), presented examples of generals in the French army who were appointed on grounds of their "nobility rather than sufficiency" with dismal consequences. Robert Barret, another effective proponent of guns, in *The Theorie and Practike of moderne warres* (1598) also called for selecting skilled men as military leaders, whatever their origins.[34] This opinion, however, won no traction.

The press reinforced the viewpoint that aristocrats should lead the military. For example, a pamphleteer declared unequivocally in 1578 that war was the province of aristocrats, that "the knowledge, and practyse of the actes and feates of armes, principallie and properlye are of the profession of noble menne, and gentlemen of great revenues."[35] In the early seventeenth century, the much admired legal scholar, John Selden, affirmed that true nobility required martial prowess joined with birth.[36] Agreeing, other writers insisted that for the king's honor, his major officers should come from high social rank, that only noblemen should command the cavalry, and that nobles alone should carry the royal standard into battle.[37] As late as World War I, war was still seen by English people as "the occupation of the nobility and gentry." It was commonly held that a "British officer should be a gentleman first and an officer second." Until World War II, the majority of officers came from the aristocracy.[38]

Service in these armies was consequential. First, for foot soldiers whose income was too low to qualify them legally to possess and use a gun in civilian life, their service offered familiarity with firearms and taught some of them who were chosen to be gunners how to care for and shoot guns effectively. The unintended and regrettable consequence, from the government's viewpoint, was the stimulation of interest in a device whose use it had tried to limit to persons of wealth. Second, the aristocracy's general acceptance of the use of guns in war was essential to the new military gun culture. Many considerations, none more important than the technological advantage of the wheel lock, combined to assure this acceptance. Aristocrats' favorable reception of the gun changed the way the cavalry fought. But the decline of cavalry forces used in battle continued apace.[39] Still, the approval of the gun in battle matched the important place firearms occupied in the personal and domestic life of the well-to-do.

Military service in the seventeenth century had the same effect, generally speaking, as it had had in the sixteenth century. It further embedded firearms in society and spread knowledge about and skill in using them to successive generations. The point is true of the three major military events that followed each other over the century. First, from 1642 to 1648 the Civil Wars brought into play armies, each composed of Englishmen of all socioeconomic standing, fighting each other.[40] Second, at the restoration of the Stuart line, King Charles II created the first professional standing army under royal authority in England's history.[41] Third, King William III and John Churchill, Duke of Marlborough, led armies that were larger than any previous one, defeated France, and established Great Britain as the greatest military power in the world. Each of these events is complex, the scholarship on each enormous. It is enough for this book to maintain that military service advanced and then anchored guns in a broad swath of society composed of men who were financially unqualified to have access to them.

Service in the county militia, the oldest and longest-lived military institution in English history, was the second military pathway that men of all social standing traveled.[42] It, too, brought them into contact with firearms. Mustered for a certain number of days each year,[43] the militia was supposed to serve only in its own county, a restriction the crown did not always honor. These county forces were generally expected to put down domestic discord and protect the nation against invasion. During the year when the Spanish Armada threatened England in 1588 and the years of continuous war from 1685 to 1703, the latter duty was genuinely significant. A recent study of these years maintained that "national defense depended on the militia."[44]

Like all military institutions, the militia was under the ultimate control of the monarch and the Privy Council. There is merit, however, in regarding it as the sum of the county bodies, each one unique, varying in strength, commitment, and leadership. The leadership of the militia in each county was in the hands of the county's Lord-Lieutenant and Deputy-Lieutenant. Elizabeth I finally regularized these offices in 1585. Drawn from county society, the Lord-Lieutenant was almost always a peer and often a member of the Privy Council, while the Deputy-Lieutenant was a member of the upper gentry.

These socially and politically prominent officers carried out their duties of mustering and training and so on with the help of lesser officers, the Captain, the Sheriff, Justices of the Peace, and on down to the Constables. Wealthy county men served as officers and in the cavalry. The structure of the militia was hierarchical like that of the pseudo-feudal army. This being the case, the pertinent questions about the militia for this study concern the composition of the militia foot and the difference that made.

Legal requirements for the militia in the sixteenth century were set forth in two laws passed in 1558 during the reign of King Philip and Queen Mary I.[45] "An Act for having of Horse Armour and Weapons" specified the militia responsibilities of men, linking their wealth and the arms they were to provide, just as the Assize of Arms (1181) had done. This law divided male subjects into ten income groups, identified the weapons for which they were responsible, and, for the first time, included firearms. Those enjoying an income of £1,000 or more were required to supply six horses or geldings with a saddle, a harness and a weapon, ten light horses or geldings, and a range of weapons, including forty pikes, thirty longbows with thirty "shefes" of arrows, twenty steel caps or skulls, and twenty haquebuttes. Nobles were also charged with stockpiling arms, a requirement that resulted in the creation of large private armories.[46] In addition, any man whose wife wore disallowed apparel, as set out in Henry VIII's statute in 1533, was obliged to find and keep certain horses. The levy on men down the income scale was mostly the same items, but in reduced amounts: a man having a yearly income of £400 was responsible for two horses, four geldings, twenty pikes, fifteen steel caps, six harquebuttes, and fifteen longbows with arrows. No firearm was required of individuals with an annual income of £10, but they had to bring one longbow, one "sheife of Arrows," one steel cap, and one black bill or halberte." Failure to comply with these rules resulted in a fine of £10 for every three months that the specified number of horses was absent.[47] Equating arms with wealth was a constant feature of military laws in early modern England. Even the poor had to shoulder some charge.

The law mandated that inhabitants of all urban areas (except persons with an income of £10 and under) should provide "at their common Chardges and Expenses" whatever "Harneis and Weapons" the Commissioners specified. It required that the equipment be kept "in suche Places as by the sayd Commissioners shalbe appointed." This meant that military supplies for urban areas bought by communal funds were publicly stored. Public storage kept the material secure and assured that firearms were regularly inspected and cleaned to protect them from rusting into nothingness. The order was a way to preserve a financial investment in guns,[48] and it also kept guns and armour and other equipment out of the hands of the less well-to-do, a constant concern of early modern English governments. In practice, the gear was kept in various places: in the city gatehouse in Hereford, entrusted to the constables in small townships, and stockpiled in churches in large towns, like Colchester, Bristol, and Taunton.[49]

Custom and law held that all "fit and able" men between sixteen and sixty years of age were liable for militia service, which meant that men all along the social spectrum could expect to serve. County militias, however, did not always meet the customary and legal requirements. A brief account of how the county militias were embodied helps explain how this happened. The first step in the creation of each county militia came from the monarch and the Privy Council, which assigned the number of men to be recruited and notified the county's Lord-Lieutenant and his deputies of the requirement. The lieutenancy, in turn, informed lesser county officers, who were responsible for filling the quota and enrolling the men. A cluster of considerations influenced what happened next. First, certain categories of persons were legally exempt from service: nobles above the rank of baron and their household servants and retainers, members of Parliament and their servants, and members of the Privy Council. Justices of the Peace, clergymen, and recusants were also excused, but they had to contribute cash.[50] These exemptions automatically removed men of high social and political standing from the militia foot. The government was sympathetic to this arrangement. In 1589, William Cecil, Lord Burghley, wrote in a memorandum entitled "Orders for the Musters" that the "late experience" at Tilbury, showed that "rich men, which have been daintily fed, and warm lodged" were less able than the poor to endure the hardships of battle and, therefore, should be spared military service.[51]

Second, counties had to balance the requirements of the Privy Council with the need to ensure that work in their fields, industries, mines, and crafts, would not be halted or even slowed at critical times of the year. Therefore, county leaders commonly exempted men from militia service who were involved in vital economic activities. Third, the most important reason that country officials did not draw upon "all fit and able" men between the ages of sixteen and sixty to fill their assigned quota was that many substantial men in the local communities paid poor men to substitute for them. The practice was so widespread that the "Acte for the taking of Musters" (the second of the Militia laws of 1558) condemned it.[52] The law pointedly complained that "a greate number" of men who are "most able and lykelyest to serve well" did not take part in the militia. It explained that "many" of them "through frendshipe or rewardes [are] released, forborne and discharged of service." And other men "not being able or mete ... [are] chosen thereunto." The result is the "great

GUN CULTURE IN EARLY MODERN ENGLAND

perill and daunger [to] this noble Realme." Therefore, the law declared that any man called to service that absents himself without a reason or appears without his proper armour, shall be jailed for ten days or fined 40 shillings for every instance. And a muster master who takes a bribe to release a person from service shall be fined ten times the money he took.

Notwithstanding these brave words, wealthy men continued to avoid service by paying the poor to substitute for them. A few persons criticized the practice. In 1579, Geoffrey Gates predicted in a printed tract that allowing the system to continue would lead to uprisings, tumults, and "ruinous theft and libertie." He insisted that only "the very householders and their sonnes" should serve in the militia.[53] In 1601, some members of Parliament proposed a law to require every man between eighteen and sixty years of age to be liable for militia service.[54] Other members, however, would hear none of this extreme idea. One pointed out that he himself should be exempt from service because he was "a lawyer and therefore unfit to be a professor of the art of war." Responding, the Speaker suggested an amendment exempting all lawyers from militia service. At this, several members, overcome with laughter, rose to move exemptions for themselves because of their professions. Predictably, the proposal failed. The debate unambiguously reveals the attitude of the majority of members of parliament toward militia service and the practice of substitution.

Sixty years later, at the Restoration, members of Parliament assumed that wealthy persons would pay a substitute to spare themselves service. By the late seventeenth century, in Norfolk, it was "generally recognized" that men of "wealth would not serve personally" and that "hirelings and substitutes" would comprise the bulk of the militia force.[55] The attitude and assumption continued, as exemplified in Buckinghamshire in the eighteenth century. An analysis of the 238 men in the 1759 Buckingham militia found that 111 men, just about half the total, were substitutes.[56] Fifty years later, 114 of the 129 men in the 1798–99 Buckinghamshire militia were substitutes.[57] The point is not that the militia foot was comprised entirely of paid substitutes, only that men from the lower reaches were a large component. Men of middling status were also in the militia foot, and some men of comfortable means were also. Individual counties varied.

All men who were chosen for militia service came into contact more or less with guns. A provision of the 1558 laws provided that the militia should be equipped with guns of different kinds, as well as pikes, halberds, swords, spears, and bows and arrows. Within fifteen years, the government increased the number of guns in the militia, so that between 1573 and 1587 the musket overtook the bow and arrow, and the increase continued. In 1587 and 1588, the government called for pikes and guns to defend against the Spanish Armada, and by the end of the century, guns were the government's weapon of choice for its military institutions. As this change took place, the number of required gunners increased automatically, and the Muster master had to choose gunners from among the militia men. It was his responsibility to match the soldier and the weapon. The rule of thumb was to assign "strong, tall, and best persons to be pikes, the squarest and broadest . . . to carry muskets, and the least and nimblest . . . the Harquebush."[58] In other words, a soldier received a weapon "as doth best agree with the proposition of [his] person," a principle that enjoyed long approval. In 1619, Edward Davies reiterated the advice.[59] Another common assumption was that townsmen should be assigned the gun or the pike, while "rustics" should use the bow and arrow, and gentlemen the pike. This belief held that townsmen were endowed with mechanical skills that would enable them to repair firearms, which, experience taught, often needed repair.[60] By 1670, however, Nathaniel Nye, "a Mathematician and Master-Gunner of the city of Worcester," tried to shift the focus away from the physical characteristics of the soldier to their mathematical aptitude. He believed that any "ingenious man may learn to be a perfect Gunner" and argued that the most important quality of a gunner was to be "skillful in arithmetic and geometry."[61] His argument reflected the growing interest in arithmetic, geometry, and instruments that came about partly because of questions that were posed by guns.[62] It also recognized the spread of mathematical literacy in sixteenth-century London and the capacity of London's citizens, including those of lower socioeconomic standing, to master the discipline.[63]

Foot soldiers were eager to be chosen as gunners. Nye noticed that "men [come forward] at the twinkling of an eye to do [that] service."[64] Their enthusiasm was clearly genuine, for until 1601 they had to pay for their gunpowder out of their wages of 8 pence per day.[65] But the price was worth it, they seemed to think. As a gunner, the foot soldier experienced the power, excitement, danger, and sense of personal empowerment and prestige that guns conferred. Moreover, they may have wanted to advance their long-term career prospects by being trained to use a gun. The process involved learning how to cast bullets, how to calculate the trajectory of a missile to hit an assigned target, and how to use the new instruments that were being developed to assist gunners. Some soldiers may also have recognized that skill with a gun was useful in a life of crime. Possibly the gunners from Nottingham also liked being draped with silk ribbons and those from Bath with lace to mark them as gunners when the militia in those places presented itself for inspection and skirmishing.[66] Whatever the reason, members of the militia foot were eager to be gunners.

The fact that wealthy men paid poor fellows to substitute for them in militia service was significant. Although the composition of each county militia was unique, more poor men than otherwise would have been the case comprised the militia foot across the nation. The result was that men down the social scale legally barred access to guns in civilian life because of their economic standing were introduced to guns and learned about them. These men brought their experiences and knowledge back with them when they returned home, thereby further spreading knowledge of firearms into the lower reaches of society.

It took a long time for the idea of the Trained Bands to be realized. In 1573, Queen Elizabeth I ordered the counties to choose at musters of the militia a "convenient and sufficient number of the most able" men and arrange that they be "taught and trained" in the use of pikes and guns.[67] The queen's directive was not the first time that such an idea had been put forward. Indeed, it may be seen as a revival of earlier proposals, the most important of which was devised in 1569 by William Cecil, now Lord Burghley, her chief minister. Cecil's project was to increase the number of guns and trained gunners in the counties. The cost of this project was to be borne by leading officials in the counties, and they expressed near universal disapproval of shouldering the expense. Within several months the government decided to withdraw the proposal. Creating the Trained Bands was arguably a way of accomplishing similar ends. While the interest in creating the Trained Bands generated by the queen's directive "established the principle of training in the militia," setting up the Trained Bands in large numbers in the counties did not go forward until 1585, when effective leadership was provided by Elizabeth's regularizing the appointment of lieutenancies in the counties.[68]

Queen Elizabeth had spelled out her idea of the composition of the Trained Bands. She wanted them to be filled with men of middling socioeconomic status: well-to-do yeomen, prosperous farmers, householders and their sons from the countryside, and artisans and tradesmen from the towns. Several considerations underlay this preference. Such men were apt to be loyal subjects, so it was "safer" to arm them than "the 'baser sort.'" They would have a stake in county affairs, and maintain a stable residence. They would meet the criterion of being "able bodie[d]." Their wealth would enable them to shoulder the expense of their arms and supplies.[69] This goal was attained in some counties. For example, Kent counted "prosperous" inhabitants in its foot bands, Norfolk and Hertfordshire had gentlemen among its foot soldiers, the "richest farmers" and their sons served in Lancashire and Cheshire, and men of "birth, credit, and qualitie" in Derbyshire.[70] The composition of the Trained Bands, however, varied across the nation's counties "with time and place." Not surprisingly, service of the substantial members of the county tended to diminish when a crisis ended or peace was at hand.[71] For the purposes of this study, however, the Trained Bands provided still another arena in which men served whose socioeconomic status was higher than that of regular militia men. The purpose of the Trained Bands was the training of the men in the use of the pike and gunpowder weapons. At the end of the seventeenth century and thereafter, service in the Trained Bands continued the spread of knowledge about guns in a systematic and organized way.

Throughout the Tudor era, military service in the "quasi feudal" army of Henry VIII and in the county militias across England brought men from all along the social scale into close proximity to firearms; that experience affected their attitudes and assumptions regarding guns. After initially rejecting guns because they were difficult to use and thought to destroy chivalry, aristocrats accepted them as technological improvements made them easier and safer to operate. In the militia, not all "fit and able" men of a certain age were liable for service, nor were those who were "fit and able" routinely chosen. Legal exemptions, economic considerations, and the practice of well-to-do men avoiding militia service by hiring poor men to substitute for them defied the terms of the Militia Laws of 1558. The result was that a large portion of the foot soldiers of the county militias came from the lower reaches of society. This meant that men, who by law were barred from possessing and using a gun in civilian life, gained knowledge of firearms and, if chosen to be a gunner, instruction in firing them. When returning home, they brought this knowledge with them. In the absence of military service, it is certain that these men would not have assimilated guns so rapidly nor learned so much about them. The new Trained Bands performed the same service for men chosen to serve, which included gentry, well-to-do farmers, and in some cases, men down the social scale.

No matter the economic and social origins of soldiers and officers, their military service promoted the process of embedding guns in the nation's society. Military service played a significant part in creating an early modern English domestic gun culture as well as military gun culture.

SIX · London

The Gun Capital of England

I N THE DECADE OF THE 1560S, probably in 1562–63, "the so-called" Agas map of London appeared in print.[1] The Agas map is a historical treasure, because it not only shows London stretched out along the River Thames, but also indicates the domestic and industrial activities of ordinary people who made this fast growing city their home. There are sketches of women laying out their washing to dry and bleach, of men herding animals, and of other men practicing their skill with the crossbow.[2] Only one activity or industry, however, is highlighted in more than one place: guns. They are indicated in four different places. Along Houndsditch Street is a picture of a house with little cannon in front of it (1) with words along the side that read: "The Gunfounder's House." Not far away to the southwest, in front of the Tower, are three cannons lined up on Tower wharf (2), where they were first placed in 1535–36.[3] Somewhat to the northeast, in the Artillery Garden, a man is practice shooting at some butts with a harquebus (3). Finally, at the corner of Thames Street and Water Lane another little cannon is shown (4), presumably to indicate the location of another gun foundry. Clearly, the map's designer believed that artillery and military guns and activities associated with them were important features of ordinary life in London, and that persons purchasing his map would expect such indications. His map establishes that by the middle of the sixteenth century, gun foundries were operating in London and had a visible presence in the city. The detail of the man practice shooting possibly indicates a popular pastime, thus showing awareness of domestic guns.

For a long time, historians have been interested in the history of London and its environs and have lavished attention on it. They have included gun-founders, gunmakers, and guns in their work. Studies by scholars at The Centre for Metropolitan History, an article, two monographs on the Ordnance Office (later the Board of Ordnance), and the *Dictionary of Gunmakers in London 1350–1850* (followed by a Supplement) provide information.[4] How-

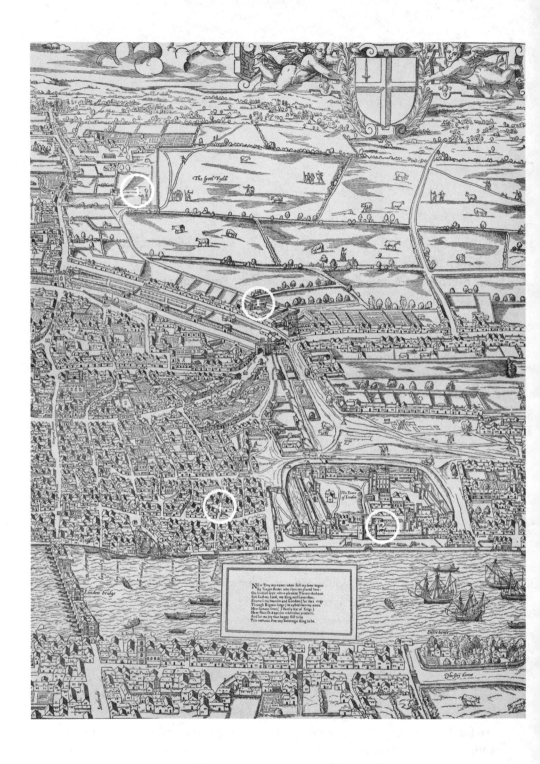

NEw Troy my name when first my fame begun,
By Trojan Brute: who then me placed here:
On Luddes hyll: where pleasant Thames doth run,
Seth Lud my Lord, my King and Lover dear,
Encreast my bounds and London (far thus wyde)
Through Regions large) he called then my name.
Have famous been (thately fear of King)
Have flourisht aye one other other proclaim,
And let me joy my happy still to be
This vertuous Fary my Soveraign King to be.

Figure 1.
Agas Map of London (1562–63) showing domestic and economic activities of the city. The map indicates the presence of guns in four different places: (1) house with cannon on Houndsditch Street, (2) three cannons on Tower wharf, (3) man shooting a harquebus in the Artillery Garden, and (4) house with cannon on Thames Street and Water Lane. (London Metropolitan Archives, City of London)

1

2

3

4

ever, many valuable studies, including major studies of London, such as Steve Rappaport's *Worlds within Worlds: Structures of Life in Sixteenth-Century London* (1989) and Lien Luu's *Immigrants and the Industries of London, 1500–1700* (2005) do not mention guns at all. No study deals with the effect that the new device had on early modern London and the lives of its residents. The present chapter does not claim that gun foundries and gunmakers' workshops, and the presence of artillery, military handguns, domestic handguns, and gunpowder transformed London, but it does argue that they and the people connected with them were responsible for significant and long-lasting change.[5] The number of gunfounders and gunmakers that made a difference to life in the city was not large, compared to the population of the city or the number of artisans in well-established crafts. It was not their number, but their activities and the government's support of artillery and military guns that were important and made a difference.

Gunfounders, gunmakers, and artisans associated with them settled in London and its environs starting in the early sixteenth century. Many of these early arrivals were Europeans whom Henry VIII had persuaded to emigrate from the Continent on the promise of work in the military gun industry and had installed in the city. Other industries especially that of cloth also attracted aliens (known as "strangers") who came to improve their economic opportunities and to escape political and religious persecution. Single men and men with wives, children, and servants fled the economic downturn in Europe, especially in Antwerp, and the political and religious turmoil: the Dutch Revolt in 1566 and the St. Bartholomew's Day massacre in France in 1572.[6] By 1571, the number of aliens in London was 4,850; it grew to 5,315 in 1573, and to 5,450 in 1593. Thus, aliens were about 3 percent of the city's population, which ranged over those years from about 152,000 to about 186,000.[7] A survey in May 1571 showed that eleven alien gunmakers were living in the city, a miniscule number compared to the total alien community.[8]

Londoners did not warmly welcome alien gunmakers, no more so than other aliens, when they first arrived. Gunmakers would have felt the effect of the Evil May Day in May 1517, a demonstration of journeymen and apprentices against all aliens. They were subject to the terms of the 1523 law, which set out restrictions on the work practices of aliens, requiring them, for instance, to hire only Englishmen and putting them under the control of the company with which they were affiliated. There was, of course, no gunmakers' guild that newly arriving gunmakers could join, but to work in London, they had to be a member of a guild. As already noted they joined the Armourers'

Guild, the Blacksmiths' Guild and the Joiners' Guild and were absorbed in the life of these three established guilds.

Like strangers working in other crafts, alien gunmakers were bound by ethnic and religious identities, as well as by craft ties.[9] They tended to settle in the same area.[10] The prominent Arcana family and other Italian gunfounders offer an early example of an ethnic enclave. They established themselves in Salisbury Square, which was located on the south side of Fleet Street near the River Thames and close to Blackfriars Bridge, and by 1533, their gun foundry was well established. The Italian community lasted there until the mid-1540s when, for unknown reasons, it dispersed.[11]

Gunmakers, whether alien or English, usually settled further east in the city. Over the early modern era, favorite areas included the street known as the Minories where 162 gunmakers lived and worked. In the nearby Tower Ward, 141 gunmakers clustered. Aldgate Ward, a little to the north, was the home of 156 gunmakers, while 106 gunmakers opted for East Smithfield.[12] Gunmakers of more independent spirit, however, chose to live in different places. For example, in 1588 Thomas Morgan lived "at the newe Maire mayde below pownd alley," and a century or so later in 1699 Richard Miles settled "near the Tennis Court, Mansell Street."[13] For their part, German and Flemish gunmakers preferred Greenwich to London, and they created their own enclaves there. Gunmakers and gun founders modified the demography and the land use of neighborhoods in which they settled and transformed the ambience by their presence. In a different way, so too did the individual gunmaker.[14]

Men and women gunmakers carried on their craft, as did other artisans, in workshops in their houses. Their workshops had special features: an announcement of George Fisher's death in 1695 stated that his "house and Shop [in the Minories] is to be let" and noticed that there were "several Conveniences for a Gunsmith, ready fixed."[15] Gunmaking required space for benches and tools, and the house of even a non-prosperous gunmaker contained "two chambers, a long room, a back room and a cellar."[16] At least one gunmaker achieved additional space by building a shed in his yard.[17] A 1660 French engraving of a gunmaker's shop enables one to visualize its possible contents, although the drawing of the shop itself is unrealistic. The print shows three gunmakers surrounded by the tools of their trade, including a file, a hammer, a chisel, and a vise, as well as by the evidence of their ongoing labor: two completed pistols hanging from an arch, a harquebus that one of them is finishing, and pistols lying on the bench. The second gunmaker is working with a hammer, while the third is busy with a vise. Words accompanying the engraving explain that one of the gunmakers' jobs is to take apart old harquebuses and

FIGURE 2. A fanciful engraving of a gunmaker's shop (French 1660) showing realistic tools, including a file, hammer, chisel, and vise as well as pistols and a harquebus. (Used by permission of the Folger Shakespeare Library)

remove the rust with a file. Using a hammer and a chisel, the gunmakers sing while they work, it is said, and when done they let out a "great cry." Fanciful though this is, the image is suggestive and merits examination.

The evolution of the Minories, where the largest number of gunmakers lived and worked, offers an example of how the gun industry affected a London neighborhood.[18] The street, located northeast of the Tower, took its name from the church of The Holy Trinity of the Minoresses; it was the site of the nunnery of the Little Sisters of St. Clare, called the Minories, established there in 1293.[19] These women were Poor Clares, Franciscan nuns. The London antiquarian, John Stow, recorded that Henry VIII dissolved the nunnery in 1539 and in its place, as we already noted, built "large storehouses for armour and habiliments of war with diuerse worke houses serving to the same purpose."[20] Such buildings would have dwarfed the small parish church and changed the ambience of the street. The shift to guns continued. In 1563, shortly after Queen Elizabeth ascended the throne, the Ordnance Office bought more buildings along the street for storage, workshops, and residences of gunmakers. During Elizabeth's reign, thirty-seven gunsmiths were practicing their trade there.[21] Artisans prospered, for the Ordnance Office "usually" gave out contracts for small arms to the gunmakers working in the Minories and East Smithfield, partly because of their convenience to the Tower and the proof yard. A hundred years or so later, in 1673, having expanded storage capacity by building depots around the country in such places as Portsmouth and Plymouth (for naval ordnance) and at Woolwich (for iron ordnance and saltpeter), the government consolidated some facilities and sold the workshops, storehouses, and officers' residences in the Minories.[22] The character of the neighborhood along the Minories changed again. The gun industry exercised a significant impact on the nature of London neighborhoods.

The area of Houndsditch, a site where gun foundries were established in the early sixteenth century, illustrates the effect gunfounders had on the use of space. Houndsditch took its name from the ditch in which Londoners had anciently dumped their garbage and trash, including dead dogs. By the early sixteenth century, it had undergone "urban renewal," with the ditch filled in and a mud wall built around it to prevent its further use as a dump. A field stretched from the mud wall towards a street, first paved in 1503, along which "a Prior of the holy Trinitie" had built small two-story cottages with backyard gardens for "poor bedred people." Stow remembered that Londoners would often walk along the street, especially on Friday evenings, for the purpose of giving alms to these unfortunates.[23] The advent of the gunfounders, however, dramatically changed the area. The government had granted certain buildings around Houndsditch to an émigré gunfounder, Peter Bawde, and later to the English Owen brothers to use for gunfounding. As a result, the area became a center for gunfounding and casting of brass. John Stow explained that the prospering of the gunfounders attracted "diverse other" entrepreneurs who "also builded there."[24] But the changes in land use that benefitted the gunfounders and other businesspersons affected the "poore bedred people" adversely. Stow, who usually regretted changes in his beloved city and especially changes to people in need of charity, reported that "their homely Cottages" were replaced by great houses." In 1553, the wide field was cut up into gardens for "many fayre . . . large houses." The mud wall was leveled, and the old ditch filled up so that both were hidden to passersby.[25] Gunfounding was the underlying reason for the change in the character of Houndsditch. The new industry acted as an employment magnet, and money poured into the community, transforming it into an upscale neighborhood. These changes in the neighborhood had harmful consequences for the "poor bedred people" and others in modest circumstances, but opened up attractive housing for people of wealth.

The Ordnance Office illustrates how firearms affected a department of the government and the Tower where its offices were located. The Tower and the Ordnance Office experienced dramatic physical growth in the sixteenth century to meet the government's need for guns and gunmakers. Its plant expanded, old buildings were refurbished, nearby existing buildings were bought up, and new ones constructed. For example, in 1512–13, some old buildings were repaired to the tune of £100.[26] In 1546–47, funds were allocated for a new building to store and guard the nation's "artillery Ordinaunce" and to provide room where the king's "Weapons of his own person shuld be kepte."[27] A number of large buildings for the use of the Board were erected along the inner side of the north walls of the Tower and in other places within the Tower precinct. In 1580, a house was built for the "Assembly of the Officers of the Ordnance, the Master Gunners, and the rest of the Queen's Gunners and Scrollers."[28] Residencies for Ordnance officers were provided. The home for the Master of Ordnance must have been grand, for it took ten years—from 1510 to 1520—to remodel the Brick Tower for that purpose.[29] Less elaborate accommodations served less high-ranking officers. Late in the next century, in 1683, officers were told "to make their ordinary habitation and abode in the houses or lodgings assigned them in or near the Tower," a requirement that assured a domestic component in the Tower complex. The order lasted until the end of the seventeenth century.[30] At the same time, gun founding took place in the Tower and did not leave until the seventeenth century. All this activity changed the appearance of the Tower grounds and the cityscape in the area of the Tower and testified to the growing importance of firearms in the work of the Ordnance Office.

Guns achieved visibility in London in a variety of other ways. In the summer of 1485, it has been said, the victorious Henry VII armed a portion of his newly created Yeomen of the Guards with a harquebus, thereby giving guns a new role and prominence.[31] It is certain that in 1534 military guns were placed on top of the Tower to command and protect the city. They did protect the city twenty years later in 1554 when they helped Queen Mary's supporters foil Wyatt's Rebellion by stopping Sir Thomas Wyatt from entering London across London Bridge.[32] In 1536, three cannons were lined up on Tower Wharf and were available for Londoners to see exactly what they looked like.[33] Of course, soldiers and militiamen would have seen cannon during their military service, and Londoners may have noticed them on board ships riding in the port of London, but now the huge guns were near at hand for residents to look at up close—perhaps even to gawk at and touch. Later in the century, on 16 February 1587, the elaborate funeral procession that threaded through the streets of London to memorialize Sir Philip Sidney provided a glimpse of firearms used by soldiers. Poet, diplomat, Master of the Ordnance, soldier, and aristocrat, connected by family and service to royalty, Sidney had died in the Netherlands from a bullet wound in his leg. To honor his memory, seven hundred high-born mourners, many carrying harquebuses, processed from the Minories to St. Paul's Cathedral where Sidney's body was interred. For Londoners who witnessed it, this procession offered visible evidence of guns. For those who were not present, the publication the next year of a series of copper plates showing the successive groups of mourners with firearms gave permanency to the event.[34]

Guns for personal use came to the attention of London residents in two rather surprising ways. One, the select number of Londoners who played the lotteries was offered richly decorated guns as prizes. John Caltrop, a merchant and citizen of London, organized a lottery, probably in 1586, that included five guns. Among them were "a moste excellent pistol graven and gilded with fine golde with all thappurtenances" and "a moste riche harquebouse of Millan with a most sumptuous flaske and toucheboxe covered with Crimsin velvet artificially wrought with goldsmythes work curiously graven and gilded with rich gold."[35] This was not the first London lottery—Queen Elizabeth organized the first in 1567[36]—but it was the first to offer guns as a prize. The lottery is a marker of the ubiquity of guns and of their popularity. They would not have been included had it not been assumed that lottery players valued them.

Guns gained visibility in a second unusual way: by being entered as an item on which to bid in auctions. On Monday, 21 December 1691, an auction was held at the Barbadoes Coffeehouse in Exchange Alley "over against the Royal Exchange in Cornhill." The title of the catalogue title announced "paintings and other curiosities,"[37] so bidders may have been surprised to see that Number 37 was "a pair of fine Horse pistols" and Number 58 "a pair of Swivel pocket pistols." These two items lack further description, but the guns were surely beautifully decorated. Probably they were slipped in under the category of "other curiosities." Three weeks later, in January 1692, John Bullord organized another auction, this one held at Wills Coffeehouse near Westminster Hall. The title for this catalogue advised that the auction offered "A Curious Collection of Paintings, By the Best masters Ancient and Modern," but bidders would have found "a curious pair of double barrel pistols" listed as Number 159. These pistols were no doubt richly decorated, their beauty justifying their inclusion in an auction of paintings. Including guns in auctions that featured paintings was a new practice, but it connects with the ongoing interest of wealthy Englishmen in collecting guns as works of art and gifting them.

The names of streets and gun shops that included the word *gun* appeared in many parts of the city and were another reminder to Londoners of the presence of firearms. One street bore the name "Gun Alley," and "Gun Yard" was used in five different areas, including Tower Hill, Petticoat Lane, and Houndsditch.[38] "Crosse gonne aley," a street identified as being close to "Whyt Chappell Barrs" in St. Botolph Aldgate, bore that name in 1593.[39] Gunshop owners would naturally be inclined to use some form of the word *gun* in their signs. Examples abound of their doing so. "Cross Guns" was a popular name for shops as well as for streets. From as early as 1582 to 1739, some form of it appeared on the signs of at least nineteen gun shops. For example, in 1592, "Crosse Goones" marked the shop of Henrick Chaffe, on High Street, Aldgate.[40] A "Cross Gonnes," owned by John Matthew 2nd, a gunmaker from Gelderland, opened for business in East Smithfield in about 1593.[41] In 1650, "Cross Gunnes" showed up on the sign of Roger Carlile's shop in Shooe Lane.[42] In 1708, Francis Smart chose for the sign of his shop in Leadenhall Street the words "The Cross Guns and the Three Crowns."[43] In 1710, a shop at the lower end of Minories near little Tower Hill, owned by James Goodby, bore the sign "The Half Moon Star and Cross Pistols."[44] The words, "Crooked Guns," apparently appealed to William Shelton, a gunmaker doing business in Covent Garden; in 1650, it was on the sign for his shop.[45] The most disarming sign for a gun store was "The Three Puppy Doggs." Jonathan Hughes, whose shop was in Monmouth Street, used it in 1734.[46] Maybe the phrase "Puppy Doggs" was intended to invoke the thought of hunting or of the dog-lock musket, used by the army until replaced by the flintlock in the 1720s. Whatever Hughes's purpose, one hopes that, at least initially, three puppies greeted customers!

Owners of book stores and print shops also used the word gun in signs for their shops. As early as 1579, Edward White, a printer, whose shop was "at the little Northe doore of Paules Church at the signe of the Gunne," printed a pamphlet by Thomas Churchyard: *A General Rehearsal of Warres*.[47] J. R. Hale noted that "the London bookseller, Grismond," sold books "at the signe of the Gun in Pauls Alley," a street close to St. Paul's Church.[48] Thus, two shops, one of a printer, the other of a bookseller, quite close to each other bore very similar signs. Furthermore, at least twelve other bookshops or print shops also incorporated the word *gun* in their signs. For example, E.D. and N.E. sold books at their shop at "the sign of the Gun" in Ivie-lane in 1652.[49] So, too, did Thomas White, also in 1652,[50] and Henry Brome in 1661.[51] Edward Leigh's tract on the kings of England was printed for Joseph Cranford at the "sign of the Gun in St. Pauls Church-yard" in 1661.[52] Another print shop, which printed a "merry" tract for Henry Brome in 1675, was located at "the sign of the Gun at the west-end of St. Paul's Church-yard."[53] That printers and book-sellers used such language to identify their shops has a broad significance, suggesting the popularity and the wide acceptance of guns among Londoners. All the street names and shop signs further integrated guns into the daily life of Londoners and helped to make firearms seem commonplace.

Practicing marksmanship in the Artillery Garden was popular with Londoners, and many people could have observed this activity.[54] The Artillery Garden traced its origins to the Guild of St. George, which King Henry VIII had incorporated in 1537 to promote regular practice in shooting the longbow, the crossbow, and the handgun. Practice took place in Spitalfields, and the men involved became known as the "gentlemen of the Artillery Garden" or the Artillery Company. Under the patronage and leadership of the royal family, the group flourished, with men vying to be admitted. For instance, in 1612 some citizens of London petitioned to be allowed to exercise armes and receive instruction in military discipline in the Artillery Garden. They won the petition. Interest continued, and two years later the size of the Artillery Company was doubled to five hundred men, but the Privy Council cautioned that members must be "knowne to be of good meanes, well affected in religion and to the servyce of his Majesty."[55] A contemporary observer, Samuel Buggs, thought they were largely "Tradesmen."[56] The men were trained by professional soldiers and often went on to become officers in the London Trained Bands. The author of *An Essay in Defence of the Female Sex* ridiculed their activities, describing the men as "these terrible Mimick of Mars" who "spend their Fury in Noise and Smoke upon a Namur, erected . . . on a Molehill, and by the help of Guns and Drums out-stink, and out-rattle Smithfield."[57] This sarcastic criticism seems gratuitous, for the Artillery Garden gave opportunity to a sizable number of men either to learn to shoot or to practice shooting regularly or both. Further, this approved activity may have siphoned off the habit, complained of so bitterly in earlier years, of indiscriminately shooting in the capital.

Guns played a role in ceremonial events of various kinds, which everyone no matter age or social standing could observe and enjoy. The boom, boom, boom of gun salutes was a new noise that assailed the ears of Londoners.[58] With the number of shots depending on the circumstances or the status of the individual, gun salutes were a new way to express honor. The government used them, as they did bonfires, as a propaganda tool and sought to control them.[59] The secretary of state was empowered to order them, and, of course, the monarch could command them. Examples abound. For instance, in January 1540, the arrival of Anne of Cleves, the unfortunate choice for King Henry's fourth wife, was marked by the shooting of guns at several intervals along the way.[60] At the proclamation of Jane as Queen of England on 10 July 1553, "shot guns [as] has nott be sene oft" marked the event.[61] In 1556, "many gonnys" were shot to welcome a visit of nine "goodly gallys and many other sheppes" from France.[62] The marriage of Ambrose Dudley, Third Earl of Warwick, the Master-General of the Ordnance Office, to Anne Russell (1548/9–1604), a lady in waiting to Elizabeth I, was a court occasion celebrated with gun salutes.[63] When King James I's son, Henry, was created Prince in 1610, a "Tryumphe [was] made before his Majestys" and a gunmaker, Thomas Laverock, provided the "smalle shott."[64] In 1624, the English welcomed the French princess, Henrietta Maria, the bride-to-be of Prince Charles, with shot from fifteen hundred great guns and with cannon fire that was the loudest the young woman had ever heard.[65] Thirty-six years later, on 30 May 1660, the nation celebrated the return from exile of Henrietta Maria's son, King Charles II. When the king stepped ashore on English soil for the first time in eleven years, Samuel Pepys reported that Navy commanders fired all their guns "round twice," and then "all the fleet" did so, too. There was "nothing in the world but going of guns almost all this day," Pepys wrote.[66] Official gun salutes continued throughout the era and beyond, and today they still welcome dignitaries.

At least one enthusiastic gunsmith shot off an unauthorized gun salute. In March 1721, "Mr. Hardwell, a Gunsmith in the Minories," celebrated the election of his friend, Humphrey Parsons, to the office of alderman of Portsoken Ward. Hardwell saluted Parsons with the roar of a gun when he was chosen and again when he walked along the Minories on his way home.[67] Apparently, Hardwell was not punished for this violation.

Ceremonial fireworks in celebration of some notable event or personage also added new scenes, sounds, and smells. They produced ever-changing images, color, and noise and became popular entertainment for everyone. Like gun salutes, they had a propaganda edge as well, of which successive governments were well aware. Like gun salutes, their use was closely regulated. Fireworks had been used in China and India for centuries, but the first recorded use of fireworks in England celebrated the coronation of Elizabeth of York (King Henry VII's consort queen) in Westminster Abbey in 1487.[68] In the procession of boats on the Thames organized by the Mayor of London, a barge "carried a dragon spouting flames of fire" in honor of the new queen. The government also celebrated the coronation of Anne Boleyn in 1533, again with

GUN CULTURE IN EARLY MODERN ENGLAND

a dragon. This one was described as a "great red dragon" that spouted "wild fire" and was accompanied by "monstrous wild men casting fire and making a hideous noise."[69] Fireworks became increasingly popular, the more so because Queen Elizabeth took great pleasure in them. The fireworks displays presented for her entertainment in 1575 when she visited the Earl of Warwick (still Master-General of Ordnance) were extraordinarily elaborate. An amazed and somewhat fearful observer wrote about them: "After a warning shot or two, was a blaze of burning darts flying to and fro, beams of stars, streams and hail of fire sparks, lightnings of wildfire on the water, and on the land, flight and shot of thunder-bolts, all with such terror and vehemence, the heavens thundered, the waters surged and the earth shook."[70]

King James I also arranged fireworks for special occasions. The fireworks at the marriage of his daughter Elizabeth to Frederick, the Prince Palatinate, in 1613, were breathtaking for their noise and marvelous ingenuity. A "most strange battell" between a "fiery Dragon" and a "St. George on Horsebacke" covered the skies in a display lasting for "an howre or more."[71] Use of fireworks continued throughout the era. On 5 November 1673, fireworks added a colorful display to the street theater organized in London to commemorate the discovery of the Gunpowder Plot. An observer reported that "the Serpents flew like Bees through the Ayre . . . flying in such numbers [that they] could scarce have room for one another to pass."[72]

Gun salutes and fireworks added to the pleasure and entertainment of the residents of London and wherever else they were used. English skill in mounting them sharpened over the years. An enthusiastic tract writer expressed unbridled admiration in 1635, writing that England exceeded "the armies of Rome in fireworks."[73] These entertaining events concealed the danger and destruction that guns and gunpowder could cause and were still another way of humanizing them.

There was, however, a serious downside to such events. Fireworks, gunpowder, and guns caused accidents that scarred London and injured or killed its residents. A combination of overconfidence, carelessness, inexperience, and ignorance explains many of these terrible events. For example, in 1560, Stow reported that in a house near St. Michael's Church a gunshot set fire to a barrel of gunpowder, with the result that "four houses were blown up and diverse others sore shattered." Eleven men and women were killed and sixteen others badly "hurt and burned."[74] About thirty years later, on 16 November 1587, a major gun accident occurred during a production of Christopher Marlowe's 2 *Tamburlaine*, probably at the theater in Shoreditch that Richard Burbage built. Carelessness and inexperience were responsible. The Lord Admiral Players had reached Act 5 of the play, where the Governor of Babylon is tied to a post and shot to death. The players had borrowed guns for this scene, but had not inspected them carefully nor practiced with them. An eyewitness related that the appropriate actor aimed his gun at the actor playing the role of the Governor of Babylon and pulled the trigger. He missed his target, killed a child and a pregnant woman on the spot, and wounded a man in the head "very sore." The accident was extraordinary. It was impossible to explain how one bullet could jump from person to person and do such horrendous damage. Charles Edelman offered a credible explanation in 2003. Focusing on the scouring stick, a ramrod used to push gunpowder down the barrel of a gun, Edelman reasoned that it had broken into pieces and accidentally remained in the barrel. When the gunpowder was ignited, it ejected the pieces of the scouring stick which sprayed all around the theater and hit the three victims.[75] It is an ingenious explanation of what almost certainly happened.

A more famous accident connected with the theater occurred at the Globe Theater on 29 June 1613 at a performance of a play called "All Is True," a version of Shakespeare's *Henry VIII*. As the audience watched, so spellbound that they did not at first notice anything was wrong, the stage directions at Act 1 sc.4, l.64 called for "Drum and Trumpet. Chambers [small cannon] discharged" to announce the arrival of the French ambassador and his entourage at the great house of Cardinal Wolsey.[76] In a letter of 2 July 1613, Sir Henry Wotton explained that a piece of smoldering paper shot from one of the cannon fell on the thatch of the roof and ignited it. The fire, he wrote, "kindled inwardly and ran around like a train, consuming within less than an hour the whole house to the very grounds."[77] Miraculously, no one was killed, but wood, straw, and a "few forsaken cloaks" were destroyed. One man's trousers caught fire, and he might have been "broiled," had not a "provident wit" put out the flames with a bottle of ale. The fire was a disaster, but the Globe Theater was rapidly rebuilt and the stage directions were not changed.

Accidents continued throughout the era. In 1604, an occasion arranged for King James I was marred by a fireworks accident. George Brough, a worker who took part in presenting the show, was "spoiled, burned and hurte" with injuries so severe that he received £3 compensation.[78] In 1650, a gun accident occurred at the artillery ground where gunners from the Ordnance Office were proving guns. A bullet from one of the guns injured or perhaps killed a child. The incident holds interest because Oliver Cromwell's Council of State awarded the child's father £10 and showed themselves sufficiently moved by the event to set aside £100 to construct a safer proving ground.[79] On 4 November 1703 a servant of a gunsmith who lived near the Horse-Guard close to Whitehall, was examining a pistol and, not knowing it was charged, removed the flint which had not fired and pushed in another, causing the pistol to go

off, killing a man who "was by accident in the shop."[80] Another accident too horrible to contemplate occurred on 24 December 1726. One Skedgwell, who worked in the Post Office, was killed at the Angler, an alehouse near Islington Church, while charging a gun by the fire. Some powder fell through the touchhole onto the floor. A coal or burning ember jumped out of the fire, ignited the gunpowder whose fire reached the gun which Skedgwell was holding "in such a manner that it discharged itself up his nostrils, so that he died immediately."[81] These accidents were awful reminders of the dangers inherent in guns and gunpowder, but no evidence has surfaced that they diminished civilians' interest in and ongoing use of them.

Gunpowder explosions followed by fires were another problem for London. Almost all explosions were accidental, but the most potentially devastating and carefully planned never happened: the Gunpowder Plot. The plot to blow up the houses of Parliament, the king, and the members of government assembled for the opening of the session on 5 November 1605 was revealed in time to forestall it. This nonevent is worth noticing, however, because today, physicists at the Centre for Explosion Studies at University of Wales, Aberystwyth, have showed that that if the thirty-six barrels of gunpowder stored in the cellar under Westminster Hall had been ignited, the explosion would have destroyed a "large part of central London."[82] No real gunpowder explosion was as devastating as this, but forty-five years later one came close.

This one happened at eight o'clock in the evening of Friday, 4 January 1650, when twenty-seven barrels of gunpowder exploded and did horrendous damage along Tower Street. According to an anonymous account,[83] Robert Porter, a ship chandler, was storing twenty-seven barrels of gunpowder in his house. The day before, on 3 January, he had put twenty barrels in his shop, which was on the first floor in preparation for delivering them the next day to the Captain of a ship to whom he had sold them. He left seven barrels in a "warehouse" located "above stairs." Somehow, a spark ignited the gunpowder in the shop and fire spread rapidly to the upstairs, so that all twenty-seven barrels exploded. The damage was extensive. Five "fair" houses located towards Tower Street were leveled. Hester Shaw, described as "a midwife of good esteem and quality," owned one of them. Ten houses behind Porter's house on People's Alley were destroyed, and twenty-six other houses were "scattered" and made uninhabitable. "At least a hundred" more houses as far away as the Tower suffered damage to their tiles and glass windows. Sixty-seven individuals were known for certain to have died, for their remains were identified between 4 and 17 January. But many more were killed who could not be identified. An untold number was injured. Hester Shaw, the midwife, was spared, because she was away tending a woman in childbirth, but her son-in-law and three grandchildren were killed, and her daughter severely burned. The anonymous author estimated the loss at about £60,000 and said that those losses were "the greatest that hath happened in London this many yeares."[84]

The unexpected consequences of this event revealed details that otherwise would have been lost. The midwife, Hester Shaw (1586?–1660), who was the daughter of a gentleman and the widow of John Shaw, the churchwarden of Allhallows parish, possessed a strong, aggressive personality. She was said to have a "good education, volubility of tongue, and natural boldness and confidence."[85] Well-respected as a midwife, Shaw claimed she lost £3,000 in midwifery earnings. She also charged that three bags of her money containing £953 6s. 8d. were blown out of her house and taken for safety to the house of her minister, Mr. Thomas Glendon, who refused to return her money. She and Glendon were on unfriendly terms before the accident, and Mrs. Shaw's charges inflamed their relationship. In 1653, Glendon published a pamphlet denying her accusations, and she responded in print. In the course of claiming the bags of money and explaining why Glendon held a grudge against her, Shaw supplied many details about the explosion and her part in trying to prevent it.

According to Shaw, she visited Porter, her next-door neighbor, at least twice to beg him to remove the gunpowder, but despite "divers hot words" between them, promises from Porter to do so, and an investigation by a constable whom Shaw called in, the gunpowder was not removed.[86] Undeterred, Shaw appeared with the constable before the Ward Moot Enquest to express her grave concerns and ask their assistance in removing the gunpowder. Members of the Ward Moot agreed to send in a team of men to investigate the matter. When from her window, Shaw saw the men arrive, she rushed out of her house, hailed them, discussed the situation with them, and extracted a promise that they would get rid of the gunpowder. But to no avail. Determined still, Shaw took her case to the Mayor of London (whom she knew personally), the Aldermen, several church ministers, and many friends. She also persuaded another constable to complain "divers times, from time to time" to the Sessions House. That body agreed to take the matter under "examination." But the examination was laid aside and nothing was done.

These details make clear the widespread ignorance of the potential danger of gunpowder. Porter was guilty of stubbornness and lies, but mostly he was hopelessly ignorant about the properties of gunpowder. So, too, were officials in the government of London; they were indifferent to the concerns raised by Mrs. Shaw and the one or two constables on her side. Shaw did understand the dangers and acted as a "whistle-blower." Her forceful and persistent interventions with London officials were highly unusual. Shaw illustrates the

prominence that a London woman of middling status could achieve, in this case by her persistent calls to remove gunpowder from a private house.

Violence characterized London streets long before the advent of guns, but firearms offered another weapon with which to commit mayhem, violence, injury, and sometimes death. Historians have attributed much of the unruliness of early modern England to the unguarded behavior of aristocrats. Lawrence Stone described aristocrats during the sixteenth century as short tempered, irascible, vengeful, and violent in language and action.[87] They carried a weapon at all times, either a dagger, a sword, or a pistol and, with a weapon always at the ready, were prone to spontaneous fighting in the countryside and in London. Of several examples of viciousness in sixteenth-century London, one may serve: in 1578, Robert Rich, Second Lord Rich, with twenty-five retainers, happened to meet his enemy, Edward Windham, in Fleet Street. Both were armed. Rich's retainers assaulted Windham, yelling "Kyll him." In return, Windham fired his pistol at Rich but missed. The move, however, gave him time to seek safety by running into the home of the French Ambassador (of all places!).[88]

Violence in London streets continued. For example, in 1655, Sir Thomas Wortley and a Mr. Skipwith, who had long quarreled over a matter that the reporter for *Mercurius Politicus* could not bring himself to mention, met by coincidence in the Strand. Confronting each other in the "open street," furious with each other, and both with pistols "ready charged in their pockets," each reached for a gun. Wortley succeeded in removing his pistol first and shot Skipwith in the upper breast, but somehow Skipwith returned fire, severely wounding Wortley, who died "presently." Skipwith was left in a "very doubtful and dangerous condition" under the care of the "chirugeon."[89]

Not all persons of wealth who carried guns used them violently. For example, in 1592 William Harrington carried a pistol because he thought it was the fashionable thing to do. In 1634 Sir Thomas Temple advised his son that there was a "gentleman" (whom he declined to identify except to say that his son knew him) who "continually carieth a case of pistols in his Pocket."[90] Presumably the unidentified gentleman carried the pistols as a protection. Temple did not suggest that he had ever used his weapons. Fifty years later, during the hysteria of the Popish Plot which gripped London from 1678 to 1681, we may be certain that men were armed, but gunfire on the streets of London did not occur. London women also carried guns, but did not use them: "the countess of Shaftesbury had always in her muff little pocket pistols, loaded, to defend her from the papists," the Earl of Ailesbury recounted. Lord Shaftesbury had urged her to do this and "most timorous ladies followed her fashion."[91]

Men far down the social scale joined aristocrats in making London a dangerous city. For instance, a person who was apparently mentally deranged wreaked havoc on a London street with his gun. On 21 September 1620, in St. Martin's-in-the Fields, an unidentified servant of a Mr. Lightgold positioned himself at a window and shot people passing by in the street. A pellet hit one William Swetman, who was innocently standing at the door of his master's house, and killed him.[92] This incident in the early seventeenth century reads very like events that occur on city streets in the early twenty-first century.

Guns were used in London in attempts to murder persons whose politics or religion offended the gunman. For instance, early in the morning of 13 November 1537, Mr. Robert Packington, a London mercer, was walking from "his howse at Soper Lane" on his way to hear mass at "St. Thomas of Acres" when he was killed "with a gunn."[93] Each of the five near-contemporary accounts was at pains to record that he was killed with a gun, surely indicating their interest that a firearm was used.[94] Packington's murder, it is said, was "in all likelihood" the "first 'gun-related murder' to be recorded" in London.[95] The incident was consequential, for not only was Packington a man of parts, successful in business and in parliamentary and London politics, he was also a believer in the reformed religion and part of Thomas Cromwell's circle.[96] John Fox kept the memory of the event alive by including it in all the editions of his Acts and Monuments. Fox charged John Incent, dean of St. Paul's Cathedral, with bribing a man £60 to shoot Packington. The fact of the matter is that the killer remained unknown. Packington's murder illuminates the intensity of religious differences in London in the 1530s.

Violence of this nature was heightened during the reign of Queen Mary I. On Sunday, 10 June 1554, a handgun was discharged "neare to" St. Paul's Churchyard at the time Dr. Henry Pendleton, a convert to Catholicism, was preaching a Paul's Cross sermon. Dr. Pendleton barely escaped death, for the "gonne shotte ... came nere [his] face." Fortunately for Pendleton, the bullet missed him and "lighte[d] on the Churche wall," close to where Sir Thomas White (1493?–1567), London's mayor, was sitting. It barely missed the mayor. One historian dismissed the shot as a "gunner's misadventure,"[97] but contemporaries wondered whether the attempt on Pendleton's life reflected hatred of his religion. A search for a gunner was made, but without success.

Fifty years later, after 1 March 1606, outside London, guns had a part in actions that showed disapproval of the Church of England during King James I's reign. Four recusants, led by John Anderton, a justice of the peace, entered a church during services, "tooke the Bible and service booke out of the Church," hid the books in an alehouse, and disrupted prayers for the king. Then, at a service honoring James's coronation, one hundred recusants entered the church armed with guns and "disturbed the preacher."[98] These inci-

dents reveal the fragility of the religious settlement; from the perspective of this study they show that guns were brought into play to express disapproval in strong terms.

Guns were used in the seventeenth century and early eighteenth century in attempts to assassinate political leaders. In every incident, however, unexpected circumstances intervened and none was successful. For example, Charles II escaped injury or death because the plans to shoot first him and his horses at the Rye House were foiled in 1683. Betrayal also saved King William III from being cut down by gunfire in the Assassination Plot of 1696.[99] A bizarre plan to assassinate Robert Harley, Earl of Oxford and Lord Treasurer, in early November 1712 was also foiled. The perpetrators of the so-called Band-Box Plot concocted a clever scheme well worth recalling. They had delivered to Harley a bandbox in which were placed two pistols; they had rigged the bandbox so that when it was opened, the pistols detonated and the person was killed. Oxford peeked in the box and said that he saw the pistols. At this, Jonathan Swift who was with him, grabbed the box, took it some distance away to a window, and using his penknife carefully defused the device, so neither Harley nor Swift was injured.[100] Guns had become the weapon of choice in assassinations.

Guns, gunfounders, and gunmakers had a significant effect on London during the early modern era. They influenced the size and demography of neighborhoods. They added to the population of aliens. They modified the cityscape by determining the removal, creation, and use of buildings, and the use of land. They attached their name to streets and to shop signs. They added the new sights, smells, and noise of gunfounding, shooting, and gunpowder, as well as the new sights, smells, and sounds of gun salutes and fireworks to the odors and sounds of the city. With other craftsmen, such as bell founders, metalworkers, paper makers, and blacksmiths, gunfounders changed the city's environment. Guns brought additional violence, crime, and personal suffering to London. They were responsible for accidents that usually resulted in death. Gunpowder accidents leveled buildings, scarred streets, and killed people.

Historians have not noticed the effect of guns on London. In my view, however, understanding the role of guns is essential to achieving an accurate view of the nature and development of the city. London, I suggest, is properly regarded as "The Gun Capital of England" in the early modern era. It lost this title in the eighteenth century and beyond, as the gun industry expanded to counties such as Sussex and Kent and moved west and north to cities such as Bristol and Birmingham.

SEVEN · "Newfangled
and Wanton Pleasure" in
the Many Lives of Men

THE SOCIAL AND PERSONAL LIVES of men took on new dimen-
sions with the advent of guns. Men all along the social scale—
monarchs, nobles, aristocrats, persons of substance in urban areas,
plebeians of modest means, and the poor in town and country—were more
or less touched by what King Henry VIII called the "newfangled and wanton
pleasure" in firearms. They owned, possessed, and used guns, or wanted to
do so. Social and economic status and political responsibilities largely determined the individual's relationship to firearms, and, therefore, guns changed
men's lives in varying ways. But men from all socioeconomic backgrounds
were guilty of gun crime, suffered the effects of gun and gunpowder accidents,
and used guns to commit suicide. This chapter addresses the impact of guns
on men's personal and social lives.

King Henry VIII took an intense interest in using guns for personal pursuits and in understanding how they worked. As difficult as it is to separate
a monarch's royal life from his private pursuits, it is clear that Henry added
guns to his personal activities at the same time that he was increasing their
number in his armies. At an uncertain date, the king began using firearms
himself and in 1536–37 ordered targets erected at Greenwich and Windsor to
"shotte at with his handgonne."[1] Apparently recognizing the king's interest in
guns, in 1540 Mighel Mercator gave Henry VIII a handgun, valued at 6s. 8d.,
no doubt to ingratiate himself with the king.[2] In November 1541, evidently
feeling the need for further instruction, Henry directed that Bernadin de
Valois from Piedmont, who had served him as gunner and servant since 1534,
should receive "powder and lead" to teach him.[3] To assure the proper care of
his guns, in 1538 the king created a new office in the Royal Household and
selected William Hunt, an English gunmaker, to be the first Keeper of the
King's Handguns and Demi-Hawks. The title probably indicates that Henry

intended to use the guns for hawking. To assure the regular production of his guns, in 1545 he appointed Allen Bawdeson, a French gunmaker in London and a member of the Armourers' Company, to be his "Crossbowmaker and Handgunmaker" and in 1547 to take charge of his firearms at Westminster.[4] In 1546–47, when funds were allocated to construct a new building on the Tower grounds to store and guard the nation's "artillery Ordinaunce," a room was set aside to store the king's weapons. Joiners were paid 53s. 4d. for "certen Rackes Whereon the Kinges Maiesties riche Weapons and Artillerye were hanged and kept," evidence that Henry had been assembling a private collection of firearms.[5] The inventory of Henry VIII's "movable property," made after the king's death in 1547, and published in a definitive edition in 1998, confirms that he had accumulated many guns for his own use. Henry possessed at least one hundred and thirteen harquebuses, twenty-nine halves (a lighter version of the harquebus), forty-four handguns, and four "dags" (the little concealable guns against which he railed in statutes and proclamations).[6]

The inventory contains short descriptions of Henry's guns, which reveal their beauty. Among the guns stored at Greenwich was a "blacke [gun] with the Stocke of Redde woods set with bone worke [i.e. staghorn] with a fier Locke in a case of crymsen vellet."[7] Another gun described by J. W. Hayward was delicately carved along the barrel and intricately incised with a rose crowned and supported by two lions, two medallion heads, Henry's initials, and the date 1537.[8] Other guns were variously incised with pictures, decorated with precious and semiprecious jewels, and damascened.[9] Such handsomely decorated guns as these would have served Henry VIII as collectibles or gifts.

The practice of political leaders at the highest reaches of society exchanging gifts among themselves was an ancient custom, going back at least to the Greeks.[10] The custom continued among monarchs and aristocrats in western Europe, but what was new in the early modern era was the addition of richly decorated handguns. In England, gift giving of guns between monarchs started early and were of two kinds: artillery or military guns and guns used for domestic pleasures. The earliest example in England of giving a gun is probably the "small gun" (costing 6s. 8d.) that King Edward III presented in 1361 to his second (surviving) son, Lionel of Antwerp (1338–1368), as the young man was going to Ireland.[11] This gift underscored the purpose of the prince's assignment: to strengthen the English colony by a "demonstration of military might."[12] It would also have testified to Edward's sophisticated knowledge of weaponry. Other early examples of military gift-guns are the "Mons Meg" that Philip the Good of Burgundy (1396–1467) presented to King James II of Scotland (1430–1460) in 1457,[13] and "Queen Elizabeth's Pocket Pistol" that Maximilian Van Egmont, Count Buren, Stadtholder of

Friesland (1509–1548), gave Henry VIII.[14] Finally, in 1480, King Louis XI of France sent a bombard to Richard, Duke of Gloucester (the brother of King Edward IV [1461–1483]). Richard thanked Louis XI, saying, "I always and still take great pleasure in artillery."[15]

Elizabeth I did not share her father's interest in guns, but in 1572 she did present to the Seigneuer of Sark, Channel Islands, a brass gun designed to fire lead shot and intended for domestic use.[16] Further, one Gylham Byliard gave her as a New Year's gift in 1577 "a proper dadge [i.e., a dag] guilt and well wrought." It was placed for safekeeping in the hands of John Asteley (1507–1596), Master of the Jewels and Plate and Gentleman of the Privy Chamber in 1558, so we may be sure that the dag was beautifully decorated.[17]

An ambassador's first meeting with the host of the country he was visiting began with the presentation of gifts from his master. To secure the friendship of Phillip II of Spain, King James I sent him a splendid present in 1604 that included "foure fowling pieces with their furniture very richly garnished and inlaid with plates of gold."[18] Stephen Russell, well known as an accomplished gilder, decorated the guns intended for domestic pleasures.[19] Another gift from James to Phillip in 1614 again included four fowling pieces also decorated by Russell, "two with massive gould." This gift had a history involving James I's elder son, Prince Henry of Wales, who was deeply interested in guns.

In 1608, the Prince paid Russell £45 for "graving, damasking and other workmanship" on two guns, one for his own use, and the other as a gift for his friend, King Christian IV of Denmark.[20] The gift may have reflected friendship, from which nothing was expected but warm camaraderie. Prince Henry was pleased with Russell's work: after his death, five years later, his account was charged £190 for "two rich damasked pieces" and "two rich white pieces cut and gilded with rich gold," which he had ordered, all made by Russell. They were "likely" the guns that his father gave Prince Philip as the second gift in 1614.[21] Hayward believed that these guns represented "the finest that could be procured in London at that time."[22]

The image of an elaborately decorated pistol dated about 1600 may serve as an example of guns designed for collecting and gifting. The wooden stock is inlaid with mother-of-pearl and decorated with leaves, flowers, and curling tendrils. Although rusted, the fluted barrel was once damascened in gold. On the barrel tang appears a man's bearded face in profile engraved in mother-of-pearl. The pistol is only eleven inches in length and weighs a trifle more than one pound.

James I also cultivated Russia's friendship by sending his emissary, Sir Thomas Smith, laden with richly decorated English guns to present to Tsar Boris Godunov (1598–1605). Russell probably decorated these guns, too.[23]

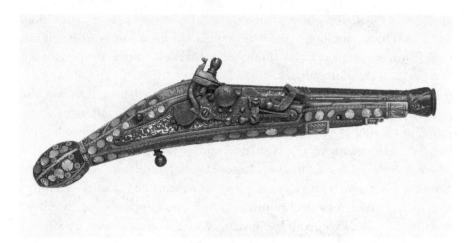

FIGURE 3. A pistol from about 1600, once damascened in gold and decorated with flowers, leaves, tendrils, and a man's bearded face in mother-of-pearl. (XII.1823 © Royal Armouries)

For his part, Smith presented a case of pistols to the Tsar's son, no doubt to ingratiate himself with the youngster and through that connection with the Tsar.[24] Who made these guns is not known, but a guess would be Russell.

Other English monarchs also used gifts of guns for diplomatic purposes. In 1664, King Charles II sent Tsar Alexis I Mikhailovich (1629–1676) a gift of three personal guns. The Ambassador to Russia, Charles Howard, Earl of Carlisle, explained that King Charles I used one of them with which to shoot. The other two had even greater significance: King Charles II himself had carried them as he rode into London in 1660 to reclaim his kingdom.[25] These guns offered an intimate gesture to encourage friendship. In 1680, King Charles II sent the Sultan of Morocco gifts that included twelve pairs of pistols, their barrels richly carved and inlaid.[26] A gunsmith named Beaver contributed three guns, together valued at £16.[27] Later, Queen Anne (1702–1714) sought to deepen this friendship by also sending guns as gifts. There was urgency in cementing the relationship. England was engaged in the War of the Spanish Succession, had established a strong naval presence in the Mediterranean under the command of Admiral Sir George Rook, and had seized the Rock of Gibraltar. In 1704, Anne ordered the dispatch of a gift of six long guns "finely wrought" made by George Trulock at a cost of £32 10s. In August of that year, Anne paid Richard Rutacht, a gilder and goldsmith, £33 for "engraving, imbossing, gilding, and Pollishing with Arabic Letters Six Gunns" and for preparing "a Damasine Simiter Gilded with Arabic letters"—all presents for the Emperor of Morocco.[28] The inclusion of guns in these diplomatic gifts shows the high regard with which firearms were held by English monarchs and their assumption that fellow monarchs the world over shared this view. Throughout the era, beautifully decorated firearms remained important as a gift in international affairs.

Collecting beautifully decorated firearms and giving them as gifts was also popular with aristocrats and wealthy gentlemen, especially after the restoration of Charles II in 1660.[29] An example is the "Horsemans pistolls . . . ye barrels . . . damasked, ye stocks inlayed and ye worke Guilt" that Captain Thomas Story received. In 1667, Lord Howe, Lieutenant-General of the Board of Ordnance, spent £93 on guns that he intended as gifts. Sir Philip Warwick received "A paire of pistols . . . with Silver Capps, the stocks inlayed and the barrels damasked." The inventory of the guns owned by Charles Stewart, Third Duke of Richmond (1639–1672), listed military handguns and personal handguns, as would be expected from a man holding a ducal title. He possessed many pistols, but the exact number is concealed in the entries: ten cases of pistols made by leading gunmakers and six cases of "Ordinary pistolls & 2 carbines." His collection contained hunting guns: three fowling guns, one made by a leading gunmaker, and two birding guns, one "very fine" and made by a distinguished Continental gunmaker. Of the eleven "screwed" guns, one was "for a ship," meaning it was a military handgun. Seven guns in the collection were gifts from fellow aristocrats. They ranged in value from £1 to £15, the most expensive being the gun for a ship.[30] In a 1690 attachment to his will, Rear Admiral Sir John Chicheley designated the guns that he wanted given to certain persons at his death. He specified that his "double Gun with the fflask topt with Silver and the green Silk String to it" should go to his "ffreind and Kinsman Henry Percy, Councellor at Law of the Temple." Another friend was to receive his "Spanish barrel Gun with Silver Loops" (identified as "barrel bands") along with his "longest Case of Pistolls." Chicheley wanted his nephew, Peter Legh of Lime in Cheshire, to inherit his "Gun with a Gold touch hole" as well as his "turne of[f] Pistolls," meaning pistols whose barrel unscrewed for loading.[31] These gentlemen chose a gun as a gift that they believed their friends and relatives would appreciate. Their doing so implies that they placed a high value on firearms. I argue that giving guns as gifts was another way that the lethal side of firearms was softened and pushed aside.

Adding guns placed an aesthetic and monetary value on firearms that lifted them to the level of things that wealthy people traditionally amassed and gave: jewels, fabrics, tapestries, silver, china, paintings, and furniture, among them.[32] In this way, political and social leaders helped to transform the perception of the gun from a device used in war to injure, destroy, and kill into a desirable treasure. These points invite a reappraisal of aristocratic values and lifestyle and give firearms an important role in them.

Guns affected the favorite sports of aristocrats—hunting and shooting. "The use of firearms for hunting," first noted in Germany in 1480 and 1504, "spread quickly" in sixteenth-century England across the social spectrum.[33] In his book, *The Gentleman's Recreation*, dedicated to King James II and addressed to the "nobility and gentry," Richard Blome had high praise for the sport. It is a "commendable Recreation," he wrote, that "all Degrees and Qualities of men, even . . . Kings and Princes" have "always . . . practiced and highly prized." A "Manly Exercise," hunting offers many health-giving qualities for the mind, the limbs, and the stomach. "No Musick is more charming to the Ears of [a Hunter] than a Pack of Hounds in full Cry," Blome declared. He omitted further encomiums, because the points were so well known and treated.[34] For these men, hunting was an activity that they thoroughly enjoyed (some passionately) and regarded as a right of their station in life. The pleasure it gave, the camaraderie it provided, and the friendly competition it engendered were important features. Whatever food their hunting contributed to the estate was an extra benefit. Further, hunting was a preparation for war. A sergeant-at-arms during Elizabeth's reign made the point bluntly when he remarked, "Hunting is a military exercise; the like stratagems are often invented and executed in war against soldiers as the hunter doth against diverse kinds of beasts."[35] Thomas Dekker (c. 1572–1632), the playwright, pamphleteer, and poet, had the same message for his generation in the poem *The Artillery Garden*, published in 1616: "Hunting is but the Ape / Doing her tricks in a lesse-fearfull shape."[36] These comments about war and hunting reinforce the point made in this study: that the small arms used by soldiers overlapped with those used by civilians.

Aristocrats were not alone in liking to hunt with a gun. Plebeians did, too, but for different reasons. Although hunting no doubt gave pleasure, their purpose was to use the gun to hunt more effectively and bring more protein and variety of food to the table. The venerable clerk of the peace in Norfolk confessed in 1550 that sixty men were out shooting each day, but his records showed that only three of the men whose annual income was below £100 were licensed to shoot, and that "none" among the sixty shooters was "worth more than £4 a year in land."[37] They defied the law to do this and scornfully rejected efforts to abide by the law. As we saw, George Knitstall offers an example. He told a Hertfordshire landowner in 1678 that if he were denied leave to hunt "he would take leave" and that he "did not care a straw for all the justices."[38]

Not everyone embraced the gun for hunting. As early as 1548, a European author of an essay on deer hunting reported that guns had frightened animals around Rome and ruined the sport.[39] In England, also in 1548, Sir Edmund Bedingfield predicted in a letter to the Earl of Bath that if shooting with guns at waterfowl was not restricted, "you wt all the rest of the nobilitie may put foorth your hawkes to breede and to keep no more."[40] Some hunters claimed that the noise and smell of firearms were so offensive to deer and fowl that they fled from forests and ponds. Neither Queen Elizabeth nor Queen Anne, King James I's consort, used a gun in hunting, preferring the crossbow. King James I, an ardent hunter, positively disliked using guns to hunt. In *Basilicon Doron*, an advice manual for his son, Prince Henry, composed in 1599 when the young boy was expected to succeed him, James declared that "it is a thievish form of hunting to shoot with guns and bows." In James's view "running hounds . . . [was] the most honourable and noblest" way to hunt.[41]

Using a gun to bring down prey was potentially dangerous, and accidents occurred that touched hunters at the lower and upper ends of the social scale. For example, in 1612 two men in Surrey were hunting rabbits and thought they spied the creatures in a thicket. They sprayed the area with gunfire, only to discover that it was a nine-year-old girl playing there, not rabbits. She suffered bullet shots in the stomach and died.[42] In 1694, one "Mr. Gerey" and his son were also hunting rabbits. The young man had climbed a tree to get a better view and, no doubt, announced that a rabbit was in range. His father handed up their gun, presenting it butt end first. Unfortunately, the cock was up, and, as the son took the gun, it went off. The bullet hit the father in the forehead and, as the diarist John Evelyn reported, "miserably slew him."[43] A decade or so later, in 1716, the Duke of Bourbon was involved in a gun-hunting accident when he was "sporting with the Duke of Berry." When the Duke of Berry shot off his fowling piece, the "shot scattered and one of [the pellets] hit [the Duke of Bourbon] in the Eye and struck it out."[44] As heartrending as were the accidents, they did not deter persons who found pleasure in using firearms in hunting.

Using a gun to shoot birds in flight became a popular method of hunting in the late seventeenth century. A different kind of approach and skill were needed, and manuals, written in Italian and Spanish, appeared in the early decades of the seventeenth century to provide instruction. Blome's *The Gentleman's Recreation* (mentioned above), available in 1686, was the first book in English to advise hunters on the best way to shoot birds in flight that included guns, as well as snares and nets. Blome argued that the "best and surest way" to bring down fowl was "to Shoot Flying." Underlining an obvious point, he declared that "when your Game is on the Wing, it is more exposed to danger, for if but one bullet hits any part of its Wings so expanded," it will fall.[45] He recommended that shooters aim at the head of the bird if it flies over them, but at the belly if it flies away from them. Always shoot with the wind, no matter where the bird is, whether in flight or on the ground. Be sure to conceal yourself, for seeing a hunter is "very offensive" to birds, Blome advised. Blome offered ingenious ideas to achieve this: train your horse to stand still and serve as your shield while you shoot. Devise a disguise that transforms you into a tree to confuse the prey. Do not hesitate when the shot looks good: "lose no time," he wrote, "but let fly." To that end, he counseled the hunter to keep his gun always cocked, but cautioned that he should keep his thumb over the cock to avoid an accidental discharge. *The Gentlemans Recreation* also offered detailed advice on gun laws, instructed readers on the best kind of hunting gun to choose, and coached them on how to care for it. Guns offered another choice for hunting deer, and rabbits, but they did not entirely displace traditional weapons such as crossbows, nets, coursing, and snares.

Another old sport—target shooting—was also transformed by the introduction of the gun. Target shooting with a bow and arrow was, of course, a venerable, much-lauded activity, which Tudor governments persistently encouraged, but with little success. Using a gun as the weapon created a new sport with its own challenges and excitement. People of all social levels engaged in target shooting. King James IV of Scotland used a "hand culverin" in 1508 to shoot seabirds and to "target practice in the great hall at Holyrood House."[46] In 1537, as we saw, King Henry VIII had targets set up for him to "shotte at with his handgonne."[47] If kings liked to shoot at targets, it is certain that individuals in and out of the court discovered a deep interest in doing so, too. In London, men shot their guns so indiscriminately that in 1540 Henry VIII ordered special marks and targets set up, and commanded that they alone be used for practice.[48] The interest in target shooting continued: when the Agas Map appeared in about 1563, it showed men target practicing in the Artillery Garden northeast of the Tower. Roger Ascham, an educator and humanist, recommended in his tract, *The Scholemaster*, published in 1570, that aristocratic boys should become proficient in shooting a gun.[49] In 1587, King James VI of Scotland (later King James I of England), encouraged the idea of target shooting by sending a model gun known as the "Siller" (Silver) gun to Kirkcudbright to be used as a prize.[50] No doubt target practice continued in the seventeenth century. In the eighteenth century, it became the "rage" for aristocrats to visit shooting galleries in London as well as other places for target practice.[51]

Aristocratic men found many ways of identifying publicly with military hardware. One was to use cannon to decorate the grounds of their estates. On a visit to Italy in 1644, John Evelyn was struck by the attention noblemen paid to beautifying their grounds, noting that "a mode much practiz'd" was to place "field artillery upon carriages" at the entry of their manors. Evelyn explained that the great men "looke on [it] as a piece of state, more than defence."[52] The cannon was a signifier of wealth and status and used to symbolize high position and authority in the state rather than to protect property and person. The physicality of the gun told anyone who passed by that the owner was a man of affairs.

In England, the practice of placing cannon on the grounds of a great house had different origins, although the symbolism of the gun was the same. The Militia Law of 1558 required aristocrats to keep arsenals of weapons for military purposes. According to Lawrence Stone, their "stockpiling" was "modest" before 1550, peaked between 1550 and 1600, and declined thereafter.[53] In conformity with the law, the Earl of Cumberland assembled fourteen cannon at Skipton in 1572, the Duchess of Suffolk displayed eleven in 1580 at her home Hellow, and in 1584 there were sixteen cannon at Lord Paget's estate, Beaudesert. These arsenals also contained a generous supply of harquebuses, dags, and powder.[54] A different kind of display of militaria was devised at Stirling Castle. On the ramparts of the castle in 1542 were statues carved in stone of men holding guns at the ready. These are said to be "the earliest" representations of guns in stone in Great Britain.[55]

Secondly, English aristocrats decorated the interior of their houses with military guns. In 1580, Wistan Browne of South Weald willed his son his "armour and weapons in Weald Hall and Rookewood Hall . . . all which I will shall remain in such studies, galleries and other rooms as they now be,"[56] indicating that he wanted them to remain on display. Reflecting the 1630s "military vogue," staircase newels in Cromwell House, Highgate, bore carvings of officers and soldiers.[57] In 1629, when Sir George Carew, Baron Carew of Clopton died, he was buried in a tomb decorated with cannon and cannonballs to signify his service as Master of the Board of Ordnance, an office he held from 1608 to 1629.[58]

In Clifton Hall, Nottinghamshire, paintings of pikemen and musketeers, inspired by Jacob de Gheyn, the engraver, testified to the military interests of the owners.[59] In 1670, Prince Rupert redecorated his private apartments at Windsor Castle by hanging the walls, including those along the "huge steppe stayres," with "pikes, muskets, pistols . . . drums, back, brest & head pieces." Evelyn pronounced the effect handsome, and "very extraordinary." The martial furniture was "all new & bright," he reported in his *Diary*.[60] The custom of using guns for home decoration continued in the early eighteenth century. In March 1741, James Brydges, First Duke of Chandos (1674–1744), whose house at Cannons is said to be the "finest house in England" at the time, wrote instructions for the "Usher of the Hall," telling him to "take care that all the Fire Arms are kept clean & bright, and laid up in their proper places over the Hall Chimney."[61] The Duke had spared no expense in building and decorating his house with the help of the most prestigious experts. That he—or perhaps they—should choose to display guns over the chimney in the hall suggests that such decorative touches were approved by the most discriminating arbiters of style. Display of a gun or two in the cottage of a plebeian man would have been possible, but dangerous, and I have found no evidence to the point.

Using guns as a decorative detail migrated to public buildings. In 1574 at Stratford-upon-Avon, the men of the city's Corporation paid "Roberte Joyner six pence for making ij [two] Rackes in the chamber to haune on the gunes."[62] The chamber was the room where officers of the corporation met. Perhaps they chose a gun motif to indicate their authority and to show their comfort with the new device. Whatever their underlying reasons, they brought guns into a public place devoted to local government and identified themselves with them. A little more than a century later, in 1685, Evelyn noted that the town hall at Portsmouth was "artificially hung round, with Armes of all sorts, like the Hall & keepe of Windsor, which looks very finely."[63]

Handguns became a fashion accessory for men, as well as a decorative item. In 1592, William Harrington, the son of a Yorkshire gentleman, who had been ordained a priest in France, returned to London for a visit. While there, he "went about as a young man of fashion, and wore a pistol."[64] Harrington's well-to-do background may have inclined him to follow what he understood to be the London fashion. George Pasfield, a wealthy merchant who carried on significant trade with Barbados from 1647 until his death in 1660, seems to have made his own fashion. He had a small pendant covered with enameled gold, set with emeralds, and fashioned in the shape of an English wheel-lock pistol to hold toilet articles. The result was a rich jewel, the only one of its kind. Hinged into the stock of the gun were a hooked tongue scraper, a tooth pick, and a small spoon for removing ear wax, of the kind made in 1590.[65] His choosing to carry these personal items in a device shaped like a gun suggests that he regarded the gun as a symbol of authority, a mark of importance, and a signal of his sophistication, status and wealth. The little case is on view now at the Victoria and Albert Museum. Another man ordered specially designed guns for his own use. William Truelock (fl. 1679) had "a little pair of Pocket Pistols with the King's Picture Engrav'd on the end." He must have treasured the pistols, because when he lost them he offered a reward of 10 shillings for their return.[66] Finally, John Tournay (d. 1745), gunstock maker, commissioned guns on which were engraved his name and address.[67]

In early modern England, it was common practice for aristocrats to engage an artist to paint their portrait. What was new in sixteenth-century England was the inclusion of a firearm. At least fourteen men and one woman (see chapter 8) chose to show themselves with a gun. The presence of a gun conveyed a symbolic meaning in all these portraits. Some portraits, however, were outright propaganda vehicles, and the gun in them had a part in transmitting the desired message. This was especially true of Captain Thomas Lee (1551/2–1601), the son of a minor gentry family and a soldier who was well-connected to powerful men at Queen Elizabeth's court. When Lee was visiting England in 1594, Marcus Gheeraerts II (1561/2–1636) painted his portrait, now at the Tate Gallery Britain. The picture aimed to exonerate Lee of suspicions that his loyalty to England was compromised during his military service in Ireland. His continuing a childhood friendship with Hugh O'Neill, Second Earl of Tyrone, the chief of Ulster, fed doubts about his loyalty, as did his proposed solutions to the Irish problem. His critics disliked his suggestion that he become England's "chief negotiator" there.[68]

Gheeraerts painted Lee standing under a spreading oak tree (a "symbol of constancy"), dressed as an Irish foot soldier without pants, hose, or shoes and armed with a handsomely decorated snaphance attached to his belt.[69] His beautifully embroidered shirt and expensive armor show that he is an English gentleman. Discernible on the leaves of the tree are the Latin words meaning "both to act and to suffer with fortitude is a Roman's part," words that (according to Livy's History of Rome) Scaevola, the Roman hero, spoke. Scaevola had entered the camp of the Etruscans, with whom Rome was at war, disguised as an Etruscan with the purpose of killing their leader, Porsena. He was captured and, to demonstrate his bravery, thrust his right hand into a fire, a move that led Porsena to make peace with Rome. This story was meant to say that Lee's activities in Ireland were those of a hero, not a traitor. Further to the point, Lee's drooping left wrist with a scar across it suggests that he has suffered an injury similar to that of Scaevola, whose hand had been badly burned. The handsome gun touches the fingers of Lee's drooping hand and implies that he has a weapon that compensates for his wound. The gun tells the viewer that Lee is well apprised of the latest technology in weaponry and that he has used the firearms against the Irish in his military efforts on behalf of England.

Another late-Elizabethan figure, the privateer and explorer Sir Martin Frobisher (1535?–1594), commissioned the artist Cornelis Ketel (1548–1616) to paint his portrait, which is now at the Bodleian Library. Ketel's rendering, said to be "the only accurate likeness of Frobisher," portrays a bearded man confidently holding a wheel-lock pistol in his right hand positioned at

his hip and pointed across the canvas.[70] He wears loosely fitting gold colored trousers buckled at the knee, a ruffle at his neck, and a barely visible sword strapped to his left side. The viewer's eye is drawn to the black pistol that stands out against the gold fabric. The date of the portrait is 1577, so the pistol relates to Frobisher's many hair-raising adventures from 1552 to 1577. During these years, he served in or commanded expeditions to the Barbary coast and Guinea (1553 to 1573) and three times led a team of ships to find a Northwest passage to the Far East (1576 to 1578). No passage was discovered, but he met a party of Inuit Indians, skirmished with them, and brought one back to England. His ships came close to a body of water later named Frobisher Bay. The pistol indicates that Frobisher's knowledge of weaponry is up-to-date, testifies to his manliness and fearlessness, and perhaps hints at his sharp temper. The portrait is arguably designed to show a man worthy of recognition and reward, things that Frobisher coveted. Later Frobisher distinguished himself in fighting the Spanish Armada in 1588 and was knighted for his exploits.

The portrait of Endymion Porter (1587–1649) painted between 1640 and

FIGURE 5.
Portrait of Endymion Porter
by William Dobson, c. 1642–5.
This country gentleman
enjoys hunting, but is also a
connoisseur of the arts.
(© Tate, London 2015)

1644 by William Dobson (1611–1646) and now at the Tate Gallery Britain, offers a different kind of self-presentation. This portrait evokes the sporting pleasures of a country gentleman, but one who is also a connoisseur of the arts. Porter is shown holding a wheel-lock hunting rifle, which Dobson has rendered in great detail to indicate its importance. The gun is half-cocked, probably to show that it was recently used to bring down the hare held by a young boy and sniffed by a dog on Porter's right. The portrait abounds in evidence of Porter's deep interest in art: it includes a carved bust of Apollo, a figure of Painting who has painted Minerva, the goddess of the Arts, and a figure of Poetry holding a pen. The portrait recognizes Porter's extensive knowledge of art and literature and reminds the viewer of his role as an adviser on such matters to King Charles I and George Villiers, First Duke of Buckingham. The combination of high culture and hunting with a gun probably means to say that Porter is a man who participates in all aspects of the life of a well-educated, sophisticated country gentleman.

Aristocratic men chose to include a firearm in their portraits, but did not elect to use an image of a firearm on their coat-of-arms. However, men beneath them socially, who were granted a coat-of-arms, emblazoned it with some kind of firearm. Such grants were awarded in the sixteenth century, a period of upheaval not only in religion, politics, and the socioeconomic position of individuals and families, but also in the College of Arms, whose heralds seemed more interested in their fees than in preserving the integrity of their responsibilities. In 1530, King Henry VIII empowered Clarenceux King Herald to grant arms to men to recognize service to the Crown or advancement in socioeconomic status. Still, such a person must not be of "vyle blood."[71] Lawrence Stone pointed out that there was "a torrent of claims for arms" and that from 1560 to 1639 altogether 3,760 were made.[72] Grants to men down the social scale continued in the seventeenth century.

None of the approximately eleven men who sought the award of a coat of arms and used some form of a gun as their motif is noticed in the *Oxford Dictionary of National Biography*.[73] For example, John Gouning, a merchant, was Mayor of Bristol in 1627, 1645, and 1654, as well as an alderman. He was eminent for his sufferings and services to King Charles I. On the shield of his coat of arms, awarded on 22 December 1662, were three silver cannon positioned horizontally.[74] The arms of Thomas Hall, son of Thomas Hall of Stonepit in Kent, awarded in 1591, incorporated the image of a hand shooting a pistol with smoke emerging from the barrel.[75] The most striking example, however, is the coat of arms that Stephan Bull of Gillingham, Kent, the Master Gunner of England, chose. Bull approached William Camden (1551–1623), Clarenceux King of Arms, the senior of three kings of arms at the College of Arms. Camden, author of the much-admired *Britannia,* was appointed to the post in October 1597 and given broad powers of authority over other heralds, who resented his advancement.[76] The geographical area of the country for which Clarenceux was responsible included Kent, where Bull lived. Bull requested Camden to research what arms he might lawfully bear without prejudice to anyone else. To recommend his candidacy, Bull pointed to his lifelong interest in things military (dating from "his youth") and noted that he had served Henry VIII, Edward VI, and Mary I, as well as Elizabeth I, who appointed him Master Gunner of England. Throughout his career, he had given "laudable service" and showed "dutyfull industry, great knowledge, valour, and fidelity."[77] He did not mention that he held property in Bubwith in northern England which the Crown by letters patent dated 30 June 1585 had leased to him.[78] Nor did he note that a painter in the circle of Marcus Gheeraerts II had painted his portrait in oil on a 44 × 36–inch panel in 1596. The half-length portrait depicts a man of substance dressed in black.[79] His petition may have found favor with Camden at least in part because of the latter's friendship with William Cecil, now Lord Burghley, who had long championed arming the militia with guns. Bull received his coat of arms on 22 August 1601 and chose to decorate its shield with three mortars standing

FIGURE 6.
Coat of arms granted in 1601 to
Stephan Bull of Gillingham, Kent,
a Master Gunner of England.
(College of Arms MS Grants
vol. 2, f. 158r. Reproduced by
permission of the Kings, Heralds,
and Pursuivants of Arms)

erect. On the crest an owl holds a linstock, a staff for holding a lighted match to light a cannon.[80] The whole is brilliantly colored in gold, red, and silver.

That these men chose to use a firearm as the motif on their coats of arms shows their active approval of the weapon and their desire to identify with it. It is further evidence of the wide popularity of guns and of the feeling that a firearm was a mark of superiority.

Guns did not create violent behavior among men. Long before guns, aristocratic and plebeian men were guilty of violence. Historians have attributed much of the unruliness of early modern England to the unguarded behavior of aristocrats. Lawrence Stone claimed that during the sixteenth century aristocrats were short tempered, irascible, vengeful, and violent in language and action.[81] They carried a weapon at all times, whether a dagger, a sword, or a pistol and, with a weapon always at the ready, were prone to spontaneous fighting. Brutality and mayhem scarred life in London and the country. Roger B. Manning, who like Stone underscored the violence of the aristocracy, argued that "the rechivalrization" of aristocratic culture was responsible. Occurring in the late sixteenth century, rechivalrization was a "culture that emphasized the martial function of the aristocracy."[82] Manning also claimed that "highway robbery" was a "distinctly aristocratic crime" and identified demobilized soldiers "especially former officers and cavalry troopers" as major perpetrators. Citing John Earle, Bishop of Salisbury, who in his *Microcosmography* (1613) had pointed out that younger sons of aristocrats were often implicated in highway robberies, Manning concluded that all these men needed for the job was "a horse and brace of pistols."[83] The multiple examples of aristocratic highwaymen that Manning adduced include Sir George Sandys, whose family was financially dependent on his success as a highway robber. Between 1616 and 1626, Sandys was in and out of jail, repeatedly found guilty of robbery. Finally he was executed for murdering one of his victims, a crime he unwisely confessed to a woman while raping her.[84] Some royalist highwaymen preyed on parliamentarians, combining a political motive with an economic one. A royalist, Captain Philip Stafford, whose estate in Berkshire had been sequestrated, tried to recover his losses by attacking parliamentarians. Another royalist, Captain Zachary Howard, also turned to highway robbery for the same reasons. His targets included members of the families of General Fairfax and Cromwell himself. Howard's career as a highway robber, however, ended in 1652, when he was arrested, tried, and hanged. Other accounts support Manning's thesis that aristocrats were heavily involved in highway robbery.

Plebeian and poor men, however, were also highway robbers. For example, in 1586, two yeoman, William Maundy and Edward Saunders, joined a gentleman named Lionel Gest in assaulting George Shellye, a gentleman, and one John Turner. They stole money and a pistol, valued at £1, among other items.[85] In 1660, two laborers were indicted for a highway robbery that had netted them money and a pistol worth 3 shillings. For this, they were sentenced to be hanged.[86] Three years later, an anonymous laborer was indicted for the same kind of crime.[87] On 21 June 1695 at about 10:00 PM, three highwaymen accosted Lord Banbury on Turnham Green. Unfortunately for them, he was armed and killed one of them, wounding the other.[88] In Oxfordshire in October 1698, a "footpad" accosted a Quaker on the highway and stole £10. As he led the man "out of the Way to be Gagg'd," the "Spirit" moved the Quaker to "trip up the heels of the Robber, which he did very dexterously" and, thus, was able to get possession of his pistols. The Quaker took the robber to a magistrate who jailed the man to await trial. Menaced by aristocrats and plebeians using guns to enforce their purpose, travelers were advised to arm themselves for a journey, and many did. The result was that guns proliferated on highways.

Pistols were used to commit other kinds of violent crime. In 1729, "a certain noble Colonel" attempted to rape a maidservant. "To frighten her into Compliance, he drew a Pistol upon her." Somehow the assault was averted, and rumor had it that the colonel would be sued for attempted rape, and also for using a "weapon altogether unlawful upon such an Occasion."[89] Men also committed manslaughter and murder with guns. In 1675, George Roper, a laborer, deliberately shot off his gun to frighten a horse that the wife of a yeoman was riding. The woman fell and died of her injuries, and Roper was found guilty of manslaughter.[90] In 1724, Thomas Arnold was indicted for attempting to murder Lord Onslow by shooting him with a fowling piece.[91]

Gun accidents occurred throughout the era in the counties as more persons possessed guns, legally or otherwise. Carelessness, lack of understanding of the operation of a gun, and the unreliability of the gun itself were partly to blame for these incidents. For example, on 23 August 1587, John Woddes, yeoman, of Binsted, Hampshire, brought a loaded birding piece into his house and laid it down on the table. It accidently went off and killed a man named Shrobbe, who was standing nearby.[92] About twenty years later, on 25 August 1606, a similar misfortune occurred: a yeoman casually discharged a birding piece he was holding. His inattention caused the bullet to hit a man in the upper arm. Predictably, the bullet wound caused the death of the fellow, but the jury in this case ruled the death by misadventure.[93] At the beginning of the eighteenth century, the *Daily Courant* reported that a servant of John Shaw, a gunsmith, whose workshop was near the Horse-Guard in Whitehall, picked up a pistol to "try the cock." Not understanding that it was charged and discovering that the flint did not strike fire, he was replacing the flint when the gun went off, killing a man who happened to be in the shop.[94] Finally, the poignant story of a gun accident involving a rich, aging farmer who lived at the edge of a village near York is worth telling.[95] As a protection against thieves who reportedly were looting the houses of the well-to-do, the man prudently kept his gun "ready charg'd." One night in 1724, hearing a "Noise in his back Yard," he got up from bed, took his gun to a window and called out, asking who was there. Receiving no answer to his repeated calls, "he let fly with a Fowling Piece" and shot dead a man in the yard. Alas, it turned out that the man was his son who had gone out to confront a presumed intruder. Grief over the accident virtually destroyed the elderly father, but, according to the account, the incident had a positive result: it "clear'd the Village of the Rogues, who found by it what they are to expect from the Inhabitants." That could have brought but cold comfort to the grieving old man. These incidents tell us that guns were enthusiastically and uncritically embraced. The individuals involved had not taken the time to learn how to handle a gun. The tragic events, however, did not apparently dampen the wholehearted acceptance of guns.

Suicide was one solution to severe personal difficulties, no matter one's social background, and adding a gun to the possible methods increased the likelihood of success, for if the initial shot did not kill the person, almost certain infection of the wound did. In 1699, a "House keeper" in Cambridge who appeared "distracted in Mind" and "very Melancholly" was in a butcher's shop. By coincidence, a young woman to whom he was attracted, was also in the shop. Apparently the relationship had stalled, either because his attentions were rejected or his family objected to the match because the young woman's "Fortune did not Merit" the man's "respect. "After some short Pause," the unhappy fellow could stand the situation no longer. "He drew a Pistol out of his Pocket and shot himself, so that he drop'd down Dead upon the Spot."[96] Another suicide occurred "a few days" before 28 December 1721. A stranger, apparently "in good Circumstances," checked into an inn at Worcester, stabled his horse, and went to a gunsmith's shop, "where he bought a pistol" and a "brace of bullets." Returning to the inn, he retired and shot himself in the head, dying "upon the spot." The paper reported that the "Cause is not yet known."[97] Finally, another distressing tale of jealousy and unrequited love came from Buckinghamshire in July 1730. An aging carpenter, who had become jealous of his "sweetheart," invited her to walk with him on the common. As they strolled along he "peremptorily" asked her if she would marry him, and when she said, "no," he put the muzzle of the fowling-piece he was carrying under his chin and, using the "end of his rule pul'd the trigger, and shot himself through the head upwards."[98]

Men from all social levels felt the influence of guns in their lives in ways that depended on their status. Wealthy men were the most deeply affected. Their political and social responsibilities brought them into regular contact with firearms and their role as military officers made their use and understanding of guns essential. They participated fully in the military gun culture that developed and gave guns a central role in their domestic lives. In ways we have seen, elite men used firearms in hunting and shooting. They collected beautifully decorated guns, admired them as works of art, sent them as gifts to heads of state and friends, and used them to decorate the interior of their houses. To show the public their status and sophistication, aristocrats placed cannon on the lawns of their estates. Men of fashion carried a gun in London in the late sixteenth century and commissioned their portraits painted with a gun. One man of wealth ordered a toiletry case made in the shape of a gun. Men of more modest social standing who received a coat of arms used the image of a firearm as its motif.

On the other hand, guns, when used in theft, murder, and manslaughter, had a destructive effect on the lives of aristocratic and plebeian men. Gun accidents also marred their lives, and gun suicides also ended some.

A consequence of all these things was that guns became deeply embedded in men's lives. Men's attitudes toward guns and their use were central components in the early modern English domestic gun culture. Their contribution to a domestic gun culture gained importance as the military role of aristocratic men began a very slow retreat before the creation and expansion of a permanent standing army of professional soldiers.

EIGHT · Guns

A Challenge to the
Feminine Ideal?

WOMEN OF ALL SOCIAL CATEGORIES were associated with guns in early modern England. Guns influenced their lives, but in different ways according to their social rank. We saw earlier that artisanal women found employment with the Ordnance Office and were enrolled in the Worshipful Company of Gunmakers. This chapter deals with the effect of guns on the personal, social, and intellectual life of royal and aristocratic women and those of middling status. Aristocratic European women embraced the gun in hunting, target shooting, and fashion as their English counterparts did not, and they are noted to underscore the contrast. Well-to-do women and those of middling status used gunpowder in cooking recipes, as a household fumigant, for personal toiletry, and for medicinal purposes. Women writers, poets, and playwrights wove the gun into their work. Women were not spared the trauma of gun crime or gun and gunpowder accidents. Moreover, they used firearms in their own acts of violence. Guns were pervasive in their lives.

The context of women's involvement with guns sits uneasily with the early modern era's model of ideal womanhood. Although losing some of its power, the ideal essentially retained its authority throughout the period and beyond. According to religious homilies, church sermons, prescriptive literature, and tracts and pamphlets written by men, the model woman was expected to embrace a restrictive lifestyle, to be demure and self-effacing in personality, largely silent in company, attentive to pleasing her husband, and devoted to her children and household. She was supposed to live in the quiet seclusion of her home in subservience to a man, first her father, or should he die prematurely, another male member of her family, and then, when she married, her husband. When she married, a woman became a femme couverte, limited in her property and civil rights. Only if she were widowed did a woman attain certain freedoms and legal rights, as a woman who never married did not. A young girl's education depended on her social status, of course, but even well-to-do girls were ill-prepared for any independent role outside the home.

An ideal woman had no place in her life for guns and other weapons of violence. When guns were first introduced in England and western Europe, their primary purpose was to wound, damage, destroy, and kill, and their primary use was in war. Long before Freud, they were regarded as a masculine symbol of power, authority, and aggression. It is therefore easy to understand why the notion that a woman could—and would want to—handle, admire, and use a gun, a dangerous and violent weapon, that depended on gunpowder, a hazardous and explosive substance, had no part in an ideal picture of womanhood.

But, ideals are one thing; reality is quite another, and it was not only with respect to guns that women violated stated norms. Scholarship over the past thirty years or so has shown that, for example, women became political critics, social activists, printers, writers, poets, and scientists, and were active in the life of many guilds.[1] In this list also belong women who, as artisanal gunmakers, made and repaired guns and served as active and responsible members of the Worshipful Company of Gunmakers. It should also include women who owned, possessed, and used guns and employed gunpowder in a variety of ways. But, if the surviving printed records that I have seen are accurate and complete, no tract or pamphlet directly denounced women for their interest in firearms, although their masculine-like role in war was ridiculed.[2] Women's connections with guns helped to minimize the sense of danger of a device and a chemical that were potentially lethal. This book argues that women's activities helped to humanize guns and gunpowder and make them widely acceptable.

Royal and aristocratic women in England initially learned about guns from the men in their lives. The political and military roles of aristocratic men, their enjoyment of hunting and target shooting, and their collecting and gift giving of beautifully decorated guns provide the context within which women became familiar with firearms. Although English royal and aristocratic women participated in horseback riding and hunting, when guns became available, they did not add them to their arsenal of hunting weapons. By contrast, Continental women did.[3] For instance, the Austrian Archduke Ferdinand and his wife Anna hunted together using guns in 1521. In Sweden, Princess Hedvig Sofia, a sister of King Karl XII (1681–1708), began hunting with a gun with her father at the age of eleven. In Germany and France, members of royalty built elaborate hunting lodges, such as Hubertusburg near Dresden, and Versailles, not far from Paris, where men and women gathered to hunt and shoot with guns.

English ladies hunted on horseback with notable skill in the sixteenth century, as they had surely done much earlier, but without using a gun. For example, Margaret Tudor (1489–1541), King Henry VIII's sister, was a superior horsewoman and an excellent shot with the crossbow. Her talents were on display in 1503, when, just fourteen years old and on her way to Scotland to marry James IV, she stopped at Alnwick, the great house of Henry Algernon Percy, the Fifth Earl of Northumberland (1478–1527), who had been appointed warden-general of the marches for the express purpose of escorting Margaret into Scotland. During her visit, the Earl arranged a hunt for her, and she brought down a buck, a feat that testified to her ability as a markswoman and rider, and her dexterity in handling a crossbow.[4] Queen Elizabeth I, a skilled rider who loved to hunt, preferred the crossbow as her weapon,[5] as did Queen Anne, King James I's consort, also an experienced horseback rider and an excellent shot.[6] If the evidence I have seen is complete and accurate, no sixteenth-century English queen or aristocratic lady used a gun in the chase. Yet, during the English Civil Wars, some women handled a gun while on horseback (see below), which makes possible the speculation that before the wars *some women* knew how to handle a gun on horseback.

European women also took a great interest in target shooting, but again, English ladies did not. In Vienna in the early eighteenth century, competitive shooting matches for court ladies were very popular.[7] Lady Mary Wortley Montagu (1689–1762) witnessed such an event when she was visiting the Viennese court in 1716. In a letter to her sister dated 14 September of that year, she described the matches as "a Diversion wholly new to me." The shoots were set up in a beautiful alley in the garden of the "Palace of Retirement" where the Empress Amalia lived. Three targets—Cupid, Fortune, and a sword, each set in an oval frame—were placed at the end of the alley. The Empress, who hosted the event, was seated on a small throne at the head of the alley, while two lines of young ladies of quality, including the two "Arch Dutchesses," ranged themselves along either side. The court ladies wore jewels in their hair and held "fine light Guns in their hands."[8] Men of the court looked on while the women took turns firing at the targets. The young Archduchess Amalia won first prize—"a fine ruby ring set round with di'monds in a Gold Snuff box." The other prizes were also elaborate and costly.[9] Although the target-shoots involved only the women of the court, they were "the favorite pleasure of the Emperor" and took place almost every week. As a result, at least in Lady Montagu's judgment, "the young Ladys [are] skilful enough to defend a fort." Lady Montagu concluded ruefully that "they laughed very much to see me afraid to handle a gun."[10]

Lady Montagu's confession that she had never before seen a shooting match involving women shows that aristocratic English ladies did not engage in them. Lady Montagu was candid in saying that she was "afraid to handle a Gun." Hunting with a gun and target shooting in a formal, organized way clearly did not interest English royal and noble women. However, too much emphasis on the point may be misplaced, because other evidence adduced below illustrates English women's familiarity with firearms.

Aristocratic European women who enjoyed guns took an active part in building up their own collections, shopping for them, and ordering them to specifications. To make hunting and shooting easier for themselves, Continental ladies ordered that guns be made shorter in length and lighter in weight. For example, Queen Christina of Sweden (1632–54) assembled an assortment of fifty-eight hunting guns. Determined to get precisely what she wanted, she commissioned Prince Raimund Montecuccoli to visit a gunmaker in Salzburg to buy a gun of advanced design. Showing sophisticated knowledge, she specified a repeating carbine that could fire thirty to forty shots.[11] European women wanted guns made to suit them. In France, King Louis XVI (1774–93) commissioned Pierre de Sainte, his "gunmaker in ordinary," to make flintlock birding guns as gifts for Queen Marie Antoinette.[12] De Sainte produced a delicate-looking gun that was light in weight and of reduced proportions. He decorated it with gilding, silver wire inlay of floral design, and red velvet fabric covering the cheek plate and the butt. The Holy Roman Empress, Maria Theresa (1745–65), also favored guns of feminized design. In Russia, both the Empress Elizabeth (1741–62) and the Empress Catherine the Great (1762–96) induced craftsmen from Germany, France, and Scandinavia to immigrate to Russia to bolster a native gunmaking industry and to make guns especially for them for hunting and target shooting. In Italy, on deposit at the Armeria Reale in Turin, are two specific examples of a feminized gun, both dated at the turn of the seventeenth century. The published supplement to the Catalogo Angelucci includes a list of objects acquired before 1890 that were previously noted only in manuscript. Entered as M. 151 is an Archibuso whose barrel length is 33.9 inches (86 centimeters) and whose weight is 4.52 pounds.[13]

By contrast, there is no gun in the vast collection at the Royal Armouries in Leeds, England, that the curators believe may be certainly identified as a woman's gun.[14] It is possible, however, that some shorter, lighter guns thought to be designed for boys were made for women. But whether or not guns were especially designed for them, some English women possessed guns that were available. For example, Margaret Spencer, a daughter of Robert Lord Spencer, shopped regularly in London for fabrics, accessories, and jewelry. Tucked among the purchases she made between 1610 and 1613 were two pairs of pistols costing 22 shillings.[15] They appeared without comment in the list of items of finery that she purchased. Although the record does not show whether the pistols were for her or a friend, the point is that Lady Spencer's casual purchase of the pistols suggests that by the early seventeenth century a young woman of fashion was comfortable buying guns in London. It is possible that other young ladies did the same.[16] The shop where the purchase was made is unknown, but gunshops dotted the streets in many parts of London, as we saw earlier. It was easy to buy a gun in the city.[17]

Later in the seventeenth century, London women continued to purchase guns. They armed themselves with little guns and carried them in their muffs as a safeguard during the Popish Plot scare. They also used guns to protect their homes from intruders, both points noted in chapter 6. When travelling, at least one lady, the Countess of Salisbury, who was journeying from Paris to Lyons in October 1699, armed her entourage with two carbines and a pair of pistols. Hearing that the roads were dangerous, the Countess promptly purchased the firearms.[18]

Aristocratic women chose to include guns in their portraits, just as men did. On the Continent, the Swedish princess Hedvig Sofia, mentioned above, presented herself in a painting dressed in clothes appropriate for hunting and cut like those of her brother.[19] The only mark of her royalty was a jewel in her hair. She holds the gun proudly in front of her with both hands as if putting it on display and advertising that, as shown on the flintlock, it was made in Stockholm. Or again, the Spanish artist, Juan Carreño De Miranda, between 1660 and 1670, painted another portrait of an aristocratic European woman who seems to be holding a gun.[20] The painting depicts a stunningly beautiful Spanish court lady, whose identity the restoration of the portrait has drawn into question. This aristocratic young lady wears an elaborate gown with a silver shirt, full ruffled sleeves with pink and silver bands, and a huge farthingale skirt that spreads out all around her. She holds a lace handkerchief in her be-ringed left hand and with her right hand reaches out to a little dog that is sitting on a table. Jewels are at her décolletage and shaped into a large bow with feathers in her long dark hair. A modern viewer is unprepared to notice that attached to her waist with a ribbon and resting on her skirt is, astonishingly, a small gold pistol. One may be further surprised to learn that the small pistol is not a functioning firearm at all, but rather a piece of jewelry used by ladies to hold powder or perfume. It has been described as an "elegant accessory."

The lady's accessory parallels in time the accessory that was in the shape of a gun that an English man used for his toiletries, described in chapter 7. The presence of the accessory indicates that the lady is comfortable presenting herself in an elaborate portrait with an object in the shape of a firearm. The little pistol adds a note of confidence, self-assurance, and fashion awareness. It titillates the viewer. Today, in the United States, items in the shape of a gun are still used as fashion accessories.[21]

In England, Queen Elizabeth I, who did not use guns herself, ordered that cannon and shot, as well as pikemen and cavalry, be included in the engraving that shows her crushing the Great Armada. The picture seems to be saying, as Elizabeth herself famously did say in addressing her troops gathered at Tilbury in 1588 to fight the Spanish Armada: "I know I have the body of a weak and feeble woman, but I have the heart and stomach of a king."[22]

The only other English woman who chose to be painted with a gun was Teresia, Lady Sherley (1590–1668), a woman of unusual talents, personality, and experience. The gun she is holding is shown as a real firearm. Lady Sherley's background clarifies the persona she presents in her portrait.[23] An English lady by marriage, not birth, she was the wife of Sir Robert Sherley (1581–1628), an eccentric, traveler, and diplomat, who, with his elder brother, Sir Anthony, journeyed to Isfahan in Persia in 1599 to visit the court of Shah Abbas I.[24] Abbas I ruled the Safavid dynasty from 1587 to 1629. The Shah sent Sir Anthony on a mission to persuade European nations to unite against his enemy, the Turks, but Sir Robert stayed on at the court, won the Shah's favor, helped him reorganize his army, and expanded his knowledge of firearms.[25] Abbas I integrated firearms, which the Safavids had utilized since 1488, into his army. In 1603 at the age of twenty-two, Sir Robert converted to Catholicism—a radical step for an Englishman—and, in 1608, married a local woman, also a radical step. His bride was Sampsonia, the eighteen-year-old daughter of a Christian chieftain, Isma'il Khan, ruler of Circassia, an area of land on the Black Sea, and a relative of one of the wives of Shah Abbas I. The Carmelite nuns baptized Sampsonia and gave her the name Teresia. Not hearing from Sir Anthony, the Shah dispatched Sir Robert on a similar mission to European capitals. Teresia had an exciting life, travelling with her husband across Europe, narrowly escaping death, and saving her husband's life twice with a gun.[26] She and Sir Robert reached England in 1611, prepared to present to King James I the Shah's proposal to give England a monopoly of the silk trade. Interested in the idea, James I entertained the couple at Hampton Court,[27] and friendly relations between them and the king developed. The Sherleys named their first and only child, born in November 1611, Henry, after James's elder son. Prince Henry and Queen Anne were friendly enough to serve as godparents.[28] Sir Robert and Lady Teresia did not linger in England. In January 1613, leaving their child with Robert's family, they sailed for Persia, and, after escaping death twice, reached the Persian court. In 1615, Abbas I again sent Sir Robert on a European mission, which took him and his wife to Spain and in 1622 to Rome, where they were painted wearing Persian dress by Sir Anthony Van Dyck and his circle. In 1624, they were back in England. During this visit, the portrait of Lady Sherley that we are about to discuss was painted by an unknown artist. Ian Eaves, noting the courtesies with which King James I received Lady Sherley and her husband, suggested that the pistol she is holding might be "a royal gift."[29] Now joined by Prince Charles (his second son), King James I continued to express interest in the proposal to give England a monopoly over the Persian silk trade, but the East India Company and the Levant Company raised strong objections. When James died in 1625 discussions faltered, and in May 1628 Sir Robert and Lady Teresia returned to Persia and received an audience with the Shah. Sir Robert, however, was stricken with a fever and died in July. Teresia retired to Rome in 1634, had her husband's remains reburied there, and died there in 1668.

Her portrait shows a strikingly handsome, self-assured, proud looking woman, with a prominent nose and large brown eyes, looking unflinchingly straight at the viewer. Lady Sherley's clothing and jewels point to her origins. She is wearing a delicately patterned dress of soft brownish fabric with brocade around the bodice, the kind of material that the Shah hoped to trade with England. Her jeweled headdress, with a large stone at the top of her high forehead and a handsome earring, is a variation of the headdress of Isfahan women.[30] A necklace encircles her rather full throat, and, with her left hand, she fingers a pocket watch, which is attached to her waist with a red ribbon. In her right hand, which rests nonchalantly on the back of a chair covered in a rich red fabric, she holds a snaphance gun.[31] The firearm is beautifully decorated: gems are set in a plain rectangular gold or gilt mounting along the sides and top of the stock. Small jewels of the same kind appear around the muzzle and the breech, the decoration suggesting that the weapon was made for a lady.

The portrait is drenched in symbolism. The red chair signifies authority. The pocket watch and the gun point to advances in technology in Europe, implying that Lady Sherley is highly intelligent and well aware of such matters. The watch may also suggest that she is counting the hours until she and her husband, who has left England, are reunited. Lady Sherley appears to be exuding pride in the gun and her skill with it. Her expertise is so assured that she holds the weapon casually, thereby implying that she is a strong woman,

FIGURE 7. Portrait of Lady Teresia Sherley, showing her casually
holding a gun. (Berkeley and Spetchley Estates, Berkeley)

easily capable of managing a firearm. The gun, arguably, means to say that in
the absence of her husband, she will use it to protect her person, her family,
and her property; with it, she will perform the duties of a man. The firearm
also may allude to her adventures with her husband, and to the credit she received for saving his life. Possibly the gun points to the fact that her husband
expanded knowledge of firearms among men at the Persian court. At the same
time, the casually displayed firearm is also a fashion accessory, a desirable object for an aristocratic lady to display. This portrait of Teresia Sherley, along

with the portraits of European ladies with guns, is a marker of the integration of firearms into the lives of some aristocratic ladies.

The question that demands consideration is: why were aristocratic English women less interested in guns than aristocratic European women? There is no certain answer. It is not that English women were incapable of handling a fire-arm expertly. The part they played in the Civil Wars proves as much, as does the fact that individual women committed murder with guns (see below). It is possible that aristocratic English women accepted and practiced the terms of the ideal woman more enthusiastically than their counterparts in Europe. Perhaps it was a matter of idiosyncratic taste with respect to how to spend one's leisure time.

Guns and gunpowder touched the imagination of women writers, poets, and playwrights. They appeared in women's literary work to advance the narrative, to explain a character, or to serve as an analogy or metaphor. Aphra Behn made the gun an integral part of the action in her most popular play, *The Rover or The Banished Cavaliers*. *The Rover* was the first play written by a woman to feature a woman wielding a firearm on stage.[32] A naughty tale of lust, love, sex, prostitution, betrayal, unfaithfulness, and revenge, it debuted on the London stage in March 1677 at the Duke of York Theater. The Restoration audience went wild over it. So, too, did King Charles II and his brother James, Duke of York, who were so enthusiastic that the king ordered two performances at court.[33] The popularity of the play among royalty attracted a large audience.

The gun sharpens the personality of the two main protagonists, Angelica Bianca, a prostitute, and Willmore, the Rover. In Act 5, scene 1, Angelica, who has fallen in love with Willmore, upbraids him for his unfaithfulness. To drive home her point, she "draws a pistol and holds it to his breast." For four pages of dialogue Angelica follows Willmore around the stage "with the pistol to his breast" or "with the pistol ready to shoot"—so say the stage directions. At one point, Willmore says nervously in an aside, "I think she's in earnest." The stage directions fail to describe the firearm that Angelica pulled from her clothing, but we may be sure that it was a small, short gun, a dag, that was easily concealed and readily available—the gun that we know the government had been trying to restrict for over a hundred years. It would have been fitted with a wheel lock or flintlock and hence would have been loaded and at the ready before Angelica used it to threaten Willmore.

Angelica's knowledgeable handling of the gun and her apparent intention to use it deepens understanding of her character. Angelica has no trouble managing the gun and keeping it pointed directly at Willmore. So long as she does not waver, she controls the scene and dominates Willmore. For a time she unnerves him, as he considers she might really shoot him. When she finally surrenders the gun, much to Willmore's relief, the relationship changes. The gun had been the great equalizer between the two of them. Angelica violates conventional norms not only because she is a prostitute but also because she demonstrates her willingness to use a violent weapon. The gun reinforces her bold, unconventional behavior and also her passion for Willmore.

No contemporary commented in print on the woman's action with the gun in *The Rover*, and no modern scholar has either. How does one explain that contemporary London playgoers and observers accepted so readily in 1677 the action that clearly violated the ideal of womanhood in early modern England? First, the silent acceptance of the narrative provides a powerful indication of how widely and deeply embedded the gun had become in London life. Second, the absence of criticism adds to other evidence that the notion of an ideal woman who should want nothing to do with a gun or with violence had lost much of its strength. Behn's play casts a particularly bright light on the relationship of women and guns.

Aphra Behn also used gunpowder in a poem entitled "On a Blew spot made in a Ladys neck by Gunpowder, by a person of Quality."[34] In this flight of poetic fancy, the poet, pointing to a blue spot on the lady's neck, queries, "What blew is that that do's so charming shew / A Hill of Saphire in a Field of Snow?" One presumes the spot is a bruise, but Behn's title makes clear that the mark was made by gunpowder "by a person of Quality." Behn has transformed gunpowder into a metaphor for passionate love, sexual desire, and fierce embrace. As Behn put it, "[Gunpowder] yet retains its wonted nature still / and from your neck, as from a Port do's kill." Gunpowder was first made for destruction, but now its power is converted to ornament and directed to personal use and passion, Behn is saying.

It seems likely that Behn's readers understood that the nitrate in gunpowder left a blue mark and probably knew that some men dandified their faces with a "gunpowder spot" or "beauty mark," a point that circulated in 1681 at about the time Behn's poem appeared.[35] Moreover, Behn's metaphor was not new. Earlier male poets had substituted a gun for Cupid's bow and arrow.[36] The military historian J. R. Hale suggests that the medieval convention of desire laying siege to the castle of chastity was revived, and that guns and gunpowder became the metaphors for love, desire, and sex.[37]

Margaret Cavendish's story, "Assaulted and pursued Chastity," also illustrates the role of the gun in a narrative. This story concerned a beautiful young woman from a wealthy family who lost her high social position when her family suffered a reversal of political and financial fortune. Washed ashore in a strange land, the young woman, now an orphan, is picked up by an old bawd, who aims to profit from her beauty by making her available to the local prince who has often used the bawd's services. Suspecting a treacherous design, the young woman decides to procure a gun to protect herself. She begs a servant girl, whom she has befriended, to get her a small pistol that makes little noise. She explains that she needs the gun because a wise old wizard had advised her to shoot off a firearm on her birthday and thereby destroy a whole year of evil. If she fails to do so, she will suffer all year. The girl believes the story and readily complies with her request.[38] That Cavendish constructs the story so that a young servant girl is able to procure a gun quite readily holds its own special interest, suggesting that by the middle of the seventeenth century, it was widely accepted that guns were easily purchased in London.

In the meantime, the old bawd tells the prince about the beautiful creature she has saved for him. He has only to see this lovely girl to fall passionately in love.[39] The girl begs him not to violate her chastity, arguing that "it's an injustice to take the Goods from the right Owners without their consents." But he is undeterred. As he moves toward her, his passions aflame, the young woman pulls out the little pistol and points it at him. The prince calculates that she would not dare use the weapon and prepares to take it away from her. But, as he approaches her more closely, she shoots him, crying out that all "young virgins will honor [me]." The prince suffers a grievous wound, but lives, and, upon his recovery, he seeks out the young woman and apologizes profusely for his importunities. He explains that in his experience women "usually ... are so tender and fearful and so far from using instruments of death as swords, guns, or the like, as they dare not look at them but turn their head aside."[40] The story goes on, the girl becomes a military leader, she and the prince meet again, and they fall in love, marry, and, let us hope, live happily thereafter.

The gun is essential to the character of both the young woman and the prince. No other weapon would have served so well. The prince's intended rape of the young woman and his statement of how he thinks women view weapons show him to be a man of his own time. The rest of the story reveals him as one capable of change. By giving the girl a gun, Cavendish establishes her immediately as a woman of courage, strength, determination, and independence. These qualities make reasonable her subsequent development into a woman with military talents and the independence of mind to forgive the prince and marry him.

These several examples illustrate how cleverly women authors weave the gun into their stories and poems and how important they are to the development of the characters and the narrative. The gun, a new device with lethal potentiality, adds excitement to these works. The stories also show how widespread the gun has become.

The record of women's domestic lives shows that women integrated gunpowder into their homes. Printed household manuals addressed to English and French women offer some astonishing, not to say alarming, directions for the use of gunpowder. The homemaker plagued with "house bugs" is advised to "take gunpowder beat small" and place it in the "crevices of [her] bedstead and fire it with a match . . . and keep the smoke in." She should follow this procedure for "an hour or more" and keep the room "close some hours after."⁴¹ When she returns to the room and opens the door, the "house bugs" would be gone (and perhaps the room as well!).

Also dangerous, albeit in a different way, was the suggestion to use saltpeter in cooking meat. William Clarke, the author of a history of saltpeter, pointed out that salt and saltpeter give meat an appetizing red color. But, he said, salt is in short supply and advised that saltpeter itself might be used. Simply mix saltpeter with a little salt and it will not only add color but also give a "more savoury taste." Clark offered the advice, he said, to "pleasure our English Ladies [who] delight in such Experiments."⁴² One can only hope his advice fell on deaf ears.

But truly terrifying was the recipe for a centerpiece that might serve at a great feast, such as a Twelfth Night party. The recipe, printed first in France, and published in England in 1685, gave directions for using gunpowder in very dangerous ways. To decorate the table, it advised the reader to use pasteboard to fashion a boat and a castle with battlements and portcullises, position guns on and around both, and place the boat and the castle far enough apart so that they can fire at each other. Next, make the little guns. Start with kickses (the hollow stems of plants), put gunpowder in them ready to be fired. Then, sprinkle the gunpowder all around the castle and on the boat. In another place, close by, position a stag, made from pasteboard; fill his body with claret wine and insert an arrow in his side. As the festivities get under way, persuade one of the ladies to "pluck out the arrow" so that the claret wine runs out like blood. This will be a frightening sight to the ladies, the recipe declares. Next the hostess should light the gunpowder! The guests will see and hear the guns firing from the boat and the castle, each pounding the other. To remove the "stinck of powder," the ladies should be provided with egg shells full of sweet water to throw at each other. Finally, the hostess should open one of the pies from which frogs skip out and then open another pie to release little birds which will fly about. All these things—the guns firing, the claret wine running like blood, the frogs leaping, the birds flying, the sweet water dampening the whole—make the "Ladies to skip and shreek" and "cause much delight and pleasure to the whole company." The author laments that "these were formerly the delights of the Nobility, before good House-keeping had left England."⁴³

There is no direct evidence that these ideas were ever tried at an important festivity, that saltpeter was used to color meat red, or that gunpowder was really used to rout house bugs, but given the fact that the instructions were included in a serious book about saltpeter and in a published household manual, it is possible that they were. Whatever the case, the point is that writers of household manuals and their readers, even if only theoretically, brought gunpowder into use in fumigating, cooking, and celebrating. In doing so, they showed ignorance of the dangers of gunpowder, but at the same time revealed how deeply this substance had penetrated their consciousness. In doing so, they also stripped away from it a sense of danger and its power to destroy.

Gunpowder appeared in other recipes connected with health and beauty. A recipe book included a medicine for "gun shott."[44] To cure a toothache, the application of gunpowder was recommended.[45] The charcoal in gunpowder was thought to clean one's teeth and sweeten one's breath. To take gunpowder marks from the face of a person who has suffered a wound, one should apply warm fresh cow dung in a thin covering and renew the plaster several times a day.[46] To make a jerking proof against a musket shot, the housewife should skin an ox's hide and cut it into the shape of armour. Then she is advised to soak the hide in vinegar for twenty-four hours, dry it in the air, and steep it in vinegar six more times, changing the vinegar each time.[47] The manual warned pregnant women to avoid the loud noise of guns to protect themselves against miscarriage.[48]

Women, no less so than men, suffered gun and gunpowder accidents whether in London or outside the capital. For example, in 1539 a yeoman named John Geynyshe, who was in London and had his gun with him, took aim at a crow that had alighted on a buoy in the River Thames. Geynyshe missed the crow but shot dead a woman who was doing her wash nearby on Westminster Bridge.[49] One wonders if Geynyshe possessed the gun legally and how experienced he was in handling and shooting it. A different kind of accident happened at the end of the century in 1691 as gunshops multiplied in number and shopping for a gun became routine. Another man named John Gray stopped by a gunshop in London to purchase "some Pistols and other things." Mary Ayres, the wife of the owner, John Ayres, was in charge of serving customers, and she offered Gray several guns to look over. As he examined them, one accidentally went off and shot Ayres "on the Right side of the Breast" killing her instantly. Gray was charged with murder and put on trial. The court brought in a verdict of "Not Guilty," on grounds that he did not know the pistols were loaded and had killed Mary Ayres "only . . . per misfortunam."[50]

Gun accidents occurred wherever there were guns and individuals who were careless in handling them. On 20 September 1592, Elizabeth Salter, spinster, and Edward Putland, husbandman, were together at the house of Thomas Welshe, a gentleman who lived in Heathfield, Sussex. Putland found a birding gun in the room and knowing very little about how a firearm worked, he did not notice that it was loaded. When he moved the firelock to discover what would happen, the gun discharged. The bullet gave Salter a "large wound" on the right shoulder, from which she died on 6 October.[51] Or again, in 1605 in Hertfordshire, Edward Bradshawe, a husbandman, accidentally shot Elizabeth Field, like him a servant of William Fishe, a gentleman.[52] In 1685, the same kind of accident occurred, this one in Kent. Benjamin Russell accidently shot and killed Elizabeth Mills when he picked up a gun and it discharged.[53] During the Civil Wars, one Captain Stagger fell into an argument with some students from Oxford University. Apparently, he took out his gun, which discharged. He claimed that his gun went off accidentally; whatever the truth of his defense, the bullet hit a woman who was purchasing meat at a butcher's shop nearby and killed her.[54] Finally, a truly bizarre gun-related accident occurred in Surrey in the 1680s. A woman was sitting in her cottage busy with her spinning, when a piece of timber which was accidentally shot from a gun foundry came through the cottage wall and decapitated her.[55]

In some cases women caused gun accidents. One well-to-do young London woman, clearly naïve and ignorant about firearms, was responsible for a devastating accident. On a Saturday in February 1680, a young army officer arrived at a Major Parry's house in St. Giles to visit Parry's daughter, his fiancée. As he waited for the young woman, he laid his pistols on a table. His fiancée, obviously excited over his visit, came into the room to greet him. She picked up one of the pistols and jestingly pointed it at her fiancé, saying, "Have at you, sir." Alas, the pistol was charged. It went off and killed her intended. The story of this poignant, personal tragedy concludes with "She is fled."[56]

In another instance, a maid in the household of a "German doctor" accidentally shot a poor man who was asking for alms at the door. She was either cleaning her employer's pistol or was presenting it in jest before the beggar, witnesses were not sure which. Whatever the truth of the matter, the woman killed the beggar and was arrested.[57]

Women were also the victims of gun crime. Murder was the purpose of one Edward Evans, a Welshman with a long, pockmarked face, who rode a bay gelding into London on 1 August 1661. Dressed all in white, he carried with him pistols and a sword. Heading toward the Rose and Crown in Cursitors Alley, he pulled up his horse at the door. When the proprietor, a Mrs. Stevenson, answered the door, he drew out one of his pistols and shot her dead.

This was first-degree murder, and a reward was offered to anyone who apprehended the man or could tell the authorities his whereabouts.[58] The bare account of the tragedy is tantalizing. It makes one curious to know more about the relationship between Evans and Stevenson and why he murdered her.

Outside London, sometime after 1671, a Warwickshire woman was murdered by a gun wielded by her husband and his servant. The husband, John Chambers, preferred "harlots" to his wife and contrived to get rid of her. He first tried to drown her, but failing in that, he persuaded his servant to assist him in dispatching his wife with a gun. The servant "shot [the woman] through the Body." As Mrs. Chambers lay dying, she accused both men of killing her. Her husband and his servant were arrested and executed. With his last breath her husband repented and warned men against prostitutes.[59]

Gun theft touched women, too. In 1584, a laborer was indicted for grand larceny. He broke into the house of Margaret Ayloff, a well-armed widow, and stole a sword, a dagger, and a gun, among other items. The gun was valued at 20 shillings, so it was probably a handsome weapon and certainly was the most valuable item that he stole.[60] In January 1622, four laborers burgled the house of a widow and stole, among other things, a gun worth 10 shillings. The court reported that two of the thieves were at large, one was dead and the other, who was found guilty, was awaiting execution by hanging.[61] These accounts of the theft of a gun in two widows' houses inspire reflection. They show that women kept guns and leave the reader to wonder why: was it for protection, to practice shooting, or perhaps because the gun had belonged to their husband and was kept for sentimental reasons?

Women, like men, were not always safe on the highways. On 7 February 1730, two footpads accosted a Mrs. James, a widow and owner of a wagon business, near Market Street in Hertfordshire as she followed her wagon at a distance on horseback. One thief held her at gun's point, while the other robbed her of £3.[62]

Women were also guilty of committing crimes with a gun, including murder. In London, on 19 April 1617, a woman identified only as Sir Richard Farmer's lady, shot "one Onely, of the Temple with a pocket pistol."[63] As with the story of Evans and Stevenson, the reader has to fill in the details and speculate why the woman killed this man. A more explicit account is provided of a murder committed by a woman using a gun at the end of the century. On Saturday, 4 December 1697, bailiffs came to a house in Lincoln's Inn Field to arrest a person living there. The doors and the windows were barricaded and when the men attempted to force them, the "woman of the house" warned that they did so at their peril. They ignored her warning and, as they continued to try to force the barricade, the woman "fired a pistol and shot one of the bailiffs." And then this virago ran a sword through the body of another bailiff. One of the men died and the other was "mortally wounded."[64]

A very different type of crime was alleged against Alice Shambrooke (the widow of William Shambrooke) and Oliver Williams. These two gunmakers faced the charge that they owed the government a quantity of guns—muskets, calivers, and pistol barrels that they had taken for repair from army garrisons at Warwick, Northampton, and other places. They were unable to account for the firearms, and the suspicion was that they had resold the stolen weapons.[65] Shambrooke and Williams were only two of several gunmakers against whom charges of such crime and corruption were brought. Their accusers were members of the Company of Gunmakers, especially John Silk, a prominent gunmaker whom we have met before. These members were no doubt concerned to preserve the reputation of their Company.[66] But this kind of corruption with guns was not unusual. What is unusual is that, according to the records I have seen, Shambrooke was the only woman to have participated in it.

In the early eighteenth century, King George I made a seldom-noticed appointment that marked a change in attitude toward women and firearms at least at the king's court. He bestowed on Elizabeth Spence (1694–1764), an unmarried aristocratic lady, who was well-known at court, the Office of Keeper of the King's Private Armoury at Westminster, a post she held from 1725 to 1759 when it was abolished. No evidence has survived to explain why the king chose Spence for the office, why she would accept it, and what exactly her duties were—if, indeed, she had any at all. Her family background permits the speculation that the appointment was meant to recognize Spence and indicate the court's approval of her. The daughter of John Spence (1663/4–1713) and Ann Trevor (d.1748), Elizabeth inherited a lineage of political service: her maternal grandfather, Sir John Trevor (1624–1672), was elected to the House of Commons from Great Bedwyn and served there from 1663 to 1672. He was also Secretary of State (south) from 1668 to his death in 1672.[67] Elizabeth's brother, Thomas Spence, was Deputy Secretary at War and Serjeant-at-Arms in the Commons from 1717 until his death in an accident in 1737. She did not marry, but moved in a circle of aristocratic women friends, including Henrietta, Duchess of Newcastle, with whom she corresponded. She remembered some of these friends in her will, a gesture indicating a close relationship.[68] Spence died at the home of the Duke of Newcastle, a further indication of high social standing. Obituaries commented on her wealth, one noticing her "considerable fortune" and another writing succinctly, "She died very rich."[69]

Prior to Spence's appointment, the position of Keeper of the King's Private

Armoury at Westminster involved some duties and carried a yearly salary of the sizable sum of £100. The Keeper appointed by Charles II was Gervase Price. James II chose Jean de Latre, and William III tapped Peter Guenon de Beaubisson.[70] When Spence took over in 1725, the post was listed just below "Housekeeping" with no indication of duties or a salary. Yet, she was listed as Keeper of the Private Armoury in *A New Present State of England* and in various editions of *The Court Kalendar*.[71] Perhaps Spence was expected to schedule and oversee the cleaning and oiling of the King's Arms to keep them in mint shape for ceremonial use. Perhaps no duties were attached to the post. Maybe Spence was pleased to accept the appointment as an honorific that conferred recognition of the high regard in which she was held. Whatever the details, the points are that the eighteenth-century court appointed a woman to a position associated with guns and that Spence herself was comfortable in accepting it. The incident marked a shift in viewpoint at that time respecting women and guns at the highest level of government.

Aristocratic English women defied the early modern idea of an ideal woman by weaving guns and gunpowder into their personal, social, and intellectual lives, but less so than their European counterparts. Their doing so suggests that guns challenged the era's traditional feminine ideal and draws into question the strength of the traditional model. Aside from one or two snide comments about women fighting in the Civil Wars, criticism of women's association with guns was minimal and did not deter them. European women evinced more enthusiasm for guns than English women did: they hunted with them, used them in target practice, and at least one court lady incorporated into her wardrobe a toiletry case shaped like a gun. European women and one English lady had their portraits painted with a firearm. But both European and English fought with guns: in the wars of religion on the Continent and in the Civil Wars in England. Both had recipes that included gunpowder in cooking, medicines, and as a fumigant. English women writers wove guns and gunpowder into their essays, stories, plays, and poems. Both English and European women were complicit in giving their children toy guns and sometimes miniature real guns, as discussed in the next chapter. The unintended consequence of these activities was to minimize the sense of danger associated with a device and a chemical that were potentially lethal. In making guns a part of their personal lives, upper-status women helped to humanize firearms. On the other hand, English women felt the effects of the dark side of guns. They suffered from gun crime and gun and gunpowder accidents. That some women were guilty of committing crimes with a gun casts a different light on early modern English women.

NINE · Guns and
Child's Play

OYS AND GIRLS ACROSS ENGLISH SOCIETY felt the presence of
guns in their lives, but guns directly affected boys more than girls.
Parents gave their sons, but not their daughters, toy guns and sometimes real miniature guns to play with. Royal and aristocratic parents saw gun
play for their sons as a preparation for adult responsibilities, which would
almost certainly include military service. They reinforced their encourage-
ment by ordering portraits of their sons holding a firearm. Sharing that attitude, a couple of schools modified their curriculum to include training in
guns. Some families down the social scale may have wanted their sons to learn
about the new weapon through play with guns. One way or another, boys in
families of moderate or meager income had guns to play with. Child's play
with guns had a dark side: gun accidents touched many youths, and some
older children used guns in crime.

The relationship between guns and children has special value for a study
of gun culture. It offers an excellent measure of how adults viewed guns, of
how pervasive firearms were in society, and of how gun culture was transmitted across generations. It has been said that toys mirror a culture and offer
"cultural messages" that are "invariably revealing."[1] The thought is particularly
applicable to gun culture.

How did children learn about firearms? Children of all ranks who grew up
in the countryside were introduced to guns in much the same way. Those of
well-to-do aristocratic families were exposed to firearms that were in storage
or on display on their family's estate or perhaps hanging on the walls of their
homes as decoration. They would have seen or heard about guns from family
members and friends who were traveling to and from militia musters or war.
They would surely have seen adults using them in hunting or target shooting. If they lived in Sussex, Surrey, or Kent they possibly saw gun founders
and gunmakers at work. In like manner, young servants in these aristocratic
households, as well as the sons and daughters of yeomen, husbandmen, and

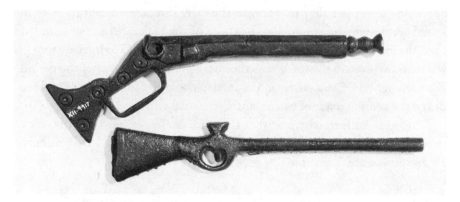

FIGURE 8. A matchlock toy musket (*top*), c. 1600, made of brass with original brass ramrod. (XII.9917 © Royal Armouries)

agricultural laborers on the manor, could have known about guns. Similarly, children who lived in or visited London, Birmingham, Bristol, and any other city in which gun founding and gunmaking took place would have had opportunities to notice the industry's workmen and to hear about gunpowder and gun accidents. They could also see and hear, surely with delight, the displays of fireworks and gun salutes that occurred with some regularity. In the normal process of growing up, children would have absorbed many things about the new weapon that, starting in the sixteenth century, was becoming an important part of English society.

In a more concrete way, children learned about firearms from the toy guns that they received as presents. Purchasing a toy gun was not difficult; they were readily available. The toy industry in London and elsewhere in England saw to that. A toy industry had developed "by at least 1300," although the word toy, meaning an object for children to play with, to amuse or instruct them, came later—in 1596. In the Middle Ages, toys became differentiated by gender.[2] Military toys were made for boys in the shape of the weapon of the period, and dolls for girls.[3] Medieval knights on horseback shifted in the seventeenth century to "small copies ... of firearms.[4] Geoff Egan, a Finds Specialist at the London Museum, maintained that "fireable hand guns and cannon, usually of copper-alloy, were the most widespread and popular of all early toys."[5] A toy musket with a fish-tail butt was a common example.

Members of the Worshipful Company of Gunmakers, however, did not profit from this new market, for they did not make toy guns as a sideline. Rather, it was artisans whose main business was making copper-alloy and pewter wares who saw the possibilities in producing toy cannon and pistols. These anonymous craftsmen are identified only by initials or a symbol. A toy

Guns and Child's Play

gun made of copper alloy probably in the early seventeenth century bore the initials R [1], which Egan took to be those of the maker.[6] Another man who used the initials IQ and, after he married, the initials IDQ to indicate that his wife was involved in the work, was the "most prolific toymaker of the period," Egan thought. IDQ was active in England in the late 1630s and 1640s and produced toy cannon made of pewter and decorated with leaves, spirals with arcs, and trefoils.[7] Unfortunately, neither the price of the toy guns nor the size of the toy business is known. The business, however, must have been profitable, for toy guns were popular.

Royal sons received military weapons, appropriate to their age, starting when they were very young. For example, in the thirteenth century, King Edward I (1239–1307) gave his five-year-old son Alfonzo a little castle and a tiny siege engine to play with. Two metal toy soldiers, each sitting on a horse and holding a sword, also date from the thirteenth century. Mass-produced, they were available to boys of artisanal families as well the well-to-do.[8] In the fifteenth century, King Henry VI (1421–1471) received eight arrows when he was five years old, and when he reached the age of seven, he was given a suit of armor. Prince Arthur, the elder son of King Henry VII, received a bow in 1492, but not a gun, even though his father was keenly interested in gunpowder weapons.[9] Interestingly, neither King Henry VIII nor his son King Edward VI (1537–1553) was given toy guns and as children did not play with toy firearms.[10] But James I's elder son, Prince Henry (1594–1612), learned "to shoot . . . in pieces [i.e., guns]" when he became interested in "manly exercises" at the age of "7, 8, 9 years" old, his tutor, Sir Charles Cornwallis, remembered.[11] The king's younger son, Prince Charles (the future King Charles I, 1600–1649), referred to "my pystolles" when he was five or six years old in a letter to his brother Henry.[12] Responding to an apparent request, Charles signed a letter (written in another hand) promising his "Sweit, sweit Brother" that he would send him the "pystolles" and "anie thing [else] that yow would hawe." Charles entrusted Henry's schoolmaster, "Maister Newton," with the delivery of the guns. In 1638 and 1639 when another Prince Charles, the future King Charles II (1630–1685), was eight or nine years old, the Foundry of London presented him with "a Train of ten Pieces of pretty little Cannon, neatly mounted on proper Carriages." The Foundry declared that the purpose of their gift was to give the Prince the materials "to practice the Art of Gunnery with."[13] Probably Charles's younger brother, James (later King James II [1633–1701]), was provided with a similar gift or, at least, played with Charles's guns and carriages.

It was almost sixty years later before another young prince was at court.

Prince William, Duke of Gloucester (1689–1700), the sickly son of Queen Anne, was fascinated with military things. From the time he was four or five years old, he played with a group of approximately ninety boys, including sons of court families, who dressed up and marched about as soldiers, and became known as "Gloucester's army." Brought up in a time of a war led by his uncle and namesake, King William III, young William avidly followed the campaigns and became, it is said, "obsessed with military matters."[14] At his tenth birthday in 1699, a contemporary poet, John Hughes (1678?–1720), celebrated his youthful warlike spirit. A poet, editor, and popular librettist, Hughes wrote "Song for the Duke of Gloucester's Birth-day 1699" in which Venus called upon Mars to "Form . . . his Mind to warlike Care." The song declared that William's "Childhood makes of War a Game" and that his "Beauty" charmed all "who burn with equal Flame for Him, as He for Arms."[15]

On the Continent, royal boys received even more elaborate gifts of guns and at an earlier age. As a little boy of three years, Louis XIII, King of France (1610–1643), received gifts of pistols, harquebuses, muskets, and cannon and began a lifelong love affair with firearms. His favorite playthings were his firearms, as recorded by Jean Heroard (Louis's physician) in a journal he kept of the boy's activities.[16] When he was three years old, Louis was allowed to fire a gun under supervision. He pinched his finger in the trigger, cried, and confessed that he was scared, but recovered himself and bravely pulled the trigger again. As an older boy, he liked nothing better than taking guns apart and putting them back together again. He became an excellent shot, successfully bringing down birds from his bedroom window. He also began collecting guns, and by the time he was fourteen years old, had assembled forty firearms, including Oriental as well as European examples.[17] Those guns formed the foundation of the magnificent collection that he completed as an adult.

As a child, the future king Louis XIV (1638–1715) was raised and schooled with twenty or so noble children, among them Louis Henri, the Count de Brienne. The count recalled in his memoirs that when the children played military games, Louis was the commander under whom they drilled, and that the boys gave him "little gifts such as swords, pistols, guns and miniature cannons of copper or other metals." De Brienne received from the king a harquebus which he treasured and carried every time the king went out for walks, so that, he explained, "I could fire it in front of him."[18] When Louis XIV became a father himself, he encouraged Monseigneur le Dauphin's interest in military matters by giving him an army of hand-painted soldiers, which comprised twenty squadrons of cavalry and ten battalions of infantry. This assemblage cost 6,000 francs. Later the king ordered a well-known silversmith to fashion the pieces in silver and include "guns and other machines of war."[19]

In the Holy Roman Empire, Archduke Maximilian (1459–1519), later the Holy Roman Emperor (1493–1519), received a toy cannon as a boy and is shown playing with it in a picture from Der Weisskunig. Another picture in that collection depicts him lighting the primer on a gun in preparation for shooting.²⁰ Russian children also played with guns. In 1664, King Charles II of England, through the agency of the English ambassador to Russia, Charles Howard, Earl of Carlisle, sent guns to the two sons of the Tsar. In addition, the earl, on his own behalf, presented the Tsarevich Feodor Alexeevich (1661–1682), who was three years old at the time, with "a hand-held zatinaya Harquebus" valued at twenty rubles.²¹ Grand Duke Alexey Alexeevich (1654–1670), then aged ten years, received a handheld rifled harquebus, also valued at twenty rubles. In the eighteenth century, the Empress Catherine the Great gave her beloved grandson, Grand Prince Alexander, a miniature gun.²² Early in life, then, little royal and noble boys in England and Europe learned that their parents approved of guns and that they were s suitable toys for them to play with.

If royal and noble parents encouraged their sons' interest in firearms by giving them guns, educators were negative, dismissive, or only mildly interested in teaching boys how to shoot and care for a gun as part of their education. Some printed treatises on the education of princes, such as Erasmus's *Institutio principis Christiani* (1516) or George More's *Principles for yong princes: Collected out of sundry authors* (1611), do not mention guns at all. Neither does Baldassare Castiglione in his *The Book of the Courtier*.²³ Sir Thomas Elyot went beyond silence and forthrightly decried the gun. In his *The Book Named the Governor* (1531), he charged England's "enemies" with bringing in "crossbows and hand guns" "to destroy the noble defence of archery." He had no interest in teaching youngsters to shoot a gun. In his view, the longbow offered much more "profit and pleasure above any other artillery."²⁴

Within about fifteen years, however, a subtle change was underway. In 1545, a year after King Henry VIII's success in using firearms at the siege of Boulogne, Roger Ascham (1515–1568), a Cambridge scholar and humanist, published his neo-Platonic dialogue, *Toxophilus the Schole of Shootinge Conteyned in Two Bookes*.²⁵ The word in the title, *Toxophilus*, meaning "lover of the bow" in Greek, put Ascham ostensibly on the side of the longbow, a position the court promoted erratically and publically, notwithstanding its behind-the-scenes emphasis on firearms. Hoping his book would win royal favor as well as a wide audience, Ascham dedicated it to Henry VIII and addressed it "To all Gentle Men and Yomen of Englande." He straddled the question of the relative value of gun and longbow, even as the court did. In a gesture to those persons favoring the longbow, he carefully listed the disadvantages of the gun, citing the cost, the weight, the "peryll of them that stand by [the gun]," and the ease in avoiding a bullet if one is "lytle" and at a distance from the shooter.[26] However, to placate the champions of firearms, he offered the thought that all weapons, including guns, should be used together as an "ayde and helpe for the other."[27] His position was a modest concession to gun lovers.

Twenty-five years later, however, in *The Scholemaster* (1570), Ascham wrote more expansively about the proper education for boys and the role of firearms in it. *The Scholemaster* set an ambitious goal for the education of "youth in [g]entlemen and noble men houses": the aim was nothing less than the creation of an educational system that mimicked that of classical Athens and Rome and sought to produce young men who were matchless in war and notable for their "worthiness, wisdom and learning." He recommended that noble and aristocratic boys be trained to handle and shoot guns as well as excel in other sports and skills. He painted a picture of boys learning "to ride [horseback] comely, to run fair at the tilt or ring, to play at all weapons, to shoot fair in bow or surely in gun."[28] He had come to believe that guns were needed to defend one's country.[29] The change in Ascham's attitude in 1570 is a measure of the steady acceptance of the gun as a weapon in war and a device used in many domestic activities.

The record of reprints of Roger Ascham's *The Scholemaster*—four between 1571 and 1589, another one in 1711—shows its popularity. The extended title of *The Scholemaster* stated that it was "specially purposed for the priuate bringing vp youth in ientlemen and noble men houses." However, aristocratic parents whose boys were tutored privately at the family's estate in the country would not have needed *The Scholemaster* to persuade them to teach their sons to shoot with a bow and a gun. Such training would have been provided as a matter of course in such a context.

On the other hand, the tract would have reinforced the decision that a couple of schools for well-to-do boys made to include shooting with a gun in their curricula. The Lincoln Grammar School hired an ex-soldier from the Low Countries to teach its students how to shoot well.[30] The school advertised that when not at their books, their pupils did not play at "childish sports," but rather "exercised in all their military postures, and in assaults and defences." Lincoln Grammar School required their students to bring their own firearms, thereby forcing them into a close relationship with their gun. Another school, The Free School at Chipping Campden, demonstrated its seriousness of purpose by collecting firearms for its own arsenal. Including guns in their educational program further legitimated firearms in the minds of young boys. It was still another way in which guns were embedded in the lives of youngsters and their potential danger veiled. On the other hand, a more famous and highly regarded school, Shrewsbury, did not include in its curriculum learning to shoot and care for a gun.[31]

The Artillery Gardens in London and in other cities and towns provided sons of merchant and middling-rank families an opportunity to learn how to handle and shoot a gun.[32] The Artillery Gardens were originally established for men to learn military arts, but in the early seventeenth century, they opened their facilities to youths. Imitating their elders, boys between the ages of nine and seventeen formed themselves into companies, picked officers, practiced with weapons that had been cut down to half-size so that they could manage them, and marched around in the Artillery field on holidays to show off their expertise.[33] In one of his poems, Ben Jonson recommended that great men send their sons to school at the London Artillery yard to "show 'hem the use of Guns; and there instruct the noble English heires / In Politique and Military Affaires."[34] Similar programs for young men were developed in the counties. King James I encouraged such efforts by attending their exercises, and King Charles I continued this practice. Youths in Chichester impressed Charles I with their expertise in a performance prepared for him. They also persuaded him to provide them with more gunpowder. Interest in providing instruction in how to shoot a gun continued. In 1665, Capt. James Roch, adjutant of the Guards, submitted a petition for a licence to set up an academy "to teach the exercise of shooting and other arms," not only to English subjects but also people of other nations.[35]

Royal and aristocratic parents expressed further approval of guns for their boys by arranging for them to be painted with a firearm or shown dressed for battle. In England in 1638, Sir Anthony Van Dyck (with help from his studio) painted a portrait of the future King Charles II as a boy of eight years old, dressed in armor with a helmet in his left hand and a gun in his right. It is the first portrait in English art of an English monarch as a child to be painted with a gun.[36] The young Charles looks straight at the viewer with a determined gaze. This portrait was a powerful piece of propaganda: it depicted the prince as a boy soldier upholding his father's side in the Civil War.

Charles fulfilled the message of the portrait, for when he was twelve years old, his tutor (Dr. William Harvey [1578–1657]), a physician and discoverer of the circulation of the blood) took him and his brother James to witness the Battle of Edgehill. There, it is said, Charles declared himself unafraid of the Parliamentary forces, brandished his pistol, and threatened to charge. A Royalist captain arrived just in time to restrain him from engaging in the fight.[37] King Charles I apparently wanted both his sons to identify with guns, for a year later in 1639 Cornelius Johnson painted a portrait of Charles's younger brother James (the future James II) at the age of six years, holding a gun.[38]

FIGURE 9. King Charles II, as a boy of eight holding a pistol,
by Sir Anthony Van Dyck and studio, 1638.
(© National Portrait Gallery, London)

A nobleman, Ambrose Dudley, Third Earl of Warwick, who served as Master of the Ordnance from 1560 to 1589, was also painted with a child holding a firearm. Executed by an unknown artist, the portrait shows Dudley standing outside a military tent resting his left hand on the shoulder of a young boy who is holding a helmet in his left hand and a pistol in his right.[39] The picture implies that Dudley is both proud and fond of the youngster, and that the boy is prepared with helmet and gun bravely to accompany him into battle.

In the next century, James Cecil, Fourth Earl of Salisbury (1666–1694), was represented in a charming, if startling, domestic scene. He is shown as a two-year-old boy, still in a long dress, sitting near his five-year-old sister Catherine, who is wearing a beautiful gown with leading strings. In this delightful rendering of childhood, a pistol is lying at James's feet. Critics of the painting do not know whether the pistol was a real gun or a toy and wonder what it meant.[40] Arguably, the gun was intended to symbolize a future military career for the youngster. Whatever the case, the gun is given a place with these two sweet, innocent-looking children, and, in such a context, the dangers inherent in a firearm are neutralized.

On the Continent, in Denmark, in 1615, Pieter Isaacsz, a Dutch painter at the court of Christian IV, portrayed the six-year-old Prince Frederik (later Frederik III) as a musketeer. The little boy holds a musket in his left hand and flourishes his hat with his right hand. The picture seems to say that the youngster is preparing to defend the land and the castle in the background. Between 1616 and 1620, Isaacsz painted another portrait of Frederik, now a little older and standing in front of cannon holding a pike in his right hand. Painting a prince with a pike, a weapon associated with the infantry, symbolized that the prince was willing to fight with his men, thereby learning their strengths and weaknesses and making himself into a better military leader. The portrait, then, sent a strong political message about the young prince. At about the same time, Isaacsz painted Duke Ulrik, Frederic's younger brother. This little boy is standing next to a mortar and is gripping a musket in the same drill position as Frederik, but with the difference that the view is from the left.[41] These three portraits were effective propaganda in showing the preparation of the young Danish princes for the military role they would play in later life.

An unknown artist of the Flemish School painted the portrait of the young son of Elizabeth of Bohemia, Frederick Henry (1614–1629), in about 1616. The two-year-old wears an elaborately woven dress featuring a motif of olive branches and a large standing collar of intricate lace. With his right hand, the child is playing with a toy cannon. The symbolism of olive branch and cannon suggests that the little boy is learning the "virtue of ruling wisely" in peace and war when he becomes king.[42]

In Spain, Velásquez painted a series of portraits of the heir to the throne, Baltasar Carlos (1629–1646), the son of King Philip IV and Isabella of Bourbon (his first wife), showing him with "his ponies, dogs and guns."[43] The portrait of the boy at the age of ten depicts the youngster in full military array, gloved in elaborate gauntlets, with a baton in his right hand, and golden spurs on his ankles. The boy is ready for battle; he is anticipating his adult responsibilities. The picture was sent to England for a political reason—to promote a marriage with the Princess Mary.

We may be sure that English boys from middling and plebeian families liked toy guns as much as wealthy children, and that they played with them, even though direct evidence is slim. Egan's remark (noted above)—that "fireable hand guns and cannon . . . were the most widespread and popular of all early toys" found in the mud of the River Thames—provides the strongest support.

FigURE 10. Prince Frederick Henry of the Palatinate (King James I's grandson), Flemish School, c. 1616. With his right hand, the child plays with a toy cannon. (RCIN 403511, Royal Collection Trust / © Her Majesty Queen Elizabeth II 2015)

Samuel Rowlands's *Satyre 4* is no more than suggestive, but still worth mentioning. Rowlands (a well-known satirist) imagines a young man who inherits his father's money. Mocking people who covet the money, he writes

> Man I dare challenge thee to throw the Sledge,
> To iumpe, or leape ouer Ditch or Hedge;
> To pich the Barre, or to shoote off a Gunne.[44]

Including shooting of a gun among everyday sports such as running and jumping suggests that shooting was also a regular sport. One may also invoke common sense about the nature of childhood to buttress the idea that children down the social scale played with toy guns.

As children grew older, the popularity of guns became certain, as illustrated by stories about boys in "play-fights." In Cornwall in 1548, a time of "religious unrest," the youngsters of Bodmin School prepared for a play-fight by dividing themselves into Catholic believers on the one hand and Protestant adherents on the other. When the ruckus was in full swing, an ingenious boy fired a "gun" that he had contrived by shoving gunpowder down a hollow candlestick. The headmaster was so appalled by this behavior that he whipped the child with a birch branch.[45] One may guess that the punishment did not destroy the child's obvious interest in guns. In another instance, in 1554, five years after Wyatt's Rebellion, about three hundred boys assembled in Finsbury Fields just outside London to replay the event, some choosing the queen's side, some Wyatt's side. Some boys were wounded by gunfire, which proved the presence of guns. Again, the authorities were aghast, arresting most of the boys and imprisoning them in the Guildhall.[46]

Finally, some boys on the cusp of adulthood became involved in highway robbery with guns. A gang consisting "of 8 or 9 young fellows [with] one old thief amongst them" used guns to harass, rob, and shoot at travelers on the highways "between London and Islington, Hampstead and Highgate." Young and indiscreet, they bragged in public about their successes, and, when they left London to live secretly in Windsor "for a while," they were overtaken, arrested in a public house, and jailed to await trial. Among them was the sixteen-year-old son of a "Tradesman" in Newgate-Market. The boy "had a Pistol about him" and offered a frank assessment of how he viewed it. He said that "he valued [the pistol] above all Things."[47]

Gun accidents touched children in all ranks of society except royal families. When a royal boy was given a gun, his nurses and tutors faced the heart-stopping possibility that the child might injure himself or others in handling it. However, apparently the supervision was so careful that gun accidents were avoided, for there is no surviving evidence that a royal boy suffered harm from playing with a gun. I found only one incident involving an aristocratic boy and a gun. This event occurred in December 1688, as the Revolution of 1688–89 was underway. A young Catholic boy named Peters, who was related to the Earl of Essex and served as an apprentice to a Mr. Manock of London, also a Catholic, brandished a gun while declaring that he "meant to kill the Prince of Orange." Peters was arrested along with another apprentice (whose actions were not explained), and the two children were sent to prison. Although someone secured a writ of habeas corpus for the boys, they were not released because the judge set the bail too high for them to meet. Roger Morrice reported that "the great lawyer" approved of what was done, saying that the law was satisfied and the prisoners were secured.[48] His comment suggests that the imprisonment of the boys was to protect them. Probably the close supervision of aristocratic as well as royal children prevented tragic gun incidents.

There is no evidence that girls played with the guns that boys in their circle of family and friends possessed, but given the nature of childhood and the fact that some young women used guns later suggests that they probably did. If so, they were either very lucky or extremely careful, for there is also no evidence that a little girl caused a gun accident. Girls were, however, victims of gun accidents. In a previous chapter, the story was recounted of a hunting accident in which a girl of nine years was shot to death by adult hunters. Young boys also accidentally killed young girls. In 1640, a thirteen-year-old boy, Daniel Fyme, who was employed as a servant in Robert Wilkins's household, used the butt end of a gun to rekindle a fire. Unaware that the gun was charged with powder and hail shot, he pulled up the cock, the gun discharged, and Mary Wilkins, a relative of his master, was killed by a shot to her breast.[49] In another incident in 1688, in London in the Parish of St. Paul's Covent Garden, John Pitts, a boy about eleven years old, and a "Maid," Martha Fryday, were together in a room where some pistols lay on a table. John picked up one and aimed it at Martha, as if to shoot her. As youngsters sometimes do, Martha laid him a bet of 6 pence that he could not shoot her. At this John "shot her dead": the bullet entered her right cheek and penetrated six inches deep. He was tried for murder, but the verdict was "Chance-medly."[50] In 1729 at Canterbury, a nine-year-old boy was examining a fowling piece. It accidentally discharged, and the bullet struck a girl of twelve in the side of the forehead and killed her.[51]

Babies were spared neither gun nor gunpowder accidents. An incident involving a one-year-old boy occurred in Chelmsford, Essex, in late June 1640. Ursula Clerke, a servant of the child's father, was seated in the hall of an inn, holding the baby in her arms. Alexander Brooke, a tailor from the town, came into the hall and, spotting a fowling piece hanging by the chimney, took it down to examine. Not knowing that it was loaded, he "did pull up the cocke," the gun discharged, and a "leaden pellet" struck the baby on the forehead and penetrated his brain. The verdict was "By misfortune."[52]

A baby girl was involved in a gunpowder accident in London in 1647. The incident occurred along Tower Street across from Barking Church: as some people were packing gunpowder into barrels the powder caught fire and caused a tremendous explosion. The fire destroyed fifty to sixty houses in the area, but spared Barking Church. The next day a cradle with a baby girl inside was found on the uppermost leads of the church. Miraculously, the child was unharmed. The baby was orphaned by the explosion, and a man of the parish raised the little girl. John Stow recorded that he met the girl when she was about eighteen years old.[53] Although babies were unlikely to be killed or injured by gunfire or gunpowder accidents, they were not immune from the dangers.

Male servants and apprentices suffered the trauma that came from accidentally killing their fellow workers and friends. These incidents happened all around the British Isles. A "very melancholy accident" was reported that took place in Edinburgh on December 26, 1728, when a fowling piece a boy was "handling unskillfully," "went off and killed two of his comrades."[54] The next year in Dublin, a boy ten or twelve years old "unfortunately" killed a child eight years old when a fowling piece they were playing with discharged, shooting the younger boy in the head.[55] Apparently, these two stories captured the interest of the reading public, or more to the point, captured publishers' attention and inspired their feeling that the stories would sell their newspapers, for the tales were reported in several papers.

In England, among other such incidents,[56] fourteen-year-old Richard Best was walking along a road toward his house in February 1647 carrying a loaded gun, when George Nash, his "fellow scholar," came walking toward him. Best's gun accidentally went off, killing Nash on the spot.[57] Another equally sad but rather different kind of accident occurred in London almost thirty years later, in mid-June 1676. This one involved a "little Boy about Twelve Years of Age" who had just come to London to take up a post as an apprentice in a shop in Fleet Street.[58] The child found his master's musket (which the latter had used that day in mustering with the Trained Bands of London) lying on the dining room table. Wanting to play at being a soldier like his master, the boy picked up the gun, shoved the gun stick into the barrel, and shook some loose gunpowder into the priming pan. At this point, his mistress called him and he rushed off to do whatever task she had for him. When he returned to the dining room, he again picked up the gun and, forgetting that the gun stick was still in the barrel, went to the window and fired the gun at random towards the outside. Unfortunately, an old man was walking along the street below and the gun stick, driven by the power of the powder, hit him in his back, a "little below the left shoulder." He died before he could be taken into a nearby shop. Unaware of the accident, the young boy was very worried that his master would scold him for losing the gun stick. He was completely unprepared when a group of people, who had witnessed the accident and identified the window from which the shot came, entered the house and confronted him. When told what had happened, the child became distraught. The law required that he be arrested and brought to trial. The jury concluded that, because the boy had fired the gun "premeditatedly and voluntarily," they had no choice but to bring in a verdict of manslaughter. Still, they recognized that the killing of the old man was accidental. Further details of what happened to the little boy were not reported, but because the original lengthy court account of the trial began by describing the lad as "an object of Pitty," perhaps his punishment was not severe.

The most tragic story about boys and guns was reported in the *Daily Post* on 28 July 1720 and involved an emotionally deranged adult in Dublin, the father of two boys aged ten and twelve.[59] The father, a Major Johnston, returned home and found his two sons playing in the parlor. He handed each one a fully loaded pistol and commanded them to shoot each other. When they refused to do so, the Major turned on them with his sword drawn and said that if they did not shoot as he commanded, he would "run them through." At this, one of the boys shot the other dead. Hearing the noise, their mother came running down the stairs into the room, whereupon the Major stabbed her and then himself. Both died later of their wounds. The story leaves so many things untold: why the father was emotionally deranged, why he targeted his sons, why he killed his wife, why he committed suicide, and what happened to the little boy who killed his brother with a gun because his father threatened to kill both boys with a sword if he did not do so. It invites readers to construct their own versions of what happened and why.

Early modern children learned early in life about the excitement and fun of guns. Parents and friends of all social standing (except perhaps the abject poor) showed their approval of firearms by giving boys authentic toy guns and sometimes real toy guns complete with gunpowder and shot. Monarchs and nobles chose children's guns as diplomatic gifts to fellow monarchs and nobles. Royal and aristocratic parents had their children painted with a firearm. The curriculum in at least two schools for the well-to-do was modified to make room for instruction in how to shoot a gun, as reformers recommended. The military yards offered boys and youth of less wealthy families an opportunity to learn about and practice shooting a gun. Such developments made firearms seem less dangerous and lethal than they actually were. Boys in the lower ranks of society were occasionally involved in gun crime. Except for royal and aristocratic sons, neither boys nor girls were immune from gun and gunpowder accidents. In short, guns were embedded in the lives of children. The relationships between guns and children became an integral part of the gun culture that developed over the era. Equally important, it was central in the process of transmitting civilian gun culture across the generations.

TEN · An Individual
Right to Arms?

The Bill of Rights (1689)

HE REVOLUTION OF 1688–89 (also known as the Glorious Revolution) marked a climax in the development of England's domestic
gun culture. Over a period of some weeks in January and February
1689, the Convention, a body irregularly elected to settle the crisis, debated
the grievances as well as the ancient rights of the nation and wrote one of
England's iconic constitutional documents, the Declaration of Rights, better
known in its statutory form as the Bill of Rights. A momentous event, its
course briefly described below, the Revolution gave England new monarchs,
King William III and Queen Mary II, formerly Prince William and Princess
Mary of Orange, and a new kingship in which political authority was shifted
to Parliament and new rights were declared.[1] One of those new rights, never
before claimed, was the right of the individual to arms, which was set out in
Article VII of the Declaration and Bill of Rights. That Article read: "That the
Subjects which are Protestants may have Armes for their defence Suitable
to their Condition and as allowed by law?" The intention of the men who
drafted Article VII and the meaning of its language are at issue today. This
chapter attends to these matters.

On 29 January 1689, Anthony Cary, Lord Falkland, a Tory member of the
House of Commons of the Convention, rose to address the assembly, which
was beginning a second day of serious work. In a short speech filled with
radical implications, Falkland urged the assembly not to think about filling
the throne until they had decided "what Power ... to give the Crown ... and
what not." The Prince of Orange has rescued us from Popery, he said, and now
we have the opportunity to "secure ourselves from Arbitrary Government."
Pressing his point later in debate, Falkland urged the need "to change things
as well as hands," to "lay the foundations" of the government anew.[2] This step

supported by both Whig and Tory members initiated discussions of the nation's liberties and rights. Tense negotiations in and between the two houses of the Convention and with William Prince of Orange ensued as members sought to settle who should be England's monarch and at the same time agree to a statement claiming the nation's alleged ancient liberties that included, for the first time in English history, a right to possess arms.

It took the political turmoil of the Revolution of 1688–89 to open up the question. As this book has shown, as far back in history as written records go, English monarchs have sought to control weapons (whatever their nature) and to limit their ownership, possession, and use to persons of a certain wealth. At no time prior to 1689 did anyone in print claim the right of English subjects to arms. The idea lacks historical, political, and legal precedent. The Petition of Right of 1628 did not mention it, nor did radical groups, such as the Levellers and the Diggers, that sprang up during the Civil War. Reformers at the time of the Exclusion Crisis (1678–83) did not claim it.[3] Neither did radical Whigs in the later seventeenth century.[4] Men who aimed to influence members of the 1689 Convention by printing tracts and pamphlets did not refer to it.[5] No one sought to remove the terms of the Game Act of 1671 in the 1689 debates. What happened to lead men who drafted Article VII to include it? The main narrative of the Revolution that follows holds clues.[6]

When King Charles II died in 1685 without leaving a legitimate heir, his Roman Catholic brother, James, Duke of York, ascended the throne as King James II. Few objections were raised, remarkably enough in view of the fervent but unsuccessful attempt just five years earlier to exclude him from the succession to the Crown because of his Catholicism. Then, the most significant protest came from James, Duke of Monmouth, the illegitimate son of King Charles II. Handsome, Protestant, and popular in western England, Monmouth led a rebellion that swept through western England in June 1685.[7] James II defeated the uprising with an army of which 10 percent of the commissioned officers were Catholic, a blatant violation of the Test Act of 1673.[8] That law required all political and military officers to take an oath denying transubstantiation, thereby protecting Protestants by assuring that no genuine Catholic could hold political or military office. In disregarding the law, James misused the royal dispensing power, his critics charged. A member of the 1685 Parliament declared that for army officers "to be employed not taking the Tests, is dispensing with all the Laws at once."[9] He implied that James had assumed the power to "dispense" with or cancel any law that he pleased. Fueling the increasing fear that James intended to disarm and replace Protestants with Catholics, in 1686 the king encamped his army on Hounslow Heath just outside of London. The army could be seen there, menacing the capital.

At the same time, similar events in Ireland prefigured what English subjects might expect: Richard Talbot, Earl of Tyrconnel (1630–1691), long James II's friend, used force to disarm Protestant officers, hand over their weapons to Catholics, and replace them with Catholics. A contemporary was certain that James's putting Irish Catholics "into Power and displacing Protestants to make room for them" was the king's worse mistake.[10]

While these issues festered, the new king's detractors took comfort from the thought that James was old (he was fifty-five), not in robust health, and was probably unable to father a healthy child. Besides, his second queen, the Catholic Mary of Modena, was apparently infertile. He had married her following the death of his first (Protestant) wife, Anne, the mother of his two Protestant daughters, Mary and Anne. He had no living sons. His elder daughter, Mary, the wife of Prince William of Orange, the leader of Protestants on the Continent, was first in line to the English throne upon her father's death. Therefore, James's successor would be a Protestant. But to the astonishment of observers, James's wife became pregnant in the fall of 1687, and the birth of a healthy baby boy on 10 June 1688 voided such pleasing assumptions. England now faced the probability of an unending succession of Catholic monarchs. Doubt was cast on the birth, as it had been on the pregnancy. Scurrilous rumors circulated that the baby boy was supposititious and had been brought into the queen's bed in a warming pan.[11] On 30 June 1688, in a stunning act of treason against their anointed king, the so-called Immortal Seven, Protestant leaders in church and state, sent a letter of invitation to Prince William of Orange, asking him to come to England and rescue the nation.[12] No specific role for the Prince was indicated. William, who was James II's nephew as well as his son-in-law and thus had his own place in the succession, accepted, assembled a fleet, and, undeterred by the failure of his first attempt to launch it because of bad weather, succeeded on the second try. He landed with an army of 15,000 men at Torbay in Devon on 5 November 1688. In December, James, suffering from nose bleeds, his nerves shattered, his propaganda campaign of tracts and pamphlets and overtures to leaders of the Church of England and to Dissenters unsuccessful, abandoned by his younger daughter Anne and by army and navy officers, and confronting the hostile presence of his elder daughter Mary and the army of his son-in-law William, sent his wife and their baby son to France. On a second attempt to escape himself, this one aided and abetted by the Prince of Orange, James successfully fled England, following his wife and son to the Court of Louis XIV.[13]

The English nation now faced an extraordinary situation. However they were interpreted, the plain facts were that their lawful king was in France, a Dutch army led by a foreign prince occupied their land, and a vacancy in the crown existed. To fill the throne was of paramount importance, but opinion as to who should do so was not unanimous. Some partisans rallied to the Prince, wanting him to rule alone; some people clung to James; others favored placing Mary on the throne alone; still others wanted Mary and William to rule together. On one thing, however, English leaders and the Prince of Orange agreed: they wanted a parliament to be summoned to take the lead in resolving these problems. Accordingly, a body as close to a regular parliament as they could come, was elected during three weeks in January 1689 and was called a Convention, as we saw at the beginning of this chapter.[14] This, then, is the broad political and religious background of the Declaration of Rights and Article VII.

In the debate following Lord Falkland's initiative, members canvassed many grievances, ranging widely over what they regarded as the arbitrary actions of King Charles II as well as King James II. In this discussion, they said nothing about arms and the right of the individual to possess them. At the end of the day (29 January), members appointed a "Rights Committee" to consider the points they had raised. On 2 February, the Rights Committee presented its first report.[15] Entitled "Heads of Grievances," the report identified twenty-three wrongs that the nation had suffered, three of which were military issues.[16] Head 5 declared that "the Acts concerning the Militia are grievous to the Subject." Head 6 held that the "raising or keeping a Standing Army within this Kingdom in time of Peace, unless it be with the Consent of Parliament, is against Law." Head 7 stated that "it is necessary for the public Safety, that the Subjects, which are Protestants, should provide and keep Arms for their common Defence; and that the arms which have been seized, and taken from them be restored." This extraordinary statement underwent substantial revision.

The prefatory statement, "it is necessary to the public safety," was dropped. No evidence is available to explain why, but probably the Prince of Orange objected because the words implied that he was unable to protect the nation. The first qualifier in the Article "Protestants" required no change. Limiting arms to Protestants mirrored a national fear and loathing of Roman Catholics that existed at least since the sixteenth-century Protestant Reformation. This deeply negative attitude intensified when Pope Pius V excommunicated Queen Elizabeth I in 1570. A yearly church service of thanksgiving for the timely discovery of the Gunpowder Plot of 1605 nourished it. The Popish Plot of 1678–83, aimed at elevating a Catholic to the English throne, had sharpened it further. A member of the House of Commons, Henry Pollexfen, well expressed the nation's anti-Catholic prejudice when he declared in debate, "Popery is the fear of the nation."[17] Actually in all the laws and proclamations regarding limiting weapons after the English Reformation, the word Protestant had not appeared. Article VII brought it forward for the first time.

Members made further changes to this first version of Head 7. The tense of the verb in "Subjects should provide and keep Arms" was changed to "may" so that the sentence read "Subjects may provide and keep Arms." The record is silent about the reasons for this revision, but it may be that "should have arms" implied that every Protestant had a right to arms, a proposition unacceptable to the Prince and the House of Lords.[18] The word "may" avoided the exhortatory sense of "should," and made the Article an allowance rather than a right.

Another issue was the meaning of the word "Armes" that Protestant subjects were allowed. According to the *Oxford English Dictionary*, the origin of the English word "Armes" was Latin *arma* and French *armes*. There is no singular. The *OED* editor defined the word as "defensive and offensive outfits for war," "things used in fighting," "instruments of offence used in war," and "weapons." Garry Wills noted that the Latin word "arma" is etymologically war "equipment."[19] Thus, according to the etymological meaning of the word and the definition in the *OED*, "armes" means weapons used for war and in fighting. As Wills wittily put it, one does not use "arms" to shoot a rabbit. Or, one may add, to bring down birds; for that sport, you use a birding gun. Arms for war and fighting are the constitutional right that Article VII guaranteed.

The bill disarming Catholics in March 1689, written just a month after Article VII was devised, adds understanding to the etymological evidence. That bill, *An Act for the better securing the Government by disarming Papists and reputed Papists*, stripped individual Catholics of all "armes, weapons, gunpowder, or Ammunition."[20] However, it left the individual Catholic "such necessary Weapons as shall be allowed to him by Order of the Justices of the Peace . . . for the Defence of his House or Person." In debate on the Act, John Maynard expressed the thought that Catholics should bring their "firearms in, unless for the necessary defence of their Houses."[21] Evidently, members of the Convention were sensitive to the natural and common law right of self-defense and did not deny it. They were aware of the need for weapons in rural communities to protect a person from animal and human predators. Probably they felt that sufficient safeguards were in place to neutralize danger from Catholics' possessing a weapon. Those protections included the imposition of an Oath of Allegiance, the requirement that the justice of the peace decide what weapons were allowed, and the understanding that if the weapon were a gun, the individual must meet the legal qualifications for possessing and using it. The pertinent point is that the act for the better securing the government and the ensuing discussion make it clear that armes and the weapon allowed for personal defense were two different things. Further reinforcing this idea is language in a letter from King Charles II to John Egerton, Second Earl of Bridgewater, dated 19 December 1660.[22] The king wrote that the court had "certain knowledge" that "persons of Loose Principles and knowne disaffection to us and our government" were so heavily armed that they must intend an uprising. He instructed Bridgewater to employ the militia to seize "any quantity [of "arms"] ... discovered in a house ... above what may reasonably be believed necessary for [the person's] safeguard and defence." Here, too, "Arms" are differentiated from what weapon an individual might need for personal defense.

As the negotiations over the document proceeded, the Rights Committee submitted a second draft that grouped the Heads into two categories: one of issues requiring new law, the other of issues reaffirming old law.[23] This step settled the fate of the three military Heads. Head 5, concerning the militia, was placed in the category requiring new law accompanied by a demand for "repealing the Acts concerning the Militia, and settling it anew." This move was probably (no evidence exists) a compromise between the two Houses. The House of Lords apparently felt that the language of Head 5 was "too generally expressed" and specifically feared that the lords-lieutenant would be unduly restricted. The lower house, wanting to avoid a break with the Lords, agreed.[24] A later decision eliminated the issues that required new law and, therefore, militia reform disappeared from the document.

Members placed Head 6 condemning standing armies in peacetime without the consent of Parliament in the category of issues that reaffirmed old law. They did so knowing that Head 6 made new law. At the Restoration when Oliver Cromwell's army was disbanded, the Disbanding Act specifically allowed the king to raise and maintain as many soldiers as he wished, so long as he paid them.[25] Further, the Militia Act of 1661 declared in emphatic language that "the sole Supreme Command and Disposition of the Militia" as well as "of all Forces by Sea and Land ... is and by the Lawes of England ever was the undoubted Right of His Majesty." The Parliament "may not pretend" to such authority.[26] To say that the king required the consent of the Parliament to raise and keep forces in peacetime was simply not true. Head 7 granting to Protestants the right to arms was also placed in the category of issues reaffirming old law. This, too, was untrue; the right was not old law.

From 9 February through 12 February, the House of Lords, assisted by a thirteen-member committee dominated by peers friendly to William, amended the draft document sent by the House of Commons.[27] They deleted the word "Common" from the phrase "their Common defence" so that it read "their defence." Records explaining this change have not survived. Joyce

Malcolm argued that removing the word was part of a "shift away from the private ownership of arms as a political duty and towards a right to have arms for individual defence."[28] This idea rests on her thesis that the old medieval duty to be ready with a weapon to assist the community in law enforcement was transformed into a right in 1689.[29] However, the fact is that the medieval duty was no longer viable in 1689. Laws, Privy Council orders, and technological change had overtaken it. The Militia Acts of 1558 set out detailed terms for militia service according to the wealth of the individual, without reference to this duty. Orders by Queen Elizabeth and her Council created the Trained Bands, a select militia, whose arms, training and duties were carefully spelled out. For years, laws and proclamations limited the possession and use of arms to persons of a certain annual income, usually set at £100. The idea that a medieval duty of all men to keep their own arms to protect their community was transformed into a right is inadmissible because no such idea was mentioned in the Convention debates, nor alluded to in the tract literature of the period. In my view, it is more likely that the Lords dropped the word "Common" because Prince William and his friends objected to the implication that Protestant subjects, rather than he, were responsible for the "common defence" of the realm.

The lords added two phrases: "Suitable to their Condition," and "as allowed by law," so that now Article VII read that "Protestant subjects may have Armes for their defence Suitable to their Condition and as allowed by law."[30] Both of these new phrases linked Article VII to restrictions on gun possession and use that were part of England's early modern gun culture. The words "Suitable to their condition" referred to the socioeconomic condition of the subject that, according to laws and proclamations, was necessary for him to own, possess, and use a gun. The amendment assured that persons whose annual income was inadequate did not win the right to have arms.

The phrase "Suitable to their condition" reminds us that the legal limitations placed on the possession and use of guns by subjects according to their annual income reflected the hierarchical nature of early modern English society. That society was shaped by titles, social gradations, status, and wealth. The social and economic prejudices of aristocratic English society had not suddenly changed in 1689. Members of the House of Lords and the House of Commons continued to embrace them. Indeed, the rampaging of a Protestant mob in London in December 1688, which had caused property and personal damage,[31] may have strengthened commitment of Members of Parliament to limiting arms to subjects "suitable to their condition." An exchange in a debate in the House of Commons further illustrates how the members regarded persons lower in the social scale. For political reasons, a member remarked that the Convention represented no more than a "4th part of the Nation," that "freeholders under 40 shillings a year & all Copyholders, & women & Children & Servants" have no share in Parliamentary elections. This comment met with indignant rejoinders, one member protesting "we represent the people fully" and speak for those that have a share in government—"or are fit to have a share in it."[32] The response encapsulated the socially conservative view that was at the heart of linking the possession of arms with wealth, "suitable to their condition."

Furthermore, the papers of two members of the Convention revealed like sentiments. Thomas Erle (c.1650–1720) spelled out his ideas in a manuscript entitled "Paper of Instructions for the Parliament Meeting after the Revolution" that was probably written in early December 1688.[33] There should be no standing army, Erle wrote, and no English monarch should have more guards than Queen Elizabeth I, King James I, or King Charles I. The nation should rely on the militia, which should be reformed to make a standing army unnecessary. Reform would also prevent an arbitrary monarch from using the militia for corrupt purposes. Only persons of wealth should be eligible to serve in a militia; since they had something to lose, they could be trusted. Substantial property holders in towns and cities should be provided with a "good musket" to protect the nation against invasion.[34] Erle's views are similar to those of members of the Convention.

Philip Wharton, Fourth Baron Wharton (1613–1696), a Whig member of the House of Lords, also left papers setting out his ideas on remodeling the government, including the militia.[35] Among the points he made was that only freeholders who had an annual income of at least £20 or held a copyhold for life of £30 should serve in the militia. Equating arms and property is a basic assumption in Wharton's thought. Neither he nor Erle believed in an unrestricted individual right to arms. Thus, in both debate and surviving papers, members of the Convention made clear that a qualification for Protestants to have a gun was their social status and economic condition.

The House of Lords insisted on adding another phrase—"as allowed by law"—which further qualified Protestant subjects' right to arms. The phrase carried two meanings. First, it summoned memory of all the old laws and proclamations going back centuries that had restricted the possession and use of a weapon according to income. The latest game law, passed in 1671, was the most restrictive law of all. Some members of the Convention had been closely connected with passing that law eighteen years before. Four members of the "Rights Committee" in the House of Commons had initiated it, and three members of the House of Lords' "Rights Committee" had served on the committee to which the Bill was referred.[36] Besides, members of both houses were generally concerned because of their socioeconomic status to preserve their game and hunting privileges and to fear the threat posed to property and person of placing arms in the hands of all Protestants. At the same time, the phrase underscored the lawmaking role of Parliament in the future. It said that Parliament, or more properly "King-in-Parliament," the nation's principal law-making body, had the authority to regulate which Protestants might have guns in the future.[37] The words underscored the power of the law and of Parliament's law-making authority in the past, the present, and the future. The terms of Article VII and of the other articles in the Declaration of Rights were subject to the overarching authority of Parliament.

These two amendments to Head 7 moved Malcolm to confess, "it is difficult to decide what to make of the new clauses tacked to the end of the article." Postulating that the Game Act of 1671 might still be in force (it was), she admitted that then "the right to have firearms would be a right merely for the wealthy." Recognizing that the militia acts were also still in force, she concluded that "the assertion of a guaranteed right for Protestants to have arms seems empty rhetoric . . . just so much fine-sounding verbiage." However, she concluded that "practical politics" accounted for the addition of the two clauses and decided that "the arms article declared a right that current law negated, with the understanding that future legislation would eliminate the discrepancy."[38] By the early eighteenth century, laws and court decisions guaranteed that all Protestants had "the right to bear arms."[39] There is not a shred of evidence of such an "understanding" in the debates. Nor is there evidence that an effort was made to revise the Declaration of Rights after it was drafted, nor to amend the Bill of Rights.

In the meantime, on 12 February the House of Commons accepted the changes made by the House of Lords. All that remained was to prepare a ceremony.[40] The Declaration of Rights was inscribed on parchment (which was given marks of importance), and the next day the document was carried in a splendid procession from Westminster to the Banqueting Hall of Whitehall Palace. There it was presented to and accepted by Prince William and Princess Mary of Orange, who were proclaimed King and Queen.[41] Ten months later, on 16 December, after months of debate and amendment of some sections, but not of Article VII, the Declaration of Rights was transformed into law, the Bill of Rights. Article VII, with all the other sections of the document, became the law of the land and took on statutory authority.

What was the fate of Article VII and the early modern gun culture that it embodied? Was the language changed to clarify its meaning? Did "early eighteenth-century legislation and court interpretation" make it clear that "an individual right to bear arms belonged to all Protestants," as has been claimed?[42] How did laws and court rulings play out?

The Convention had been transformed into the Convention Parliament at the end of February 1689,[43] and members were now sitting to take up the pressing issues that confronted the new government. Guns were not discussed for three years, until the Game Act of 1692,[44] which, it is said, offered an "opportunity to bring game law into line with the right of Protestants to have firearms."[45] A Whig, no doubt Thomas Norris (1653–1700), introduced a rider at the third reading "to enable every Protestant to keep a musket in his House for his defence, notwithstanding this or any other Act."[46] He won support from four other men who argued that the rider promoted the security of the government and that all Protestants should be able to defend themselves.[47] Sir Christopher Musgrave and Sir Joseph Tredenham, both Tories, sharply opposed the rider and were joined by Sir John Lowther, who probably represented the views of King William, who would have opposed it. They insisted that presenting the rider was irregular and that it was "not proper for this bill, which is for the preservation of the game." Moreover, the rider "savoured of the politics to arm the mob, which . . . is not very safe for any government."[48] The rider was decisively defeated, one hundred and sixty-nine votes to sixty-five.[49] The implications of the discussion and the vote are that while sentiment existed for arming all Protestants and an effort was made to modify the Game Law to that end, a large majority opposed the move. For the rest of the decade, Game Laws and guns were not discussed, nor was an effort made to modify the terms of Article VII. At the turn of the eighteenth century, Article VII remained intact.

Claims for the right of Protestant subjects to have arms were raised during the eighteenth century. This happened in discussions of the terms of the Game Laws. For example, the Game Act of 1706 omitted guns from the list of weapons that were prohibited, because, as explained later, a Member of Parliament had objected to prohibiting them because "it might be attended with greate inconvenience."[50] A gun was "frequently necessary to be kept and used for other purposes, as the killing of noxious vermin and the like."[51] The court ruled that a gun should be disallowed only when it was used for hunting. In 1689, one remembers, a gun was allowed for self-protection, even for Catholics, and in 1706 it was allowed for killing vermin. However, it could not be used in hunting. As the historian of the Game Laws remarked, "the spirit of the Game Laws . . . was very much alive in the eighteenth century,"[52] a point nicely illustrated in discussions regarding this Game Act. Article VII was not mentioned.

Another venue for discussing an individual's right to a gun was cases brought before the law courts. *Rex v. Gardner*, argued before King's Bench in 1739, serves as an example. A justice of the peace had convicted Gardner of keeping a gun, in violation of a Game Law, 5 *Anne, c. 14*. The Solicitor General, for the plaintiff, declared that a gun was an "engine to destroy game" and therefore the guilty verdict should stand. The lawyer for Gardner, however, argued that a gun was "not properly an engine to destroy game, unless it is put to that use." The justices agreed, one pointing out that "farmers are generally obliged to keep a gun, and are no more within the Act for doing so than they are for keeping a cabbage-net." The conviction was "quashed" and Gardner was allowed to keep his gun. The decision reiterated the point made in the discussions regarding the Game Act of 1706: a man may keep a gun if it is necessary for his work, but he may not use it in hunting. The point at issue was whether restrictions imposed by Game Laws had been violated. The case had nothing to do with Article VII of the Bill of Rights.

Tracts published during the run-up to the Militia Bill of 1757 kept alive the issue of gun possession. In 1755, John Shebbeare, a Tory polemicist, who was critical of the government's slowness to proceed with militia reform, wrote a series of letters to and about the English people, in which he fumed against the Game Laws for depriving "people of Arms to defend themselves, and thus [making] them slaves by robbing them of the power of resistance."[53] He said it was a "breach" of the Bill of Rights to disarm the populace.[54] It was the first time that the Bill of Rights was invoked in such discussions. Shebbeare and other Tories bitterly attacked the use of standing armies and foreign troops, condemned the denial of arms to the people, and demanded a national militia.[55] They appropriated the anger over that denial and used it with other points as a propaganda ploy. Tories and Patriot Whigs pressed hard for arming the people for service in a militia, which they confidently predicted would not only remove the need for German mercenaries but also train the nation in civic virtue. Public opinion, thus aroused, propelled William Pitt to power and led to the passage of the Militia Bill. Ironically, the new militia, although driven by popular and libertarian sentiments, proved unpopular, provoked serious riots, and influenced political alignments.[56] The printed tracts and the debates concerning the Militia Bill of 1757 illustrate the polemical uses of claiming a right to arm. Nothing was done, however, to amend Article VII of the Bill of Rights.

The Gordon Riots of 1780 was another occasion that provoked outbursts of vehement support for the right of the individual to possess arms. The context was this:[57] the government of Lord North had fallen under increasingly sharp criticism because of military reverses in America and serious problems with France, Spain, and neutral nations. The opposition, under the leadership of such men as Charles James Fox, became radical and factious. In 1778 in an effort to motivate Catholics to enlist in the army, North's government promoted the passage of the Catholic Relief Act, which removed several disabilities from Catholics. Tapping into the deep vein of anti-Catholicism, the Protestant Association, led by its president, the erratic Lord George Gordon, young son of a Scottish noble, organized a mass petition, said to contain one hundred and twenty thousand signatures, for the repeal of the Act. When Parliament refused an immediate hearing, the crowds gathered outside Westminster turned angry. Violence soon spread throughout the city. From Friday, 2 June, to the following Thursday, 8 June, great damage was done to Catholic chapels, houses, and businesses. Over three hundred people were killed in the melee, and more injured. Some cities in the counties also erupted in riot and mayhem. Order was restored only when the army was finally ordered to act. An army officer, Jeffrey Lord Amherst, commanded his lieutenant-colonel in London to disarm all residents except those in the militia and others specifically designated to defend the city. Charles Lennox, the Third Duke of Richmond, responded indignantly to this move. In speeches in the House of Lords later in the month, he claimed that the Bill of Rights guaranteed that "every Protestant subject shall be permitted to arm himself for his personal security, or for the defence of his property."[58] He moved that the order of the army officer be branded as "unwarrantable" because it had violated the "sacred right" of Protestant subjects "to have arms for their defence, suitable to their conditions, and as allowed by law."[59] It is clear that in his confused speech he ultimately claimed nothing different from the restricted right allowed by Article VII. The Earl of Carlisle, Lord Stormont, and the Lord Chancellor defended the army's actions, and Richmond's motion was defeated.

Protests favoring the right of Protestant subjects to be armed occurred outside of Parliament in liberal political circles. In the summer of 1780, the Yorkshire Association condemned any attempt "to disarm peaceable subjects" who were Protestant.[60] When asked to give his opinion in July 1780, the recorder of London registered his approval of the associations and of the right of Protestants individually to have arms "and to use them for lawful purposes." It was a right, he said, that "may, and in many cases must, be exercised collectively." Malcolm regarded his remarks as "perhaps the clearest summation of the right of Englishmen to have arms" at that time.[61] It seems more likely that the recorder's use of the words "for lawful purposes" and his reference to "exercising" the right "collectively" signaled that he wanted to guarantee the right of individual Protestants to be armed for service in the associations. In any case, these remarks did not end the matter. Two years later, an anonymous tract, *Dialogue between a Scholar and a Peasant* (1782), written by William

Jones, again regretted that Englishmen did not have guns and urged them to be prepared—that is, armed—to defend themselves in associations against the government. The radical Society for Constitutional Information published the tract and translated it into Welsh.[62] These moves provided powerful propaganda. However, the moment passed; people turned away from extralegal activities, disavowed radicalism, and lost interest. The government took charge, and the associations in the counties and in London dissolved. Jones was charged with libel and sedition. The fervent expressions of the right of the individual Protestant to be armed came to nothing.

Further to support her thesis, Malcolm called on the work of a great legal figure in English history, the jurist Sir William Blackstone,[63] declaring that in his *Commentaries on the Laws of England* (1765–69) he "expanded the role of an armed citizenry beyond the individual's own preservation to the preservation of the entire constitutional structure."[64] Is this really what Blackstone wrote and meant to say? Blackstone began Book I, chapter I of the *Commentaries* with a discussion of Great Britain's rights, also known, he said, as her liberties. After identifying "three principal or primary articles: the right of personal security, the right of personal liberty and the right of private property," he noted that "to secure their actual enjoyment" were five other "auxiliary subordinate rights."[65] "The fifth and last auxiliary right of the subject," Blackstone wrote, "is that of having arms for their defence, suitable to their condition and degree, and such as are allowed by law. Which is also declared by [Article VII of the Bill of Rights] and is indeed a public allowance, under due restraints, of the natural right of resistance and self-preservation, when the sanctions of society and laws are found insufficient to restrain the violence of oppression."[66] In the first part of this statement, the language follows exactly the language of the Bill of Rights, making clear that Blackstone did not regard the right of having arms as unrestricted. He accepted Article VII's two significant qualifiers and actually strengthened the socioeconomic requirement by adding the word "degree" to the phrase "suitable to their condition." He went further in saying that the right to have arms applies only "when the sanctions of society and laws are found insufficient to restrain the violence of oppression." In other words, Blackstone limited the right to have arms to a time when violent oppression [that is, tyranny] was rampant. In the last part of the statement Blackstone joined his belief in natural law to the terms of the Bill of Rights,[67] making the fifth right "a public allowance, under due restraints, of the natural right of resistance and self-preservation." These words placed even the "natural right of resistance and self-preservation" "under due restraints." Blackstone's language shows that he was not advocating an unrestricted right of the individual to have arms.

In sum, over the eighteenth century, voices were raised, tracts written, and law cases decided in favor of the right of the individual to have a gun within the terms of the Game Laws. These instances, however, did not rise to the level of constitutional change. People may express their outrage over an issue in Parliamentary debate; they may print tracts and pamphlets insisting on their viewpoint; they may bring their complaints before law courts; and judges may decide an issue in ways that please the people. However, none of these things creates a constitutional right. The constitutional right of the individual to hold arms at the end of the eighteenth century had not changed one iota. It remained a right restricted by religion, socioeconomic standing, and law.

The climax of Malcolm's argument was that an individual right to have arms was an inheritance that "Englishmen took with them to the American colonies."[68] Malcolm contended that America's Founding Fathers went beyond the English precedent and in shaping the Second Amendment to the American Constitution "swept aside" the restrictions of religion, socioeconomic condition, and "as allowed by law" and, thereby, removed "any infringement" on the right of the individual to have arms.[69] The idea that the Second Amendment grants every individual the right to arms has been the subject of heated debate, but the point is now settled, at least for the time being, by the Supreme Court's five to four decision in 2008 in the case of *The District of Columbia, et al. v. Dick Anthony Heller.* The Court ruled that the Second Amendment grants an individual right to arms.

My disagreement here is not with the interpretation that the Second Amendment granted an individual right to arms, but with the idea that the Second Amendment is a legacy of Article VII of the English Bill of Rights. I agree, as perhaps every historian would, that the American colonists were deeply indebted to Great Britain's political ideas and constitutional documents. Magna Carta, the Petition of Right, and the Bill of Rights, it is said, were "the models in hand, or at least in mind" when the American Constitution and Bill of Rights were under draft.[70] No one would doubt that James Madison, generally credited with leading the effort to write a Bill of Rights, and members of the First Congress were familiar with the provisions of each of these documents. They also knew many other writings, such as the radical tracts from the period of the Civil War and the works of Sir Edward Coke, Algernon Sidney, Henry Care, John Locke, and the eighteenth-century Commonwealth men. All of the colonial leaders were well versed in English political ideas and government. Some delegates to the First Congress insisted that they had a claim to all the rights of Englishmen. There is no doubt that the Bill of Rights and all its Articles permeated the thinking of the delegates.

Nonetheless, Article VII did not figure in the debates of the First Congress as members drafted the Second Amendment.[71] The debates and other pertinent documents relating to the creation of the American Bill of Rights contain no direct reference to Article VII. When discussing military matters, delegates expressed strong objections to a standing army, favored a reliable militia, and worried over the issue of conscientious objectors.[72] The absence of reference to Article VII suggests that its terms, which in 1789 were exactly what they were in 1689, were not relevant. If the Americans "swept" away the restrictions of religion, socioeconomic status, and "as allowed by law," then, logically, they were not following the terms of Article VII. Why should they? Article VII did not offer an unrestricted individual right to arms. It reflected a political system and a social order in which only 2 percent of English subjects could legally possess a gun. It embodied the major terms of early modern English gun culture. The colonists found so little in Article VII that they jettisoned its central terms.

If the Americans did grant an individual right to arms, as the United States Supreme Court ruled, they got that idea from someplace other than the 1689 English Bill of Rights.

Conclusion

Defining Gun Culture in Early Modern England

THE DOMESTIC GUN CULTURE THAT BEGAN in the sixteenth century in England and evolved over the next two hundred years did not capture the attention of either academic or military historians. *Gun Culture in Early Modern England* is the first book to attempt to navigate these unchartered waters. In undertaking to discover, explain, and describe the characteristics of the nation's domestic gun culture, this study embraced men, women, and children from across the social spectrum and focused on the effect the gun had on their social, economic, cultural, and political lives. Equally important to the investigation was the attitude and policies of the government toward its subjects' legal possession and use of firearms. Guns made for personal pleasures followed the establishment of an active native gun industry whose purpose was to produce artillery and military handguns. Military and domestic guns were closely related to each other, but obviously their purposes and implications were different. At the end of the era, domestic gun culture influenced Article VII of England's iconic constitutional document, the Bill of Rights of 1689, which settled the Revolution of 1688–89. This broad perspective offered an unrivalled opportunity to observe how domestic gun culture began and developed, how complex its nature became, and how far-reaching was its significance. It made possible a definition of England's early modern gun culture and answers to questions that first inspired this book.

A striking feature of England's early modern gun culture was its restrictive nature: English subjects whose socioeconomic standing was below a certain level (usually an annual income of £100) were legally disallowed to possess or use a firearm. This limit affected about 98 percent of the population. In other words, only 2 percent of the population had the legal right to possess and use handguns. Disallowing people of middling and lower socioeconomic standing to possess weapons was deeply ingrained in English history. A law of 1389 articulated it. England's strong hierarchical social structure with recognizable and accepted gradations of honor at the top, distinctions throughout, and sharp differences between wealthy aristocrats and the rest of society underlay this attitude. The monarch and members of the Privy Council, Parliament, and other national and local political and social institutions shared it. Persons at the upper reaches of society equated political loyalty with wealth, an assumption inspired by the fear that allowing men of modest or poor means access to firearms would imperil the nation, threaten its leaders, further uprisings, and endanger the population. In view of the domestic violence of sixteenth-century England, which was roiled by persistent and widespread religious, political, social, and economic grievances, and the Civil Wars of the mid-seventeenth century, such fears were a constant factor.

In addition, royal, noble, and aristocratic men shared the determination, sometimes verging on hysteria, to protect their hunting preserves from people who invaded or threatened them. The use of firearms in hunting multiplied the danger of violating these preserves and further sharpened tensions.

Given that restrictions on gun possession and use appeared in repeatedly issued statues and proclamations, the immediate question becomes: how could subjects on whom the limits fell learn about firearms, become skilled in their use, and show their approval of them? It was essential that men of middling and lower social standing should learn about guns, because had they not done so, a domestic gun culture would not have begun in the sixteenth century. They discovered firearms in multiple ways. The most important pathway to guns was their service in the military organizations of the era. A large number of foot soldiers, who were barred from possessing and using guns in civilian life because their annual income was insufficient, served in the derelict feudal array that Henry VIII inherited and revived in a different form, in the county militias where they were often paid substitutes, and in the ad hoc armies raised for a purpose and then disbanded. The weapons of these military institutions were increasingly artillery and military handguns. Thus, all soldiers were exposed to firearms and, if chosen to be gunners, were trained to shoot and maintain them. When they returned to civilian life, they brought back with them knowledge about and interest in firearms, which domestic guns could satisfy. This effect on successive generations of men from the lower reaches of society continued in the nonprofessional county militias, and with a difference in the permanent, paid standing army that King Charles II established at the Restoration. Service in the standing army transformed the subject into a professional soldier.

Equally important to spreading knowledge of guns was the entrepreneurial and employment opportunities in the gun industry that became available to men from all levels of English society and to plebeian women (mostly widows) who worked as gunmakers. The government's contracts for military guns, arranged through the Office of Ordnance, provided many jobs as long as war, unsettled international relations, or domestic unrest existed. In years of peace, making and repairing guns for civilian purposes, and crafting elaborate pieces encrusted with jewels and damascened for collecting, gift giving, and decoration took up the slack. Over the years, men and women working for the Office of Ordnance and as members of the Worshipful Company of Gunmakers from its inception in 1637 learned intimately about the mechanism of firearms. This study contends that gun workers' close relationship to guns and reliance on them for their livelihood veiled in their minds the violence for which guns were made and cloaked their inherent danger. Learning about guns through military service and employment in the gun industry helped to define gun culture.

Another feature of England's early modern gun culture was its urban character. Except for instances in Surrey and Sussex, gunmaking was centered in cities such as London, Bristol, and later Birmingham. London and its residents felt the presence of guns in numerous ways that touched their daily lives. Artillery was on view: cannon lined the wharf in front of the Tower and the roof of the Tower as well. People could see up close what these big military guns looked like. The demographics and ambience of neighborhoods changed as gunmakers, gun founders, or others associated with the business of guns moved into them. Some of these workers produced artillery and military handguns; others turned out domestic handguns. Artisans gave their shops where guns were sold names that incorporated some form of the word *gun*. A testimony to the popularity of guns is that owners of bookshops and print shops also used the word *gun* in their signs. Moreover, the streets of the city were given names that included the word *gun*. Guns were features of a lottery and a couple of auctions. The entire city could hear the gun salutes welcoming an international dignitary or celebrating a special event or watch fireworks powered by gunpowder. Guns permeated London. Until the end of the era, the city was "The Gun Capital" of England.

Subjects on whom gun restrictions fell responded with grudging acceptance, willful disobedience, angrily expressed outrage, and written requests for change. A defiant person could circumvent the restrictions on hunting by ignoring the law and taking a chance at not being caught. Court records show that many did just that, and it is reasonable to think that there must have been many more who violated the laws but escaped detection. Other men revealed their resentment by using violent words. A third response was to make a case for the repeal of the restraints in writing. The most notable instance occurred in 1536 when the leaders of the Pilgrimage of Grace used the Pontefract Articles (their petition to the authorities regarding twenty-four important religious, political, and economic grievances) to call for a repeal of gun laws. Including a request to repeal gun restrictions in such a document indicates how deep the dislike of them was. The effort remains significant even though it failed.

None of these instances of defiant disobedience, oral denunciation, and written requests for repeal of the restrictions resulted in change. The habit of deference, the condition of powerlessness and poverty, and the absence of effective leadership were powerful limitations on any demand for alteration in gun laws.

Another mark of English domestic gun culture was the wide-ranging influence guns had on the personal lives of noble and aristocratic men. Of all the parts of society, these men felt the effect of guns the most. The advent of the domestic gun changed the nature of their two favorite sports: hunting and shooting. They added beautifully decorated guns to their longstanding practice of buying silver, tapestry, furniture, and jewelry, and used them for collecting, gift giving, and decorating. Aristocratic men identified with guns in other ways. They ordered that an image of a gun be included in their portraits. At least one gentleman had his toiletry case shaped like a gun and adorned with jewels. Men of wealth, if not of lengthy family lineage, chose the image of guns for their coats of arms.

Aristocratic English women were less enthusiastic about firearms than their European counterparts were. They did not use a gun in hunting or shooting. Yet a few women of upper status were capable of operating a pistol in the Civil Wars with deadly effect, and some carried a small gun in their purse during the Popish Plot frenzy. They were complicit in giving their sons toy guns and in having them painted with a gun. Margaret Cavendish, Duchess of Newcastle, based one of her stories on the heroine's mastery of a pistol. Their knowledge of the medicinal and household properties of gunpowder was extensive. Firearms figured in the work and lives of women of less exalted social rank. A gun had a prominent part in one of Aphra Behn's most popular plays, *The Rover*.

The children of early modern England were an important component of the nation's gun culture. Their parents and friends introduced them to guns by giving them toy guns, some so realistic that they were capable of firing a tiny bullet. Royal children developed an intense interest in guns, as exampled by the eight-year-old Charles (later King Charles II) who threatened to attack his father's enemy with his gun in an early Civil War battle. Prince William (Queen Anne's son) also possessed an intense interest in firearms and battles. Matching this royal enthusiasm was the son of a "Tradesman" who proudly said that he valued his pistol "above all Things."

Another overarching characteristic of early modern English gun culture was the genuine liking people had for guns. Regrettably, no essay has survived to explain why English subjects looked upon firearms so fondly, but their actions are equally revealing of their attitude. People of wealth considered firearms as a means of protecting person, family, and property, a view shared by all socioeconomic groups. The wealthy regarded the possession and use of guns as an entitlement of their station in life and as a status symbol. They favored the expensive wheel-lock handgun and prized firearms that artisans transformed into pieces of art by embellishing them with pictures and adorning them with gold, silver, bone, and precious and semi-precious jewels. Monarchs, nobles, and aristocrats selected these guns as gifts to exchange with each other, confident that firearms would please the recipient. They identified with guns by including them in their portraits. They perpetrated the tradition by giving toy guns to their sons and by having their young boys' portraits painted with a gun.

Persons of modest socioeconomic standing liked guns, too, and expressed their feelings in equally obvious ways according to their means. The gun helped them hunt more effectively and bring more protein to the table, whatever pleasure hunting offered. They opposed the restrictive Game Laws; their actions indicating their desire to possess and use guns. Target shooting with a gun was a new sport that less well-to-do men practiced enthusiastically in London as early as the third decade of the sixteenth century. Gun accidents and crime did not destroy the general approval and use of domestic guns.

Finally, England's domestic gun culture took on a constitutional dimension at the time of the Revolution of 1688–89, when it shaped the terms of Article VII of the Declaration of Rights and the Bill of Rights. Embedded in Article VII were major parts of the nation's gun culture. This book maintains that the Article did not secure a constitutional right to every Protestant subject to have arms. Rather it secured a right to suitably qualified men to have "Armes"—the kind used in war—"for their defense." To qualify one had to meet certain criteria: in religion (Protestant), socioeconomic standing ("suitable to their condition") and "according to the law." The men who drafted the Article were upper-status Protestants who had their own interests and the welfare of the nation at heart. For centuries, Englishmen had passed laws and proclamations that legally kept guns out of the hands of persons of modest or little income. The gun culture of early modern England shaped an article in one of England's iconic constitutional documents.

This book proposes a different perspective on the historical narrative of early modern England at a time when traditional emphases on religion, politics, and Parliament are beginning to make room for diverse viewpoints, different integrating questions, and new kinds of sources. A focus on domestic gun culture, I believe, will enrich the discussion. In my view, some prevailing generalizations will require adjustment as studies of the era go forward. The government's restrictive policies toward its less well-to-do subjects' legal possession and use of guns added to popular discontent. Guns for civilian purposes came in the wake of guns made for military purposes; they, too, introduced changes in the economy that require notice. Men found entrepreneurial and, with artisanal women, employment opportunities in the renovated gunmaking industry and with the government's agency, the Ordnance Office or Department. The Worshipful Company of Gunmakers was an important addition to the guild system in London. Gunmakers and gun founders, many of them aliens, modified the demography and ambience of London's neighborhoods and affected the city's noise level, smells, street signs, and shop signs, points that enlarge understanding of the capital city. Domestic guns affected the lifestyle of men, women and children of all socioeconomic standings, but that of aristocratic men the most. The impact of guns on children modifies one's perception of early modern childhood. Gun accidents and gun crime affected all levels of society and requires integration into historical accounts of that society. Finally, this book contends that domestic gun culture shaped the meaning of Article VII of the Declaration of Rights and Bill of Rights of 1689. I hope these matters will attract the attention of historians of Early Modern England.

APPENDIX A

What Is a Gun?

What *was* a handgun that existed four to five hundred years ago in early modern England? What did it look like? How did it work? How was it made, and
by whom? Thanks to the work of museum curators and directors, the collections of gun enthusiasts, and the scholarly research of specialists in the history of firearms, answers are at hand. While only a few guns used by ordinary
folk have survived, those that wealthy persons owned are on view at museums
in England, Europe, and the United States.[1] Usually, catalogues that accompany museum exhibits are lavishly illustrated. Pictures of guns illustrating
how they operate appear in contemporary drill manuals and books on the
history of gun. A few pictures are reproduced in this book. Based on these
physical, visual, and written resources, this appendix describes the appearance
of guns and explains how they operated, examines the nature of gunpowder,
and discusses the steps taken by members of the gun industry to produce a
handgun.

A handgun of whatever type is basically a metal tube designed to exploit
the propulsive capability of gunpowder in ejecting a missile. A gun has three
parts—the lock, stock, and barrel—as in the familiar saying. Gunpowder, the
gun's essential ingredient, also has three components: saltpeter (potassium nitrate), charcoal (carbon), and sulfur. If these ingredients are mixed in a certain
proportion, they have propulsive powers, and, when confined within a vessel
that is fitted with a touchhole so that fire can reach them, they are capable of
propelling a projectile some distance. The principle of the gun, according to a
firearms expert, is unique: only in the gun does the "propulsive force [depend]
on the expansion of gas due to the combustion of explosive material and is
independent of torsional or gravitational force."[2] In other words, as another
expert put it, the "chemical energy" is converted to "mechanical force" capable
of pushing a projectile out of the tube.[3] A further unique characteristic is that
the nitrate compound, saltpeter, "provides oxygen for the explosion,"[4] and,
thus, the mixture does not depend upon air as the oxidant. This combination

of elements was used all over the world to fire a gun until the nineteenth century.

Two of the three elements that comprise gunpowder were readily available in England and the West. Mineral springs in England and volcanos in southern Italy supplied sulfur.[5] Charcoal required wood that was "easy to pulverize" and produced little ash, such as willow, alder, hazel, and beech, which, too, were at hand in England.[6] But saltpeter, the essential element of the three, was in short supply. To reduce the nation's dependence on importing saltpeter, the government took steps, especially in the early seventeenth century, to harvest a supply from the contents of dovecotes and stables, a story recounted recently by David Cressy in his *Saltpeter: The Mother of Gunpowder.*

Saltpeter, carbon, and sulfur can be mixed in different proportions to make a product called gunpowder that is different from the gunpowder used to shoot a gun. This substance can create decorative and celebratory fireworks, send signals, dig a tunnel, excavate a canal, and demolish a building. But it will not have the force to eject a missile from a metal tube. The secret to creating gunpowder capable of propelling a missile lay in increasing the proportion of saltpeter (the nitrate compound) relative to the two other components, carbon and sulfur. To achieve explosive power the saltpeter content must be greater than the other two ingredients: ideally, the proportion is 75 percent saltpeter, 15 percent charcoal, and 10 percent sulfur.[7]

A device stuffed with the appropriate mixture and capable of expelling a missile appeared in England sometime in the late thirteenth century to early fourteenth. Gunpowder, however, was first developed in China in the ninth century by anonymous scientists who had focused their attention on nitrates. The date of the creation of the gun by the Chinese is no longer in dispute: both Geoffrey Parker and Jack Kelly believe that it happened in the thirteenth century.[8] Theories about how this knowledge moved from East to West multiplied in early modern England and Europe, and some are quite fanciful. But two things are certain about guns in these early centuries in England. One is that Roger Bacon (c.1214–1292[?]) was the first person in England and Western Europe to refer to gunpowder in writing. In a letter to Pope Clement VII in 1267, Bacon wrote of "a child's toy of sound and fire made in various parts of the world with powder of saltpetre, sulphur, and charcoal of Hazelwood." Showing intimate knowledge of the device, he referred to the "horror of the sounds" it made and noted that if the instrument were large, "no one could stand the terror of the noise and flash."[9] The second point beyond dispute is that the first illustration in the West of a firearm appeared in the bottom margin of the last page of an English illuminated manuscript, *De Nobilitatibus, Sapientiis et Prudentiis Regnum* (Concerning the majesty, wisdom and pru-

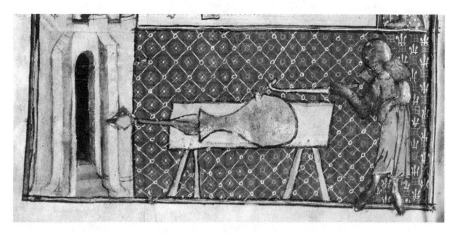

FIGURE 11. A cannon set horizontally on a trestle (with a man in medieval mail holding a taper to the touchhole and an arrow projecting from its muzzle) appeared in Walter de Milemete's *De Nobilitatibus, Sapientiis et Prudentiis Regnum* in 1326. (MS 92 fol. 70v. © Governing Body of Christ Church, Oxford)

dence of kings). This manuscript was presented in 1326 to Prince Edward, the year before he became King Edward III (1327–1377), by Walter de Milemete, his chaplain.[10] A similar drawing appeared in China in 1332, suggesting that interested parties in West and East were in touch with each other.

The Milemete drawing depicts a pear-shaped object lying on its side on a rectangular table with a wick protruding from a touchhole at the top of the object. To the right of the table stands a soldier dressed in medieval mail using a red-hot iron to ignite the wick. A large arrow (possibly made of leather) with a four-sided iron head and metal feathers (probably made of brass) has come out of the mouth of the vase and is targeting the area on the left where there is a castle door surmounted by a tower. Scholars do not know who made this object or where it was made, but speculation has it that the artisan was a bell founder.[11] Nothing is known of who rendered the drawing. But one may discern the origins of a cannon in this drawing. The arrow protruding from the muzzle illustrates the overlap between old and new weapons.

From these simple beginnings, firearms developed over a period of two hundred years, largely in Europe but also in England, until by the 1530s a "consensus" regarding the appearance and performance of guns was achieved.[12] This "early modern ordnance synthesis" lasted with important adjustments, but without fundamental change, throughout the Tudor-Stuart era. As a result, artillery and handguns became easier to handle, less dangerous to fire, more serviceable in war, and more adaptable to civilian use.

Several craftsmen, some with names describing almost exactly their task,

What Is a Gun?

were responsible for producing these firearms. A gun founder took the first step. To make a cannon, a gun founder forged sheets of metal that were bound together with metal strips into the desired shape.[13] In a similar way, the first step in making a handgun, whether for military or personal use, required the gunsmith to pour molten metal into a mold, from which it would emerge in the desired shape of a barrel. Gunmakers put together the various parts—the lock, the stock, the barrel—to make either a military or a domestic handgun.

Early anonymous persons experimented with the size and shape of the device. In doing so, they traveled along two paths. On the one hand, they created cannon of varying size for military use on the battlefield. A small cannon was developed in the fourteenth century and given the name *ribald*, an Anglo-Norman word in origin, meaning "a person of low social status" and inferring that the cannon was small and insignificant.[14] King Edward III ordered ribalds for his campaign against France in the Hundred Years' War in 1345–46.[15] No doubt, it was an anonymous soldier or soldiers who, seeing great possibilities for the ribald, designed a contraption called a ribaudequin. This apparatus was a cart on whose four sides up to a dozen small ribalds were mounted. The cart could be pivoted around from one side to the other as each set of ribalds was fired. A ribaudequin could produce a murderous effect when all the ribalds were fired in sequence.

At the other end of the scale, some cannon were enormous in size, as exampled by the "Mons Meg," still seen on display at Edinburgh Castle. Built in 1449 and sent in 1457 by Philip the Good, Duke of Burgundy, as a gift to his nephew by marriage, King James II of Scotland, the device, called a bombard, is thirteen feet, two inches in length, weighs approximately five tons, and has a bore diameter of nineteen and one half inches. It is capable of firing a stone shot weighing 330 pounds up to two miles away.[16] In 1682, the bombard burst in firing a salute in honor of James, Duke of York, whom King Charles II had sent to Scotland, but it did not injure the Duke.[17] Another huge cannon is "Queen Elizabeth's Pocket Pistol," which was cast in Utrecht in 1544 and presented to King Henry VIII by Maximilian Van Egmont, Count Buren, Stadtholder of Freisland. Subsequently, Henry gave it to his daughter Elizabeth.[18] Disagreement over the details (including who gave the gun to whom) threads through the sources that describe this device. The cannon, called a *culverin*, meaning a "long, slender piece of artillery" designed to "carry balls to a great distance," is also described as a "basilisk, a large brass—or (preferably) bronze-cannon." The piece measures twenty-four feet in length, has a bore diameter of four and three-quarters inches, and with two degrees of elevation using eighteen pounds of powder, it can project a ten-pound ball from twelve hundred to two thousand yards, to as far as seven miles, the fanciful distance of across the English Channel to the French shore! When one hundred years old, "Elizabeth's Pocket Pistol" saw action in the English Civil War. It was used by King Charles I's forces at the siege of Hull in 1643, where it was captured by the Parliamentarians and used by them at the siege of Sheffield in 1644. The cannon was retired in the eighteenth century and moved to Dover Castle, where it was mounted on the cliff's edge, and there it remains.

The second line of development was the handgun, which by definition was a firearm that one person could discharge with or without a rest (OED). The word *handgun* is first recorded in English records in 1386, a date discovered by T. F. Tout, thus proving that a handheld weapon was known in England toward the end of the fourteenth century, a generation earlier than had been thought.[19] Tout hypothesized that the handgun existed even before it got its name, for it developed easily from early cannon, whose first name was *manualia ingenia*.[20] In the early fifteenth century, the first pictorial rendering of a handgun appeared: Conrad Kyeser's drawing, "Bellifortis," 1405.[21] It shows a long, slender, cannon-like object mounted on an elongated stock, supported by a rest. A man is lighting the charge using a handheld match at the touchhole located along the top of the barrel. The drawing is reminiscent of the Milemete drawing.

Technical advancements in the nature of gunpowder and lock mechanisms were necessary to make handguns effective. Serpentine or mealed powder was unsuitable for a short gun because it exploded fast and uncontrollably.[22] By the early sixteenth century, corned gunpowder was developed. In the corning process, the three ingredients of gunpowder—saltpeter, charcoal, and sulfur—were mixed together, moistened, rolled out into balls of a desired size or pushed through a sieve to achieve a specific size, and then thoroughly dried.[23] The advantage of corned gunpowder was that the balls were resistant to moisture, thereby making the powder less subject to spoilage in storage and hence of longer life. Further, when the powder was lit, the explosion was almost instantaneous, and the general uniformity of the balls made it uniform along the barrel. Thus, the velocity of the missile was maintained longer. Although corned gunpowder was more powerful than mealed powder, the gunner could more effectively control the size of the grain and thereby regulate the speed of the combustion. The strength of corned gunpowder could be—as indeed it had to be—adjusted to the length of the barrel of the gun, the diameter of the bore, and the kind of shot used.[24]

Some handguns were used for both military and domestic purposes.[25] One, the harquebus, had a barrel about forty inches long, used corned gunpowder and lead bullets (which were light in weight), and was forged from iron, not cast in bronze.[26] The size varied; to shoot a large harquebus required a tripod or forked "rest" to lessen the weight on the shooter and reduce the effect of the recoil. Both soldiers and hunters used the harquebus.[27] Another was the caliver, a lighter version of the harquebus. It could be fired without a rest and was popular in the late sixteenth century. In length, it measured about thirty-eight inches.[28] A third was the musket. This firearm was defined by its long barrel and heavy weight. It was fired from either a soldier's shoulder or chest or a rest.[29] Sir Roger Williams advised that the recoil of the gun did not harm a soldier if he placed his thumb between the stock of the gun and his face, assuming that he had "any discretion." Williams preferred the musket to the caliver by two to one.[30]

Two more handguns, which stand somewhat apart because of their small size, were in common use. The pistol, a small version of the harquebus, measured about twenty inches and was used for military and domestic purposes. The dag was shorter, measuring five or six inches, and could be concealed in a pocket or cloak. The government rightly considered the dag highly dangerous and tried without much success to ban it entirely.

Essential to the development of a practical handgun was the replacement of the manual procedure for igniting the charge with a mechanical system. The first mechanical device was the matchlock.[31] Known from 1411, it was invented by German gunsmiths, and refined over the century. The matchlock operated this way: a measure of gunpowder was poured down the barrel of the gun and was followed by a missile of some kind—an arrow, a stone, a hail shot, or, later, a bullet. Both the gunpowder and the missile were rammed into the breech of the gun with a ramrod or scourer. A length of cord saturated with saltpeter was clamped to one end of a curved metal lever (called a serpentine) which in turn was attached to the stock of the gun so that it could pivot. The other end of the cord was fastened to a trigger (tricker in English). Along the side or the top of the barrel was affixed a little "flash pan" containing a small quantity of fine grained priming powder. The gunner lit the end of the cord, using either a glowing pipe or generating a spark with a piece of flint and steel that he carried with him, thereby causing the saltpeter to burn. When he pulled the trigger, the lever or serpentine pivoted and dropped the smoldering cord into the flash pan, thereby igniting the priming powder, which communicated through the touchhole to the gunpowder charge. The powder charge caught fire, exploded, and expelled the missile from the gun. The whole process took between twenty and thirty seconds.

The matchlock suffered from several disadvantages. The gunner had to keep the cord smoldering at all times or have a pipe or piece of flint at the ready to light it. If the matchlock were used in battle, the smoldering cord could betray the soldier's presence. Soldiers tended to light both ends of the cord to assure that if one end went out, another would be at the ready, which increased the likelihood of burning their fingers, setting their clothing on fire, or revealing their location. Rain, excessive fog, or dew could dampen the cord or the priming powder or both and end in failure to ignite the charge. The major advantages of the matchlock were that it was relatively inexpensive and easy to maintain. As a result, English soldiers used firearms fitted with the matchlock until the end of the seventeenth century.

The second mechanical advance, the wheel lock, marked a decided improvement over the matchlock.[32] Indeed, it has been described as a "milestone in the history of firearms."[33] This mechanism originated in the early sixteenth century and although both Germany and Italy claim credit for inventing it, the honor should probably go to Italy because in about 1500 Leonardo da Vinci sketched a drawing of a wheel-lock device. As its name suggests, a wheel lock is a small wheel (twenty-five to forty millimeters in diameter) with a serrated edge. It fits into a little slot at the bottom of the flash pan with the priming powder. The wheel contains an intricate arrangement of springs and gears, likened to that in a watch. Near it is a lever, with a little clamp at one end that holds a piece of iron pyrite. A spring is fastened to the wheel by a short chain that the gunner winds up by hand using a "spanner" and is held in place ready for firing. With this procedure, the firearm is referred to as "spanned." Pulling the trigger releases the spring, causing the cover of the flash pan to shoot back and the wheel to rotate rapidly against the pyrite. This friction produces sparks of fire, thereby igniting the priming powder, which, as in the matchlock, communicates with the main charge through the touchhole and causes it to detonate.

There were many advantages to the wheel lock. It eliminated the need to keep a match cord saturated with saltpeter smoldering. The wheel lock also made possible the development of the pistol, a shorter, lighter version of the harquebus. It enabled the gunner to prepare his weapon for firing (by spanning it) in anticipation of using it and carry it in readiness on his person, concealed, if desired. When spanned, a gun with a wheel-lock mechanism was not supposed to detonate. It was much safer than the matchlock. These features greatly benefitted the cavalryman, the hunter, and the crook. A cavalryman could place the spanned wheel lock on his person or in holsters attached to the saddle and ride into battle, ready to fire. This capability changed the way the cavalry operated, and it went far to change the attitude of aristocrats toward firearms. The same kind of advantage accrued to the hunter and to the crook.

The wheel lock, however, also had disadvantages. First, because the mechanism was complex and required high standards of manufacture,[34] the wheel lock was expensive. Only the wealthy could afford a wheel-lock gun, which meant that in the military, only cavalrymen used it. Second, if the wheel lock were in the spanned condition for a long time—say overnight—it might not fire.[35] Finally, pyrite tended to crumble, with the result that sometimes the gun failed to fire.

A solution to one of the disadvantages of the wheel lock—crumbling pyrite—was the flintlock mechanism, the third technical advance in locks. Developed in the seventeenth century, the flintlock substituted a piece of flint for the pyrite. The flint was clamped to the end of a cocked pivoted arm, and when the gunner pulled the trigger, the arm was released to allow the flint to strike a rough plate above the firing pan so that the resulting sparks dropped down and ignited the priming powder, which, as with the other locks, communicated through the touchhole with the major charge. The advantage was that the flint was a stronger substance and did not crumble with use. The various kinds of guns that were available to soldiers and civilians were fitted with one of these locks.

How did these early modern guns perform? Tests conducted in 1988–89 in Graz, Austria, using the collection of early modern guns held by the Steiermarkisches Landeszeughaus provided some answers for military guns and indirectly for guns used for domestic pursuits.[36] The muzzle velocity—that is, the speed with which the bullet leaves the barrel—was very high, about the same as for modern weapons. Air resistance causes the speed of all bullets to lose kinetic energy the further the distance to the target.[37] This was especially true of spherically shaped bullets, which decelerated rapidly, losing about half of their energy in the first 100 meters. This contributed to the poor accuracy, which was associated with the range of the weapon. Bert Hall figured that a musketeer could expect to hit a target "with 10–20 percent of [his] shots" and probably "more like 5 percent."[38] A. R. Hall agreed that the range for small arms to be effective was between one hundred and fifty to two hundred yards.[39] This confirmed the calculations of a contemporary military man, Humphrey Barwick, who reckoned that if good powder and bullet were used and the gunner was trained and skillful, a musket could kill a man in armour at two hundred yards.[40]

Tests, however, that controlled for the skill of gunner showed that the weapon accounted for the poor showing. The only way to improve accuracy was to rifle the barrel. Rifling involved cutting grooves down the interior length of the barrel to give the bullet a controlled spin as it traveled along the grooves. Following the practice of medieval fletchers, gunsmiths experimented with rifling at the end of the fifteenth century. The trajectory of the missile was improved, but rifling was not easy, and rifled guns took longer

APPENDIX A

to load. Therefore, they were seldom used during the early modern era. The rate of fire, however, depended upon the skill and level of concentration of the gunner. Under ideal conditions, it took between twenty to thirty seconds to prepare to fire. Misfires, averaging one in every four to six shots, impeded achieving this rate of fire. Guns were also capable of firing more than one bullet, a capability achieved by adding more than one barrel. Hail shot was also available, and was widely favored, despite a law banning its use in hunting. After about fifty years on the books, the law restricting hail shot was cancelled at the end of the sixteenth century.

To sum up, guns of different sizes and gunlocks of different design were available for military and domestic use. Their accuracy was reliable only at short distances, no matter the skill of the gunner. Rifling, known from the end of the fifteenth century, improved accuracy, but the process was costly and not much used. The period witnessed no significant change in the design of the gun or the lock or of the performance. The guns of the sixteenth century established a pattern that lasted until the nineteenth century.

APPENDIX B

Naming the Gun

The presence of guns and gunpowder enlarged and enriched the language of England and European nations. The new mechanism in the shape of a tube and the new explosive it contained had to have a name. The onomastic process, a technical term referring to names and naming, was natural and essential.

English people chose the word *gun* for the new device.[1] According to the *Oxford English Dictionary*,[2] an anonymous clerk responsible for keeping the record of weapons stored at Windsor Castle referred in 1330–31 to a "great ballista" (a device capable of heaving a missile by the mechanical means of releasing tightly bound cords) as Domina Gunhildr, a Scandinavian woman's name that combined Gunn-r and Hild-r, both meaning "war." Gunna or Gonne was the diminutive. Giving a woman's name to a weapon was an old and widespread tradition that is still found today. Perhaps it softened the terror of war and created a sense that the weapon would provide loving protection. Nine years later, in 1339, a second anonymous clerk employed by the city of London and charged with compiling an inventory of the "Munitions of war provided by the City" held in the Chamber of the Guildhall listed "six instruments of latone usually called gonnes" along with thirty-two pounds of gunpowder for the "said instruments."[3] The point is that the clerk regarded the word *gonnes* as the usual name for the six instruments that used gunpowder. The *OED* editor explains that it is "likely" that the word *Gunhildr* was regularly applied to a ballista before 1330, so that when a weapon appeared using gunpowder, the words *gunna* or *gonne* were "naturally" employed to name it. He dismisses the thought that either the old French word *mangonne* or Middle English word *gunne* was the origin of the word. Bert S. Hall suggests that the word *gun* became confused with the word *gin*, from *engine*, that was applied to siege weapons like catapults, and migrated to gunpowder arms.[4]

In the fourteenth century, the practice began of assigning specific names to specific types of firearms. For example, in 1339, the French were the first to apply the word *cannon* to a large firearm.[5] Derived from the Latin *canna*, meaning tube, it migrated to England, an example of transnational fertilization. *Cannon* appeared in English in *Piers Plowman* (written between 1362 and 1390) and in Chaucer's poems (composed between 1375 and 1400). By 1387, the English language had absorbed it. However, as Sir Francis Walsingham (1530–1590) pointed out, in a remark reflecting national self-consciousness about the names of weapons, the English preferred the word *gun* while the French favored *cannon*. The word *artillery* was used in both England and France, first for bows and arrows, then for cannon.

The English word *harquebus* (or hackbut), also spelled *arquebus*, was the name for a gun popular during the reign of Elizabeth I. *Harquebus* came from the German *hackenbuschse* or "hook gun," first mentioned in 1418 in both Braunschweig and Frankfurt and used by German cities to defend their walls.[6] The "hook" was used to attach the gun to a wall to support its weight and reduce the recoil. A gun with a hook attached became known as an *arquebus a croc*. If the hook were removed, the gun was called a harquebus and that word was applied generally to all portable firearms in the sixteenth century.[7] The military and civilians used the harquebus. The Dutch word was *Hakkenbusse*, the French word (*h*)*arquebuze*, and the Italians called this kind of gun a *scopietti*.[8]

The word *caliver* referred to a smaller, lighter harquebus widely used in late-sixteenth-century England. A humorous story connected with the origins of *caliver* holds that the word *calibre* in French, refers to the size of the bullet, not the gun. An English soldier, not understanding French, thought that *calibre* meant the gun, so he called the device a *caliver*, a mistake that stuck. For their part, the French called the gun a *Peece de calibre*, meaning a gun with a bigger bullet.[9]

Two other words appeared in the sixteenth century as descriptors of the small handguns noted in Appendix A. One word was *pistol*, or its variant *pistolet*. The *OED* states that the word *pistolet* appeared first, but does not offer a specific date. It is said that *pistol* derived from a Bohemian word, *pistala*, meaning "firing tube."[10] In Western Europe, the word *pistol* was first found in French in 1566. The English probably derived their word *pistol* from French, and it was in use by 1570. The other term, *dag*, occurred first in England in a proclamation of 23 January 1549 issued by King Edward VI and his Privy Council.[11] Its derivation is unknown. Sometimes the term became *pocket dag* to indicate that the device was small enough to be concealed in a person's pocket. Some pocket dags were no more than five or six inches in length. The English government regarded the pocket dag as a very dangerous weapon (which it was) and took repeated steps to ban it.

The word *gunner* meant two things in the early modern era. The preferred meaning in the *OED* was a man who fires a cannon. An acceptable meaning was a man who fires a handgun. I have used the term in both senses.

By the beginning of the fifteenth century, the word *gunpowder* had a place in the English language. In 1404, the mixture was known in English records as *pulvere pro guerra*, but by 1411, clerks in the Exchequer were using the word *gunpowder*.[12] In 1611, Thomas Heywood, referring to the sharpness of saltpeter, remarked that "an old woman is better . . . then [sic] Saltpeter for making gun-powder."[13] Perhaps he was alluding to the role urine played in making saltpeter and joined it to the idea of incontinent old women; perhaps he was thinking of the sharp, short temper of some senior women. Gunpowder continued to be described as an old woman in 1690 and 1785.[14]

A minor contretemps occurred in the press over the English habit of adopting foreign words for military terms. Sir John Smythe, the major defender of the longbow and a participant in the debate about the relative merits of the longbow and the gun, at the end of Queen Elizabeth I's reign, was indignant over this development. He fumed that the words "the body of the watch, or 'standing watch' as we were wont to term it, is called corps du garde. As though our English nation, which hath been so famous in all action military many hundred years, were now but newly crept into the world, or as though our language were so barren that it were not able of itself to afford convenient words."[15]

Sir Roger Williams, also a participant in the longbow versus gun debate, answered him in conciliatory terms. He explained that the use of foreign words were necessary for some things because "there are fewe [words] or none at all in our language" that are appropriate. There was also the matter of communicating with military men in Europe. If he, an Englishman, called a "Rampier a wall [Europeans] would thinke I lied," he said. Williams urged fairness: "as most languages call London and Bristol as we do, so it is best for us to call their inventions as they do."[16]

The use and meaning of the word *gun* expanded as it appeared in metaphor and slang. Among the numerous examples, the following sample illustrates the point. As early as 1551, the phrase "out of gunshot," was recognized as meaning out of danger, and it continued to appear in that sense throughout the seventeenth century.[17] *Gun* was used to intensify or underscore an expression. For example, in 1622, Fletcher wrote in *The Prophetess*, Act 1, scene 3, "You are right, master. Right as a gun." Fifty-nine years later, in 1681, Dryden used the word in the same sense in *The Spanish Friar*, Act 3, scene 2. This practice continued until 1892.[18] "As sure as a gun" was another turn of phrase referring to the dependability of guns.[19] In 1633, in Jonson's *The Tale of a Tub*, Act 2, scene 1, appeared the remark, "'Tis right; he has spoke as True as a Gun, believe it." William Congreve (1670–1729), Henry Fielding (1707–1754), and John Gay (1685–1732) also turned to the expression to stress certainty in their dialogues.[20] John Breval used it effectively in his *The Play Is the Plot* (1718) to show that Sir Barnaby is certain that he has discovered that his daughter and Captain Daredevil are scheming to elope. Barnaby expostulates, "Another Plot laid by my Daughter and Captain Daredevil . . . as sure as a Gun! But I'll put a Spoke in their Wheel."[21]

By 1645, the words *gun* and *great gun* had migrated to wine or ale and meant a "Flagon" or bottle of spirits.[22] John Evelyn recorded in his diary on 7 August 1645 that he had enjoyed a dinner on board a boat headed for Turkey from Venice. The meal was of "English pouderd beefe and other good meate with a store of Wine, & greate Gunns, as the manner is."[23] Samuel Pepys also recalled a fine dinner he had with friends in March 1662, noting that the toasts drunk to their wives' health were "seven or nine guns" apiece.[24] By 1700, to be "in the gun" was to be drunk.[25]

The word *gun* took on other meanings. In Thomas Fuller's *Gnomologia*, no. 1824, in 1732 it conveyed the idea of strength, as in "He carries too big a Gun for me; I must not engage him."[26] Sailors picked up the word and used it in a "gunner's daughter," to mean the cannon to which a sailor was lashed when he was punished by flogging. "To marry the gunner's daughter" was to be flogged. The turn of phrase "flash in the pan" came directly from the unsuccessful operation of a matchlock gun. Sometimes the priming powder failed to reach the powder charge in the barrel because it was damp or the touchhole was clogged; in these circumstances the priming powder simply flared or flashed up in the pan with no result. A vivid account of the arrest of some highwaymen on 20 December 1720 uses these precise words to describe what happened. As the constable and others entered Black Horse Inn in Westminster, one of the "rogues . . . offered to fire his [pistol] close against the Breast of the Master of the Inn, but it flash'd in the Pan," and the constable was able to seize the men.[27] The phrase "flash in the pan" also came to mean a person who displays early brilliance but falters along the way or fails to live up to his or her promise. No date of first use is known, but it would have been before 1720. The phrase continues in use today.[28]

Using the word *gun* in aphorisms continued into the modern world, far beyond the period of this study. However, one or two examples are worth noting. The phrase "Son of a gun" began as a pejorative term used in the British Navy in the early 1800s to refer to a sailor's bastard baby boy born on deck amid gun emplacements to a female slave or prostitute. ("Son of a bitch" came into the English language at about the same time.) By 1867, a British admiral, who explained that wives of officers who accompanied their husbands would give birth under the gun carriages, sanitized this account. Today, the meaning has evolved into an affectionate greeting between good friends, as in, "Great to see you, you old son of a gun."[29] Another familiar phrase, "Stick to one's guns," means not to give up, not to change one's mind; it appeared first in 1839.[30]

The device that we know in English as a gun has borne that name for approximately 670 years and traces its origins back to a Scandinavian woman's name Gunhildr meaning war; Gunna or Gonne were its diminutives. *Gun* became the generic term for different kinds of firearms, which received specific names as well. The use of the word *gun* in metaphor in early modern England continued throughout the era, with new meanings being added, even in the modern world. Nothing so well illustrates how deeply firearms penetrated society than that the word *gun* appears in so many idioms, proverbs, and metaphors that ordinary people use. This made the gun a normal part of everyday life and helped to humanize it by masking its original purpose of killing and destruction in war.

NOTES

Abbreviations

BC   Burney Collection of Seventeenth- and Eighteenth-Century Newspapers (digitized), British Library

BL   British Library

CJ   Parliament, Great Britain, *Journals of the House of Commons*, 11 volumes

CSPD   *Calendar of State Papers, Domestic Series*, 1553–1714

DNB   H. C. G. Matthew and Brian Harrison, eds., *Oxford Dictionary of National Biography*, 60 volumes

HEHL   Henry E. Huntington Library, San Marino, California

HMSO   Her or His Majesty's Stationery Office

NA   National Archives, London

OED   *Oxford English Dictionary*

SP   State Papers

SR   Alexander Luders et al., eds., *Statutes of the Realm*, 11 volumes

Introduction

1. A gun founder worked in a gun foundry casting artillery (cannon). A gunmaker (either a man or a woman) put together the parts of a firearm—the barrel, the stock, and the lock—to make a gun.

2. Bert S. Hall, *Weapons and Warfare in Renaissance Europe: Gunpowder, Technology, and Tactics* (Baltimore: Johns Hopkins University Press, 1997), 99. Howard L. Blackmore, *Hunting Weapons from the Middle Ages to the Twentieth Century* (Mineola, NY: Dover Publications, Inc., 2000), 217.

3. *SR*, 3: 132. A mark was worth about two-thirds of a pound (*OED*, s.v. "mark").

4. Lawrence Stone, *Crisis of the Aristocracy 1558–1641* (Oxford: At the Clarendon Press, 1965), 239–40.

5. The word "gunner" means two things: first, a man who fires a cannon; second, a man who fires a handgun (*OED*, s.v. "gunner").

6. Abigail Kohn, "Their Aim Is True. Taking Stock of America's Real Gun Culture," *Reason Magazine Online*, May 2001. http://reason.com/archives/2001/05/01/their-aim-is-true.

7. Peter Burke, *Varieties of Cultural History* (Ithaca, NY: Cornell University Press, 1997), chaps. 1, 3, 8, and 11.

8. J. R. Hale, "Gunpowder and the Renaissance: An Essay in the History of Ideas," in *From the Renaissance to the Counter-Reformation*, ed. Charles H. Carter (New York: Random House, 1965), 113–44.

9. Lisa Jardine, *The Awful End of Prince William the Silent* (London: Harper Collins, 2005), 85–92.

10. I presented a paper on this material at the Renaissance Society of America meeting in 2008 and hope to publish it in the future.

11. Henry J. Webb, *Elizabethan Military Science: The Books and the Practice* (Madison: University of Wisconsin Press, 1965) is the classic study.

12. Lady Sherley's name is spelled variously. I have followed the spelling preferred by Sheila R. Canby, *Shah 'Abbas The Remaking of Iran* (London: British Museum Press, 2009), 57.

13. Howard L. Blackmore, *Gunmakers of London 1350–1850* (York, PA: George Shumway, 1986). Blackmore, *Gunmakers of London, Supplement 1350–1850* (Bloomfield, Ontario: Museum Restoration Service, 1999).

14. Charles Ffoulkes, *The Gun-Founders of England: With a List of English and Continental Gun-Founders from the XIV to the XIX Centuries* (Cambridge: Cambridge University Press, 1937); J. F. Hayward, "The Huguenot Gunmakers of London," *Journal of Arms and Armour Society* 6, no. 4 (1968): 117–43; A. N. Kennard, *Gunfounding and Gunfounders* (London: Arms and Armour Press, 1986); R. E. G. Kirk and Ernest F. Kirk, eds., *Return of Aliens Dwelling in the City and Suburbs of London* (Aberdeen: University Press for the Huguenot Society of London, 1902); W. E. May, "Some Board of Ordnance Gunmakers," *Journal of Arms and Armour Society* 6, no. 7 (1969): 201–4; W. Keith Neal and D. H. W. Back, *Great British Gunmakers 1540–1740* (London: Lund Humphries, 1984); and Richard W. Stewart, *The English Ordnance Office 1585–1625: A Case Study in Bureaucracy* (London: Royal Historical Society/Boydell Press, 1996).

15. Natalie Deibel, then a graduate student in History at the George Washington University, first constructed the spreadsheets, and Adrienne Shevchuk, then a staff member of the Institute at the Folger Shakespeare Library, maintained and expanded them.

16. David Cressy, *Saltpeter: The Mother of Gunpowder* (Oxford: Oxford University Press, 2013). Jack Kelly, *Gunpowder: Alchemy, Bombards, and Pyrotechnics* (New York: Basic Books, 2004).

1. Re-creating and Developing a Gun Industry

1. Neither J. S. Scarisbrick (*Henry VIII* [London: Eyre & Spottiswoode, 1970]) nor John Guy (*Tudor England* [Oxford: Oxford University Press, 2008]) mentions the matter. David Starkey (*Henry: Virtuous Prince* [London: Harper Press, 2008], 314, 316) and Lucy Wooding (*Henry VIII* [London: Routledge, 2009], 69) note Henry's concern. Howard L. Blackmore credits the king with advancing the gun industry in *Gunmakers of London 1350–1850* (York, PA: George Shumway, 1986), 11–12.

2. Their choice of name shows that the word *Gunmaker* was descriptive of a craft and also bore a generic connotation that covered subspecialties within the industry (see Appendix A).

3. T. F. Tout, "Firearms in England in the Fourteenth Century," *English Historical Review* 26 (1911): 670–72.

4. See Bert S. Hall, *Weapons and Warfare in Renaissance Europe: Gunpowder, Tech-

nology, and Tactics (Baltimore: Johns Hopkins University Press, 1997), 44, and OED, s.v. "ribaudequin."

5. Hall, Weapons and Warfare in Renaissance Europe, 678, 679, 683. Blackmore, Gunmakers of London, 10, 206.

6. Tout, "Firearms in England," 673–74. Hall, Weapons and Warfare in Renaissance Europe, 45–46.

7. John Charlton, ed., The Tower of London: Its Buildings and Institutions (London: HMSO, 1978), 18. Blackmore, Gunmakers of London, 142.

8. Blackmore, Gunmakers of London, 66.

9. Ibid., 10.

10. David Grummitt, "The Defence of Calais and the Development of Gunpowder Weaponry in England in the Late Fifteenth Century," War in History 7, no. 3 (2000), 253–72. I used Grummitt's article reproduced in Historical Abstracts with full Text, pp. 1–20. http://web.b.ebscohost.com.proxygw.wrlc.org/ehost/delivery?sid=96942149-155b -4578-a4. Grummitt, Historical Abstracts, 1–2, 3.

11. Grummitt, Historical Abstracts, 6–9.

12. Ibid., 10, 12–13.

13. Ibid., 11, 12.

14. James Raymond, Henry VIII's Military Revolution (London: Tauris Academic Studies, 2007), 29.

15. David Cressy, Saltpeter: The Mother of Gunpowder (Oxford: Oxford University Press, 2013), 42.

16. Raymond, Henry VIII's Military Revolution, 28.

17. Grummitt, Historical Abstracts, 10, 11, 12.

18. Scarisbrick, Henry VIII, 21–30.

19. Ibid., 23.

20. Steven Gunn, "The French Wars of Henry VIII," in Origins of War in Early Modern Europe, ed. Jeremy Black (Edinburgh: John Donald Publishers, 1987), 45–47. Gunn offers a complex analysis of Henry's war policy.

21. Ibid., 37–40.

22. Ibid., 32–33.

23. Raymond, Henry VIII's Military Revolution, 28.

24. Howard L. Blackmore, Armories of the Tower of London, 2 vols. (London: HMSO, 1976), 1:4.

25. Charles Ffoulkes, The Gun-Founders of England: With a List of English and Continental Gun-Founders from the XIV to the XIX Centuries (Cambridge: Cambridge University Press, 1937), 29, for the Poppenruyter contracts. Scarisbrick, Henry VIII, 51, for Thomas Spinelly.

26. Ffoulkes, Gun-Founders of England, 4.

27. Blackmore, Gunmakers of London, 75.

28. Ibid., 69.

29. Ffoulkes, Gun-Founders of England, 108.

30. Ibid., 4–5. Also Blackmore, Armouries of the Tower of London, 1:4.

31. Letters and Papers, Foreign and Domestic, of the Reign of Henry VIII, 21 vols. (London: HMSO, 1864–1924), vol. 18, part 1, 564. Baude's name is spelled variously, and I have followed Ffoulkes, Gun-Founders of England, 117.

32. DNB, s.v. "Sir William Paget (1505/6–1563)." For Sir John Russell, Scarisbrick, Henry VIII, 127, 129, 131, 344, 359.

33. *Letters and Papers, Henry VIII*, vol. 19, part 2, 5 August 1544, Russell to Paget, 37.

34. Ibid., 20 August 1544, Russell to Paget, 117.

35. Adrian B. Caruana, *Tudor Artillery: 1485–1603*, Historical Arms Series no. 30 (Alexandria Bay, NY: Museum Restoration Service, 1992), 4.

36. Raymond, *Henry VIII's Military Revolution*, 30, identifies Damsell.

37. *Letters and Papers, Henry VIII*, vol. 19, part 2, 1544, 156.

38. In this instance, the word *gunner* identifies Baude as working with artillery.

39. Ffoulkes, *Gun-Founders of England*, 45.

40. *Letters and Papers, Henry VIII*, vol. 5, 306. "Treasurer of the Chamber's Accounts."

41. John Stow, *A Survey Of London*, ed. Charles Lethbridge Kingsford, 2 vols. (Oxford: At the Clarendon Press, 1908), 2:288, 128n.

42. *Letters and Papers, Henry VIII*, vol. 12, part 1, *Grants in April 1537*, 1103 (sub-items 21, 22).

43. *The Diary of Henry Machyn, Citizen and Merchant-Taylor of London, From A.D. 1550 to A.D. 1563*, ed. John Gough Nichols (London: Printed for the Camden Society by J. B. Nichols and Son, 1848), 36.

44. Blackmore, *Armouries of the Tower*, 7.

45. Stow, *Survey of London*, 1:128.

46. Joan Thirsk, *Economic Policy and Projects: The Development of a Consumer Society in Early Modern England* (Oxford: Clarendon Press, 1978), 24.

47. Ffoulkes, *Gun-Founders of England*, 46. *DNB*, s.v. "Ralph Hogge."

48. *DNB*, s.v. "William Levett" and "Ralph Hogge."

49. A. R. Hall, *Ballistics in the Seventeenth Century* (Cambridge: Cambridge University Press, 1952), 10–11. For a different view, see Blackmore, *Armouries of the Tower*, 5.

50. Hall, *Weapons and Warfare in Renaissance Europe*, 99. A harquebus was a handgun used by soldiers and by persons for private pleasures.

51. Howard L. Blackmore, *Hunting Weapons: From the Middle Ages to the Twentieth Century* (Mineola NY: Dover, 2000), 217.

52. *SR*, 3:132.

53. In this context, *wanton* means lawless, reckless, and willful: see *OED*, s.v. "wanton."

54. Paul L. Hughes and James F. Larkin, eds., *Tudor Royal Proclamations*, 3 vols. (New Haven, CT: Yale University Press, 1964), 1:121. An earlier proclamation on the same topic in 1526 was addressed to officials in London. Ibid., 107.

55. Ibid., 1:194.

56. Steven Gunn, "Archery Practice in Early Tudor England," *Past and Present* 209 (2010): 77.

57. Ibid., 78.

58. A personal e-mail from the Joiners Guild confirmed that no published study of the company exists. Its website, however, offers information at The Worshipful Company of Joiners and Celiers (www.joinersandceilers.co.uk). The word *celiers* (not in the *OED*) is related to Anglo Norman French, Middle English and Medieval Latin and means "carver."

59. These figures were generated by the spreadsheet from data provided by Blackmore, *Gunmakers of London*.

60. R. Campbell, *The London Tradesman: Being a Compendious View of all the Trades, Professions, Arts, both Liberal and Mechanic, now practiced in the Cities of London and Westminster* (London: Printed by T. Gardner, 1747), 242.

61. Hall, *Ballistics*, 12–14.

62. Gunmakers' Company Minutes, 1691–1704, MSS 5206, 124, Guildhall.

63. Renter Warden's Accompts, Gunmakers' Company, fol. 37, MSS 5219/1, Guildhall.

64. SP 12/147, fol. 85r, NA. Duplicate in SP 12/147, fol, 186r, NA. Neither document is signed or dated. *CSPD*, 1581–90, 8, offers the date, 1681, without proof. Proof is provided by Armourers Company Court Book, 1559–1621, 395, MSS 12071/2, Guildhall Library. At the meeting of 17 January 1580/81 the gunmakers' "sutt for ther Corporation" was discussed.

65. Blackmore, *Gunmakers of London*, 13. Parker was named a "Viewer of Firearms" on the gunmakers' draft proclamation of 1589.

66. Armourers Company Court Book, 1559–1621, 395, MSS 12071/2, Guildhall Library. 17 January 1580/81. Francis Russell, Second Earl of Bedford, (1526/7–1585) was a member of the Privy Council.

67. Lindsay Boynton, *Elizabethan Militia, 1558–1638* (London: Routledge, 1967), 69. C. G. Cruickshank, *Elizabeth's Army*, 2nd ed. (Oxford: Oxford University Press, 1966), 115.

68. Warwick was appointed Master of Ordnance in 1560. He was Francis Bedford's son-in-law. *DNB*, s.v. "Ambrose Dudley, Earl of Warwick."

69. SP 12/147, fol. 187r, NA.

70. Walsingham was a Privy Councilor. Quotation from *DNB*, s.v. "Sir Francis Walsingham."

71. Armourers Company Court Book, 1559–1621, 412, MSS 12071/2, Guildhall Library.

72. Blackmore, *Gunmakers of London*, 13.

73. Armourers Company Court Book, 1559–1621, 412, MSS 12071/2, Guildhall Library.

74. Ibid.

75. Ibid.

76. Ibid.

77. Ibid., 413.

78. Lansdowne MS. 59, no 78, fol. 211r–231r, British Library. Fol. 211r for this paragraph. The report and the petition are described and summarized in the draft proclamation.

79. Blackmore, *Gunmakers of London*, 117.

80. Lansdowne MS. 59, no. 78, fol. 211r and fols. 216r–217r, British Library.

81. Ibid., fol. 230r.

82. Walter M. Stern, "Gunmaking in Seventeenth-Century London," *Journal of Arms and Armour Society* 1, no. 5 (1954), 71–73.

83. Gunmakers Court Minutes, unfoliated, MSS 5220/2, Guildhall Library.

84. Blackmore, *Gunmakers of London*, 15.

85. Ibid. Also Stern, "Gunmaking in Seventeenth-Century London," 73.

86. Bankes Mss., Bundle 12, 24 (pagination irregular), Bodleian Library.

87. L. O. J. Boynton, "Charter of the Company of Gunmakers. London," *Journal of the Society for Army Historical Research* (London, 1927), 79–92.

88. "The Oath of every Member at his Admission into the Company of Gunmakers," Gunmakers MSS C 37/T, Guildhall Library.

89. Stern, "Gunmaking in Seventeenth-Century London," 73. Blackmore, *Gunmakers of London*, 15–16.

90. Blackmore, *Gunmakers of London*, 16.

91. Ibid.

92. Gunmakers Court Minutes, 28 August 1651, 5220/2, Guildhall Library.

93. Stern, "Gunmaking in Seventeenth-Century London," 75.

94. Armourers Court Minute Books, 1621–1675, fol. 197v, MSS 12071/3, Guildhall Library. Some words are illegible.

95. Gunmakers Court Minutes, 30 August 1655, 5220/2, Guildhall Library.

96. Armourers Court Minute Books, 1621–1675, fol. 213r, 12071/3, Guildhall Library.

97. Blackmore, *Gunmakers of London*, 65.

98. Gunmakers Court Minutes, 12 June 1656, 5220/2, Guildhall Library.

99. Stern, "Gunmaking in Seventeenth-Century London," 77.

2. Economic Opportunities for Men and Women

1. Geoffrey Parker, *The Military Revolution: Military Innovation and the Rise of the West, 1500–1800*, 2nd ed. (Cambridge: Cambridge University Press, 1996), 1, 2n. Roger B. Manning, *The Swordsmen: The Martial Ethos in the Three Kingdoms* (Oxford: Oxford University Press, 2003), 1–3nn2–3.

2. Penry Williams, *The Tudor Regime* (Oxford: Clarendon Press, 1991 paperback), chap. 10. Williams, "Rebellion and Revolution in Early Modern England," in *War and Society, Essays in Honour and Memory of John Western*, ed. M. R. D. Foot (London: Elek, 1973), 223–40.

3. Richard W. Stewart, *The English Ordnance Office, 1584–1625: A Case-Study in Bureaucracy* (London: The Royal Historical Society/Boydell Press, 1996); H. C. Tomlinson, *Guns and Government: The Ordnance Office under the later Stuarts* (London: Royal Historical Society, 1979).

4. Sarah Barter, "The Board of Ordnance," in *The Tower of London: Its Buildings and Institutions*, ed. John Charlton (London: HMSO, 1978), 106–7.

5. Stewart, *English Ordnance Office*, 6.

6. Stow, *A Survey Of London*, 1:125–26.

7. *Account of Sir Francis Flemynge, Lieutenant of the King's Ordnance in the Tower of London*. Additional Charter 16334, 1546. British Library.

8. Raymond, *Henry VIII's Military Revolution*, 275 9n.

9. *DNB*, s.v. "Thomas Seymour."

10. Raymond, *Henry VIII's Military Revolution*, 177.

11. Tomlinson, *Guns and Government*, 46–47.

12. Stewart, *English Ordnance Office*, 8.

13. It is notable that bullets play a role in Sidney's poetry.

14. Stewart, *English Ordnance Office*, Appendix 1. Tomlinson, *Guns and Government*, Appendix.

15. Stewart, *English Ordnance Office*, tables 1, 9.

16. Raymond, *Henry VIII's Military Revolution*, 164–79. *DNB*, s.v. "Christopher Morris."

17. Tomlinson, *Guns and Government*, 46–47.

18. Ibid., 6.

19. Ibid., 16.

20. Stewart, *English Ordnance Office*, 13, 16.

21. *DNB*, s.v. "Sir John Davis."

22. Stewart, *English Ordnance Office*, Appendix 1, 152.

23. Tomlinson, *Guns and Government*, 3.

24. Stewart, *English Ordnance Office*, 9, 15–16.

25. Ibid., 16.

26. Blackmore, *Armories of the Tower of London*, Vol. 1: *Ordnance*, 18.

27. Tomlinson, *Guns and Government*, 49.

28. SP 12/15, fols. 30r–31r, NA.

29. Ibid.

30. Caruana, *Tudor Artillery*, 4–5.

31. Ibid., 18–36.

32. Ibid., 19.

33. Ibid., 21–23.

34. Ibid., 24–26.

35. Stewart *English Ordnance Office*, Appendix 1, 150, 153.

36. *Journals of the House of Lords*, vol. 7, 6 May 1645.

37. *CJ*, vol. 4, 9 May 1645.

38. The occupations of apprentices' fathers from 1656 to 1800 reported in London Livery Company, *Apprenticeship Registers*, Abstracted and indexed by Cliff Webb, vol. 8, *Gunmakers' Company 1656–1800* (London: Society of Genealogists, 1997), were overwhelmingly in crafts and trades. These data cover a later date, but almost certainly the socioeconomic profile was roughly the same earlier.

39. These figures are based on Blackmore's *Gunmakers of London*.

40. London Livery Company, *Apprenticeship Registers*, vol. 41, abstracted and indexed by Cliff Webb, "Blacksmiths' Company 1605–1800." Some women were listed as masters of the Blacksmiths Company.

41. Stewart, *English Ordnance Office*, Appendix 2.

42. Ibid., 155, 157; Blackmore, *Gunmakers of London*, 117.

43. Stewart, *English Ordnance Office*, Appendix 2, 157, 183.

44. Accounts of the Ordnance Office 1585–1625, MS Eng. hist. c. 191, fol. 22r, Bodleian Library. See fols. 21v and 22v for Staunton and male gunmakers.

45. Blackmore, *Gunmakers of London*, 207.

46. Stewart, *English Ordnance Office*, Appendix 2, 158.

47. Ibid., 156.

48. Ibid., 159, 161.

49. WO 51/76v, NA.

50. Stern, "Gunmaking in Seventeenth-Century London," Appendix 1, 96–97. See 59 for orders in 1638 and 1639.

51. Ibid., 59–60.

52. Ibid., Appendix 2, 98–99.

53. Tomlinson, *Guns and Government*, 110.

54. Blackmore, *Gunmakers of London*, 93.

55. Ibid., 168.

56. Ibid., 180.

57. Ibid., 197.

58. Ibid., 95, 97.

59. Ibid., 181.

60. Names of women masters that I compiled differ in a few instances from those of Webb in *London Apprentices: Gunmakers' Company*.

61. Blackmore, *Gunmakers of London*, 99.

62. Ibid., 128.

63. Webb, *London Apprentices: Gunmakers' Company*, 31.

64. Company of Gunmakers Minutes, 1691–1704, MS 5220/6, 28, Guildhall Library. Blackmore, *Gunmakers of London*, 115.

65. Webb, *London Apprentices: Gunmakers' Company*, 18. Blackmore, *Gunmakers of London*, 134, 189.

66. Company of Gunmakers Minutes, 1691–1704, MS 5220/6, 28, Guildhall Library. Blackmore, *Gunmakers of London*, 105.

67. Webb, *London Apprentices: Gunmakers' Company*, 22. Blackmore, *Gunmakers of London*, 157.

68. Company of Gunmakers Minutes, 1691–1704, MS 5220/6, 28, Guildhall Library.

69. Blackmore, *Gunmakers of London*, 56, 61, 183.

70. Court Minutes 1681–1691, MS 5220/5, fol. 97v, Guildhall Library.

71. Ibid., fol. 98v

72. Ibid. fol. 97.

73. Ibid., fol. 113. Where Mrs. Stace sat is not recorded.

74. Company of Gunmakers, Quarterage Book, 1673–1737, MS 5226/1, Guildhall Library, lists twelve widows, but the symbols and written comments are difficult to decipher.

75. Renter Warden's Accompts 1664, MS 5219/1, fol. 3v, 6, 8, Guildhall Library; Blackmore, *Gunmakers of London*, 48.

76. Company of Gunmakers, Minutes, 1691–1704, MS 5220/6, 96, Guildhall Library.

77. Ibid. 207.

78. Ibid., 28. Blackmore, *Gunmakers of London*, 102, 111.

79. Court Minutes 1681–1691, MS 5220/5, fol. 76r, Guildhall Library.

80. Ibid., fol. 101r. Blackmore, *Gunmakers of London*, 102.

81. Index of Apprentices, MS 5220/5–7, B2:B53, Guildhall Library.

82. Steve Rappaport, *Worlds within Worlds: Structures of Life in Sixteenth-Century London* (Cambridge: Cambridge University Press, 1989), 37, 39.

83. Ibid., 41.

84. Hilda L. Smith, *All Men and Both Sexes: Gender, Politics, and the False Universal in England, 1640–1832* (University Park: Penn State University Press, 2002), 77–78.

85. Company of Gunmakers, Court Minutes, 1637–1663 (fair copy), MS 5220/2, 22 January 1656/57; 30 April 1657, Guildhall Library. Blackmore, *Gunmakers of London*, 39, 79.

86. Blackmore, *Gunmakers of London*, 42.

87. Howard L. Blackmore, *Gunmakers of London 1350–1850, A Supplement* (Bloomfield, Ontario: Museum Restoration Service, 1999), 48, 55. A Beadle, one of four officers reporting to the Master of the Company, had ceremonial duties and was responsible for organizing guild meetings.

88. Blackmore, *Gunmakers of London 1350–1850, A Supplement*, 57.

89. Renterwardens' Accounts, 1663–1745, MS 5219/1, fols.1v, 14v, Guildhall Library.

90. Blackmore, *Gunmakers of London*, 103.

91. Ibid., 72.

92. Ibid., 77.

93. Ibid., 93.

94. Hughes and Larkin, *Tudor Royal Proclamations*, 1:121.

95. Gunn, "Archery Practice," 77.

96. Hughes and Larkin, *Tudor Royal Proclamations*, 3:218.

97. "Cecil Papers: October 1601," in *Calendar of the Cecil Papers in Hatfield House*, Vol.

14, *Addenda*, ed. E Salisbury (London, 1923), 185–189. http://www.british-history.ac
.uk/cal-cecil-papers/vol14/pp185-189. Accessed 18 June 2015.

98. Neil Younger, *War and Politics in the Elizabethan Counties* (Manchester: Manchester University Press, 2012), 1–2, 24–25, 160–66.

99. MSS Eng. Hist. C.191, Bodleian Library.

100. *CSPD*, 1625–26, 184.

101. Blackmore, *Gunmakers of London*, 16, 65.

102. J. F. Hayward, *The Art of the Gunmaker*, 2 vols. (London: Barrie and Rockliff, 1962) 1:236. *Calendar of Assize Records*. James I, ed. J. S. Cockburn (London: HMSO, 1980–82), Kent Indictments, item 799.

103. Hayward, *Art of the Gunmaker*, 1:236.

104. Stern, "Gunmaking in Seventeenth-Century London," 82–84.

105. Blackmore, *Gunmakers of London*, 60.

106. Ibid., 41.

107. Derek Stimpson, ed., *The Worshipful Company of Gunmakers or The Gunmakers' Company: A History* (London: Worshipful Company of Gunmakers, 2008), 14–15. The size of the penalty is not given.

108. Blackmore, *Gunmakers of London*, 87.

109. Ibid., 139.

110. Ibid.

111. BC, *London Gazette*, 27 October 1692 (no. 2814).

112. BC, *Post Man and Historical Account*, 6 March 1712 (no. 2104). Isaac Maynard, a French gunsmith naturalized in 1700, 140.

113. BC, *Daily Post*, 26 June 1721 (no. 542); 30 June 1721 (no. 546).

114. MS 5220/1, fols.50v, 51r–v, Guildhall Library.

115. Gunmakers Company Minutes, 1691–1704, MS 5220/6, Court of Assistants, 226–27, Guildhall Library.

116. Court of Assistants and Order of the Court, MS. 5220/6, Guildhall Library. Four names added after 3 June 1703 brought the total to eighty.

117. Robert Latham and Williams Matthews, eds. *The Diary of Samuel Pepys*, 10 vols. (Berkley: University of California Press, 1970–83), 8:137 1n. The gunmaker was Edmund or George Trulocke, the date, 29 March 1667.

118. Blackmore, *Gunmakers of London*, 179.

119. Ibid., 67.

120. PROB 11/387, NA.

121. PROB 4/635, NA.

122. The church was destroyed in the Fire of 1666, but Cristopher Wren rebuilt it in 1670.

123. Blackmore, *Gunmakers of London*, 61.

124. PROB 11/395, NA.

125. Blackmore, *Gunmakers of London*, 46.

126. PROB 4/18344, NA.

127. PROB 4/4250, NA. A "Boltinge Mill" was a device for sifting coarse meal from flour. The *Oxford English Dictionary* does not directly define the term.

128. Blackmore, *Gunmakers of London*, 154. PROB 4/20583, NA.

129. *British Journal*, 20 July 1723 (no. 44). *London Gazette*, 23 July 1723 (no. 6184).

130. Blackmore, *Gunmakers of London*, 182.

3. Regulating Domestic Guns with "Good and Politic Statutes"

1. The word "ownership" does not appear in the limitations imposed on subjects by the statutes.

2. Paul L. Hughes and James F. Larkin, eds., *Tudor Royal Proclamations*. 3 vols. (New Haven, CT: Yale University Press, 1964–69), 1:171, 194.

3. R. W. Heinze, *Proclamations of the Tudor Kings* (Cambridge: Cambridge University Press, 1976), 153–77. Scholars now agree that the Statute of Proclamations (1539 to 1547) aimed primarily to improve the enforcement of statutes, not to override law.

4. Edward Berry, *Shakespeare and the Hunt* (Cambridge: Cambridge University Press, 2001), ix.

5. Chester and Ethyn Kirby, "The Stuart Game Prerogative," *English Historical Review* 46, (1931): 239–40.

6. *SR*, 2:65.

7. Alistair Dunn, *The Great Rising of 1381: The Peasants' Revolt and England's Failed Revolution* (Charleston, SC: Tempus, 2002).

8. *SR*, 3:132.

9. Ibid., 215–16.

10. Hughes and Larkin, *Tudor Royal Proclamations*, 1:121. An earlier proclamation on the same topic in 1526 was addressed to officials in London and other places. 1:107.

11. *SR*, 3:833, 835.

12. Hughes and Larkin, *Tudor Royal Proclamations*, 1:247, 254.

13. Ibid., 284.

14. *SR*, 4, Part 1, 58.

15. William Lambarde, *Eirenarcha, or: The Office of the Justices of the Peace*, 4th ed. (1599), 296.

16. William Dalton, *Countrey Justice, Conteyning the practice of the Justices of the Peace out of their Session* (London: Printed for the Society of Stationers, 1618), 50.

17. Hughes and Larkin, *Tudor Royal Proclamations*, 2:804.

18. Arthur MacGregor, "The Household Out Of Doors: The Stuart Court and the Animal Kingdom," in *The Stuart Courts*, ed. Eveline Cruickshanks (Phoenix Mill, Gloucestershire: Sutton Publishing, 2000), 86–117, presents a broad picture of animals at court.

19. P. B. Munsche, *Gentlemen and Poachers* (Cambridge: Cambridge University Press, 1981), 11–12.

20. Elizabeth Read Foster, ed., *Proceedings in Parliament 1610*, 2 vols. (New Haven, CT: Yale University Press), 1:51.

21. Edmund S. Morgan, *Inventing the People: The Rise of Popular Sovereignty in England and America* (New York: W. W. Norton & Co., 1988), 23.

22. The Act is conveniently found in J. P. Kenyon, ed., *The Stuart Constitution 1603–1688: Documents and Commentary*, 2nd ed. (Cambridge: Cambridge University Press, 1986), 457–58.

23. Munsche, *Gentlemen and Poachers*, 16–19.

24. Ibid., 63–64, for this paragraph.

25. Steven Gunn, "Archery Practice in Early Tudor England," *Past and Present*, No. 209 (2010), 79.

26. Ibid.

27. J. S. Cockburn, ed., *Calendar of Assize Records. Elizabeth I*, 5 vols. (London: HMSO, 1975–80), vol. 3, item 2478.

28. J. S. Cockburn, ed., *Calendar of Assize Records, James I,* 5 vols. (London: H.M.S.O, 1975–82), vol. 4, item 1139.

29. S. C. Ratcliff and H. C. Johnson, eds., *Warwick County Records,* 9 vols. (Warwick: L. Edgar Stephens, 1935–64), 6:7.

30. Ibid., 49.

31. Arthur MacGregor, "Animals and the Early Stuarts: Hunting and Hawking at the Court of James I and Charles I," *Archives of Natural History* 16 (1989): 308.

32. Ibid.

33. Ibid.

34. J. S. Cockburn, ed., *Calendar of Assize Records, Kent Indictments, Charles II,* 1660–1675 (London: HMSO, 1995), items 1093, 1255, 1275–77.

35. J. A. Sharpe, ed., "'William Holcroft, His Booke': Local Office-holding in Late Stuart Essex," *Essex Record Office Publication* 90, (1986), 25–27, 29, 32–33, 35, 61.

36. Ratcliff and Johnson, eds. *Warwick County Records,* Quarter Sessions, vol. 9, 125.

37. Joseph Stileman to Sir Robert Cecil 29 July 1598, Cecil Papers, CP 62/99: 8:280, Hatfield House.

38. Hertford County Records, *Notes and Extracts from the Sessions Rolls 1581–1698,* ed. W. J. Hardy (Hertford: Published by C. E. Longmore, Clerk of the Peace Office, 1905), 906.

39. Munsche, *Gentlemen and Poachers,* 64.

40. Ibid.

41. SP 15/20, fol. 54r, NA.

42. J. J. Scarisbrick, *Henry VIII* (London: Eyre and Spottiswoode, 1970), 39–46. John Guy, *Tudor England* (Oxford: Oxford University Press, 1988), 149–53.

43. Stephen Gunn, David Grummitt, and Hans Cools, eds., *War, State, and Society in England and the Netherlands, 1477–1559* (Oxford: Oxford University Press, 2007), 320, for quote. Guy, *Tudor England,* 150, for figure.

44. Richard Hoyle, *The Pilgrimage of Grace and the Politics of the 1530s* (Oxford: Oxford University Press, 2001), 460–63, for the Pontefract Articles; 347–53 for analysis.

45. 7 April 1537, Privy Council to the Duke of Norfolk, in *Miscellaneous State Papers from 1501 to 1726,* ed. Philip Yorke, Earl of Hardwicke, 2 vols. (London: W. Strahan & T. Cadell, 1778), 1:43–45.

46. I have written an article on this important proposal, which I hope to publish.

47. SP 12/59, fols. 1v–2r, NA.

48. *SR,* 4, part 1, 548.

49. Ibid., *An Acte concerning shooting in Long Bows,* 1:25–26.

50. Ibid., vol. 4, part 1, 285.

51. Hughes and Larkin, *Tudor Royal Proclamations,* 1:108.

52. Ibid., 121.

53. C. G. Cruickshank, *Elizabeth's Army* (Oxford: Oxford University Press, 1966), 103.

54. Lindsay Boynton, *Elizabethan Militia* (London: Routledge and Kegan Paul, 1967), 66–69, for this paragraph.

55. Gunn, "Archery Practice," 55, 57.

56. Boynton, *Elizabethan Militia,* 58–59.

57. Cruickshank, *Elizabeth's Army,* 109.

58. Boynton, *Elizabethan Militia,* 67.

59. *Harquebuz* and *caliver* are words for guns defined in Appendix B.

60. Boynton, *Elizabethan Militia,* 66.

61. Frederick Darby Cleaveland, *Notes on the Early History of The Royal Regiment of Artillery* (Woolwich: Printed by the author, 1892), 18.

62. Ibid., 112.

63. Sir John Smythe, *Certain Discourses Military, written by Sir John Smythe, Knight; Concerning the formes and effects of diuers sorts of weapons* (London: Richard Johnes, 1590), 81.

64. Ibid., 74.

65. Ibid., 23–24, 28.

66. Ibid., proem.

67. See Maurice J. D. Cockle, *A Bibliography of English Military Books up to 1642 and of Contemporary Foreign Books*, (London: Holland Press, 1978). Henry J. Webb, *Elizabethan Military Science: The Books and the Practice* (Madison: University of Wisconsin Press, 1965). G. Geoffrey Langsam, *Martial Books and Tudor Verse* (New York:King's Crown Press, 1951), and Paul A. Jorgensen, *Shakespeare's Military World* (Berkeley: University of California Press, 1956).

68. Humphrey Barwick, *Concerning The Force And Effect Of Manuall Weapons Of Fire* (London: E. Allde, 1594?), B.

69. Ibid., Bv.

70. Ibid., B2.

71. Robert Barret, *The Theorike and Practike of Moderne Warres, Discourse in Dialogue wise* (London: Printed for William Ponsonby, 1598), 4.

72. Ibid., 17.

73. Peter Edwards, *Dealing in Death: The Arms Trade and the British Civil Wars, 1638–52* (Phoenix Mill, Gloucestershire: Sutton Publishing, 2000), 4–5, finds a greater role for bows than does Barbara Donagan, *War in England, 1642–1649* (Oxford: Oxford University Press, 2008), 74.

74. Hughes and Larkin, *Tudor Royal Proclamations*, 1:108.

75. Heinze, *Proclamations of the Tudor Kings*, 91.

76. *SR*, 4: part 1, 285.

77. *Calendar of the Patent Rolls, Queen Elizabeth I: Preserved in the Public Record Office, 1558–82*, 9 vols. (London: HMSO, 1939–86), 4: item 538.

78. Ibid., 6: item 962.

79. Ibid., item 3106.

80. Paul L. Hughes and James F. Larkin, eds., *Tudor Royal Proclamations*, 3 vols. (New Haven, CT: Yale University Press, 1964–69), 1:194.

81. *SR*, 3:832–35. A demyhake is a handgun of "about three-quarters of a yard long." *OED*, s.v. "demyhake."

82. Journal of Court of Common Council, COL/CC/01/10/15, vol. 15 (1543–48), Fol. 77v, London Metropolitan Archives, for this proclamation, which, curiously, is not included in Hughes and Larkin, *Tudor Royal Proclamations*.

83. See Heinze, *Proclamations of the Tudor Kings*, 186.

84. Hughes and Larkin, *Tudor Royal Proclamations*, 1:271.

85. *SR*, 4, part 1, 58.

86. Hughes and. Larkin, *Tudor Royal Proclamations*, 1:320.

87. H. Robinson, ed., *Original Letters Relative to the English Reformation Society*, 2 vols. (1846–47), 2, no. 301, 648.

88. *DNB*, s.v. "Thomas Seymour, Baron Seymour of Sedeley."

89. Andy Wood, *The 1549 Rebellions and the Making of Early Modern England* (Cam-

bridge: Cambridge University Press, 2007). Jane Whittle, "Lords and Tenants in Kett's Rebellion, 1549," *Past and Present* 207, (2010): 3–52.

90. N. M. Sutherland, "The Assassination of Francois Duc de Guise, February 1563," *Historical Journal* 24, 2 (June 1981): 279–82.

91. Lisa Jardine, *The Awful End of Prince William the Silent: The First Assassination of a Head of State with a Handgun* (London: Harper Collins, 2005), 99–115.

92. Multiple-firing pistols had been developed. See Appendix A.

93. Guy, *Tudor England*, 277–78.

94. Ibid., 285, 331, 334. Also *DNB*, s.v. "William Cecil, first Baron Burghley," and "Francis Walsingham."

95. Hughes and Larkin, *Tudor Royal Proclamations*, 2:459.

96. Ibid., 611.

97. Ibid., 641.

98. Ibid., 3:766.

99. James F. Larkin and Paul L. Hughes, eds., *Stuart Royal Proclamations*, 2 vols. (Oxford: Clarendon Press, 1973), 1:126.

100. H. M. C., *MSS of the Duke of Buccleuch and Queensberry preserved at Montagu House, Whitehall*, 1:239–40. Cited in Ian Eaves, "Further Notes on the Pistol in Early Seventeenth Century England," *Journal of the Arms and Armour Society* 8 (June 1976): 288.

101. Larkin and Hughes, *Stuart Royal Proclamations*, 1:160.

4. Domestic Gun Licenses Issued "As if under the Great Seal"

1. *SR*, 3:132–33. 6 Henry VIII.c.13. The *OED* uses "plagard" and "placard" interchangeably. It defines the word as "a formal license giving authority or permission for something; a warrant, a permit, letters patent, letters of placard: a letter under seal." The date of the first use of "placard" is 1482, and of "plagard," 1481–90.

2. Records of the gun licenses are found in the Patent Rolls.

3. Three hundred marks in 1514, and £100 in subsequent laws.

4. *SR*, 3:457–58. 25 Henry VIII.c 17.1533.

5. "A forme for a placarde to be graunted to any person to shoote in Crosse bowes and handgunnes," SP 12/15, fol. 57, NA.

6. "Concerning Crossbows and Handguns," *SR*, 3:835. 33 Henry VIII.c.6.1541.

7. Memorandum from Queen Elizabeth to Sir Nicholas Bacon, Keeper of the Great Seal, May 1561, C82/1092, NA. The queen refers only to "certen causes and consideracons us movinge" to issue a license.

8. Henry VIII did so in 1511. *SR*, 3:32–33, 3 Henry.c.13.

9. *SR*, 3:215–21; 14 Henry VIII.c.7.1523; *SR*, 3:457–58; 25 Henry VIII.c.17.1533; *SR*, 3:834; 33 Henry VIII.c.6.1541.

10. *SR*, 3:834–85; 33 Henry VIII.c.6, Addenda, 1541.

11. Paul L. Hughes and James F. Larkin, *Tudor Royal Proclamations*, 3 vols. (New Haven, CT: Yale University Press, 1964–69), 1:271.

12. Sir Edgar Stephens, *The Clerks of the Counties, 1360–1960* (London: Society of Clerks of the Peace, 1961), 36.

13. *SR*, 4, part 1, 58. 2 & 3 Edward VI.c.14.

14. "Hawk's meat" refers to food for hawks kept for hunting.

15. *SR*, 4, part 2, 1055. 1 Jac.c.27.1604.

16. SP 15/20, fol. 54v, NA. Also, as a point of interest, the Gun Licence Act of 1870 set the cost at 10 shillings.

17. *SR*, 3:33. Parenthetically, between thirty thousand and forty thousand game licenses were bought each year during the decade of the 1820s. Munsche, *Gentlemen and Poachers*, 196, n.1.

18. John Strype, *Life of the learned Sir John Cheke*, (Oxford: Clarendon Press, 1821), 90. I thank John McDiarmid for this reference.

19. Privy Council to Suffolk Muster commissioners, Greenwich, 20 June 1569, Harleian MSS 309, fol. 102r, BL.

20. John Abbot of Faversham to [Thomas] Cromwell, 20 February 1532, *Letters and Papers Foreign and Domestic, of the Reign of Henry VIII*, 21 vols. (London: HMSO, 1864–1920), 5:812.

21. Ibid., vol. 20, pt. 1, 1166 (25).

22. The dowager countess is not noticed in the *DNB*. She merits an entry.

23. *DNB*, s.v. "Thomas Howard."

24. *The Complete Peerage*, (London: St. Catharine Press, 1945), vol. 10:245, note b.

25. Peter Gwyn, *The King's Cardinal: The Rise and Fall of Thomas Wolsey* (London: Barrie and Jenkins, 1990), 173.

26. *Letters of Royal and Illustrious Ladies of Great Britain*, ed. Mary Anne Everett Wood, 3 vols. (London: Henry Colburn, 1846), 2:10–12, letter 5.

27. Ibid., 13–14, letter 6 and editor's notes.

28. *Letters and Papers of Henry VIII*, 6:68.

29. Gwyn, *King's Cardinal*, 294, 296.

30. *Letters and Papers of Henry VIII*, 6:381.

31. Ibid., vol. 20, part 2, 995, 492.

32. Ibid., part 1, 1166 (25).

33. Ibid., part 2, 332 (41).

34. *Calendar of the Patent Rolls Preserved in the Public Records Office. Edward VI*, 6 vols. (London: HMSO, 1921), 1:216–17. The license was dated 16 September 1547.

35. *Calendar of the Patent Rolls Preserved in the Public Records Office. Philip and Mary*, 4 vols. (London: HMSO, 1936–39), 3:258. *DNB*, s.v. "Sir Richard Southwell."

36. *Calendar of the Patent Rolls. Philip and Mary*, 1:328; *Calendar of the Patent Rolls Preserved in the Public Records Office, 1558–82. Elizabeth I*, 9 vols. (London: HMSO, 1939–86), 2:510.

37. *Calendar of the Patent Rolls. Philip and Mary*, 1:328, 2:80, 3:181, 487.

38. Ibid., 3:360.

39. *Calendar of Patent Rolls, Elizabeth I*, 4: item 317.

40. Ibid., item 109. I thank John F. McDiarmid for this information.

41. Ibid., 5: item 1815.

42. *Calendar of Patent Rolls*, 43 Elizabeth I (1600–1601), 2 vols., ed. Simon R. Neal and Christine Leighton (Great Britain: List and Index Society, 2011), Vol. 339, item 483.

43. *CSPD, Elizabeth 1581–1590* (1865), 149.

44. *Calendar of Patent Rolls, Philip and Mary*, 2:118.

45. SEAX, Essex Record Office, Essex Archives Online, 1604, Q/SR 169/57.

46. *Calendar of the Patent Rolls. Philip and Mary*, 3:280.

5. Military Service

1. Steven Gunn, "The French Wars of Henry VIII," in *Origins of War in Early Modern Europe*, ed. Jeremy Black (Edinburgh: John Donald Publishers, 1987), 28–29.

2. The military prerogative of the monarchy underwent change in the early modern era. The Militia Bill and Ordinance of 1641–42 stripped it from the king; the Militia Act of 1660 reaffirmed it; and the Bill of Rights of 1689 qualified it.

3. John Guy, *Tudor England* (Oxford: Oxford University Press, 1988), 168.

4. Penry Williams, *The Tudor Regime* (Oxford: Clarendon Press, 1979), 113, 119. James Raymond, *Henry VIII's Military Revolution* (London: Tauris Academic Studies, 2007), 118–22. C. G. Cruickshank, *Army Royal: Henry VIII's Invasion of France, 1513* (Oxford: Clarendon Press, 1969), 28.

5. *Letters and Papers, Foreign and Domestic of the Reign of Henry VIII*, 21 vols. (London: HMSO, 1864–1920), "The Army against France," 1544, vol. 5, part 1, 273, for the numbers.

6. Paul E. J. Hammer, *Elizabeth's Wars: War, Government and Society in Tudor England, 1544–1604* (Basingstoke, Hampshire: Palgrave Macmillan, 2003), 28. Steven Gunn, "Archery Practice in Early Tudor England," *Past and Present* 209 (2010): 76.

7. Hammer, *Elizabeth's Wars*, 9, for quote; 26, for number.

8. Raymond, *Henry VIII's Military Revolution*, 34.

9. Ibid. Cruickshank, *Army Royal*, 64, 66–67.

10. Raymond, *Henry VIII's Military Revolution*, 178. Hammer, *Elizabeth's Wars*, 18, for quote.

11. Gunn, "Archery Practice," 76.

12. Hammer, *Elizabeth's Wars*, 28–29, for the weaknesses of the system and its implications.

13. Keith Thomas, "Arms and the Man," chap. 2 in *The Ends of Life: Roads to Fulfillment in Early Modern England* (Oxford: Oxford University Press, 2009), 44–77.

14. Cruickshank, *Elizabeth's Army*, 3.

15. *The historie of Orlando Furioso... As it was plaid before the queens Maiestie* (London: Iohn Danter, 1594). *The historie of Orlando Furioso... As it was plaid before the queens Maiestie* (London: Simon Stafford, 1599).

16. Barbara Reynolds, ed., introduction to *Orlando Furioso*, by Ludovico Ariosto. (Baltimore: Penguin, 1975), 74–82.

17. William Camden, *Remains Concerning Britain* (Printed by John Legatt for Simon Waterson: London, 1614), 241–42. Thomas Montagu (1388–1428) was wounded in the face by a stone cannonball at Orléans on 24 October 1428, and died on 3 November 1428. Camden's book was issued five times before 1640, so his views were well known.

18. Samuel Buggs, *Miles Mediterraneus. The Mid-land Souldier. A Sermon Preached... In The Military Garden in the... Citie of Coventry* (1622), 27. Buggs expected his audience to know the story of Abimelech, told in Judges 9:50–57. When Abimelech, a murderous king, ruthlessly attempted to subdue the city of Thebez, the people took refuge in the tower. Abimelech prepared to burn it down. But from the tower's ramparts a woman threw down a millstone that landed on his head. Realizing that he was doomed, Abimelech commanded his armour bearer to run him through with his sword so no one could say that he died at the hands of a woman.

19. David Person, "Of Armies and Battels," in David Person, ed., *Varieties: or, A surueigh of rare and excellent matters, necessary and delectable for all sorts of persons* (London: Richard Badger [and Thomas Cotes], 1635), 115.

20. Henry J. Webb, *Elizabethan Military Science: The Books and the Practice* (Madison: University of Wisconsin Press, 1965) 113.

21. Bert S. Hall, *Weapons and Warfare in Renaissance Europe: Gunpowder, Technology, and Tactics* (Baltimore: Johns Hopkins University Press, 1997), 193–94, for this paragraph.

22. Sir Humphrey Gilbert, *Queene Elizabethes Achademy* (London: Published for the Early English Text Society, 1898), 4.

23. Harleian MSS 6844, fol. 16, excerpted in Cruickshank, *Elizabeth's Army*, 24.

24. *CSPD*, 1598–1601, 248.

25. *DNB*, s.v. "John Cruso."

26. Cruso, *Militarie Instructions for the Cavallrie*, A3.

27. Ibid., 27.

28. Hall, *Weapons and Warfare in Renaissance Europe*, 190.

29. *DNB*, s.v. "John Cruso." Subjects who wished to hunt effectively with a gun would have found Cruso's book helpful.

30. *Journal of the Siege of Rouen*, ed. J. G. Nichols (Camden Miscellany I, 1847), 40, cited in J. R. Hale, "Gunpowder and the Renaissance: An Essay in the History of Ideas," in *From the Renaissance to the Counter-Reformation*, ed. Charles H. Carter (New York: Random House, 1965), 127.

31. George Lawder, *The Scottish Souldier* (Edinburgh, 1629), fol. A4t, cited in Hale, "Gunpowder and the Renaissance," 127n72.

32. *Letters and Papers of Henry VIII*, vol. 19, part 1, 1544, #575.

33. Sir Roger Williams, *A Briefe Discourse of Warre, With his opinion concerning some parts of the Martiall Discipline* (London: Thomas Orwin, 1590), 43.

34. Webb, *Elizabethan Military Science*, 6–7, 54, 56–57, 70.

35. T. Proctor, *Of the Knowledge and Conducte of Warres* (London: Richard Tottelli, 1578), preface.

36. Roger B. Manning, *Swordsmen: The Martial Ethos in the Three Kingdoms* (Oxford: Oxford University Press, 2003), 15–16.

37. Ibid., 10, 23–24.

38. See David Cannadine, *The Decline and Fall of the British Aristocracy* (New Haven, CT: Yale University Press, 1990), 264, 265, 280.

39. Webb, "Cavalry," chapter 5 in *Elizabethan Military Science*, 108–23.

40. The Civil Wars have attracted historians since the seventeenth century. Charles Carlton supplies a brief overview of the scholarship in *Going to The Wars: The Experience of the British Civil Wars 1638–1651* (London: Routledge, 1994), 2–3. See also Barbara Donagan, *War in England, 1642–1649* (Oxford: Oxford University Press, 2008).

41. John Childs, *The Army of Charles II* (London: Routledge and Kegan Paul, 1976).

42. Studies of the militia include: I. F. W. Beckett, *The Amateur Military Tradition, 1558–1945* (Manchester: Manchester University Press, 1991); Lindsay Boynton, *Elizabethan Militia, 1558–1638* (London: Routledge, 1967); Mark Charles Fissel, *English Warfare, 1511–1642* (London: Routledge, 2001); Hammer, *Elizabeth's Wars*; and Neil Younger, *War and Politics in the Elizabethan Counties* (Manchester: Manchester University Press, 2012). Researchers have not studied all county militias. Except for general properties, each county militia was unique.

43. Musters usually occurred once a year, but sometime more often, and sometimes only every three years.

44. Younger, *War and Politics*, 13.

45. *SR*, vol. 4, part 1, 4 & 5 Philip and Mary, c.2 (*An Act for having of Horse Armour and Weapons*), 316–20, and ibid., 4 and 5 Philip and Mary, c.3 (*An Act for taking of Musters*), 320–21.

46. Lawrence Stone, *The Crisis of the Aristocracy 1558–1641* (Oxford: Clarendon Press, 1965), 219–22, for comment.

47. *SR* vol. 4, part 1, 4 & 5 Philip and Mary, c.2 (*An Act for having of Horse Armour and Weapons*), 317–18.

48. Boynton, *Elizabethan Militia*, 21, 23.

49. Ibid., 22–23.

50. Cruickshank, *Elizabeth's Army*, 24.

51. H.M.C., *Calendar of the Manuscripts of the Most Hon. The Marquis of Salisbury*, (London: HMSO, 1892), part 4, 17–18.

52. *SR*, vol. 4, Part 1, 4 & 5 Philip and Mary, c.2 (*An Act for the taking of Musters*), 320–21, for this paragraph.

53. Geoffrey Gates, *The Defence of the Militarie Profession. Wherein is eloquently shewed the due commendation of Martiall prowess* (London: Printed for Henry Middleton, 1579), 54–55.

54. Cruickshank, *Elizabeth's Army*, 9.

55. *Norfolk Lieutenancy Journal 1676–1701*, transcribed and edited by B. Cozens-Hardy (Norwich: Norfolk Record Society, 1961), 30:12.

56. I. F. W. Beckett, "Buckinghamshire Militia Lists for 1759: A Social Analysis," *Records of Buckinghamshire*, ed. G. R. Elvey, vol. 20, pt. 3 (1977): 464.

57. Lois G. Schwoerer, "The Grenville Militia List for Buckinghamshire, 1798–1799," *Huntington Library Quarterly*, vol. 68, no. 4 (2005): 672–73.

58. Howard L. Blackmore, *British Military Firearms 1650–1850* (London: Herbert Jenkins, 1961), 18.

59. Edward Davies, *The Art of War, and Englands Traynings* (London: Edward Griffin, 1619).

60. Boynton, *Elizabethan Militia*, 107, 111–12.

61. Nathaniel Nye, *The Art of Gunnery* (London: Wiliam Leak, 1670), 36, 41.

62. Jim Bennett and Stephen Johnston, *The Geometry of War 1500–1750* (Oxford: Museum of the History of Science, 1996) is a catalogue of an exhibit of instruments developed to assist the gunner.

63. Deborah E. Harkness, *The Jewel House: Elizabethan London and the Scientific Revolution* (New Haven, CT: Yale University Press, 2007), 140–41.

64. Nye, *The Art of Gunnery*, 35.

65. Cruickshank, *Elizabeth's Army*, 116. Soldiers tried to reduce the cost of gunpowder by declining to fire their gun in practice, a step counterproductive to their learning to shoot.

66. Boynton, *Elizabethan Militia*, 27.

67. Ibid., 91.

68. Younger, *War and Politics*, 105–7.

69. Ibid., 133. Boynton, *Elizabethan Militia*, 108–9, 111.

70. Younger, *War and Politics*, 133–34.

71. Ibid., 136, 142–45.

6. London

1. For the history and character of the Agas Map, see Adrian Prockter and Robert Taylor, comps., *The A to Z of Elizabethan London* (London: London Topographical Society, 1979), v–vi.

2. Later maps do not show this kind of social detail.

3. John Charlton, ed., *The Tower of London: Its Buildings and Institutions* (London: HMSO, 1978), 35.

4. Walter M. Stern, "Gunmaking in Seventeenth-Century London," *Journal of Arms and Armour Society* 1, no. 5 (1954): 55–99. Richard W. Stewart, *The English Ordnance Office, 1584–1625: A Case Study in Bureaucracy* (London: Royal Historical Society/Boydell Press, 1996). H.C Tomlinson, *Guns and Government: Ordnance Office under the Later Stuarts* (London: Royal Historical Society, 1979). Harold L. Blackmore, *Gunmakers of London, 1350–1850* (York, PA: George Shumway, 1986).

5. For different purposes, Vanessa Harding examines the changes in London's shape in "City, Capital, and Metropolis: The Changing Shape of Seventeenth-Century London," in *Imagining Early Modern London: Perceptions and Portrayals of the City from Stow to Strype, 1598–1720*, ed. J. F. Merritt (Cambridge: Cambridge University Press, 2001): 117–43.

6. Laura Hunt Yungblut, *Strangers Settled Here amongst Us: Policies, Perceptions and the Presence of Aliens in Elizabethan England* (London: Routledge, 1996), 15–18. Yungblut does not mention gunmakers.

7. Steve Rappaport, *Worlds Within Worlds: Structures of Life in Sixteenth-Century London* (Cambridge: Cambridge University Press, 1989), 55–56. Numbers are drawn from surveys of aliens ordered by the Privy Council. Lien Luu's figures are higher in her monograph *Immigrants and Industries in London, 1500–1700* (Aldershot, Hants, England: Ashgate, 2005), 92.

8. I have deduced this number from pages in the following work: R. E. G Kirk and Ernest F. Kirk, eds., *Returns of Aliens Dwelling in the City and Suburbs of London from the Reign of Henry VIII to that of James I*, 4 vols. (Aberdeen: University Press for the Huguenot Society of London, 1900–1908), 1: 425, 427, 451, 457, 458, 463, 466, 472.

9. J. F. Hayward, "The Huguenot Gunmakers of London," *Journal of the Arms and Armour Society* 6, no. 4 (December 1968): 117–43, for gunmakers who came for religion.

10. M. J. Power, "The Social Topography of Restoration London," in *London 1500–1700: The Making of the Metropolis*, eds. A. L Beier and Roger Finlay (London: Longman, 1986), 216, 218, 221, validates this point for the occupations he studied.

11. Charles Ffoulkes, *The Gun-Founders of England: With a List of English and Continental Gun-Founders from the XIV to the XIX Centuries* (Cambridge: Cambridge University Press, 1937), 44, 45.

12. The numbers were developed by entering data in Blackmore, *Gunmakers in London*, into the Spreadsheet on Locations, noted in the introduction.

13. Blackmore, *Gunmakers of London*, 142, 145.

14. An article on the contribution of aliens to gunmaking and gun founding would be worthwhile.

15. Blackmore, *Gunmakers of London*, 93.

16. See above, chap. 2.

17. Blackmore, *Gunmakers of London*, 77.

18. Martha Carlin, "St. Botolph Aldgate Gazetteer: Minories, East Side; Holy Trinity

Minories" (Unpublished, Institute of Metropolitan Studies, 1987). I thank Owen Myhill, Institute of Metropolitan Studies, for sending me an electronic copy. This highly detailed analysis of each property on the street would serve as a basis for a close study of each parcel connected to gunmaking.

19. Gillian Bebbington, *London Street Names* (London: Batsford, 1972), 222.

20. John A. Stow, *A Survey of London* (1603), 2 vols. Reprint., with introduction and notes by Charles Lethbridge Kingsford (Oxford: At the Clarendon Press, 1908–71), 1:125–26.

21. Stern, "Gunmaking in Seventeenth-Century London," 55.

22. Tomlinson, *Guns and Government*, 109, 118–19, 122.

23. Stow, *Survey of London*, 1:128.

24. Ibid.

25. Ibid., 128–29.

26. Ffoulkes, *Gun-Founders of England*, 44, 45.

27. Sarah Barter, "The Board of Ordnance," in *The Tower of London: Its Buildings and Institutions*, ed. John Charlton (London: HMSO, 1978), 107.

28. Ibid., 148. Also Adrian B. Caruana, *Tudor Artillery: 1485–1603*, Historical Arms Series no. 30 (Alexandria Bay, NY: Museum Restoration Service, 1992), 16, 11n.

29. Charlton, *Tower of London*, 35.

30. Barter, "Board of Ordnance," 110.

31. See Clive Harris, *The History of the Birmingham Gun-Barrel Proof House*, 2nd ed. 1949, 4, cited in Stern, "Gunmaking in Seventeenth-Century London," 2n. However, Anita Hewerdine, *The Yeomen of the Guard and the Early Tudors: The Formation of a Royal Bodyguard* (London: I. B. Tauris, 2012), does not mention it.

32. See Howard L. Blackmore, *Armouries of the Tower of London*, 2 vols. (London: HMSO, 1976), 1:10. Sir Thomas Wyatt (c.1521–1554) was the son of the poet, Sir Thomas Wyatt (c.1503–1542). *DNB*, s.v. "Sir Thomas Wyatt (c.1521–1554)."

33. Charlton, *Tower of London*, 35.

34. *The Funeral Procession of Sir Philip Sidney Febr. 1586*, n.p., 15224, Folger Shakespeare Library.

35. J. F. Hayward, *The Art of the Gunmaker*, 2 vols. (London: Barrie and Rockliff, 1962) 1:34, 120–21.

36. David Dean, "Elizabeth's Lottery: Political Culture and State Formation in Early Modern England," *Journal of British Studies* 50, no. 3 (2011): 587–611.

37. *A Curious Collection of Paintings and other Curiosities will be sold by auction, at the Barbadoes Coffee-House in Exchange Alley, over against the Royal Exchange in Cornhill* (London: 1691). Wing C7659.

38. John Fisher and Roger Cline, comps., Place Name Index to *The A to Z of Restoration London* (Lympne Castle, Kent: Harry Margary/Guildhall Library, 1992), 84.

39. MSS 9234/4, fols. 11v, 49r, 71r, Guildhall Library.

40. Blackmore, *Gunmakers of London*, 69.

41. Ibid., 140.

42. Ibid., 67.

43. Ibid., 180.

44. Ibid., 101.

45. Ibid., 177.

46. Ibid., 119.

47. Thomas Churchyard, *A General Rehearsal of Warres, wherein is five hundred Sev-*

erall Services of Land and Sea: as Sieges, Battailles, Skirmiches, and Encounters (London: Imprinted by Edward White, dwelling at the little Northe doore of Paules Church, at the signe of the Gunne, 1579).

48. J. R. Hale, "Gunpowder and the Renaissance: An Essay in the History of Ideas," in *From the Renaissance to the Counter-Reformation*, ed. Charles H. Carter (New York: Random House, 1965), 132. Dated early Stuart England.

49. John Downame, *Brief concordance, or table to the Bible of the Last Translation* (London: Printed by W. Du-Gard, and are to bee sold by E. D. and N. E. at the sign of the Gun in Ivie-lane, 1652).

50. Thomas White, *Practice of Christian perfection* (London: printed for Jos. Cranford at the sign of the Gun in Ivy Lane, 1653 [i.e., 1652]).

51. *Sir Arthur Haselrig's Last Will and Testament, With a Briefe Survey of his Life and Death* (London: Printed for Henry Brome, and are to be sold at his shop at the sign of the Gun in Ivy-lane, 1661).

52. Edward Leigh, *Choice Observations of all the Kings of England from the Saxons to the Death of King Charles the First* (London: Printed for Joseph Cranford, at the sign of the Gun in St. Pauls Church-yard, 1661).

53. Charles Cotton, *Burlesque upon burlesque: or, The scoffer scoft* (London: Printed for Henry Brome at the sign of the Gun at the west-end of St. Paul's Church-yard, 1675).

54. Justine Taylor, "The Origins of the Honourable Artillery Company: Part I—King Henry VIII and the 'Fraternity or Guild of Artillery,'" *The Honourable Artillery Company Journal* 86 (Autumn 2009): 105–15, and "The Origins of the Honourable Artillery Company: Part II—The Heirs of the 1537 'Fraternity or Guild of Artillery of Longbows, Crossbows and Handguns,'" *The Honourable Artillery Company Journal* 87 (Autumn 2010): 101–12.

55. *Acts of the Privy Council*, ed. John Roche Dasant et al., 46 vols. (London: HMSO, 1890–1964), 33:667, 668.

56. Samuel Buggs, *Miles Mediterraneus. The Mid-land Souldier. A Sermon* (London: John Dawson for John Bellamie, 1622), 33.

57. *An Essay in Defence of the Female Sex . . . In a Letter to a Lady. Written by a Lady* (London: Printed for A. Roper and E. Wilkinson, 1696), 92–93.

58. See Bruce Smith, *The Acoustic World of Early modern England: Attending to the O-factor* (Chicago: University of Chicago Press, 1999).

59. David Cressy, *Bonfires and Bells: National Memory and the Protestant Calendar in Elizabethan and Stuart England* (Berkeley: University of California Press, 1989). *Weekly Packet*, 4–11 March 1721, No. 453.

60. *Letters and Papers, Foreign and Domestic, of the Reign of Henry VIII*, 21 vols. (London: HMSO, 1864–1920), 14: item 14.

61. *The Diary of Henry Machyn, Citizen and Merchant-Taylor of London, From A.D. 1550 to A.D. 1563*, ed. John Gough Nichols (London: Printed for the Camden Society by J. B. Nichols and Son, 1848), 35.

62. *OED*, s.v. "Guns."

63. Frederick Darby Cleaveland, *Notes on the Early History of The Royal Regiment of Artillery* (Woolwich: Printed by the author, 1892), 18. Robert Thomas, Master Gunner of England, oversaw the firing and was killed by the explosion.

64. Blackmore, *Gunmakers of London*, 131.

65. Edith Hamilton, *Henrietta Maria* (London: Hamish Hamilton, 1976), 53.

66. Robert Latham and Williams Matthews, eds. *The Diary of Samuel Pepys*, 10 vols. (Berkley: University of California Press, 1970–83), 1:153.

67. *Weekly Packet*, 4–11 March 1721, No. 453.

68. Alan St. H. Brock, *A History of Fireworks* (London: George G. Harrap & Co., Ltd., 1949), 32.

69. Ibid.

70. Ibid., 34.

71. Ibid., 35–36.

72. *The Burning of the Whore of Babylon, As it was Acted, with great Applause, in the Poultrey, London, on Wednesday Night, being the Fifth of November Last, at Six of the Clock* (London: Printed and to be sold by R.C., 1673), 2.

73. David Person, "Of Armies and Battels," in David Person, ed., *Varieties: or, A surueigh of rare and excellent matters, necessary and delectable for all sorts of persons* (London: Richard Badger [and Thomas Cotes], 1635), 115.

74. Stow, *Survey of London*, 1:222.

75. Charles Edelman, "Shoot at Them All at Once," *Theatre Notebook: A Journal of the History and Technique of the British Theatre* 57 (2003): 78–81. I thank Irene Dash for calling my attention to this essay.

76. *Henry VIII*, eds. Barbara A. Mowat and Paul Werstine (New York: Washington Square Press, 2007), 50–51. Wotton thought the cannons went off to announce the arrival of King Henry VIII.

77. Logan Pearsall Smith, ed., *The Life and Letters of Sir Henry Wotton*, 2 vols. (Oxford: At the Clarendon Press, 1907), 2: 33. John Nichols, *Progresses, Processions, and Magnificent Festivities of King James the First*, 4 vols. (London: Printed by and for J. B. Nichols, Printer to the Society of Antiquaries, 1828), 1:155, in also reported the event.

78. Howard L. Blackmore, *Gunmakers of London, Supplement 1350–1850* (Bloomfield, Ontario: Museum Restoration Service, 1999).

79. Stern, "Gunmaking in Seventeenth-Century London," 64.

80. BC, *Daily Courant*, 5 November 1703 (no. 485).

81. BC, *Weekly Journal or British Gazetteer*, 24 December 1726 (no. 85).

82. Damian Carrington, "Gunpowder Plot Would have Devastated London." *Newscientist.com*, 5 November 2003. http://www.newscientist.com/article/dn4338-gunpowder-plot-would-have-devastated-london.html#.VTcW1FoNL4M.link.

83. *Death's Master-peece: or, a True Relation of that Great and Sudden Fire in Tower Street, London, which by the Fiering of Gunpowder, on Friday the 4th of January, 1649* (London: Printed for Francis Grove, 1649 [i.e,. 1650]), 1–6.

84. Ibid., 6

85. *DNB*, s.v. "Hester Shaw."

86. Hester Shaw, *A Plaine Relation of my Sufferings. By that Miserable Combustion, which happened in Tower-street through the Unhappy Firing of a Great Quantity of Gunpowder, there the 4. of January 1650.* (London, 1653).

87. Lawrence Stone, *The Crisis of the Aristocracy 1558–1641* (Oxford: Clarendon Press, 1965), 223–34.

88. Ibid., 226.

89. BC, *Mercurius Politicus Comprising the Summ of All Intelligence*, 13–20 March 1655 (no. 301).

90. Sir Thomas Temple, 1st Bart., to his son Sir Peter Temple, 8 August 1634. MSS STT 2333, HEHL.

91. *Memoirs of Thomas, Earl of Ailesbury. Written by Himself.* 2 vols. (Westminster: Printed for the Roxburghe Club, 1895), 1:29.

92. *CSPD*, 1619–23, 179.

93. William Douglas Hamilton, ed., *A Chronicle of England during the Reigns of the Tudors, from A.D. 1485–1559. By Charles Wriothesley, Windsor Herald.* 2 vols. (Westminster: Printed for the Camden Society, 1875), 1:59.

94. Peter Marshall, "The Shooting of Robert Packington," *Religious Identities in Henry VIII's England*, ed. Peter Marshall (Aldershot, Hants: Ashgate, 2006), 62.

95. Ibid.

96. Ibid., 64–65

97. Hamilton, *Chronicle of England*, 2:117. *Diary of Henry Machyn*, 65. *Chronicle of the Grey Friars of London*, ed. John Gough Nichols (Westminster: Printed for the Camden Society, 1852), 90.

98. Hatfield House: e-resource: Archive Doc: CP 197/52. Calendar Reference: 24:70.

99. Jane Garrett, *The Triumphs of Providence: The Assassination Plot, 1696* (Cambridge: Cambridge University Press, 1980).

100. Bertrand A. Goldgar and Ian Gadd, eds., *The Cambridge Edition of the Works of Jonathan Swift*, English Political Writings 1711–1714 (Cambridge: Cambridge University Press, 2008), 321–32. Comment by editors, 26–27.

7. *"Newfangled and Wanton Pleasure" in the Many Lives of Men*

1. Harold L. Blackmore, *Hunting Weapons from the Middle Ages to the Twentieth Century* (Mineola, NY: Dover Publications, Inc., 2000), 217.

2. *Letters and Papers, Foreign and Domestic of the Reign of Henry VIII*, 21 vols. (London: HMSO, 1864–1920), 16: item 380, 170.

3. Howard L. Blackmore, *Royal Sporting Guns at Windsor* (London: HMSO, 1968), 217. The word "demi-hawk" is not in the *OED*.

4. Harold L. Blackmore, *Gunmakers of London, 1350–1850* (York, PA: George Shumway, 1986), 11, 49.

5. Account of Sir Francis Flemynge, Lieutenant of the King's Ordnance in the Tower of London, authorized by late King Henry VIII, Additional Charter 16334, BL.

6. David Starkey, ed., *The Inventory of King Henry VIII*, 2 vols. (London: Harvey Miller for Society of Antiquaries, 1998).

7. Ibid., no. 8269.

8. J. F. Hayward, *The Art of the Gunmaker*, 2 vols. (London: Barrie and Rockliff, 1962) 1:115–16.

9. Starkey, *Inventory of King Henry VIII*, vol. 1, no. 8271–8276, 8284 (two dags), 8315.

10. Natalie Zemon Davis, *The Gift in Sixteenth-Century France* (Madison: University of Wisconsin Press, 2000), 10, 22, 32.

11. T. F. Tout, "Firearms in England in the Fourteenth Century," *English Historical Review* 26 (1911): 674, 682. Tout thought this gift was the first firearm seen in Ireland.

12. *DNB*, s.v. "Lionel of Antwerp." He was made Duke of Clarence in 1362.

13. Bert S. Hall, *Weapons and Warfare in Renaissance Europe: Gunpowder, Technology, and Tactics* (Baltimore: Johns Hopkins University Press, 1997), 59–61.

14. Both guns are described in Appendix A.

15. David Grummitt, "The Defence of Calais and the Development of Gunpowder Weaponry in England in the Late Fifteenth Century," *War in History* 7, no. 3 (2000), 258.

16. Adrian B. Caruana, *Tudor Artillery: 1485–1603*, Historical Arms Series no. 30 (Alexandria Bay, NY: Museum Restoration Service, 1992), 9n.

17. Jane A. Lawson, ed., *The Elizabethan New Year's Gift Exchanges 1559–1603*. Records of Social and Economic History New Series 51 (Oxford: Oxford University Press, 2013), 279.

18. William Reid, "Present of Spain: A Seventeenth-Century Royal Gift," *Connoisseur* (August 1960), 23.

19. Blackmore, *Gunmakers of London*, 171.

20. Hayward, *Art of the Gunmaker*, 1:127. Blackmore, *Gunmakers of London*, 171.

21. Reid, "Present of Spain," 23. For a picture of the gun, now in the Royal Armoury, Madrid (K. 128), see Blackmore, *Gunmakers of London*, 172.

22. Hayward, *Art of the Gunmaker*, 1:127.

23. Ibid.

24. Ian Eaves, "Some Notes on the Pistol in Early Seventeenth Century England," *Journal of Arms and Armour Society*, 6 (1970): 288.

25. Elena Yablonskaya, "Seventeenth-Century English Firearms in the Kremlin," in *Britannia and Muscovy: English Silver at the Court of the Tsars*, eds. Olga Dmitrieva and Nataly Abramova (New Haven, CT: Yale University Press, 2006), 135.

26. Robert Elgood, *Firearms of the Islamic World* (London: I. B. Tauris Publishers, 1995), 70.

27. Howard L. Blackmore, *Gunmakers of London, Supplement 1350–1850* (Bloomfield, Ontario: Museum Restoration Service, 1999).

28. Elgood, *Firearms of the Islamic World*, 70. Blackmore, *Gunmakers of London*, 171.

29. See Blackmore, *British Military Firearms*, 28 for these examples.

30. Hayward, *Art of the Gunmaker*, 235–36.

31. Claude Blair, "Admiral Sir John Chicheley's Firearms, 1690," *Journal of Arms and Armour Society* 11, no. 5 (1985), 255.

32. Linda Levy Peck, *Consuming Splendour: Society and Culture in Seventeenth-Century England* (Cambridge: Cambridge University Press, 2005), 15–16, 18, 29, 230, 266. Maija Jansson, "Ambassadorial Gifts," in Dmitrieva and Natalya Abramova, *Britannia and Muscovy*, 198–206.

33. Hall, *Weapons and Warfare in Renaissance Europe*, 99. Blackmore, *Hunting Weapons*, 217, 220.

34. Richard Blome, *The Gentlemans Recreation. In Two Parts: The First being an Encyclopedy of the Arts and Sciences. The Second Part, Treats of Horsemanship, Fowling, Hawking, Fishing, Hunting, Agriculture* (London: S. Rotcroft, 1686), 67.

35. Charles Carlton, *This Seat of Mars: War and the British Isles, 1485–1746* (New Haven, CT: Yale University Press, 2011), 33.

36. Thomas Dekker, *The Artillery Garden. 1616.* (Oxford: Printed in the Bodleian, 1952), C3v.

37. Steven Gunn, "Archery Practice in Early Tudor England," *Past and Present* 209 (2010): 79.

38. P. B. Munsche, *Gentlemen and Poachers* (Cambridge: Cambridge University Press, 1981), 64.

39. Blackmore, *Hunting Weapons*, 220.

40. Ibid.

41. *The Basilicon Doron of King James I*, ed. James Craigie, 2 vols. (Edinburgh and London: Printed for Scottish Text Society, 3rd Series, 1944–50) 1:189. A recent, more accessible edition is *Law of Free Monarchies and Basilikon Doron*, ed. Daniel Fischlin and Mark Fortier (Toronto: Center for Reformation and Renaissance Studies, 1996), 167.

42. Cockburn, ed., *Calendar of Assize Records. Surrey Indictments*, James I, item 777.

43. *The Diary of John Evelyn*, ed. E. S. de Beer, 6 vols. (Oxford: Clarendon Press, 1955), 5:199.

44. BC, *Daily Courant*, 15 September 1716 (no. 4651).

45. Blome, *Gentlemans Recreation*, 125.

46. Geoffrey Parker, *The Military Revolution: Military Innovation and the Rise of the West, 1500–1800*, 2nd ed. (Cambridge: Cambridge University Press, 1996), 17.

47. Blackmore, *Hunting Weapons*, 217.

48. Paul L. Hughes and James F. Larkin, *Tudor Royal Proclamations*, 3 vols. (New Haven, CT: Yale University Press, 1964–69), 1:194.

49. Ascham and his work are discussed below.

50. Reported by bbc.uk/ahistoryoftheworld/objects/9/16/2010. When Kirkcudbright celebrates a national event today, it organizes shooting matches with the Siller gun as a prize.

51. Norman Dixon, *Georgian Pistols: The Art and Craft of the Flintlock Pistol, 1715–1840* (London: Arms and Armour Press, 1971), 23.

52. *Diary of John Evelyn*, 2:252–53.

53. Lawrence Stone, *The Crisis of the Aristocracy 1558–1641* (Oxford: Clarendon Press, 1965), 220.

54. Ibid.

55. On separate visits, Jackson Boswell and I heard the guide make this assertion. Efforts to confirm the story were unsuccessful.

56. F. G. Emmison, *Elizabethan Life: Home, Work and Land from Essex Wills and Sessions and Manorial Records* (Chelmsford: Essex County Council, 1976) 64.

57. Lindsay Boynton, *Elizabethan Militia, 1558–1638* (London: Routledge, 1967), 264.

58. Richard W. Stewart, *The English Ordnance Office, 1584–1625: A Case Study in Bureaucracy* (London: Royal Historical Society/Boydell Press, 1996), 10, 13n.

59. Boynton, *Elizabethan Militia*, 264.

60. *Diary of John Evelyn*, 3:560.

61. Miscellaneous, Box 1, folder 2, no. 7, STB Military, HEHL. Also *DNB*, s.v. "James Brydges."

62. Chamberlains' Accounts in Stratford-upon-Avon for 17 Feb. 1574, in "Minutes and Accounts of the Corporation of Stratford-upon-Avon and Other Records," ed. Richard Savage, 2:1566–77, *Publications of the Dugdale Society* (Oxford: Printed for the Dugdale Society, 1924), 3:75. I thank Lena Orlin for this reference.

63. *Diary of John Evelyn*, 4:473.

64. Richard Simpson, ed., *The Rambler, 1858: A Catholic Journal of Home and Foreign Literature*, vol. 10 (London: Forgotten Books, 2013), 399. I thank Gerard Kilroy for this reference.

65. The jewel was first mentioned in Pasfield's will, dated 1660. The enamel was damaged by fire in 1817, but the goldwork and the emeralds survived.

66. Blackmore, *Gunmakers of London*, 192.

67. Ibid., 191.

68. *DNB*, s.v. "Thomas Lee." Karen Hearn, ed., *Dynasties: Painting in Tudor and Jacobean England* (London: Tate Publishing, 1995), 176.

69. Karen Hearn, *Marcus Gheeraerts II: Elizabethan Artist* (London: Tate Publishing, 2002), 18–21, 59n. Hayward, *Art of the Gunmaker*, 1:123–24.

70. James McDermott, *Martin Frobisher* (New Haven, CT: Yale University Press, 2001), was a well-received biography. Hayward, *Art of the Gunmaker*, 1:120, identified the pistol as a wheel lock.

71. Rodney Dennys, *Heraldry and the Heralds* (London: Jonathan Cape, 1982), 155.

72. Stone, *Crisis of the Aristocracy*, 67.

73. Dr. Lynsey Darby, Archivist at the College of Arms, identified all but one of the men.

74. The College of Arms, "Grant of Arms to John Gouning, Mayor of Bristol," Miscellaneous Grants, 2:166.

75. A Collection of 500 Coats of Arms . . . Sixteenth Century, no. 366, fol. 47: Crest of Thomas Wall, Kent, 1591, V.b.256, FSL.

76. *DNB*, s.v. "William Camden."

77. The College of Arms, "Grant of Arms to Stephen Bull of Gillingham, Kent, Master Gunner of England. 1601," Miscellaneous Grants, vol. 2, fol. 580.

78. www.bubwith.net.

79. The portrait was in the London National Portrait Gallery, "National Portrait Exhibition, 1866."

80. *OED*, s.v. "linstock."

81. Stone, *Crisis of the Aristocracy*, 223–34.

82. Roger B. Manning, *Swordsmen: The Martial Ethos in the Three Kingdoms* (Oxford: Oxford University Press, 2003), 60–61.

83. Ibid., 157–58.

84. Ibid., 158–60, for the examples in this paragraph.

85. Cockburn, *Calendar of Assize Records: Elizabeth I*, vol. 5, item 1813.

86. Cockburn, *Calendar of Assize Records: Charles I. Kent Indictments*, vol. 1, item 14.

87. Ibid., item 467.

88. BC, *Post Boy and Historical Account*, 22 June 1695 (no. 19).

89. BC, *Fog's Weekly Journal*, 6 December 1729 (no. 64).

90. Cockburn, ed., *Calendar of Assize Records: Kent Indictments Charles II 1660–1675*, vol. 2, item 33.

91. BC, *Evening Post*, 3 March 1724 (no. 2279). Also reported by BC, *Weekly Journal or Saturday's Post*, 7 March (no. 280).

92. Cockburn, *Calendar of Assize Records: Elizabeth I*, vol. 5, item 1889.

93. Cockburn, *Calendar of Assize Records: Surrey Indictments, James I*, item 145.

94. BC, *Daily Courant*, 5 November 1703 (no. 485).

95. BC, *Parker's London News or the Impartial Intelligencer*, 12 October 1724 (no. 921). BC, *Newcastle Courant*, 17 Oct. 1724 (no. 226).

96. BC, *London Post with Intelligence Foreign and Domestick*, 8 Nov. 1699 (no. 68).

97. BC, *London Journal*, 28 December 1723 (no. 231).

98. BC, *Grub Street Journal*, 23 July 1730 (no. 29).

8. Guns

1. For example, Elizabeth H. Hageman, "Family Matters: Isabella and Geffrey Whitney's Advice to Their Siblings—and Adriana's Plight in "The Comedy of Errors" in *Renaissance Historicisms: Essays in Honor of Arthur F. Kinney*, ed. James M. Dutcher and Anne Lake Prescott (Newark: University of Delaware Press, 2008), 173–92. Lois G. Schwoerer, "Women's Public Political Voice in England: 1640–1700," in *Women Writers and the Early Modern British Political tradition*, ed. Hilda Smith (Cambridge: Cambridge University Press, 1998), 56–74. Hilda L. Smith, *All Men and Both Sexes: Gender, Politics, and the False Universal in England, 1640–1832* (University Park, PA: Penn State University Press, 2002). Melinda Zook, *Radical Whigs and Conspiratorial Politics in late Stuart England* (University Park: Penn State University Press, 1999), and *Protestantism, Politics, and Women in Britain, 1660–1714* (Houndsmill, Baskingstoke: Palgrave Macmillan, 2013).

2. Katherine Usher Henderson and Barbara F. McManus, eds., *Half Humankind: Contexts and Texts of the Controversy about Women in England, 1540–1640* (Urbana: University of Illinois Press, 1985). Linda Woodbridge, *Women and the English Renaissance: Literature and the Nature of Womankind, 1540–1620* (Urbana: University of Illinois Press, 1984). Sandra Clark, "Hic Mulier, Haec Vir, and the Controversy over Masculine Women," *Studies in Philology* 82 (1985), 157–83.

3. R. L. Wilson, *Silk and Steel: Women at Arms* (New York: Random House, 2003), 4, 13, 22, for what follows.

4. Bridget Clifford and Karen Watts, eds., *An Introduction to Princely Armours and Weapons of Childhood* (Leeds: Royal Armouries, 2003), 47. *DNB*, s.v. "Margaret Tudor."

5. Carole Levin, *The Reign of Elizabeth I* (New York: Palgrave, 2002), does not mention guns. She believes that Elizabeth never shot a gun (personal conversation).

6. Arthur MacGregor, "Animals and the Early Stuarts: Hunting and Hawking at the Court of James I and Charles I," *Archives of Natural History* 16 (1989): 305–18. John Nichols, ed., *Progresses and Public Processions of Queen Elizabeth*, 3 vols. (New York: B. Franklin, 1966), 2:671.

7. Competition in weaponry, including the pistol, was part of Viennese court entertainment. At a "great tournament" in 1699 attended by heads of state, the King of the Romans "took the prize of the Pistol." BC, *Flying Post or the Post Master*, 1 August 1699 (no. 660).

8. Their guns were probably made by Caspar Zeiner (1661–1745), the head of the Vienna Guild of Gunmakers in 1695, two of whose guns "made for the court shoots" have survived. See Wilson, *Silk and Steel*, 11, for pictures of them.

9. Lady Mary Wortley Montagu, *Complete Letters*, 3 vols., ed. Robert Halsband (Oxford: At the Clarendon Press, 1965–67), 1:268.

10. Ibid., 1:269.

11. Wilson, *Silk and Steel*, 10, 13

12. Ibid., 10, 17.

13. *Primo Supplemento al Catalogo Angelucci Elenco Degli Oggetti Acquisiti Dalla Armeria Reale Di Torino Dopo il 1890*, ed. Giorgio Dondi (Torino, 2005), M151 and also M152

14. Personal conversation with Graeme Rimer.

15. Linda Levy Peck, *Consuming Splendour: Society and Culture in Seventeenth-Century England* (Cambridge: Cambridge University Press, 2005), 69–70. I thank Peck for this reference.

16. Lorna Weatherill, "A Possession of One's Own: Women and Consumer Behavior in England, 1660–1740," *Journal of British Studies*, 25 (1986): 131–56.

17. Perhaps Lady Spencer bought the guns at the Royal Exchange (founded in 1565), which, according to Lindsay Boynton, "certainly included shops that sold armor, guns, and ammunition." Lindsay Boynton, *Elizabethan Militia, 1558–1638* (London: Routledge and Kegan Paul, 1967), 69–70. However, the report on gunshops compiled for the years 1676–1704 does not mention a gunshop at the Royal Exchange.

18. Payments in Paris and on the journey from Paris to Lyons, Oct. 1699, Accounts 173, # 20, Hatfield House. I thank Linda Levy Peck for this reference.

19. Wilson, *Silk and Steel*, 13.

20. See Carmen Gimenez and Francisco Calvo Serraller, eds., *Spanish Painting from El Greco to Picasso: Time, Truth, and History* (Catalogue for exhibit at the Guggenheim Museum, New York, Spring 2007), 176.

21. See Amazon.com, where pistol gun cufflinks set in silver are on offer for $60.00 and a "smoking gun bangle watch" sells for $105.00. Also Chee Pearlman, "Nine of a Kind: Purse Pistols," *New York Times Magazine*, 20 March 2011, 19. As more citizens in the United States are allowed to carry concealed weapons, guns are made "flashier, more feminine and easier to pop into a handbag." Nine guns are pictured, one showing roses on the barrel, another decorated with Swarovski crystals. Prices range from $352.00, to $4,000 for a "Freedom Arms .22," customized with jewels.

22. The picture is now in the Ashmolean Museum in Oxford. Thomas Cecil was the engraver. The quotation is from Anne Somerset, *Elizabeth I* (New York: St. Martin's Press, 1991), 464.

23. The Sherleys attracted contemporary interest. Tracts were written about Sir Robert and his brothers and plays about Lady Sherley. The *DNB*, includes an entry for Sir Robert, but not for Lady Sherley.

24. Portraits of the Sherleys were included in an exhibit held at the British Museum, 19 February–14 June, 2009. For the exhibit catalogue, see: Sheila R. Canby, *Shah 'Abbas: The Remaking of Iran* (London: British Museum Press, 2009).

25. *DNB*, s.v. "Sir Robert Sherley." Ian Eaves, "Further Notes on the Pistol in Early Seventeenth Century England," *Journal of the Arms and Armour Society* 8 (June 1976): 292, for reference to firearms. Kenneth Chase, *Firearms: A Global History to 1700* (Cambridge: Cambridge University Press, 2008), 117–19.

26. Canby, *Shah 'Abbas*, 57, citing the opinion of Edward Faridany.

27. Eaves, "Further Notes on the Pistol," 294.

28. Ibid.

29. Ibid.

30. Canby, *Shah 'Abbas*, 57.

31. Eaves, "Further Notes on the Pistol," 292.

32. Male playwrights, notably John Webster, had earlier used guns as stage props and placed them in the hands of female characters. For example, in Webster's *The White Devil*, ed. Christina Luckyi (London: Methuen Drama, 2008), two women fire pistols at the man who brought them a case of pistols for a suicide pact that they have no intention of fulfilling. Also, in Webster's *The Duchess of Malfi*, ed. Leah S. Marcus (London: Arden Shakespeare, 2009), Julia, mistress of the Cardinal, pulls a gun on Bosola in Act 5, scene 2.

33. Aphra Behn, *Oroonoko, The Rover, and Other Works*, ed. Janet Todd (London: Penguin Books, 1992), 11. Also *DNB*, s.v. Aphra Behn.

34. Aphra Behn, *Poems upon Several Occasions* (London: R. Tonson and J. Tonson, 1697), 168–69.

35. *OED*, s.v. "gunpowder."

36. It is commonly said that Spenser was the first poet to substitute gunshot for Cupid's arrow.

37. J. R. Hale, "Gunpowder and the Renaissance: An Essay in the History of Ideas," in *From the Renaissance to the Counter-Reformation*, ed. Charles H. Carter (New York: Random House, 1965), 132–34.

38. Margaret Cavendish, Duchess of Newcastle, "Assaulted and pursued Chastity," in *Nature's Pictures drawn by fancies pencil to the life. Written by the thrice noble, illustrious, and excellent princess, the lady Marchioness of Newcastle.* (London: printed for J. Martin and J. Allestrye, 1656), 220.

39. Ibid., 222–23, for this paragraph.

40. Ibid., 227.

41. *The Compleat English and French Vermin-Killer, Being a Necessary Family-Book* (London: Printed by G. Conyers, at the Ring in Little-Britain, 1707), 3. Featured in Jean Miller et al, eds., *The Housewife's Rich Cabinet: Remedies, Receipes, and Helpful Hints*, Catalog of Exhibition, 27 August 1997–31 January 1998 (Washington, DC: Folger Shakespeare Library, 1997).

42. William Clarke, *The Natural History of Nitre: Or, A Philosophical Discourse of the Nature, Generation, Place, and Artificial Extraction of Nitre* (London: Printed by E. Okes for Nathaniel Brook at the Angel in Cornhill near the Royal Exchange, 1670), 92.

43. Robert May, *The Accomplish'd Cook, or The Art & Mystery of Cookery*, 5th ed. (London, Odabiah Blagrave, 1685), n.p.

44. V.a.388, 200, Folger Shakespeare Library.

45. John Webster, *The Duchess of Malfi*, Act 3, scene 2, 17–19, cited in Hale, "Gunpowder and the Renaissance," 132.

46. Robert Boyle, *Medicinal Experiments* 3rd ed. (London, 1696), cited in Miller et al., *The Housewife's Rich Cabinet*, 112.

47. Nicolas Lemery, *New Curiosities in Art and Nation* (London, 1711) cited in Miller et al., *The Housewife's Rich Cabinet*, 74–75.

48. R.C., *The Complete Midwife's Practise Enlarged*, 4th ed., enlarged (London, 1680), cited in Miller et. al., *The Housewife's Rich Cabinet*, 92–93.

49. Howard L. Blackmore, *Hunting Weapons: From the Middle Ages to the Twentieth Century* (Mineola NY: Dover Publications, Inc., 2000), 219.

50. *Old Bailey Proceedings Online* (www.oldbaileyonline.org, version 7.2, 5 June 2015), April 1691, trial of John Gray (t16910422-9). This John Gray is not listed in the Gunmakers' list of gun shopkeepers nor does he appear in Harold L. Blackmore's *Gunmakers of London, 1350–1850* (York, PA: George Shumway, 1986). Perhaps he is related to two earlier John Ayres in Blackmore's book.

51. R. F. Hunnisett, ed., *Sussex Coroners' Inquests 1558–1603* (Kew, Surrey: PRO Publications, 1996), item 444.

52. J. S. Cockburn, *Calendar Assize Records, Hertfordshire Indictments. James I* (London: HMSO, 1980–82), item 88.

53. Cockburn, *Calendar Assize Records, Kent. Charles II*, item 1191.

54. Charles Carlton, *Going to The Wars: The Experience of the British Civil Wars, 1638–1651* (London: Routledge, 1994), 207.

55. *The Victoria History of the County of Surrey*, ed. H. E. Malden, 4 vols. (Westminster: A. Constable and Co., Ltd., 1902–14), 2:325.

56. Newdigate Newsletters, L.c.1039, London, 8 February 1680, Folger Shakespeare Library.

57. BC, *Flying Post or the Post Master*, 24 June 1699 (no. 644).

58. BC, *Kingdomes Intelligencer*, No. 31, 29 July–5 August 1661.

59. *Bloody-minded husband; or The cruelty of John Chambers, who lately lived at Tanworth, in Warwick-shire, and conspir'd the death of his wife*, in *The Pepys Ballads*, ed. Hyder Edward Rollins, 8 vols. (Cambridge, MA: Harvard University Press, 1930), 3:202–5. After 1671.

60. Cockburn, *Assize Records, Elizabeth I*, vol. 3, item 1482.

61. Cockburn, *Assize Records, Essex Indictments*, King James I, item 1626.

62. BC, *London Evening Post*, 7 February 1730 (no. 339).

63. CSPD, 91:460–61. Probably the murdered man was John Onley from Tottenham, Middlesex, who was admitted to the Inner Temple in 1605. See *Students Admitted to The Inner Temple, 1547–1660* (London: William Clowes and Sons, 1877), 174. Neither Sir Richard Farmer nor John Onley is noticed in the *DNB*.

64. BC, *Post Boy*, 4 December 1697 (no. 404).

65. Walter M. Stern, "Gunmaking in Seventeenth-Century London," *Journal of Arms and Armour Society* 1, no. 5 (1954): 62.

66. Ibid., 61–62.

67. *DNB*, s.v. "Sir John Trevor."

68. Her will reveals that she owned manors, lands, tenements, and messuages in Sussex and Kent and personal items, such as a rose diamond ring. It does not show total value. PRO, PROB 11/904, fols. 304r–305v, NA.

69. BC, *London Chronicle*, 16 October 1764 (no. 1221); BC, *Public Advertiser*, 26 October 1764 (no. 9355).

70. CSPD, 1663–64, 221; CSPD, 1664–65, 171; CSPD, 1689–90, 65. For De Latre, see Blackmore, *Gunmakers of London*, 81.

71. *A New Present State of England*, 2 vols. (London, 1750), 2:45; and *The Court Kalendar* (London, 1744), 88; for 1757, 78. Spence's name is not included in lists of court office-holders, such as John Chamberlain's *Magnae Britanniae Notitia* or Guy Meige's *Present State of Great Britain*.

9. Guns and Child's Play

1. John Brewer, "Childhood Revisited: The Genesis of the Modern Toy," *History Today*, 30 (December 1980): 33.

2. Nicholas Orme, "Child's Play in Medieval England," *History Today*, 51, no. 10 (October 2001): 51.

3. Ibid., 50.

4. Geoff Egan, "Miniature Toys of Medieval Childhood," *British Archaeology*, ed. Simon Dinson, no. 35 (1998): 8. www.britarch.ac.uk/ba/ba35/ba35feat.html.

5. Geoff Egan, *Playthings from the Past, Toys from the A. G. Pilson Collection c. 1300–1800* (London: Jonathan Horne, 1996), n.p.

6. Geoff Egan, letter to the author, 13 August 2009.

7. Egan, *Playthings*, n.p.

8. Orme, "Child's Play," 50, 52.

9. Ibid., 52.

10. Their biographies do not mention toy guns. J. J. Scarisbrick, *Henry VIII* (London: Eyre and Spottiswoode, 1970). *Life and Raigne of King Edward Sixth by John Hayward*, ed. Barrett L. Beer (Kent, Ohio: Kent State University Press, 1993).

11. *The Basilicon Doron of James I*, ed. James Craigie, 2 vols. (Edinburgh and London: W. Blackwood and Sons, 1944–50), 2, 264. *The True Law of Free Monarchies; and Basilikon doron*, ed. Daniel Fischlin and Mark Fortier (Toronto: Centre for Reformation and Renaissance Studies, 1996) 166, 60n.

12. Charles Stuart, Letter to Henry Stuart, 1605/6, Harleian MSS 6986:85, folio 154r, BL. This is the earliest surviving letter of Prince Charles's correspondence, Aysha Pollnitz thinks. I thank her for the reference. "Maister Newton" was the learned Scotsman, Sir Adam Newton, first baronet (d. 1630), who served Prince Henry as tutor and then secretary, when he was given his own establishment in 1612. *DNB*, s.v. "Sir Adam Newton."

13. Descriptive paper XIV.24, 1638/9, Leeds Armory. Five of the guns were made by John Browne, the Royal Gunfounder, and five by Thomas Pitt.

14. *DNB*, s.v. "William, Duke of Gloucester."

15. John Hughes, *Poems on Several Occasions*, 2 vols. (London: J. Tonson and J. Watts, 1735), 1:93–94. *DNB*, s.v. "John Hughes."

16. Elizabeth Marvick, *Louis XIII: The Making of a King*, (New Haven, CT: Yale University Press, 1986), 64–66, for what follows.

17. Leonid Tarassuk, "The Cabinet d'Armes of Louis XIII: Some Firearms and Related Problems," *Metropolitan Museum Journal* 21 (1986): 65.

18. Cited in Mark Edward Motley, *Becoming a French Aristocrat* (Princeton: Princeton University Press, 1990), 63–64, 69–70, 172–73.

19. Emily Jackson, *Toys Of Other Days* (New York: Charles Scribner's Sons, 1908), 100.

20. Bridget Clifford and Karen Watts, *Introduction to Princely Armours and Weapons of Childhood* (Leeds: Royal Armouries, 2003), 39.

21. Elena Yablonskaya, "Seventeenth-Century English Firearms in the Kremlin," in *Britannia and Muscovy: English Silver at the Court of the Tsars*, eds. Olga Dmitrieva and Nataly Abramova (New Haven, CT: Yale University Press, 2006) 135.

22. R. L. Wilson, *Silk and Steel: Women at Arms* (New York: Random House, 2003),22.

23. Baldassare Castiglione, *The Book of the Courtier* (London: David Nutt, 1516), 52–53. The book was translated into English by Thomas Hoby in 1561.

24. Sir Thomas Elyot, *The Book Named the Governor. English Linguistics 1500–1800: A Collection of Facsimile Reprints*, ed. R. C. Alston (Menston: Scolar Press Ltd., 1970), 246:93–94.

25. Roger Ascham, *Toxophilus*, ed. Peter E. Medine (Tempe, AZ: Arizona Center for Medieval and Renaissance Studies, 2002), 19–20. The essay was reprinted in 1571 and 1589.

26. Ibid., 74.

27. Ibid., xii.

28. Roger Ascham, *The Scholemaster or plaine and perfite way of teachyng children, to understand, write, and speake, the Latin tong, but specially purposed for the priuate bringing vp youth in ientlemen and noble men houses*, ed. John Daye (London: John Daye, 1570), 47, 48, 52, 53. The Folger copy is signed by Margaret Ascham, Roger's wife. Written between 1563 and 1568, the essay was published posthumously in 1570.

29. Ibid., 19–20.

30. Lindsay Boynton, *Elizabethan Militia, 1558–1638* (London: Routledge and Kegan Paul, 1967), 265, for the two examples.

31. Mike Morrogh, Archivist at Shrewsbury School, letter to the author, April 26, 2011.

32. There were four artillery gardens in London and others outside the city.

33. Justine Taylor, "The Origins of the Honourable Artillery Company," *The Honourable Artillery Company Journal*, 2009–10, pt. 1, 105–15, and pt. 2, 101–12.

34. Boynton, *Elizabethan Militia*, 265, for the paragraph.

35. *CSPD*, 1665–66, 161.

36. The portrait of Charles's brother, Henry, entitled *Henry, Prince of Wales, on Horseback*, the first large equestrian royal portrait in English art, painted in 1611, shows Henry holding a pike, not a firearm. Timothy Wilks, ed., *Prince Henry Revived: Image and Exemplarity in Early Modern England* (London: Paul Holberton with Southampton Solent University, 2007), 146–79, 180–211.

37. *DNB*, s.v. "William Harvey."

38. King James II. N.P.G. 5104. www.npg.org.uk/collections. Elizabeth Hageman called my attention to Cornelius Johnson's work. I thank her.

39. *DNB*, s.v. "Ambrose Dudley, Earl of Warwick." Portrait.

40. Clifford and Watts, *Introduction to Princely Armours*, 27.

41. Timothy Wilks, "The Pike Charged: Henry as Militant Prince," in Wilks, *Prince Henry Revived*, 190–94.

42. Anna Reynolds, *In Fine Style: The Art of Tudor and Stuart Fashion* (London: Royal Collection Trust of Queen Elizabeth II, 2013), fig. 9, pp. 21, 126, 129.

43. Lionel Cust, "Notes on Pictures in the Royal Collections—XXXIII. The Portrait of Prince Baltasar Carlos, by Velázquez," *Burlington Magazine for Connoisseurs* 28, no. 152 (Nov. 1915): 56–57.

44. Samuel Rowlands, *The Letting of Humours' Blood in the Head-vaine* (London: W. White, 1600), n.p.

45. Orme, "Child's Play," 5.

46. Ibid.

47. BC, *Weekly Journal or British Gazetteer*, 25 July 1730 (no. 229).

48. Mark Goldie, ed. *The Entr'ing Book of Roger Morrice 1677–1691*, 7 vols. (Woodbridge: The Boydell Press/Parliamentary History Yearbook Trust, 2007–9), 4:442.

49. Cockburn, *Calendar Assize Records, Elizabeth I*, vol. 1, item 1892.

50. *The Proceedings of the Old Bailey. London's Central Criminal Court, 1674–1913*, 31 August 1688, #t16880831-19. www.oldbaileyonline.org.

51. BC, *Flying Post or the Weekly Medley*, 18 January 1729 (no. 16).

52. SEAX, June 1640, T/A 418/117/35. Essexcc.gov.uk.

53. *Gentleman's Magazine and Historical Chronicle*, ed. Edward Cave (London: F. Jeffries et al., 1736–1833), 18 (September 1748): 404.

54. BC, *London Evening Post*, 2 January 1729 (no. 168).

55. BC, *St. James's Evening Post*, 16 August 1729 (no. 2225).

56. As, for example, Cockburn, *Calendar of Assize Records, Hertfordshire Indictments, James I*, item 124.

57. Cockburn, *Calendar of Assize Records*, vol. I, item 2406.

58. *The Proceedings of the Old Bailey*. June 28, 1676. #t16760628-4. www.oldbaileyonline.org.

59. BC, *Daily Post*, 28 July 1720 (no. 257).

10. An Individual Right to Arms?

1. Lois G. Schwoerer, *The Declaration of Rights, 1689* (Baltimore: Johns Hopkins University Press, 1981), Appendix 1.

2. Anchitell Grey, *Debates of the House of Commons, from the year 1667 to the year 1694*, 10 vols. (London: Printed for D. Henry, 1763), 9:30, 33. John Somers, "Notes of Debate, January 28, January 29," in *Miscellaneous Papers, from 1501 to 1726*, ed. Philip Yorke, Earl of Hardwicke, vol. 2 (London, 1778), 414, 417.

3. B. Behrens, "The Whig Theory of the Constitution in the Reign of Charles II," *Cambridge Historical Journal* 7 (1941): 42–71. O. W. Furley, "The Whig Exclusionists: Pamphlet Literature in the Exclusion Campaign, 1689–81," *Cambridge Historical Journal* 13 (1957): 19–36.

4. Melinda Zook, *Radical Whigs and Conspiratorial Politics* (University Park: Penn State University Press, 1999).

5. Mark Goldie, "The Revolution of 1689 and the Structure of Political Argument," *Bulletin of Research in the Humanities* 83 (1980): 473–564. Schwoerer, *Declaration of Rights, 1689*, chapter 8, "Rights and Reform" Pamphlets, 153–68.

6. Studies of the Revolution of 1688–89 reach back to Lord Macaulay's *History of England from the Accession of James II*, ed. C. J. Firth, 6 vols. (London: Macmillan and Co., 1913–15), and earlier. Recent work includes Eveline Cruickshanks, ed., *By Force or by Default? The Revolution of 1688–1689* (Edinburgh: John Donaldson Publishers, Ltd., 1989); Tim Harris, "'The Greatest Revolution that was Ever Known': The Revolution Settlement in England," chapter 8 of *Revolution: The Great Crisis of the British Monarchy 1685–1720* (London: Penguin Books, 2006), 308–63; Steve Pincus, *1688: The First Modern Revolution* (New Haven, CT: Yale University Press, 2009); Schwoerer, *Declaration of Rights, 1689*, part 3, and *The Revolution of 1688–89: Changing Perspectives* (Cambridge: Cambridge University Press, 1992); William A. Speck, *Reluctant Revolutionaries* (Oxford: Oxford University Press, 1988).

7. Peter Earle, *Monmouth's Rebels: The Road to Sedgemoor, 1685* (New York: St. Martin's Press, 1977). Harris, *Revolution*, 78–93.

8. Harris, *Revolution*, 192, gives the numbers of Catholic officers.

9. Grey, *Debates of the House of Commons*, vol. 8, 358.

10. Harris, *Revolution*, 101.

11. Rachel J. Weil, "The Politics of Legitimacy: Women and the Warming-pan Scandal," in Schwoerer, *The Revolution of 1688–89*, 65–82.

12. Harris, *Revolution*, 271–73, gives their names and spheres of influence.

13. Schwoerer, *Declaration of Rights, 1689*, 120–27.

14. For the election and the opening of the Convention on 22 January 1688/89, see Schwoerer, *Declaration of Rights, 1689*, chapters 6, 7, and 9.

15. Ibid., 203–13, for these events.

16. The Committee used the word "Heads" to indicate that the points under discussion were "but heads and no law," as one member put it. Grey, *Debates*, 9:42.

17. Grey, *Debates*, 9:27, 34. Harris believes that the phase was "probably . . . an allusion" to the dreadful events in Ireland. Harris, *Revolution*, 343. Also Patrick J. Charles, "'Arms for Their Defence?': An Historical, Legal and Textual Analysis of the English Right to Bear Arms and Whether the Second Amendment Should Have Been Incorporated in McDonald v. City of Chicago," *Cleveland State Law Review* 57 (2009), 359.

18. Charles, "'Arms For Their Defence?,'" 381.

19. Gary Wills, "To Keep and Bear Arms," *New York Review of Books*, 42 (21 September 1995): 64–65.

20. *SR*, 1 William and Mary, c.15.

21. Charles, "'Arms For Their Defence?,'" 401–2.

22. STT Military Box 1, item 37, Temple Papers, HEHL.

23. *CJ*, 10:22.

24. Lois G. Schwoerer, *"No Standing Armies!"* (Baltimore: Johns Hopkins University Press, 1981), 149–50.

25. *SR*, 5:238; *CJ*, 8:71.

26. *SR*, 5:308–9.

27. For a discussion of the Lords' Rights Committee, see Schwoerer, *Declaration of Rights*, 237–43.

28. Joyce Lee Malcolm, *To Keep and Bear Arms: The Origins of an Anglo-American Right* (Cambridge, MA: Harvard University Press, 1994), 119.

29. Ibid., 4–6.

30. *CJ*, 10:25.

31. William Sachse, "The Mob and the Revolution of 1688," *Journal of British Studies* 4 (1964): 23–40. Robert Beddard, "Anti-Popery and the London Mob, 1688," *History Today* 38 (1988): 36–39; Tim Harris, "London Crowds and the Revolution of 1688," in *By Force or by Default? The Revolution of 1688–1689*, ed. Eveline Cruickshanks (Edinburgh: John Donaldson Publishers, Ltd., 1989), 44–64.

32. Lois G. Schwoerer, "A Jornall of the Convention at Westminster Begun the 22 of January 1688/89," *Bulletin of the Institute of Historical Research* 44 (1976): 252.

33. Erle MSS 4/4, Churchill College, Cambridge University. The modern edition is Mark Goldie, ed., "Thomas Erle's Instructions for the Revolution Parliament, December 1688," *Parliamentary History*, 14 (1995): 337–47.

34. Ibid., 344–45.

35. Carte MSS 81, fol. 766, Bodleian Library. Wharton's untitled paper is discussed further in Schwoerer, *Declaration of Rights, 1689*, 238–39.

36. *CJ*, 9:219; *Journals of the House of Lords*, 12:481. See Schwoerer, *Declaration of Rights, 1689*, 78.

37. Carl Bogus, "The Hidden History of the Second Amendment," *University of California Davis Law Review* 31 (1998), 383–85.

38. Malcolm, *To Keep and Bear Arms*, 120.

39. Ibid., 122.

40. *CJ*, 10:25.

41. Schwoerer, *Declaration of Rights, 1689*, 248–63.

42. Malcolm, *To Keep and Bear Arms*, 121, 122.

43. See Lois G. Schwoerer, "The Transformation of the Convention into a Parliament, February 1689," *Parliamentary History* 3 (Fall 1984): 57–76.

44. The bill moved through the House of Commons in February 1693. *CJ*, 10:801, 805, 807, 824.

45. Malcolm, *To Keep and Bear Arms*, 126. Henry Horwitz, ed. *The Parliamentary Diary of Narcissus Luttrell* (Oxford: Clarendon Press) 444, identified the participants in this exchange. For comment, see *The History of Parliament: The House of Commons 1660–1690*, 7 vols. ed. Basil Duke Henning (London: Secker & Warburg, 1983), 3:148. Also Henry Horwitz, *Parliament, Policy and Politics in the Reign of William III* (Manchester: Manchester University Press, 1977), Appendix C.

46. The quotation is from *CJ*, 10:824.

47. Horwitz, *Diary of Narcissus Luttrell*, 444. The other three were the Hon. Goodwin Wharton (1653–1704), an eccentric, known as an "influential" Whig at this time; Mr. Howe, impossible to identify because one of three "Howes" in the Parliament; and Mr. Clarke, probably Sir Gilbert Clarke (c. 1645–1701), a Tory. See *History of Parliament*, ed. Henning, 3: 695–96; 2:82.

48. Horwitz, *Diary of Narcissus Luttrell*, 444.

49. Ibid.

50. Richard Burn, *The Justice of the Peace, and Parish Officer: by Richard Burn, Clerk, One of His Majesty's Justices of the Peace for the County of Westmorland* (A Millar: London, 1755), 1:442–43.

51. Ibid.

52. P. B. Munsche, *Gentlemen and Poachers* (Cambridge: Cambridge University Press, 1981), 32, 80, 81, 82.

53. John Shebbeare, *A Fifth Letter to the People of England, on the subversion of the constitution: and the necessity of its being restored* (1757), 34–35. The same point was made even more passionately in his *A Letter to the People of England, on the present situation and conduct of national affairs* (1755), 16.

54. Shebbeare, *A Third Letter to the People of England* (1756), 49, 57.

55. See Eliga H. Gould, *The Persistence of Empire: British Political Culture in the Age of the American Revolution* (Chapel Hill: University of North Carolina Press, 2000), 46, 51, 82.

56. Gould, *Persistence of Empire*, chapter 3, "Patriotism Established: The Creation of a 'National Militia' in England," 72–105. Especially note pages 75, 79, 81, 84, 86, 89.

57. T. A. Critchley, *The Conquest of Violence: Order and Liberty in Britain* (New York: Schocken Books, 1970), 81–90. Christopher Hibbert, *King Mob: The Story of Lord George Gordon and the London riots of 1780* (Cleveland: World Publishing Co., 1958).

58. William Cobbett, ed., *The Parliamentary History of England*, 36 vols. (London: R. Bagshaw, 1806–20), 21:727.

59. Ibid., 728.

60. For what follows, see Gould, *The Persistence of Empire*, 174, 176.

61. Malcolm, *To Keep and Bear Arms*, 134, for quote and comment.

62. Gould, *The Persistence of Empire*, 173–74, 176.

63. Bogus, "Hidden History," 396nn458–460.

64. Malcolm, *To Keep and Bear Arms*, 143.

65. The other four auxiliary rights were the "constitution, powers, and privileges of parliament"; the limitation of the king's prerogative; the right to apply to the courts for redress; and the right to petition the king or either house of parliament.

66. William Blackstone, *Commentaries on the Laws of England*, 4 vols., ed. Stanley N. Katz (Chicago: University of Chicago Press, 1979), 1:139.

67. Bogus, "Hidden History," 397.

68. Malcolm, *To Keep and Bear Arms*, 134.

69. Ibid., 162.

70. Forrest McDonald, *Novus Ordo Seclorum: The Intellectual Origins of the Constitution* (Lawrence: University Press of Kansas, 1985), 40.

71. Kenneth R. Bowling, "'A Tub To the Whale': The Founding Fathers and Adoption of the Federal Bill of Rights," *Journal of the Early Republic* 8 (1988): 223–51, does not mention Article VII.

72. *Creating the Bill of Rights: The Documentary Record from the First Federal Congress*, ed. Helen E. Veit, Kenneth R. Bowling, and Charlene Bangs Bickford (Baltimore: Johns Hopkins University Press, 1991), 4, 12, 17, 19, 22, 30, 38–39n13, 48, 182–84.

Appendix A

1. For example, the Royal Armouries Museum in Leeds; in London, the Tower, the Victoria and Albert Museum and the Wallace Collection. In Europe: the Armeria Reale in Turin, Italy, and the Heeresgeschichtliches Museum in Vienna. In the United States: the Metropolitan Museum of Art in New York and the National Rifle Association Museum in Virginia.

2. O. F. G. Hogg, *English Artillery 1326–1716: Being the History of Artillery in this Country Prior to the Formation of the Royal Regiment of Artillery* (London: Royal Artillery Institution, 1963), 6. "Torsional" refers to early weapons capable of hurling an object by mechanical means.

3. Jack Kelly, *Gunpowder: Alchemy, Bombards, and Pyrotechnics* (New York: Basic Books, 2004), 8.

4. David Cressy, *Saltpeter: The Mother of Gunpowder* (Oxford: Oxford University Press, 2013), 10.

5. Ibid., 12.

6. Kelly, *Gunpowder*, 33. Cf. Cressy, *Saltpeter*, 12.

7. Kelly, *Gunpowder*, 25 37.

8. Geoffrey Parker, *The Military Revolution: Military Innovation and the Rise of the West, 1500–1800*. 2nd ed. Cambridge: Cambridge University Press, 1996), 83. Kelly, *Gunpowder*, 17.

9. Kelly, *Gunpowder*, 25. J. R. Partington, *History of Greek Fire and Gunpowder* (Cambridge: W. Heffer, 1960), 64–79.

10. Oxford University, Christ Church Library, MS 92, fol. 70v. For another version of the manuscript with the same date, see BL, MS. Add. 47680, fol. 44v.

11. John Keegan, *The Face of Battle* (New York: Vintage Books, 1977), 320.

12. Bert S. Hall, *Weapons and Warfare in Renaissance Europe: Gunpowder, Technology, and Tactics* (Baltimore: Johns Hopkins University Press, 1997), 87 (quote), 94–95. Major Hugh B. C. Pollard, *History of Firearms* (London: Geoffrey Bles, 1926), 1.

13. Adrian B. Caruana, *Tudor Artillery: 1485–1603*, Historical Arms Series no. 30 (Alexandria Bay, NY: Museum Restoration Service, 1992), 5–10. A. R. Hall, *Ballistics in the Seventeenth Century* (Cambridge: Cambridge University Press, 1952).

14. Hall, *Weapons and Warfare in Renaissance Europe*, 44. OED, s.v. "Ribald."

15. T. F. Tout, "Firearms in England in the Fourteenth Century," *English Historical Review* 26 (1911): 670.

16. www.edinburghcastle-history.co.uk/mons-meg.html for photograph and details. Also Hall, *Weapons and Warfare in Renaissance Europe*, 59–61.

17. A crack in the side of the bombard is still visible. See Charles Ffoulkes, *The Gun-Founders of England: With a List of English and Continental Gun-Founders from the XIV to the XIX Centuries* (Cambridge: Cambridge University Press, 1937), 23.

18. John Latta, *Queen Elizabeth's Pocket Pistol*. 30 September 2007. Dover Castle. www.panoramio.com/photo/5381732.

19. Tout, "Firearms in England," 684.

20. Ibid.

21. Hall, *Weapons and Warfare in Renaissance Europe*, 96.

22. Charles Trollope, "Design and Evolution of English Cast-iron Guns," *Journal of Ordnance Society* 14 (2002): 51–64.

23. Hall, *Weapons and Warfare in Renaissance Europe*, 68–73, 102, for a description of the process. See Herbert J. Jackson, *European Hand Firearms of the Sixteenth, Seventeenth and Eighteenth Centuries* (London: Martin Hopkinson & Co., 1923), frontispiece for an illustration.

24. Hall, *Weapons and Warfare in Renaissance Europe*, 87.

25. The names of these weapons are discussed in Appendix B.

26. Hall, *Weapons and Warfare in Renaissance Europe*, 95–99. *OED*, s.v. "harquebus."

27. Hall, *Weapons and Warfare in Renaissance Europe*, 97.

28. *OED*, s.v. "caliver."

29. *OED*, s.v. "musket."

30. Sir Roger Williams, *A Briefe Discourse of Warre, With his opinion concerning some parts of the Martiall Discipline* (London: Thomas Orwin, 1590), 40–43.

31. Hall, *Weapons and Warfare in Renaissance Europe*, 95–96, 149, 212, for the matchlock.

32. Graeme Rimer, *Wheellock Firearms of the Royal Armouries* (Leeds: Royal Armouries, 2001), has many illustrations.

33. Jack Kelly, *Gunpowder: Alchemy, Bombards, and Pyrotechnics* (New York: Basic Books, 2004), 76.

34. Rimer, *Wheellock Firearms*, 8.

35. Brian C. Godwin, "An English Wheellock—by Association?" in *The Nineteenth Park Lane Arms Fair Catalogue*, 35.

36. Hall, *Weapons and Warfare in Renaissance Europe*, 134–56, for the results.

37. Ibid., 137.

38. Ibid., 138–47.

39. Hall, *Ballistics*, 8.

40. Boynton, *Elizabethan Militia*, 114.

Appendix B

1. The first word for the device was "*crakys*," an onomatopoeia of the noise of the device. John Barbour, the archdeacon of Aberdeen, used the word in a couplet about the 1327 war between England and Scotland: "The other crakys were of war / That they before heard never air." Today we use the word "firecracker." Frederick Darby Cleaveland, *Notes on the Early History of The Royal Regiment of Artillery* (Woolwich: Printed by the author, 1892), 2. *Crakys* does not appear in the *OED*.

2. *OED*, s.v. "Gun." Exchequer Accounts, Q.R. Bundle 18, no. 34. *The Middle English Dictionary*, ed. Hans Kurath (Ann Arbor: University of Michigan Press, 2001), concurs.

3. Henry Thomas Riley, ed., *Memorials of London and London life, in the XIIIth, XIVth, and XVth centuries. Being a series of extracts, local, social, and political, from the early archives of the city of London, A. D. 1276–1419*, (Longmans, Green and Co.: London, 1868), 204–5, 207. The word *latone* refers to "latten," an alloy of copper and tin (with traces, perhaps of zinc and lead), meaning a bronze device. See *OED*, s.v. "latone."

4. Bert S. Hall, *Weapons and Warfare in Renaissance Europe: Gunpowder, Technology, and Tactics* (Baltimore: Johns Hopkins University Press, 1997), 44.

5. J. R. Partington, *History of Greek Fire and Gunpowder* (Cambridge: W. Heffer, 1960), 116, and for the names on this page.

6. Hall, *Weapons and Warfare in Renaissance Europe*, 98–100.

7. *OED*, s.v. "harquebus."

8. Hall, *Weapons and Warfare in Renaissance Europe*, 89.

9. Francis Grose, *Military Antiquities: Respecting a History of the English Army from the Conquest to the Present Time*, 2 vols. (London: Stockdale, 1800) 1.

10. Hall, *Weapons and Warfare in Renaissance Europe*, 193.

11. Paul L. Hughes and James F. Larkin, eds., *Tudor Royal Proclamations*, 3 vols. (New Haven, CT: Yale University Press, 1964–69), 1:320. But the *OED* gives the first date as 1561.

12. *OED*, s.v. "gunpowder," 1, 1a.

13. Morris Palmer Tilley, *The Proverbs in England in the Sixteenth and Seventeenth Centuries* (Ann Arbor: University of Michigan Press, 1950), 742. Thomas Heywood, *Golden Age* (London: 1611), vol. 4, 72.

14. J. S. Farmer and W. E. Henley, *Slang and Its Analogues*, 7 vols. (New York: Arno Press, 1970), 3:236.

15. Sir John Smythe, *Certain Discourses Militarie* (London, 1600), 41–42.

16. Sir Roger Williams, *A Briefe discourse of Warre* (London, 1590), 48–49.

17. Tilley, *Proverbs in England*, 277–78.

18. *OED*, s.v. "gun."

19. Tilley, *Proverbs in England*, 278–79.

20. Farmer and Henley, *Slang and Its Analogues*, 3:235.

21. John D. Breval, *The Play Is the Plot. A Comedy* (London: J. Tonson, 1718), 2.1.

22. *OED*, s.v. "gun" and "great gun."

23. *The Diary of John Evelyn*, ed. E. S. de Beer, 6 vols. (Oxford: Clarendon Press, 1955), 1:469. "Pouderd" beef is salted or preserved beef.

24. Robert Latham and Williams Matthews, eds. *The Diary of Samuel Pepys*, 10 vols. (Berkley: University of California Press, 1970–83), 3:50.

25. *OED*, s.v. "gun."

26. Ibid.

27. BC, *Weekly Journal or Saturday's Post*, 24 Dec. 1720 (no. 108).

28. Robert Hendrickson, ed., *The Facts on File: Encyclopedia of Word and Phrase Origins*, 3rd ed., (New York: Checkmark Books, 2004), 265.

29. Ibid., 675–76.

30. Ibid., 690.

BIBLIOGRAPHY

Primary Sources

Unpublished Primary Sources

Bodleian Library, Oxford University
Bankes MSS, Bundle 12
Carte MSS 81, fol. 766
MS Eng. hist. c. 191

British Library, London
Add Ch 16334
Harley MS 309
Harley MS 6986, item 85
Lansdowne MS 59, no. 78
MS Add. 47680

Christ Church Library, Oxford University
MS 92

Churchill College, Cambridge University
Erle MSS 4/4

College of Arms, London
C.21
C.27
Camden Grants, vols. 1-3
EDN 56
Grants, vol. 2
Miscellaneous Grants 2
Walker's Grants

Folger Shakespeare Library, Washington, D.C.
An ordinary of arms, with an index of families. 1580. V.a.253.
Cooke, Robert. Ordinary of arms. 1580. V.b.103.
Guillim, John. A display of heraldry. 1610. V.b.171

STC 15224
V.b.256, no. 366
Z.d.12-17

Hatfield House, Hertfordshire, England
Cecil Papers, 186.60

Huntington Library, San Marino, California
Hastings Correspondence. HA Boxes 45 and 48
MSS STT 2333. Sir Thomas Temple, 1st Bart., to his son Sir Peter Temple, 8 August 1634.
ST 138. Grenville Papers. Bucks Militia, 1619–1806, item 7
ST 144. Grenville Papers, vol. 1

London Metropolitan Archives
COL/CC/01/   MS 5220/6
MS 5219/1   MS 5220/5-7
MS 5220/1   MS 5226/1
MS 5220/2   MS 12071/2
MS 5220/5   MS 12071/3

The National Archives, London
The Proceedings of the Old Bailey, London: 1674–1834. Old Bailey Proceedings Online. www.oldbaileyonline.org. Version 7.
SP 12/15
SP 12/146
SP 12/147

PRINTED PRIMARY SOURCES

Acts of the Privy Council of England. Edited by John Roche Dasant et al. 46 vols. London: HMSO, 1890–1964. Volume 33.

Ailesbury, Thomas. *Memoirs of Thomas, Earl of Ailesbury: Written by Himself.* 2 vols. Westminster: The Roxburghe Club, 1895.

Allen, Marion E., ed. *Wills of the Archdeaconry of Suffolk 1620–1624.* Suffolk Records Society, Vol. 31. Woodbridge, Suffolk: The Boydell Press, 1989.

———. *Wills of the Archdeaconry of Suffolk 1625–1626.* Suffolk Records Society, Vol. 37. Woodbridge, Suffolk: The Boydell Press, 1995.

Ariosto, Leonardo. *The historie of Orlando Furioso . . . As it was plaid before the queens Maiestie.* London: John Danter, 1594.

———. *The historie of Orlando Furioso . . . As it was plaid before the queens Maiestie.* London: Simon Stafford, 1599.

Ascham, Roger. *The Scholemaster or plaine and perfite way of teachyng children, to understand, write, and speake, the Latin tong, but specially purposed for the priuate bringing vp youth in ientlemen and noble men houses.* London: John Daye, 1570.

———. *Toxophilus or the Schole of Shooting in two bookes (1545).* Edited by Peter E. Medine. Tempe: Arizona Center for Medieval and Renaissance Studies, 2002.

Ashcroft, M. Y., comp. *To escape the monster's clutches.* North Yorkshire County Council, 1977.

Atkinson, J. C., ed. *Quarter Sessions Records.* 9 vols. London: Publication of the North Riding Record Society, 1884–92.

Axon, E., ed. *Manchester Sessions: Notes of Proceedings before Oswald Mosley.* Manchester: Record Society of Lancashire and Chester, 1901.

Ayscough, Anne. *Account of the Behaviour and Confession of Mr. Leonard Revel.* Nottingham: The author, 1723.

Babington, John. *Pyrotechnia. Or, A Discourse of Artificial Fire-works.* London: Thomas Harper, 1635.

Barret, Robert. *The Theorike and Practike of Moderne Warres.* London: William Ponsonby, 1598.

Barriff, William. *Military Discipline: Or, The Young Artillery Man.* London: Thomas Harper, 1635.

Barwick, Humphrey. *A Breefe Discourse, Concerning the Force and Effect of All Manuall Weapons of Fire.* London: E. Allde, 1592.

The Basilicon Doron of King James I. Edited by James Craigie. 2 vols. Edinburgh and London: Printed for the Scottish Text Society by W. Blackwood and Sons, 1944–50.

Behn, Aphra. *Oroonoko, The Rover, and Other Works.* Edited by Janet Todd. London: Penguin Books, 1992.

———. *Poems on Several Occasions.* London: R. Tonson and J. Tonson, 1684.

Bennett, J. H. E., and J. C. Dewhurst, eds. *Quarter Sessions Records.* Manchester: Printed for the Record Society of Lancashire and Cheshire, 1940.

Blackstone, William. *Commentaries on the Laws of England.* 4 vols. Edited by Stanley N. Katz. Chicago: University of Chicago Press, 1979.

Blome, Richard. *The Gentlemans Recreation. In Two Parts The First being an Encyclopedy of the Arts and Sciences. The Second Part, Treats of Horsemanship, Fowling, Hawking, Fishing, Hunting, Agriculture.* London: S. Rotcroft, 1686.

Boyle, Robert. *Medicinal Experiments.* 3rd ed. London, 1696.

Boynton, L. O. J. "The Charter of the Company of Gunmakers London." *Journal of the Society of Army Historical Research* 6 (1927): 79–92.

Breval, John D. *The Play Is the Plot. A Comedy.* London: J. Tonson, 1718.

Brown, Rawdon, ed. *Calendar of State Papers and Manuscripts, Relating to English Affairs, Existing in the Archives and Collections of Venice.* London: Longman & Co, 1873.

Buggs, Samuel, *Miles Mediterraneus: The Mid-land Souldier.* London: John Dawson, 1622.

Burn, Richard. *Justice of the Peace and Parish Officer.* London: Henry Lintot, Law Printer to the King, 1753.

Burney Collection of Seventeenth- and Eighteenth-Century Newspapers. The British Library.

The Burning of the Whore of Babylon, As it was Acted, with great Applause, in the Poultrey, London, on Wednesday Night, being the Fifth of November Last, at Six of the Clock. London: Printed and to be sold by R.C., 1673.

Calendar of the Cecil Papers in Hatfield House. Volume 14: Addenda (1923), 263–344.

Calendar of State Papers, Domestic Series. 1553–1714.

Camden, William. *Remaines Concerning Britaine. 7th impression. Edited by John Philipot.* London: John Legett, 1614.

Campbell, R. *The London Tradesman: Being a Compendious View of all the Trades, Professions, Arts, both Liberal and Mechanic, now practiced in the Cities of London and Westminster.* London: Printed by T. Gardner, 1747.

Case of the Company of Gun-Makers of the City of London. N.p., n.d.

Cavendish, Margaret, Duchess of Newcastle. "Assaulted and pursued Chastity." In *Nature's Pictures drawn by fancies pencil to the life. Written by the thrice noble, illustrious, and excellent princess, the lady Marchioness of Newcastle.* London: Printed for J. Martin and J. Allestrye, 1656.

Chamberlains' Accounts in Stratford-upon-Avon for 17 Feb. 1574. In "Minutes and Accounts of the Corporation of Stratford-upon-Avon and Other Records," edited by Richard Savage, 2:1566–77. *Publications of the Dugdale Society.* Oxford: Printed for the Dugdale Society, 1924.

Churchyard, Thomas. *A Generall rehearsal of warres, wherein is five hundred severall services of land and sea: as sieges, battailles, skirmiches, and encounters.* London: Edward White, 1579.

Cirket, A. F. D. *English Wills, 1498-1526. Publications of the Bedfordshire Historical Record Society.* Volume 37. 1947.

Clarke, William. *The Natural History of Nitre: Or, A Philosophical Discourse of the Nature, Generation, Place, and Artificial Extraction of Nitre.* London: Printed by E. Okes for Nathaniel Brook at the Angel in Cornhill near the Royal Exchange, 1670.

Clendon, Thomas. *Justification Justified: or The Doctrine of Justification.* London: Robert Ibbitson, 1653.

Cobbett, William, ed. *The Parliamentary History of England: From the Norman Conquest in 1066, to the year 1803.* 36 vols. London: Printed by T. C. Hansard, 1806–20.

Cockburn, J. S., ed. *Calendar of Assize Records, Elizabeth I.* 5 vols. London: HMSO, 1975–80.

———. *Calendar of Assize Records, Hertfordshire Indictments, James I.* London: HMSO, 1980–82.

———. *Calendar of Assize Records: Kent Indictments, Charles II 1660–1675.* 3 vols. London: HMSO, 1995.

A Collection of the Yearly bills of Mortality, from 1657 to 1768 inclusive. Together with several other Bills of an earlier Date. London: A. Millar, 1759.

Comber, Thomas. *Discourse of DUELS, shewing The Sinful Nature And Mischievous Effects of Them*. London: Samuel Roycroft, 1687.

Cotton, Charles. *Burlesque upon burlesque: or, The scoffer scoft*. London: Henry Brome, 1675.

Cox, Nicholas. *The Gentleman's Recreation, In Four Parts; viz. Hunting, Fowling, Hawking, Fishing*. London: Printed C. Flesher, 1674.

Cramer, J. A., trans. *Second Book of the Travels of Nicander Nucius, of Corcyra*. London: Printed for the Camden Society by J. B. Nichols and Son, 1841.

Crocker, Glenys, and Alan Crocker. *Gunpowder Mills: Documents of the Seventeenth and Eighteenth Centuries*. Bristol: J. W. Arrowsmith Ltd., 2000.

Cruso, John. *Militarie Instructions for the Cavallrie: Or rules and Directions for the Service of Horse*. Cambridge: Printers to the Universitie of Cambridge, 1632.

Curious Collection of Paintings, By the Best Masters Ancient and Modern Will be Sold by Aucion at Wills Coffee-house on Wednesday, the 13th of this instant January. London, 1691.

Danielsson, Bror, ed. *William Twiti: The Art of Hunting, 1327*. Stockholm, Sweden: Almqvist & Wiksell International, 1977.

Davis, Norman, ed. *Paston Letters and Papers of the Fifteenth Century*. 2 vols. Oxford: At the Clarendon Press, 1971.

Death's Master-Peece: or, A true Relation of that great and sudden Fire in Towerstreet, London, which came by the fiering of Gunpowder, on Friday the 4th of January, 1649. London: Francis Grove, 1649/50.

Dekker, Thomas. *The Artillery Garden. 1616. Library*. Oxford: Printed in the Bodleian, 1952.

Delaune, Sir Thomas. *The Present State of London: Or, Memorials comprehending A Full and Succinct Account*. London: George Larkin, 1681.

Dondi, Giorgio, ed. *Primo Supplemento al Catalogo Angelucci Elenco Degli Oggetti Acquistati Dalla Armeria Reale Di Torino Dopo il 1890*. Turin: Armeria Reale, 2005.

Downame, John. *Brief concordance, or table to the Bible of the Last Translation*. London: Printed by W. Du-Gard, and are to bee sold by E. D. and N. E. at the sign of the Gun in Ivie-lane, 1652.

Dunn, Richard Minta, ed. *Norfolk Lieutenancy Journal 1660–1676*. Norfolk Record Society. Volume 45. 1977.

Earwaker, J. P., ed. *Lancashire and Cheshire Wills and Inventories 1572–1696, Now preserved at Chester*. Manchester: Printed for the Chetham Society. 1893.

Elyot, Sir Thomas. *The Book Named the Governor*. Edited by John Major. New York: Teachers College Press, 1969.

Emmison, F. G., ed. *Elizabethan Life: Disorder Mainly from Essex Sessions and Assize Records*. Chelmsford: Essex County Council, 1970.

———. *Elizabethan Life: Wills of Essex Gentry and Merchants Proved in the Prerogative Court of Canterbury*. Chelmsford: Essex County Council, 1978.

English Brothers, Sir Thomas, Sir Anthony, Mr. Robert Shirley. As it is now play'd by her Maisties Servants. London: John Wright, 1607.

Evelyn, John. *The Diary of John Evelyn*. Edited by E. S. deBeer. 6 vols. Oxford: Clarendon Press, 1955.

Fiennes, Celia. *Through England on a Side Saddle in the Time of William and Mary*. London: Field & Tuer, Leadenhall Press, 1888.

Foster, Elizabeth Read, ed. *Proceedings in Parliament, 1610*. 2 vols. New Haven, CT: Yale University Press, 1966.

Gates, Geoffrey. *The Defence of the Militarie Profession. Wherein is eloquently shewed the due commendation of Martiall prowesse*. London: Henry Middleton, 1579.

A general Bill for this present year, ending the 19 of December 1665, according to the Report made to the Kings most Excellent Majesty, By the Company of Parish Clerks of London. London, 1665.

A General Bill of all the Christnings and Burials, from the 16th of December 1685 According to the Report made to the KINGS Most Excellent MAJESTY By the Company of Parish-Clerks of London. London, 1685.

Gentlemans Academie, or, The Booke of S. Albans containing three most exact and excellent Bookes: the first of Hawking, the second of all the proper terms of Hunting, and the last of Armorie; all compiled by Juliana Barnes, in the yere from the incarnation of Christ 1486. And now reduced into a better method, by G.M. London: Humfrey Lownes, 1595.

Gentleman's Magazine and Historical Chronicle. Edited by Edward Cave. London: F. Jeffries et al., 1736–1833. Vol. 18.

Gilbert, Sir Humphrey. *Queene Elizabethes Achademy*. London: Published for the Early English Text Society, 1898.

Goldie, Mark, ed. *The Ent'ring book of Roger Morrice 1677–1691*. 7 vols. Woodbridge, Suffolk: The Boydell Press, with the Parliamentary History Yearbook Trust, 2007–9.

———. "Thomas Erle's Instructions for the Revolution Parliament, December 1688." *Parliamentary History* 14 (1995): 337–47.

Goring, Jeremy, and Joan Wake, eds. *Northamptonshire Lieutenancy Papers and Other Documents, 1580–1614*. Gateshead: Northumberland Press, 1975.

Great Britain. Parliament. *Journals of the House of Commons*. Volumes 1–11. London: HMSO, 1803.

———. *Journals of the House of Lords*. Volumes 1–19. London: HMSO, 1803.

Great Britain. Public Record Office. *Calendar of the Patent Rolls, Edward VI. Preserved in the Public Record Office*. 6 vols. London: HMSO, 1924.

———. *Calendar of the Patent Rolls, Philip and Mary. Preserved in the Public Record Office*. 4 vols. London: HMSO, 1937–39.

———. *Calendar of the Patent Rolls, Elizabeth I. Preserved in the Public Record Office*. 9 vols. London: HMSO, 1939–86.

———. *Letters and Papers, Foreign and Domestic, of the Reign of Henry VIII*. 21 vols. London: HMSO, 1864–1920.

Grey, Anchitell. *Debates of the House of Commons, from the year 1667 to the year 1694*. 10 vols. London: Printed for D. Henry, 1763.

Gun-Smiths QUERIES. Printed in the year 1710.

Hamilton, William Douglas, ed. *A Chronicle of England during the Reigns of the Tudors, From A.D. 1485–1559. By Charles Wriothesley, Windsor Herald*. Volume 2. Westminster: Printed for the Camden Society, 1877.

Hartley, T. E., ed. *Proceedings in the Parliaments of Elizabeth I*. 3 vols. Wilmington, DE: M. Glazier, 1981.

Haselrig, Sir Arthur. *Sir Arthur Haselrig's last will and testament, With a briefe survey of his life and death*. London: Printed for Henry Brome, 1661.

Hertford County Records. Notes and Extracts from the Sessions Rolls 1581–1698. Edited by W. J. Hardy. Hertford: Published by C. E. Longmore, Clerk of the Peace Office, 1905.

Hickeringill, Edmund. *The Test or, Tryal of the Goodness & Value of Spiritual Courts, in Two Queries.* London: George Larkin, 1683.

Historical Manuscripts Commission. *Calendar of the Carew Manuscripts.* 6 vols. Edited by J. S. Brewer and William Bullen. London: Longman & Co., 1873.

———. *Calendar of the Manuscripts of the Most Hon. The Marquis of Salisbury.* London: HMSO 1892.

———. *The Manuscripts of the Earl of Dartmouth, Fifteenth Report.* 3 vols. London: HMSO, 1896.

———. *Report on the Manuscripts of Lord de l'Isle and Dudley Preserved at Penshurst Place.* 6 vols. London: HMSO, 1925.

———. *Supplementary Report on the Manuscripts of His Grace the Duke of Hamilton.* Edited by Jane Harvey McMaster and Marguerite Wood. London: HMSO, 1932.

Horwitz, Henry, ed. *The Parliamentary Diary of Narcissus Luttrell.* Oxford: Oxford University Press, 1972.

Hughes, Paul L., and James F. Larkin, eds. *Tudor Royal Proclamations.* 3 vols. New Haven, CT: Yale University Press, 1964–69.

Hughes, John. *Poems on Several Occasions.* 2 vols. London: J. Tonson and J. Watts, 1735.

Hughey, Ruth, ed. *Correspondence of Lady Katherine Paston 1603–1627.* Norwich: Norfolk Record Society, 1941.

Hunnisett, R. F., ed. *Sussex Coroners' Inquests, 1558–1603.* Kew, Surrey: PRO Publications, 1996.

Kirk, R. E. G., and Ernest F. Kirk, eds. *Return of Aliens Dwelling in the City and Suburbs of London.* Aberdeen: The University Press, 1908.

Lad, John. "A Rule of Gunners Art." In *Tudor Artillery 1485–1603,* edited by Adrian B. Caruana. Historical Arms Series No. 30. Alexandria Bay, NY: Museum Restoration Service, 1992.

Lambard, William. *Eirenarcha, or Of the office of the iustices of peace, in foure bookes: reuised, corrected, and enlarged.* London: Printed for the Companie of Stationers, 1619.

Lant, Thomas. *The Funeral Procession of Sir Philip Sidney 16 Febr. 1586.* London, 1588.

Larkin, James F., and Paul L. Hughes, eds. *Stuart Royal Proclamations.* 2 vols. Oxford: At the Clarendon Press, 1973–83.

Latham, Robert, and Williams Matthews, eds. *The Diary of Samuel Pepys.* 10 vols. Berkley and Los Angeles: University of California Press, 1970–83.

Lawson, Jane A. ed. *Elizabethan New Year's Gift Exchanges 1559–1603.* Records of Social and Economic History New Series 51. Oxford: Oxford University Press, 2013.

Leigh, Edward. *Choice Observations of all the Kings of England from the Saxons to the Death of King Charles the First.* London: Printed for Joseph Cranford, at the sign of the Gun in St. Pauls Church-yard, 1661.

List of the Names of all the Commodities of English Product and Manufacture, That was Exported to France 1702. London: Printed for B. Tooke, 1713.

Luders, Alexander, et al., eds. *Statutes of the Realm.* 11 vols. London: Dawsons of Pall Mall, 1810–28.

Machyn, Henry. *The Diary of Henry Machyn Citizen and Merchant-Taylor of London, From A.D. 1550 to A.D. 1563.* Edited by John Gough Nichols. London. Printed for the Camden Society by J. B. Nichols and Son, 1848.

Macpherson, C. B., ed. *Hobbes Leviathan.* New York: Penguin Books, 1978.

McClure, Norman Egbert, ed. *Letters of John Chamberlain.* Philadelphia: American Philosophical Society, 1939.

Malthus, Thomas. *A Treatise of Artificial Fire Works Both For Warres and Recreation: with divers pleasant Geometricall observations.* London: Printed for Richard Hawkins, 1629.

Manwood, John. *A Treatise of the Laws of the Forest.* 3rd ed. London: Printed for the Company of Stationers, 1665.

Markham, Garvase. *Country Contentments: Or, The Husbandmans Recreations.* 5th ed. London: Thomas Harper, 1633.

May, Robert. *The Accomplish'd Cook, or The Art & Mystery of Cookery.* 5th ed. London, Odabiah Blagrave, 1685.

Millar, Oliver, ed. "Inventories and Valuations of the King's Goods 1649–1651." *The Walpole Society 43.* Glasgow: The University Press, 1972.

Miller, Jean, Francis Owens, and Rachel Doggett, eds. *The Housewife's Rich Cabinet: Remedies, Recipes, & Helpful Hints.* Washington, DC: The Folger Shakespeare Library, 1997.

Montagu, Lady Mary Wortley. *The Complete Letters.* Edited by Robert Halsband. 3 vols. Oxford: At the Clarendon Press, 1965–67.

Mulcaster, Richard. *Positions Concerning the Training Up of Children (1581).* Edited by William Barker. Toronto: University of Toronto Press, 1994.

Munday, Richard, and Jan A. Stevenson, eds. *Guns and Violence: The Debate before Lord Cullen.* Brightlingsea, Essex: Piedmont Publishing, Ltd., 1996.

Newcastle, Margaret Cavendish. *Natures pictures drawn by fancies pencil to the life. Written by the thrice noble, illustrious, and excellent princess, the lady Marchioness of Newcastle.* London: Printed for J. Martin and J. Allestrye, 1656.

Newcastle, William Cavendish. *An English Prince: Newcastle's Machiavellian Political Guide to Charles II.* Edited by Gloria Italiano Anzilotti. Pisa: Giardini Editori e Stampatori, 1988.

Nichols, John Gough. *Chronicle of the Grey Friars of London.* London: Printed for Camden Society, 1852.

Norfolk Lieutenancy Journal 1676–1701. Transcribed and edited by B. Cozens-Hardy. Norwich: Norfolk Record Society, 1961.

Nye, Nathaniel. *The Art of Gunnery.* London: Printed for William Leak, 1670.

Peacham's Compleat Gentleman (1634). Cambridge: Clarendon Press, 1906.

Pepys, Samuel. *The Diary of Samuel Pepys.* Edited by Robert Latham and Williams Matthews. 10 vols. Berkley: University of California Press, 1970–83.

Person, David. "Of Armies and Battlels." In David Person, *Varieties: or, A surueigh of rare and excellent matters, necessary and delectable for all sorts of persons,* 97–123. London: Richard Badger [and Thomas Cotes], 1635.

Pollard, A. F., ed. *The Reign of Henry VII from Contemporary Sources.* 3 vols. London: Longmans, Green and Co., Ltd., 1913–14.

Prynne, William. *A Summary Collection Of the principal Fundamental Rights Liberties, Proprieties Of All English Freemen.* London: Printed for the author, 1656.

Rawski, Conrad H., trans. *Petrarch's Remedies for Fortune Fair and Foul. A Modern English Translation of De remediis utriusque Fortune, with a commentary by Conrad H. Rawski.* Bloomington: University of Indiana Press, 1991.

Reasons for a New Bill of Rights: Humbly submitted to the Consideration of the Ensuing Session of Parliament. London, 1692.

Rich, Barnaby. *Allarme to England, foreshewing what perilles are procured, and where the people liue without regarde of Martiall lawe.* London: Printed by Christopher Barker, Printer to the Queenes Maiestie, 1578.

Rich Cabinet, With Variety of Inventions: Unlock'd and open'd for the Recreation of Ingenious Spirits at their vacant hours. As also Variety of Recreative Fire −works both for Land, Air, and Water. Collected by J. W. [J. White]. 4th ed. London: William Whitwood, 1668.

Riley, Henry Thomas, ed. Memorials of London and London life, in the XIIIth, XIVth, and XVth centuries. Being a series of extracts, local, social, and political, from the early archives of the city of London, A.D. 1276–1419. London: Longmans, Green and Co., 1868.

Rollins, Hyder Edward, ed. Bloody−minded husband; or The cruelty of John Chambers, who lately lived at Tanworth, in Warwick-shire, and conspir'd the death of his wife. In The Pepys Ballads, 3:202–5. 8 vols. Cambridge, MA: Harvard University Press, 1930.

———. "The High-way Mans Advice To His Brethen, Or, Nevison's Last Legacy to the Knights of the High-Padd." In The Pepys Ballads, 3:123–30. Cambridge, MA: Harvard University Press, 1930.

———. The Pepys Ballads. 8 vols. Cambridge, MA: Harvard University Press, 1930.

———. Tottel's Miscellany (1557–1587). 2 vols. Cambridge, MA: Harvard University Press, 1963.

———. "The York-shire Rogue, Or, Capt. Hind Improv'd'; In the Notorious Life, and Infamous Death, of that Famous Highway-Man, William Nevison." In The Pepys Ballads, 3:206–9. 8 vols. Cambridge, MA: Harvard University Press, 1930.

Rowlands, Samuel. The Letting of Humours' Blood in the Head-vaine. London: W. White, 1600. Reprint. Edinburgh: James Ballantyne and Co., 1814.

Roy, Ian, ed. The Royalist Ordnance Papers 1642–1646. Oxford: Oxfordshire Record Society, 1975.

Schwoerer, Lois G., ed. "Journal of the Convention at Westminster begun the 22 of January 1688/89." Bulletin of the Institute of Historical Research 49 (1976): 242–63.

Shaw, Hester. A Plaine Relation of my Sufferings. By that Miserable Combustion, which happened in Tower-street through the unhappy firing of a great quantity of Gunpowder, there the 4. of January 1650. London, 1653.

Shaw, W. A., et al., eds. Calendar of Treasury Books, 1660–1718. 32 vols. London: HMSO, 1904–62.

Shebbeare, John. A Letter to the People of England, on the Present Situation and conduct of National Affairs. Letter I. London: J. Scott, 1755.

———. A Third Letter to the People of England. On Liberty, Taxes, And the Application of Public Money. London: J. Scott, 1756.

———. A Fifth Letter to the People of England, on the Subversion of the Constitution: And The Necessity of it's being restored. London: J. Morgan, 1757.

Smith, Thomas. The Military Guide for Young Officers. The Arte Of Gunnerie. London: Richard Field, 1600 [i.e., 1601].

Smythe, Sir John. Certain Discourses Military, written by Sir John Smythe, Knight; Concerning the formes and effects of diuers sorts of weapons. London: Richard Johnes, 1590.

Somers, John. "Notes of Debate, January 28, January 29." In Miscellaneous State Papers: From 1501 to 1726, edited by Philip Yorke, second Earl of Hardwicke. 2 vols. 2:401–25. 1778.

Speed, Robert. A Briefe Treatise, To prooue the necessitie and excellence of the use of archerie. Abstracted out of ancient and Moderne Writers. London: Richard Johns, 1596.

Sprat, Thomas. History of the Royal Society. Edited by Jackson I. Cope and Harold Whitmore Jones. St. Louis, MO: Washington University Studies, 1958.

Starkey, David, ed. The Inventory of King Henry VIII. 2 vols. London: Harvey Miller Publishers for The Society of Antiquaries, 1998.

Strong, James. *Joanereidos: or, Feminine valour eminently discovered in westerne women.* London, 1645.

Strype, John. *Life of the learned Sir John Cheke [1705].* Oxford: Clarendon Press, 1821.

Stow, John. *Survey Of London. Reprinted from the text of 1603.* Edited by Charles Lethbridge Kingsford. 2 vols. Oxford: At the Clarendon Press, 1908–71.

Stubbe, Henry. *Legends no Histories: Or, A Specimen Of some Animadversions Upon the History of the Royal Society.* London, 1670.

Students Admitted to The Inner Temple, 1547–1660. London: William Clowes and Sons, 1877.

Tartaglia, Nicholas. *Three Bookes of Colloquies Concerning the Arte of Shooting in Great and Small Pieces of Artillerie.* Translated by Cyprian Lucar, Gent. London: John Harrison, 1588.

Thomson, Gladys Scott, ed. *The Twysden Lieutenancy Papers, 1583–1668.* Ashford: Headley Brothers, 1926.

Trenchard, John. *A Short History of Standing Armies in England.* London: A. Baldwin, 1698.

True and Exact Particular and Inventory Of All and Singular The Lands, Tenements, and Hereditaments, Goods, Chattels, Debts and Personal Estate of William Astell, Esq. Late one of the Directors of the South-Sea Company. London: Jacob Tonson, 1721.

The True Law of Free Monarchies; and Basilikon doron. Edited by Daniel Fischlin and Mark Fortier. Toronto: Center for Reformation and Renaissance Studies, 1996.

True relation of a most desperate murder, committed on the body of Sir John Tindall Knight . . . Who with a pistol charged with 3.Bullets was slaine. London: Edw. All-de, 1617.

Veit, Helen E., Kenneth R. Bowling, and Charlene Bangs Bickford, eds. *Creating the Bill of Rights: The Documentary Record from the First Federal Congress.* Baltimore: Johns Hopkins University Press, 1991.

Wake, Joan, ed. *Muster, beacons, subsidies, etc. in the county of Northampton.* Kettering: Printed for the Northamptonshire Record Society by T. Beaty Hart, 1926.

Webster, John. *The Duchess of Malfi.* Edited by Leah S. Marcus. London: Arden Shakespeare, 2009.

———. *The White Devil.* Edited by Christina Luckyi. London: Methuen Drama, 2008.

White, J. *ART'S Treasury of Rareties, and Curious Inventions.* London: Printed for G. Conyers, n.d.

White, Thomas. *Practice of Christian perfection.* London: printed for Jos. Cranford at the sign of the Gun in Ivy Lane, 1653 (i.e., 1652).

Williams, Sir Roger. *A Briefe discourse of Warre. With his opinion concerning some parts of the Martial Discipline.* London: Thomas Orwin, 1590.

Wood, Mary Anne Everett, ed. *Letters of Royal and Illustrious Ladies of Great Britain.* 3 vols. London: Henry Colburn, 1846.

Wotton, William. *Reflections upon Ancient and Modern Learning.* London, J. Leake, 1697.

Youngs, Frederic A., Jr., ed. *The Proclamations of the Tudor Queens.* Cambridge: Cambridge University Press, 1976.

Secondary Sources

Alford, Stephen. *Burghley: William Cecil at the Court of Elizabeth I.* New Haven, CT: Yale University Press, 2011.

Anglo, Sydney. "Court Festivals of Henry VII." *Bulletin of the John Rylands Library* 43, no. 1 (1960): 1–4.

————. "Foundation of the Tudor Dynasty." *Guildhall Miscellany* 2, no. 1 (1960): 1–9.

————. *Spectacle, Pageantry, and Early Tudor Policy.* 2nd ed. Oxford: Clarendon Press, 1997.

Archer, Ian. "London Lobbies in Later Sixteenth Century." *Historical Journal* 31, no. 1 (1998): 17–44.

Ariès, Phillipe. *Centuries of Childhood.* London: J. Cape, 1962.

Baker, J. H. "Criminal Courts and Procedure at Common Law." In *Crime in England 1550–1800,* edited by J. S. Cockburn, 28–46. London: Methuen, 1977.

————. *Introduction to English Legal History.* 2nd ed. London: Butterworths, 1979.

Baldick, Robert. *The Duel.* London: Chapman & Hall, 1965.

Barnes, T. G. "Examination before a Justice in the Seventeenth Century." *Somerset and Dorset Notes and Queries* 27 (1955): 39–42.

Barter, Sarah. "The Board of Ordnance." In *Tower of London,* edited by John Charlton, 106–16. London: HMSO, 1978.

Beaver, Daniel. *Hunting and the Politics of Violence.* Cambridge: Cambridge University Press, 2008.

Bebbington, Gillian. *London Street Names.* London: Batsford, 1972.

Beckett, I. F. W. *Amateur Military Tradition, 1558–1945.* Manchester: Manchester University Press, 1991.

————. "Buckinghamshire Militia Lists for 1759." *Records of Buckinghamshire.* Edited by G. R. Elvey. Issue 20, no. 3 (1977): 460–69.

Beddard, Robert. "Anti-Popery and the London Mob, 1688." *History Today* No. 38 (1988): 36–39.

Beier, A. L., and Roger Finlay, eds. *London 1500–1700.* London: Longman, 1986.

Ben-Amos, Ilana Krausman. "Women Apprentices in the Trades and Crafts of Early Modern Bristol." *Continuity and Change* 6 (1991): 227–52.

Berry, Edward. *Shakespeare and the Hunt.* Cambridge: Cambridge University Press, 2001.

Bindoff, S. T., ed. *History of House of Commons: 1509–1558,* 3 vols. London: Secker & Warburg, for the History of Parliament Trust, 1982.

Blackmore, Howard L. *Armories of the Tower of London.* 2 vols. London: HMSO, 1976.

————. *British Military Firearms 1650–1850.* London: Herbert Jenkins, 1961.

————. *Gunmakers of London 1350–1850.* York, PA: George Shumway, 1986.

————. *Gunmakers of London, Supplement 1350–1850.* Bloomfield, Ontario: Museum Restoration Service, 1999.

————. *Hunting Weapons from the Middle Ages to the Twentieth Century.* Mineola, NY: Dover Publications, Inc., 2000.

————. *Royal Sporting Guns at Windsor.* London: HMSO, 1968.

Blair, Claude. "Admiral Sir John Chicheley's Firearms, 1690." *Journal of Arms and Armour Society* 11, no. 5 (1985): 255.

Bogus, Carl. "Hidden History of the Second Amendment." *University of California Davis Law Review* 31 (1998): 311–408.

Bonavita, Roger Vella. "The English Militia, 1558–1580." M.A. thesis, Victoria University of Manchester, April 1972.

Boulton, Jeremy. *Neighbourhood and Society.* Cambridge: Cambridge University Press, 1987.

————. "Wage Labour in Seventeenth-Century London." *Economic History Review* 40, no. 2 (1996): 268–90.

Bowling, Kenneth R. "'A Tub to the Whale': Founding Fathers and Adoption of Federal

Bill of Rights." *Center for Public Service, University of Virginia.* Reprinted from *Journal of the Early Republic* 8 (1988): 223–51.

Boynton, Lindsay. *Elizabethan Militia, 1558–1638.* London: Routledge and Kegan Paul, 1967.

Brailsford, Dennis. *Sport and Society.* London: Routledge and Kegan Paul, 1969.

Brander, Michael. *Hunting and Shooting.* London: Weidenfeld & Nicholson, 1972.

Brewer, John. *Sinews of Power: War, Money and the English State: 1668–1783.* New York: Knopf, 1988.

Brock, Alan St. H. *History of Fireworks.* London: George G. Harrap, 1949.

Brodsky, Vivien. "Widows in Late Elizabethan London." In *The World We Have Gained,* edited by Lloyd Bonfield, Richard M. Smith, and Keith Wrightson, 122–54. London: Basil Blackwell, 1986.

Bromley, John. *Armorial Bearings of the Guilds of London.* London: Frederick Warne & Co., 1960.

Burke, Peter. *Varieties of Cultural History.* Ithaca, NY: Cornell University Press, 1997.

Butler, Martin. *The Stuart Court.* Cambridge: Cambridge University Press, 2009.

Canby, Sheila R. *Shah 'Abbas I: Remaking of Iran.* London: British Museum Press, 2009.

Cannadine, David. *Decline and Fall of the British Aristocracy.* New Haven, CT: Yale University Press, 1990.

Carlin, Martha. "St. Botolph Aldgate Gazetteer: Minories, East Side; Holy Trinity Minories." Unpublished. London: Institute of Metropolitan Studies, 1987.

Carlton, Charles. *Going to the Wars.* London: Routledge, 1994.

———. *This Seat of Mars: War and the British Isles, 1485–1746.* New Haven, CT: Yale University Press, 2011.

Carrington, Damian. "Gunpowder Plot Would have Devastated London." *Newscientist.com,* 5 November 2003. Http://www.newscientist.com/article/dn4338-gunpowder-plot-would-have-devastated-london.html#.VTcW1FoNL4M.link.

Caruana, Adrian B. *Tudor Artillery: 1485–1603.* Historical Arms Series, No. 30. Alexandria Bay, NY: Museum Restoration Service, 1992.

Chambers, E. K. *Elizabethan Stage.* 4 vols. Oxford: At the Clarendon Press, 1923.

Charles, Patrick J. "'Arms for Their Defence.'" *Cleveland State Law Review* 58 (2009): 352–460.

———. "Faces of the Second Amendment." *Cleveland State Law Review* 60 (2012): 1–55.

Charlton, John, ed. *The Tower of London: Its Buildings and Institutions.* London: HMSO, 1978.

Chase, Kenneth. *Firearms.* Cambridge: Cambridge University Press, 2008.

Childs, John. *Army of Charles II.* London: Routledge & Kegan Paul, 1976.

———. *Army of James II and the Glorious Revolution.* New York: St. Martin's Press, 1980.

Chitty, Joseph. *A Treatise on the Game Laws, and Fisheries: with An Appendix containing all the Statutes and a Copious collection of Precedents.* 2nd ed. London: Samuel Brooke, 1826.

Cipolla, Carlo M. *Guns and Sails.* London: Collins, 1965.

Citino, Robert M. "Review Essay. Military Histories Old and New: A Reintroduction." *American Historical Review* 112 (2007): 1070–90.

Clark, Sandra. "Hic Mulier, Haec Vir." *Studies in Philology* 82 (1985): 157–83.

Clay, C. G. A. *Economic Expansion and Social Change.* 2 vols. Cambridge: Cambridge University Press, 1984.

Cleaveland, Frederick Darby. *Notes on the Early History of The Royal Regiment of Artillery.* Woolwich: Published by the author, 1892.

Clifford, Bridget, and Karen Watts, eds. *Introduction to Princely Armours and Weapons of Childhood*. Leeds: Royal Armouries, 2003.

Clode, Charles M. *Military Forces of the Crown*. 2 vols. London: John Murray, 1869.

Cockburn, J. S. *History of English Assizes: 1558–1714*. Cambridge: Cambridge University Press, 1972.

Cockle, Maurice J. D. *Bibliography of Military Books up to 1642*. London: Holland Press, 1978.

Coleman, D. C. *Industry in Tudor and Stuart England*. London: Macmillan Press, 1975.

Cooper, John S. *For Commonwealth and Crown: English Gunmakers*. Dorset: Wilson Hunt, 1993.

Cressy, David. *Bonfires and Bells: National Memory and the Protestant Calendar in Elizabethan and Stuart England*. Berkeley: University of California Press, 1989.

———. *Literacy and the Social Order: Reading and Writing in Tudor and Stuart England*. Cambridge: Cambridge University Press, 1980.

———. "Saltpetre, State Security and Vexation." *Past and Present* 1 (2011): 73–111.

———. *Saltpeter: The Mother of Gunpowder*. Oxford: Oxford University Press, 2013.

Critchley, T. A. *The Conquest of Violence: Order and Liberty in Britain*. New York: Schocken Books, 1970.

Crocker, Glenys, and Alan Crocker. *Damnable Inventions*. Bristol: J. W. Arrowsmith Ltd., 2000.

Cruickshank, C. G. *Army Royal: Henry VIII's Invasion of France 1513*. Oxford: At the Clarendon Press, 1969.

———. *Elizabeth's Army*. 2nd ed. Oxford: Oxford University Press, 1966.

Cust, Lionel. "Notes on Pictures in the Royal Collections—XXXIII. The Portrait of Prince Baltasar Carlos, by Velázquez." *Burlington Magazine for Connoisseurs* 28, no. 152 (1915): 56–57, 59–60.

Davies, C. S. L. "Peasant Revolt in France and England: A Comparison." *Agricultural History Review* 21 (1973): 122–34.

Davies, D. W. *Elizabethans Errant: Strange Fortunes of Sir Thomas Sherley and His Three Sons*. Ithaca: Cornell University Press, 1967.

Davis, Natalie Zemon. *The Gift in Sixteenth-Century France*. Madison: University of Wisconsin Press, 2000.

Dean, David. "Elizabeth's Lottery: Political Culture and State Formation in Early Modern England." *Journal of British Studies* 50, no. 3 (2011): 587–611.

Dennys, Rodney. *Heraldry and Heralds*. London: Jonathan Cape, 1982.

Dessen, Allan C., and Leslie Thomson, eds. *A Dictionary of Stage Directions in English Drama 1580–1642*. Cambridge: Cambridge University Press, 1999.

DeVries, Kelly. *Guns and Men in Medieval Europe: 1200–1500*. Aldershot, Hampshire: Ashgate, 2002.

DeVries, Kelly, and Robert D. Smith. *Medieval Military Technology*. Toronto: University of Toronto Press, 2012.

Dixon, Norman. *Georgian Pistols: The Art and Craft of the Flintlock Pistol, 1715–1840*. London: Arms and Armour Press, 1971.

Dmitrieva, Olga, and Natalya Abramova, eds. *Britannia and Muscovy: English Silver at the Court of the Tsars*. New Haven, CT: Yale University Press, 2006.

Dmitrieva, Olga, and Tessa Murdoch, eds. *Treasures of the Royal Courts: Tudors, Stuarts and the Russian Tsars*. London: Victoria & Albert Publishing, 2013.

Donagan, Barbara. *War in England, 1642–1649*. Oxford: Oxford University Press, 2008.

Duffy, Maureen. *Passionate Shepherdess: Aphra Behn, 1640–89.* New York: Avon Books, 1977.

Dugaw, Diane. *Warrior Women and Popular Balladry, 1650–1850.* 2nd ed. Chicago: University of Chicago Press, 1996.

Dunn, Alistair. *Great Rising of 1381.* Charleston, SC: Tempus, 2002.

Earle, Peter. *Monmouth's Rebels: The Road to Sedgemoor, 1685.* New York: St. Martin's Press, 1977.

Eaves, Ian. "Some Notes on the Pistol in Early Seventeenth Century England." *Journal of Arms and Armour Society* 6, no. 11 (1970): 277–344.

———. "Further Notes on the Pistol in Early 17th c. England." *Journal of Arms and Armour Society* 8, no. 5 (1976): 269–329.

Edelman, Charles, ed. *Shakespeare's Military Language.* London: Athlone Press, 2000.

———. "Shoot at Them all at once." *Theatre Notebook: A Journal of the History and Technique of the British Theatre* 57 (2003): 78–81.

Edwards, Peter. *Dealing in Death.* Phoenix Mill, Gloucestershire: Sutton Publishing, 2000.

Egan, Geoff. "Miniature Toys of Medieval Childhood." *British Archaeology.* Edited by Simon Dinson. No. 35 (1998). www.britarch.ac.uk/ba/ba35/ba35feat.html.

———. *Playthings from the Past: Toys from the A. G. Pilson Collection, c.1300–1800.* Jonathan Horne, 1996.

Elgood, Robert. *Firearms of the Islamic World.* London: I. B. Tauris Publishers, 1995.

Eisenstein, Elizabeth L. *Printing Press: Agent of Change.* Cambridge: Cambridge University Press, 1979.

Elton, G. R. *The Parliament of England, 1559–1581.* Cambridge: Cambridge University Press, 1986.

———. *Reform and Reformation.* London: Arnold, 1977.

———. *The Tudor Constitution: Documents and Commentary.* Cambridge: Cambridge University Press, 1960.

Emberton, Wilfred. "Close and Perilous Siege of Basing House." Basingstoke: W. J. Emberton, 1972.

Emmison, F. G. *Elizabethan Life: Disorder Mainly from Essex . . . Records.* Chelmsford: Essex County Council, 1970.

———. *Elizabethan Life: Home, Work and Land from Essex Wills and Sessions and Manorial Records.* Chelmsford: Essex County Council, 1976.

Erickson, Amy Louise. "Married Women's Occupations in Eighteenth-Century London." *Continuity and Change* 23, no. 2 (2008): 267–307.

Fairclough, K. R. "The Hard Case of Sir Polycarpus Wharton." *Surrey Archaeological Collections* 83 (1996): 125–35.

Farmer, J. S., and W. E. Henley, eds. *Slang and Its Analogues.* 7 vols. New York: Arno Press, 1970.

Ffoulkes, Charles. *The Gun-Founders of England: With a List of English and Continental Gun-Founders from the XIV to the XIX Centuries.* Cambridge: Cambridge University Press, 1937.

Finlay, Roger. *Population and Metropolis: The Demography of London 1580–1650.* Cambridge: Cambridge University Press, 1981.

Finlay, Roger, and Beatrice Shearer. "Population Growth and Suburban Expansion." In *London 1500–1700,* edited by A. L. Beier and Roger Finlay, 37–59. London: Longman, 1986.

Fissel, Mark Charles. *English Warfare 1511–1642*. London: Routledge, 2001.

———. *War and Government in Britain: 1598–1650*. Manchester: Manchester University Press, 1991.

Forbes, Thomas Rogers. *Chronicle from Aldgate: Life and Death in Shakespeare's London*. New Haven, CT: Yale University Press, 1971.

Fraser, Antonia. *History of Toys*. London: Delacorte Press, 1966.

———. *Weaker Vessel*. New York: Alfred A. Knopf, 1984.

Froide, Amy. *Never Married: Single Women in Early Modern England*. Oxford: Oxford University Press, 2005.

Gadd, Ian Anders, and Patrick Wallis. "Reaching beyond the City Wall: London Guilds and National Regulation, 1500–1700." In *Guilds, Innovation, and the European Economy, 1400–1800*, edited by S. R. Epstein and Maarten Prak, 288–315. Cambridge: Cambridge University Press, 2008.

Garrett, Jane. *The Triumphs of Providence: The Assassination Plot, 1696*. Cambridge: Cambridge University Press, 1980.

Gentles, Ian. *The New Model Army*. Oxford: Blackwell, 1992.

Gimenez, Carmen, and Francisco Calvo Serraller, eds. *Spanish Painting from El Greco to Picasso*. New York: Guggenheim Museum, 2007.

Glass, D. V. *London Inhabitants within the Walls, 1695*. London: London Record Society, 1966.

Godwin, Brian C. "An English Wheellock—by Association." *The Nineteenth Park Lane Arms Fair—17th February 2002*.

Goldgar, Bertrand A., and Ian Gadd, eds. *English Political Writings 1711–1714: The Conduct of the Allies and Other Works*. Cambridge: Cambridge University Press, 2008.

Goldie, Mark. "The Roots of True Whiggism 1688–94." *Journal of Political Thought* 1 (1980): 195–236.

Goodwin, J. "The Newdigates of Arbury." *Gentleman's Magazine* 226 (1869). New York: AMS Press, Inc., 1968: 289–301.

Goring, J. J. "The General Proscription of 1522." *English Historical Review* 86, no. 341 (1971): 681–705.

———. "Social Change and Military Decline in Mid-Tudor England." *History* 60 (1975): 185–99.

Gould, Eliga H. *The Persistence of Empire: British Political Culture in the Age of the American Revolution*. Chapel Hill: University of North Carolina Press, 2000.

———. "To Strengthen the King's Hands: Dynastic Legitimacy, Militia Reform and Ideas of National Unity in England, 1745–1760." *Historical Journal* 34, no. 2 (1991): 329–48.

Grancsay, Stephen V. "A Wheellock Pistol Made for the Emperor Charles V." *Metropolitan Museum of Art Bulletin*, New Series 6, no.4 (1947): 117–22.

Graves, Michael A. R. *Burghley: William Cecil, Lord Burghley*. London: Longman, 1998.

Griffiths, Paul. *Lost London: Change, Crime and Control in the Capital City, 1550–1660*. Cambridge: Cambridge University Press, 2008.

Grose, Francis. *Military Antiquities: Respecting a History of the English Army from the Conquest to the Present Time*. 2 vols. London: Stockdale, 1800.

Grummitt, David, "The Defence of Calais and the Development of Gunpowder Weaponry in England in the Late Fifteenth Century." *War in History* 7, no. 3 (2000): 253–72. In *Historical Abstracts with Full Text*, pp. 1–20. Http://web.b.ebscohost.com.proxygw.wrlc.org/ehost/delivery?sid=96942149-155b-4578-a4.

Gunn, Steven. "Archery Practice in Early Tudor England." *Past and Present* 209, (2010): 53–82.

———. "The French Wars of Henry VIII." In *Origins of War in Early Modern Europe,* edited by Jeremy Black, 28–51. Edinburgh: John Donald Publishers, 1987.

Gunn, Steven, David Grummitt, and Hans Cools, eds. *War, State, and Society.* Oxford: Oxford University Press, 2007.

Guy, John. *Tudor England.* Oxford: Oxford University Press, 1988.

Gwyn, Peter. *The King's Cardinal: The Rise and Fall of Thomas Wolsey.* London: Barrie and Jenkins, 1990.

Hacker, Barton C. "Women and Military Institutions in Early Modern Europe." *Signs* 6, no. 41 (1981): 643–71.

Hageman, Elizabeth H. "Family Matters." In *Renaissance Historicisms,* edited by James M. Dutcher and Anne Lake Prescott, 173–92. Newark: University of Delaware Press, 2008.

Hale, J. R. *Artists and Warfare in the Renaissance.* New Haven, CT: Yale University Press, 1990.

———. "Gunpowder and the Renaissance: An Essay in the History of Ideas." In *From the Renaissance to the Counter-Reformation,* edited by Charles H. Carter, 113–44. New York: Random House, 1965.

———. "War and Public Opinion in the Fifteenth and Sixteenth Centuries." *Past and Present* (1962): 18–33.

Hall, A. R. *Ballistics in the Seventeenth Century.* Cambridge: At the University Press, 1952.

———. "Military Technology." In *History of Technology.* Volume 3, 347–76. Oxford: Clarendon Press, 1957.

Hall, Bert S. *Weapons and Warfare in Renaissance Europe: Gunpowder, Technology, and Tactics.* Baltimore: Johns Hopkins University Press, 1997.

Hamilton, Edith. *Henrietta Maria.* London: Hamish Hamilton, 1976.

Hammer, Paul E. J. *Elizabeth's Wars: War, Government and Society in Tudor England, 1544–1604.* Houndsmill, Hampshire: Palgrave Macmillan, 2003.

Hanawalt, Barbara A. "Men's Games, King's Deer: Poaching in Medieval England." In Hanawalt, *"Of Good and Ill Repute": Gender and Social Control in Medieval England,* 142–57. Oxford: Oxford University Press, 1998.

Harding, Vanessa. "City, Capital, and Metropolis: Changing Shape of Seventeenth-Century London." In *Imagining Early Modern London: Perceptions and Portrayals of the City from Stow to Strype, 1598–1720,* edited by J. F. Merritt, 117–43. Cambridge: Cambridge University Press, 2001.

Harkness, Deborah E. *The Jewel House: Elizabethan London and the Scientific Revolution.* New Haven, CT: Yale University Press, 2007.

Harris, Tim. "London Crowds and the Revolution of 1688." In *By Force or by Default? The Revolution of 1688–1689,* edited by Eveline Cruickshanks, 44–64. Edinburgh: John Donaldson Publishers, Ltd., 1989.

———. *Restoration: Charles II and His Kingdoms, 1660–1685.* London: Penguin, 2006.

———. *Revolution: The Great Crisis of the British Monarchy, 1685–1720.* London: Penguin, 2007.

Hassell-Smith, A. "Militia Rates and Militia Statutes, 1558–1663." In *English Commonwealth, 1547–1640,* edited by Peter Clark, Alan G. R. Smith, and Nicholas Tyacke, 93–110. New York: Barnes & Noble Books, 1979.

Hayward, J. F. *The Art of the Gunmaker.* 2 vols. London: Barrie and Rockliff, 1962.

Hearn, Karen, ed. *Dynasties: Painting in Tudor and Jacobean England*. London: Tate Publishing, 1995.

———. *Marcus Gheeraerts II: Elizabethan Artist*. London: Tate Publishing, 2002.

Heinze, R. W. *Proclamations of the Tudor Kings*. Cambridge: Cambridge University Press, 1976.

Henderson, Katherine Usher, and Barbara F. McManus, eds. *Half Humankind: Contexts and Texts of the Controversy about Women in England, 1540–1640*. Urbana: University of Illinois Press, 1985.

Hendrickson, Robert, ed. *The Facts on File: Encyclopedia of Word and Phrase Origins*. 3rd ed. New York: Checkmark Books, 2004.

Hewerdine, Anita. *Yeomen of the Guard and the Early Tudors: The Formation of a Royal Bodyguard*. London: I. B. Tauris, 2012.

Hibbert, Christopher. *King Mob: The Story of Lord George Gordon and the London Riots of 1780*. Cleveland, OH: World Publishing Co., 1958.

Historical Society of West Wales. *West Wales Historical Records*. 9 vols. Edited by Francis Green. Carmarthen: W. Spurrell and Son, 1910–29.

The History of Parliament: The House of Commons 1660–1690. 7 vols. Edited by Basil Duke Henning. London: Secker & Warburg, 1983.

Hogg, O. F. G. *English Artillery, 1326–1716: Being the History of Artillery in this Country Prior to the Formation of the Royal Regiment of Artillery*. London: Royal Artillery Institution, 1963.

Holdsworth, Sir William. *History of English Law*. 3rd. ed. 17 vols. London: Methuen & Co., 1922–72.

Horwitz, Henry. *Parliament, Policy and Politics in the Reign of William III*. Manchester: Manchester University Press, 1977.

Houston, R. A. *Population History of Britain and Ireland*. London: Macmillan Press, 1992.

Hoyle, R. W. *The Pilgrimage of Grace and the Politics of the 1530s*. Oxford: Oxford University Press, 2001.

Hyde, Ralph, John Fisher, and Roger Cline. *A to Z of Restoration London*. Lympne Castle, Kent: London Topographical Society, 1992.

Innes, Joanna. "Domestic Face of the Military-Fiscal State." In *Imperial State at War: Britain From 1689 to 1815*, edited by Lawrence Stone, 96–127. London: Routledge, 1994.

Jackson, Emily. *Toys of Other Days*. New York: Charles Scribner's Sons, 1908.

Jackson, Herbert J. *European Hand Firearms of the Sixteenth, Seventeenth and Eighteenth Centuries*. London: Martin Hopkinson & Company, 1923.

Jansson, Maija. "Ambassadorial Gifts." In *Britannia and Muscovy: English Silver at the Court of the Tsars*, edited by Olga Dmitrieva and Natalya Abramova, 198–206. New Haven, CT: Yale University Press, 2006.

Jardine, Lisa. *The Awful End of Prince William the Silent: The First Assassination of a Head of State with a Handgun*. London: Harper Collins, 2005.

Jorgensen, Paul A. *Shakespeare's Military World*. Berkeley: University of California Press, 1956.

Keegan, John. *The Face of Battle*. New York: Vintage Books, 1977.

Kelly, Jack. *Gunpowder: Alchemy, Bombards, and Pyrotechnics*. New York: Basic Books, 2004.

Kelso, Ruth. *Doctrine of the English Gentleman in the Sixteenth Century*. Urbana: University of Illinois Press, 1929.

Kennard, A. N. *Gunfounding and Gunfounders: A Directory of Cannon Founders from the Earliest Times to 1850.* London: Arms and Armour Press, 1986.

Kenyon, J. P., ed. *Documents and Commentary to The Stuart Constitution 1603–1688.* 2nd ed. Cambridge: Cambridge University Press, 1986.

Kiernan, V. G. *The Duel in European History: Honour and the Reign of Aristocracy.* Oxford: Oxford University Press, 1988.

Kirby, Chester. "The English Game Law System." *American Historical Review* 38 (1933): 240–62.

Kirby, Chester, and Ethyn Kirby. "The Stuart Game Prerogative." *English Historical Review* 46 (1931): 239–54.

Kirk, R. E. G., and Ernest F. Kirk, eds. *Return of Aliens.* 4 vols. Aberdeen: University Press, 1902.

Kohn, Abigail. "Their Aim Is True. Taking Stock of America's Real Gun Culture," *Reason Magazine Online.* May 2001. Http://reason.com/archives/2001/05/01/their-aim-is -true.

Kurath, Hans, ed. *The Middle English Dictionary.* Ann Arbor: University of Michigan Press, 2001.

Langsam, Geoffrey G. *Martial Books and Tudor Verse.* New York: King's Crown Press, 1951.

Laslett, Peter. *The World We Have Lost.* New York: Charles Scribner's Sons, 1972.

Latta, John. *Queen Elizabeth's Pocket Pistol.* 30 September 2007. Dover Castle, Kent. www.panoramio.com/photo/5381732.

Lavin, James D. "The Gift of James I to Felipe III of Spain." *Journal of Arms and Armour Society* 14 (1992): 64–88.

Lawrence, D. R. *Complete Soldier: Military Books and Military Culture in Early Stuart England, 1603–1645.* Leiden: Brill, 2009.

Levin, Carole. *The Reign of Elizabeth I.* New York: Palgrave, 2002.

London Livery Company. Apprenticeship Registers. Abstracted and indexed by Cliff Webb. Vol. 22, *Armourers and Brasiers' Company 1610–1800.* London: Society of Genealogists, 1998.

London Livery Company. Apprenticeship Registers. Abstracted and indexed by Cliff Webb. Vol. 41, *Blacksmiths' Company 1605–1800.* London: Society of Genealogists, 2004.

London Livery Company. Apprenticeship Registers. Abstracted and indexed by Cliff Webb. Vol. 8, *Gunmakers' Company 1656–1800.* London: Society of Genealogists, 1997.

Luu, Lien Bich. "Assimilation or Segregation: Colonies of Alien Craftsmen in Elizabethan London." *Proceedings of the Huguenot Society of Great Britain and Ireland* 26, no. 2 (1995): 160–72.

———. *Immigrants and Industries in London, 1500–1700.* Aldershot, Hants: Ashgate, 2005.

Macaulay, Lord Thomas. *History of England from the Accession of James II.* 6 vols. Edited by C. J. Firth. London: Macmillan and Co., 1913–15.

Maclure, Millar. *The Paul's Cross Sermons.* Toronto: University of Toronto Press, 1958.

MacDonald, Michael, and Terence R. Murphy. *Sleepless Souls: Suicide in Early Modern England.* Oxford: Clarendon Press, 1990.

Macfarlane, Alan. *The Justice and the Mare's Ale.* New York: Cambridge University Press, 1981.

MacGregor, Arthur. "Animals and the Early Stuarts: Hunting and Hawking at the Court of James I and Charles I." *Archives of Natural History* 16 (1989): 305–18.

———. "The Household Out Of Doors: The Stuart Court and the Animal Kingdom."
In *The Stuart Courts*, edited by Eveline Cruickshanks, 86–117. Phoenix Mill, Gloucestershire: Sutton Publishing, 2000.

———. *Late King's Goods: Collections, Possessions, and Patronage of Charles I in the Light
of the Commonwealth Sale Inventories*. Oxford: Oxford University Press, 1989.

Malcolm, Joyce Lee. *Guns and Violence*. Cambridge, MA: Harvard University Press,
2002.

———. *To Keep and Bear Arms: The Origins of an Anglo-American Right*. Cambridge,
MA: Harvard University Press, 1994.

Malden, H. F., ed. *Victoria History of the County of Surrey*. 4 vols. Westminster: A. Constable and Company, Ltd., 1902–14.

Manning, Roger B. *Hunters and Poachers: A Social and Cultural History of Unlawful
Hunting in England, 1485–1640*. Oxford: Clarendon Press, 1993.

———. *The Swordsmen: Martial Ethos in the Three Kingdoms*. Oxford: Oxford University
Press, 2003.

———. *Village Revolts: Social Protest and Popular Disturbances*. Oxford: Clarendon Press,
1988.

Marshall, Peter. "The Shooting of Robert Packington." In *Religious Identities*, edited by
Peter Marshall, 61–79. Aldershot, Hants: Ashgate, 2006.

Marvick, Elizabeth. *Louis XIII*. New Haven, CT: Yale University Press, 1986.

Matthew, H. C. G., and Brian Harrison, eds. *Oxford Dictionary of National Biography*. 60
vols. Oxford: Oxford University Press, 2004.

May, W. E. "Some Board of Ordnance Gunmakers." *Journal of Arms and Armour Society*
6, no. 7 (September 1969): 201–4.

McDermott, James. *Martin Frobisher*. New Haven, CT: Yale University Press, 2001.

McDonald, Forrest. *Novus Ordo Seclorum: The Intellectual Origins of the Constitution*.
Lawrence: University Press of Kansas, 1985.

Merritt, J. F., ed. *Imagining Early Modern London*. Cambridge: Cambridge University
Press, 2001.

Millar, Gilbert John. *Tudor Mercenaries and Auxiliaries, 1485–1547*. Charlottesville: University Press of Virginia, 1980.

Miller, Jean, et al., eds. *The Housewife's Rich Cabinet: Remedies, Receipes, and Helpful
Hints*. Washington, DC: Folger Shakespeare Library, 1997. Exhibition Catalog.

Miller, John. *After the Civil Wars*. New York: Longman, 2000.

———. "Militia and Army in the Reign of James II." *Historical Journal* 16 (1973): 659–79.

Morgan, Edmund S. *Inventing the People: The Rise of Popular Sovereignty in England and
America*. New York: W. W. Norton & Company, 1988.

Morrill, J. S., and J. D. Walter. "Order and Disorder in English Revolution." In *Order
and Disorder*, edited by Anthony Fletcher and John Stevenson, 137–65. Cambridge:
Cambridge University Press, 1985.

Morrissey, Mary. *Politics and the Paul's Cross Sermons*. Oxford: Oxford University Press,
2011.

Mowat, Barbara A., and Paul Werstine, eds. *Henry VIII*. New York: Washington Square
Press, 2007.

Munsche, P. B. *Gentlemen and Poachers*. Cambridge: Cambridge University Press, 1981.

Neal, W. Keith, and D. H. L. Back. *Great British Gunmakers, 1540–1740*. London: Lund
Humphries, 1984.

Nichols, John. *Progresses, Processions, and Magnificent Festivities of King James the First*. 4

vols. London: Printed by and for J. B. Nichols, Printer to the Society of Antiquaries, 1828.

———, ed. *Progresses and Public Processions of Queen Elizabeth.* 3 vols. New York: B. Franklin, 1966.

Nolan, John S. "Muster of 1588." *Albion* 23 (1991): 387–407.

Officer, Lawrence H., and Samuel H. Williamson. "Purchasing Power of British Pounds from 1270 to Present." *Measuring Worth.* 2015. www.measuringworth.com/ppoweruk/.

Orme, Nicholas. "Child's Play in Medieval England." *History Today* 51 (2001): 49–55.

Ormrod, David. *The Dutch in London.* London: HMSO, 1973.

Papworth, John. *Alphabetical Dictionary of Coats of Arms Belonging to Families in Great Britain and Ireland.* London, 1858.

Parker, Geoffrey. *The Military Revolution: Military Innovation and the Rise of the West, 1500–1800.* 2nd ed. Cambridge: Cambridge University Press, 1996.

Parkes, Joan. *Travel in England in the Seventeenth Century.* Oxford: Oxford University Press, 1925.

Partington, J. R. *History of Greek Fire and Gunpowder.* Cambridge: W. Heffer, 1960.

Pearlman, Chee. "Nine of a Kind: Purse Pistols." *New York Times Magazine,* 20 March 2011.

Peck, Linda Levy. *Consuming Splendour: Society and Culture in Seventeenth-Century England.* Cambridge: Cambridge University Press, 2005

Peltonen, Markku. *The Duel in Early Modern England.* Cambridge: Cambridge University Press, 2003.

Perry, Curtis, ed. *Material Culture and Cultural Materialisms in the Middle Ages and Renaissance.* Turnhout, Belgium: Reports, 2001.

Pevsner, Nikolaus. *The Buildings of England: Middlesex.* Harmondsworth, Middlesex: Penguin Books, 1951.

Philip, Chris. *Bibliography of Firework Books: Works on Recreative Fireworks from the Sixteenth to the Twentieth Century.* Dingmans Ferry, PA: American Fireworks News, 1988.

Pincus, Steven. *The First Modern Revolution.* New Haven, CT: Yale University Press, 2009.

Plowden, Alison. *Women All On Fire: The Women of the English Civil War.* Phoenix Mill, Gloucestershire: Sutton Publishing, 1998.

Pocock, John G. A. *The Ancient Constitution and the Feudal Law: A Study of English Historical Thought in the Seventeenth Century. A Reissue with a Retrospect.* Cambridge: Cambridge University Press, 1987.

———, ed. *Commonwealth of Oceana, and a System of Politics: James Harrington.* Cambridge: Cambridge University Press, 1992.

Pollard, Hugh B. C. *History of Firearms.* London: Geoffrey Bles, 1926.

Power, M. J. "The Social Topography of Restoration London." In *London 1500–1700,* edited by A. L. Beier and Roger Finlay, 199–223. London: Longman, 1986.

Prior, Mary. "Women and the Urban Economy: Oxford 1500–1800." In *Women in English Society 1500–1800,* edited by Mary Prior, 93–117. London: Methuen, 1985.

Prockter, Adrian, and Robert Taylor, comps. *The A to Z of Elizabethan London.* London: London Topographical Society, 1979.

Rappaport, Steve. *Worlds within Worlds: Structures of Life in Sixteenth-Century London.* Cambridge: Cambridge University Press, 1989.

Raymond, James. *Henry VIII's Military Revolution.* London: Tauris Academic Studies, 2007.

Read, Conyers. *Mr. Secretary: Cecil and Queen Elizabeth.* London: Jonathan Cape, 1955.

Reid, William. "Present of Spain: a Seventeenth-Century Royal Gift." *Connoisseur* (August 1960): 21–26.

Rimer, Graeme. *Wheellock Firearms of the Royal Armouries.* Leeds: Royal Armouries, 2001.

Rimer, Graeme, et al., eds. *Henry VIII: Arms and the Man.* Leeds: Royal Armouries Museum, 2009.

Rogers, Clifford J., ed. *The Military Revolution Debate: Readings on the Military Transformation of Early Modern Europe.* Boulder, CO: Westview Press, 1995.

Rogers, Nicholas. "Popular Protest in Early Hanoverian London." *Past and Present* 73 (1978): 70–100.

Sachse, William. "The Mob and the Revolution of 1688." *Journal of British Studies* 4 (1964): 23–40.

Scarisbrick, J. S. *Henry VIII.* London: Eyre & Spottiswoode, 1970.

Schrijver, Elka. "The Siege of Haarlem." *History Today* 23 (1973): 507–12.

Schwoerer, Lois G. *Declaration of Rights, 1689.* Baltimore: Johns Hopkins University Press, 1981.

———. "The Grenville Militia List for Buckinghamshire, 1798–1799." *Huntington Library Quarterly* 68 (2005): 667–75.

———. *"No Standing Armies!": The Antiarmy Ideology in Seventeenth-Century England.* Baltimore: Johns Hopkins University Press, 1981.

———. "To Hold and Bear Arms." *Chicago-Kent Law Review* 76 (2000): 27–60. Reprinted in *The Second Amendment in Law and History: Historians and Constitutional Scholars on the Right to Bear Arms.* Edited by Carl Bogus, 207–27. New York: New Press, 2002.

———. "Women and Guns in Early Modern London." In *Challenging Orthodoxies,* edited by Sigrun Haude and Melinda S. Zook, 33–52. Farnham, Surrey: Ashgate, 2014.

———. "Women's Public Political Voice in England: 1640–1700." In *Women Writers,* edited by Hilda Smith, 56–74. Cambridge: Cambridge University Press, 1998.

Shammas, Carole. *The Pre-industrial Consumer in England and America.* Oxford: Clarendon Press, 1990.

Sharpe, J. A. *Crime in Early Modern England, 1550–1750.* London: Longman, 1999.

———. *Crime in the Seventeenth Century: A County Study.* Cambridge: Cambridge University Press, 1983.

Sharpe, Kevin. *Reading Revolutions: The Politics of Reading in Early Modern England.* Cambridge: Cambridge University Press, 2000.

———. *Selling the Tudor Monarchy: Authority and Image in Sixteenth-Century England.* New Haven, CT: Yale University Press, 2009.

Shepard, Alexandra. *Meanings of Manhood in Early Modern England.* Oxford: Oxford University Press, 2003.

Simpson, Richard, ed. *The Rambler, 1858: A Catholic Journal of Home and Foreign Literature.* Vol. 10. London: Forgotten Books, 2013.

Singer, Charles, E. J. Holmyard, A. R. Hall, and Trevor I. Williams, eds. *The History of Technology.* Vols. 1 and 3. Oxford: Clarendon Press, 1956.

Singer, Dorothea Waley. "On a 16th Century Cartoon concerning the Devilish Weapon of Gunpowder." *Ambix: The Journal of the Society for the Study of Alchemy and Early Chemistry* 7, no. 1 (1959): 25–33.

Skinner, Quentin. *Foundations of Modern Political Thought.* 2 vols. Cambridge: Cambridge University Press, 1978.

Smith, Bruce. *Acoustic World of Early Modern England.* Chicago: University of Chicago Press, 1999.

Smith, Hilda L. *All Men and Both Sexes: Gender, Politics, and the False Universal in England, 1640–1832.* University Park, PA: Penn State University Press, 2002.

Smith, Logan Pearsall, ed. *The Life and Letters of Sir Henry Wotton.* 2 vols. Oxford: At the Clarendon Press, 1907.

Somerset, Anne. *Elizabeth I.* New York: St. Martin's Press, 1991.

Speck, William A. *Reluctant Revolutionaries.* Oxford: Oxford University Press, 1988.

Spence, Craig. *London in the 1690's: A Social Atlas.* London: Institute of Historical Research, University of London, 2000.

Starkey, David. *Henry: Virtuous Prince.* London: Harper Press, 2008.

———, ed. *The Inventory of King Henry VIII.* 2 vols. London: Harvey Miller, for Society of Antiquaries, 1998.

Stater, Victor Louis. *Noble Government: Stuart Lord Lieutenancy and the Transformation of English Politics.* Athens: University of Georgia Press, 1994.

Stephens, Sir Edgar. *The Clerks of the Counties, 1360–1960.* London: Society of Clerks of the Peace, 1961.

Stern, Walter M. "Gunmaking in Seventeenth-Century London." *Journal of Arms and Armour Society* 1, no. 5 (1954): 55–99.

Stewart, Richard W. *The English Ordnance Office 1584–1625: A Case Study in Bureaucracy.* London: The Royal Historical Society/Boydell Press, 1996.

Stimpson, Derek, ed. *The Worshipful Company of Gunmakers or The Gunmakers' Company: A History.* London: Worshipful Company of Gunmakers, 2008.

Stone, Lawrence. *Crisis of the Aristocracy, 1558–1641.* Oxford: At the Clarendon Press, 1965.

Strype, John. *Life of the Learned Sir John Cheke.* Oxford: Clarendon Press, 1821.

Sutherland, N. M. "The Assassination of François Duc de Guise, February 1563." *Historical Journal* 24, no. 2 (June 1981): 279–82.

Tarassuk, Leonid. "The Cabinet d'Armes of Louis XIII." *Metropolitan Museum Journal* 21 (1986): 65–122.

Taylerson, A. W. G. "The London Armoury Company." *Journal of Arms and Armour Society* 23 (1956): 45–56.

Taylor, Justine. "The Heirs of the 1537 'Fraternity or Guild of Artillery of Longbows, Crossbows and Handguns.'" *Honourable Artillery Company Journal* 87, no. 479 (2010): 101–12.

———. "The Origins of Honourable Artillery Company." *Honourable Artillery Company Journal* 86, no. 477 (2009): 105–16.

Thirsk, Joan. *Economic Policy and Projects.* Oxford: Clarendon Press, 1978.

———, ed. *The Agrarian History of England and Wales.* Volumes 4–6. Cambridge: Cambridge University Press, 1967–89.

Thomas, Keith. *The Ends of Life: Roads to Fulfillment in Early Modern England.* Oxford: Oxford University Press, 2009.

———. "Numeracy in Early Modern England." *Royal Historical Society* 37 (1987): 103–32.

Tilley, Morris Palmer. *Proverbs in England.* Ann Arbor: University of Michigan Press, 1950.

Tomlinson, H. C. *Guns and Government: Ordnance Office under the Later Stuarts*. London: Royal Historical Society, 1979.

———. "Wealden Gunfounding." *Economic History Review* 34, no. 3 (1976): 383–400.

Tout, T. F. "Firearms in England in the Fourteenth Century." *English Historical Review* 26 (1911): 666–702.

Trim, D. J. B. "Fighting Jacob's Wars: The Employment of English and Welsh Mercenaries in the European Wars of Religion in France and the Netherlands, 1562–1610." Ph.D. diss., King's College, University of London, 2002.

Trollope, Charles. "Design and Evolution of English Cast-iron Guns." *Journal of Ordnance Society* 14 (2002): 51–64.

Vale, Malcolm. *War and Chivalry: Warfare and Aristocratic Culture in England, France, and Burgundy at the End of the Middle Ages*. Athens: University of Georgia Press, 1981.

Walton, Clifford. *History of British Standing Army*. London: Harrison and Sons, 1894.

Ward, Joseph P. *Metropolitan Communities: Trade Guilds, Identity, and Change in Early Modern London*. Stanford CA: Stanford University Press, 1997.

Weatherill, Lorna. "A Possession of One's Own." *Journal of British Studies* 25 (1986): 131–56.

Webb, Henry J. *Elizabethan Military Science: The Books and the Practice*. Madison: University of Wisconsin Press, 1965.

Weigall, David. "Women Militants in the English Civil War." *History Today* 22, no. 6 (1972): 434–38.

Weigel, Gail Capitol. "Equestrian Portrait of Prince Henry." In *Prince Henry Revived*, edited by Timothy Wilks, 146–79. London: Southampton Solent University/Paul Holberton, 2007.

Weil, Rachel J. "The Politics of Legitimacy: Women and the Warming-pan Scandal." In *The Revolution of 1688–89: Changing Perspectives*, edited by Lois G. Schwoerer, 65–82. Cambridge: Cambridge University Press, 1992.

Werrett, Simon. *Fireworks: Pyrotechnic Arts and Sciences in European History*. Chicago: University of Chicago Press, 2010.

Western, J. R. *The English Militia in the Eighteenth Century: The Story of a Political Issue*. London: Routledge and Kegan Paul, 1965.

Whittle, Jane. "Lords and Tenants in Kett's Rebellion, 1549." *Past and Present* 207 (2010): 3–52.

Wilks, Timothy, ed. *Prince Henry Revived*. London: Southampton Solent University/ Paul Holberton, 2007.

Williams, A. R. "Some Firing Tests with Simulated 15th c. handguns." *Journal of Arms and Armour Society* 8 (1974): 114–20.

Williams, Penry. "Rebellion and Revolution in Early Modern England." In *War and Society: Essays in Honour and Memory of John Western*, edited by M. R. D. Foot, 223–40. London: Elek, 1973.

———. *The Tudor Regime*. Oxford: Clarendon Press, 1979.

Willmoth, Francis. "Mathematical Sciences and Military Technology: The Ordnance Office in the Reign of Charles II." In *Renaissance and Revolution: Humanists, Scholars, Craftsmen and Natural Philosophers in Early Modern Europe*, edited by J. V. Field and Frank A. J. L. James, 117–31. Cambridge: Cambridge University Press, 1993.

Wills, Gary. "To Keep and Bear Arms." *New York Review of Books* 42 (21 September 1995): 62–73.

Wilson, Derek. *The Tower: 1078–1978*. London: Book Club Associates, 1978.

Wilson, R. L. *Silk and Steel: Women at Arms.* New York: Random House, 2003.

Wood, Andy. *The 1549 Rebellions and the Making of Early Modern England.* Cambridge: Cambridge University Press, 2007.

Woodbridge, Linda. *Women and the English Renaissance.* Urbana: University of Illinois Press, 1984.

Wooding, Lucy. *Henry VIII.* London: Routledge, 2009.

Wrigley E. A., and R. S. Schofield. *Population History of England 1541–1871: A Reconstruction.* Cambridge: Cambridge University Press, 1989.

Wrightson, Keith. *English Society, 1580–1680.* New Brunswick, N.J.: Rutgers University Press, 1988.

Yablonskaya, Elena. "Seventeenth–Century English Firearms in the Kremlin." In *Britannia and Muscovy: English Silver at the Court of the Tsars,* edited by Olga Dmitrieva and Natalya Abramova, 134–43. New Haven, CT: Yale University Press, 2006.

Younger, Neil. *War and Politics in the Elizabethan Counties.* Manchester: Manchester University Press, 2012.

Yungblut, Laura Hunt. *Strangers Settled Here amongst Us: Policies, Perceptions and the Presence of Aliens in Elizabethan England.* London: Routledge, 1996.

Zook, Melinda. *Protestantism, Politics, and Women in Britain.* Houndsmill, Basingstoke: Palgrave Macmillan, 2013.

———. *Radical Whigs and Conspiratorial Politics.* University Park: Penn State University Press, 1999.

INDEX

Italicized page numbers refer to illustrations.

Index   255

Gordon Riots, 166–67
Gouning, John, 119
Granville, George, 29
Gray, John, 137, 218n50
Green, Dorothy, 37
Green, William, 39
Greene, Robert, 76
Grey, Jane, 98
Groome, Margaret, 35, 36
Grummitt, David, 12–13
Guild of St. George, 97
Guise, Francis, Duke of, 61–62
gun, etymology and usage, 10, 186–90; "crakys," 226n1
gun culture, domestic: ceremonial and decorative uses of guns, 95, 97–98, 113–16; defined, 4–5; economics of, 26–45; guns as gifts and collectibles, 107–11, 109, 128, 144–45; gun statutes and proclamations, 6, 9, 17, 21, 39–40, 46–50, 53–55, 58–64, 67, 69, 75, 98, 107, 162, 163, 172, 176, 187, 194n54, 200n3, 200n10; in literature, 76, 133–35, 148, 151, 174, 187, 188–89, 196n13, 217n32; lotteries and, 95; personal and social aspects, 106–24, 174–75; status and, 7, 103, 110, 114–15; terror of guns softened, 4, 33, 97, 110, 186. See also children and guns; gun culture, military; handguns and pistols; London; women and guns
gun culture, military, 1–2, 5–6, 11, 14–16, 20, 26–26, 56–57, 60, 74–77, 114, 123; battlefield conditions, 57, 77–78; gun performance, 182–85; hunting and, 111; service, 3, 9, 22, 72, 74, 77–86, 95, 172. See also militia
gunfounding, 7, 8, 9, 12–16, 33, 90, 93–94, 180, 191n1
gun laws, 2–3, 6, 9, 18, 39, 46–73, 75, 157, 187; against concealed weapons, 52, 62–63; registration, 49
gun licenses, 6, 9, 50–51, 60, 65–73, 204n17
gunmakers and gunmaking, 3, 4, 7, 8–9, 17–18, 90, 140, 173, 179–82, 191n1, 192n2; apprenticeship, 21, 22, 24, 31, 35–38; corruption, 140; employment figures, 32–33, 35; foreign, 14–16, 31, 32, 90; production

figures, 34, 40; proofing, 18, 21, 22–23; shop, 92; standardization and regulations, 21, 22, 24, 63; working conditions, 91–92. See also London
gunmakers' guild. See Worshipful Company of Gunmakers
Gunn, Steven, 17, 39, 55
gunpowder, 4, 7, 8, 27, 32, 77, 99–103, 153, 177–78, 181–82, 188; women's use of, 125, 134, 136–37
Gunpowder Plot, 99, 101
gun-related crime, violence, and accidents, 1, 9–10, 18–19, 20, 39, 57, 99–105, 112, 120–23, 137–40, 152–55
gun rights. See right to arms
gun sales and marketing, 18–19, 26, 39–41
gun shops. See under London; gunmakers and gunmaking

Hale, J. R., 5, 96, 134
Hall, A. R., 184
Hall, Bert S., 184, 186
Hall, Thomas, 119
Hamilton, Thomas Watt, 1
handguns and pistols, 2, 3, 5, 11, 17, 22, 24, 39, 71–73, 92, 97, 109, 149; dags, 61, 62–63, 107, 108, 187; as fashion accessories, 115, 129–30, 132, 217n21; pistol etymology, 187; regulations for, 48, 62–64; technical aspects, 177–78, 180, 181–85
Hardwell, Mr. (gunsmith), 98
Harington, John, 76
Harley, Robert, 105
harquebuses, 14–15, 17, 19, 58, 84, 87, 89, 91, 92, 94, 95, 107, 114, 145–46, 181–82, 187
Harrington, William, 103, 115
Harris, Barbara, 73
Harvey, William, 148
Haynes, Thomas, 36
Hayward, J. W., 107, 108
Hede, James, 13
Hedvig Sofia, 126, 129
Henneage, Thomas, 71
Henrietta Maria, 98
Henry III (of France), 62
Henry V, 13, 27